Advance Praise for Designing Social Interfaces

"A fabulous resource for companies looking to take advantage of the powers of the social web! This is a must-read for engineers and designers new to developing for social media, and an excellent reference for the seasoned designer."

—Abby Kirigin,
Interaction design consultant/Product strategy advisor

"Erin and Christian have put together an astounding collection of the most important social design patterns in use today. I recommend it for anybody building a social website or application... I wish I had this book three years ago!"

—Joshua Porter,
Founder of Bokardo Design and author of Designing for the Social Web *(New Riders)*

"Christian and Erin have pulled together the current thinking on social design into a common language for driving interactions via usable open standards, open source, open processes, and interoperabilit"

David Recordon,
'D Foundation

*"With this   lone and
Crumlish   proceed to
tease out   source on my
shelf. I wi*

—Bill Scott,
Veb Interfaces

Di

Designing Social Interfaces

Designing Social Interfaces

Christian Crumlish and Erin Malone

O'REILLY®

Beijing · Cambridge · Farnham · Köln · Sebastopol · Taipei · Tokyo

Designing Social Interfaces
by Christian Crumlish and Erin Malone

Published by O'Reilly Media, Inc., 1005 Gravenstein Highway North, Sebastopol, CA 95472.

O'Reilly books may be purchased for educational, business, or sales promotional use. Online editions are also available for most titles (*http://mysafaribooksonline.com*). For more information, contact our corporate/institutional sales department: 800-998-9938 or *corporate@oreilly.com*.

Editor: Mary Treseler

Production Editor: Rachel Monaghan

Copyeditor: Genevieve d'Entremont

Proofreader: Rachel Monaghan

Production Services: Newgen North America

Indexer: Julie Hawks

Cover Designer: Karen Montgomery

Interior Designer: Ron Bilodeau

Illustrator: Robert Romano

Printing History:

    September 2009: First Edition.

 This book uses Repkover,™ a durable and flexible lay-flat binding.

ISBN: 978-0-596-15492-9

[TI]

Contents

Part IV. A Beautiful Day in the Neighborhood

Preface

Why We Wrote This Book

We wrote this book because we needed a book like this and we knew there wasn't one on the market yet. Our own pattern collection and documentation and arrangement of "social user experience interface" design patterns grew large and complex enough that we felt it warranted a book-length treatment and presentation. We wrote this book to build on the work we were doing at Yahoo! and the work of the social design community at large. We wrote this to propose a large macro-landscape for organizing and discussing these interaction patterns and to help build a consensus on a common language and set of conventions for discussing social design. We wrote this book because every web designer and developer on the planet today is being asked to consider the social dimension of their work, and we wanted to help.

What This Book Is About

This book is not about designing social behaviors, although many of the interactions are either dependent on or drive specific social behaviors. Many of the principles in the first section of this book talk about different kinds of user behavior, but are best considered across the landscape of the entire pattern collection.

This book is about *interaction design*, specifically designing *social* interactions and interfaces on the Web and in mobile environments (although we primarily focus on the Web).

The collection of patterns is a distillation of many years of experience in designing social and community products for the Web that have led us to define this set of best practices, principles, and patterns for social interfaces. We focus on consumer-facing interactions, primarily because that's where our experience lies. We touch on enterprise and mobile applications toward the end of the book, to remind designers that all the things discussed can be applied in the enterprise and in devices, provided the problems and solutions are viewed with the appropriate lens and set of constraints.

This collection is emerging, evolving, and continues to grow with time and technical innovations.

Why Do We Refer to Yahoo! So Much?

We refer to Yahoo! across the book because: we developed the Yahoo! Pattern Library and believe that designers can benefit from using interaction patterns in their process; several of the patterns in this book come from the Yahoo! Pattern Library, and others will be published back into the library as part of that collection; we both participated in defining and building social interactions and social tools that are found embedded in Yahoo! properties across all its offerings; and we feel that many of the patterns gain their credibility because we have seen them heavily and successfully user-tested and implemented at scales that support hundreds of millions of users.

Although this may mean some of the considerations are a little bit pedestrian for the early adopter or hard core advanced users, we feel good in our recommendations because we know these solutions and considerations work for the average user out there.

However, despite using many examples from Yahoo!, we have tried to include visual examples from many sources around the Internet to illustrate the interactions of various patterns and pieces of patterns. They say a picture is worth 1,000 words, so wherever possible we try to *show* how something can be accomplished instead of just talking about it.

How This Book Is Organized

This book is organized into five parts. The first introduces the concept of user interface design patterns and outlines some high-level principles for social design that we believe inform all the subsequent patterns. The next three parts each introduce a major cluster of related patterns, grouped together by theme, and the final part explores some emerging considerations that have not yet attained the status of patterns but that warrant close attention.

Part I: What Are Social Patterns?

In Chapter 1, we lay out exactly what we mean when we're talking about patterns in the design of interfaces for social user experiences and how to work with them. In Chapter 2, we cover some of the broad, overarching principles that can make the difference between a successful, thriving online community and a ghost town.

Part II: I Am Somebody

One of the building blocks of social experiences are representations of individual people in the system. Just as in *Monopoly*®, each "player" needs a "token" that represents him in the "game." Chapter 3 explores how to engage users and get them to register for and sign into your service, thus establishing the beginnings of a new "self" in your system. Chapter 4 offers patterns for the representation of an individual identity, using things such as profiles and avatars. Chapter 5 discusses ways to indicate presence and show people in your application who else is there. Chapter 6 presents a family of reputation patterns that can help encourage the sort of behaviors you wish to foster.

Part III: The Objects of Our Desire

This is the largest chunk of the book, where we get into the actual behaviors that people engage in online and introduce the concept of social objects: those "conversation pieces" that anchor and give meaning to social interactions online. Chapter 7 addresses how people may collect objects in your application. Chapter 8 looks at how sharing and gift-giving work. Chapter 9 presents interfaces for publishing and broadcasting found objects and original content. Chapter 10 examines techniques for enabling people to give one another feedback on their contributions. Chapter 11 talks about communication and how it is bound to social objects. Chapter 12 looks at collaboration and how people can work together to create and evolve shared objects. Chapter 13 takes a step back to discuss larger social media ecosystems and interfaces that help people make sense of them.

Part IV: A Beautiful Day in the Neighborhood

The third cluster of patterns addresses relationships and the communities that can grow out of them. Chapter 14 examines relationship terminology and models of reciprocity or asymmetry, and how to enable users to find one another and form and declare relationships. Chapter 15 presents interfaces for community management and moderation, and models for collaborative filtering. Chapter 16 explores how to enable people to meet one another in the real world and create shared events.

Part V: Further Considerations

In the final part, we approach the leading edge of social design and discuss some of the considerations you may encounter there. In Chapter 17, we look at many models of openness and the benefits and consequences of embracing them in your social architecture. In Chapter 18, we look to the frontiers of "social in the enterprise," mobile application development, generational change (at both ends of the age spectrum), and what we can learn from game design.

Sidebar Essays

Just as we have approached the collection of patterns as both authors and as curators of information from many sources, we have curated a collection of different voices from around the Internet to share alternative opinions, more in-depth exploration, and thoughts about social user behavior that provide seasoning around the patterns in each chapter. Look for continued conversations on these topics on our wiki and on the individual essayists' personal blogs.

Who Should Read This Book

Anyone involved in building social interactions will be interested in this book.

User experience and interaction designers will find the detailed interaction patterns useful in their arsenal of tools. The explanations in the patterns and the related principles will provide the designer with a full spectrum of details to consider when making decisions for designing the social experience. The patterns don't always prescribe how to design the thing, but they will offer up all the things the designer needs to think about when designing, as well as what trade-offs may need to be made to design a great experience given a specific business and audience context.

Although this book does not go into technical details for how to build these interfaces, the web developer will appreciate the patterns, as they can be mapped to specific code solutions and provide the "why" behind design decisions.

Everyone on the product team will benefit from this book, as it provides a common vocabulary around social interactions and offers rich explanations and real-world examples that can benefit team discussions and communication.

Using the Interaction Patterns

You can read this book cover to cover. It's arranged with a narrative flow in which ideas build on one another. But we designed it to work just as well as a reference. You can zero in on a particular section of interest or just read about a specific interface pattern, exploring related concepts through cross-references and the index.

This book is here to help you get your job done. In general, you may use the patterns in this book in your programs and documentation. Not all patterns should be used for every application; different ideas and social objects will require different solutions. Ideally, you will sample from each of the categories and will add more complex features and concepts as the community grows and as you learn what is successful and useful for its needs. We believe that the entire collection gives context to the social landscape and provides information about what types of things you should consider as you are making design decisions.

You do not need to contact us for permission unless you're reproducing a significant portion of the text of the patterns. For example, creating a pattern repository that uses several patterns or excerpts of patterns from this book does not require permission. Selling or distributing a CD-ROM of examples from O'Reilly books does require permission. Answering a question by citing this book and quoting the patterns does not require permission. Incorporating a significant amount of pattern material from this book into your product's documentation does require permission.

We appreciate, but do not require, attribution. An attribution usually includes the title, author, publisher, and ISBN, for example, "*Designing Social Interfaces*, by Christian Crumlish and Erin Malone. Copyright 2009 Yahoo!, Inc., 978-0-596-15492-9."

What Comes with This Book

This book has a companion website (*http://designingsocialinterfaces.com*) that offers an open forum for conversation around the patterns presented here; an addendum containing updated examples; additional thoughts about emerging patterns and principles; and helpful links to articles, resources on designing social interfaces, and discussions on specific topics touched on in this book by us or our many guest essayists.

All the book's diagrams and figures are available under a Creative Commons license for you to download and use in your presentations. You'll find them at Flickr (*http://www.flickr.com/photos/socialpatterns/sets*).

How to Contact Us

Please address comments and questions concerning this book to the publisher:

O'Reilly Media, Inc.
1005 Gravenstein Highway North
Sebastopol, CA 95472
800-998-9938 (in the United States or Canada)
707-829-0515 (international or local)
707 829-0104 (fax)

We have a web page for this book, where we list errata, examples, and any additional information. You can access this page at:

http://www.oreilly.com/catalog/9780596154929

To comment or ask technical questions about this book, send email to:

bookquestions@oreilly.com

For more information about our books, conferences, Resource Centers, and the O'Reilly Network, see our website at:

http://www.oreilly.com

Safari® Books Online

 Safari Books Online is an on-demand digital library that lets you easily search over 7,500 technology and creative reference books and videos to find the answers you need quickly.

With a subscription, you can read any page and watch any video from our library online. Read books on your cell phone and mobile devices. Access new titles before they are available for print, and get exclusive access to manuscripts in development and post feedback for the authors. Copy and paste code samples, organize your favorites, download chapters, bookmark key sections, create notes, print out pages, and benefit from tons of other time-saving features.

O'Reilly Media has uploaded this book to the Safari Books Online service. To have full digital access to this book and others on similar topics from O'Reilly and other publishers, sign up for free at *http://my.safaribooksonline.com.*

Acknowledgments

We'd like to thank Mary Treseler at O'Reilly, who initially acquired the manuscript from us, helped us develop the outline and voice for the book, and shepherded us through the publishing process, encouraging and gently nudging us all along the way. I think it's fair to say that without her support and guidance we would not have been able to pull this off. The consummate editor, Mary was really a pleasure to work with.

Sanders Kleinfeld answered our endless anxious questions about DocBook and XML that failed to validate even when we yelled at it.

Rachel Monaghan steered us crisply through production and Genevieve d'Entremont copyedited a prodigious mound of pages in a shockingly brief amount of time, somehow paying close attention to subtle inconsistencies, cross-references, and infelicities of style. Jacque Quann helped us track the contract terms and shake loose the advance checks (yay).

Havi Hoffman, who manages Yahoo! Press, worked a lot of behind-the-scenes magic to incubate and nurture this book through an elaborate process. She made some of the earliest suggestions about doing a book of this kind and kept the relationship among the authors (one a Yahoo! employee, the other not), the publisher, and the imprint on a healthy footing. We'd also like to thank Chris Yeh, who runs the Yahoo! Developer Network (where the Yahoo! Pattern Library lives); Neal Sample, the chief architect for YOS; and Jay Rossiter, who runs the consumer platforms group that houses YOS, YDN, and Yahoo! Press.

Dan Brodnitz of about-creativity.com and Lynda.com offered helpful advice and coaching in the initial proposal phases of the project.

Thanks to Matt Leacock and Bryce Glass, earlier collaborators on this project and the Yahoo! Social Media Toolkit that was one of its ancestors, and ongoing contributions (Matt helping to design a social patterns card game with us and Bryce contributing the drafts of the reputation patterns and some visualizations of the entire social design landscape).

Thanks to Bill Scott from Netflix, Abby Kirigin from Tipjoy, Adina Levin from SocialText, and Paul Kroft from MITRE, who reviewed the first draft of the manuscript for technical and market viability and offered detailed, thorough feedback and suggestions that consistently improved the quality of the book. Thanks also to Paul Pedrazzi from Oracle, who reviewed our material on social patterns in the enterprise and offered valuable comments and pointers.

Thanks to the flourishing community of UX designers and strategists we're connected to via Twitter, the IA Institute, the IxDA, LinkedIn, Facebook, blogs, zines, and plenty of face-to-face events, who collectively encouraged us as we were writing this book, offered feedback on wiki drafts, linked to our project, asked for advice, interviewed us, and generally helped make the writing of the book itself a social experience.

From Christian

I'd like to thank Briggs, who knew what she was getting into when I agreed to write a book in my "copious spare time" and through both forbearance and numerous small kindnesses made it possible for me to take on this ambitious effort.

My collaborator, Erin Malone, has been by far the best coauthor I've ever partnered with, but even before this project came into being, Erin mentored me, recruited me to curate the Yahoo! Pattern Library, encouraged my exploration of social design patterns, and gamely agreed to come on board to help write the book. Through thick and thin, Erin has been the mainstay of this project and a wonderful person to work with.

I'd like to thank George Oates, the original designer for Flickr, who sat down with me for a couple of hours over a nice long lunch, talking about the fundamental principles of social design as she sees it and has lived it. Much of the content of Chapter 2 and insights sprinkled throughout the book found their genesis in that conversation.

Elizabeth Churchill from Yahoo! Research also helped me clarify my thinking on a number of related topics over the course of several wide-ranging conversations.

The organizers of BarCamp Block in Palo Alto in October of 2007 provided a great environment for brainstorming the original "tree of patterns" that evolved into this book. Many of the patterns identified that day survived into the latest version of the taxonomy. Likewise, the organizers of BayCHI's monthly program and Ignite SF also provided opportunities to rehearse some of the ideas about social patterns, social anti-patterns, anti-social patterns, and so on, over a series of presentations.

I'd like to thank my family and friends who also cut me a great deal of slack as I became incommunicado at best and irritable at worst.

I'd also like to thank Micah Laaker, who runs the user experience design team for the Yahoo! Open Strategy (where I work) and contributed an essay on openness to Chapter 17.

Among our essayists, I'd also like to single out Matte Scheinker, a mentor to me while he was still at Yahoo! and contributor of a nuanced essay on the ethical implications of this type of design work.

From Erin

Big, big, thanks to my coauthor, Christian, for bringing this project into our team in the first place, for being a champion of the Pattern Library and for stirring the pot around the social taxonomy before this became a book idea, for cheering me on as a coauthor when I decided that I wanted to work on this with him, and for making this process fun and collaborative. Extra thanks for openly sharing his publishing experiences so that I knew what to expect at each phase of the publishing process. Cowriting has never seemed so easy.

To my business partners at Tangible ux, James Young and Bruce Charonnat, for giving me the time and support to disappear and write this book instead of doing client work. And to my clients for encouraging me on this journey and allowing me to try out and test many of these patterns in real-world design situations.

To my family; my sister, Sheila; and my parents, Diane and Rick; for putting up with my writing over the holidays and on vacations the last several months.

Heartfelt thanks go to Irene Au and Christina Wodtke for bringing me into Yahoo! in the first place to design and build the Yahoo! Pattern Library, an event in time that changed my life; and thanks to Larry Tesler for continuing to believe in the project, especially when we wanted to open the curtains to the world and share the library as an open resource. Without that experience I would not have felt qualified to write this book. To Christina, extra thanks for giving me advice and the foreknowledge that the book would take over my life for a while.

Special thanks to Matt Leacock, for helping me realize the Yahoo! Pattern Library into being and for keeping community applications and social software a constant in our team across six and a half years at AOL and Yahoo!.

Thanks to Lucas Pettinati, for the amazing work designing and testing Yahoo!'s registration process and forms, and for defining a set of best practices around this work.

Thanks to Bill Scott for pushing through the vision of an open pattern library from Yahoo!, for the continued support as an evangelist even though he doesn't work there anymore, and for taking the time to read our manuscript and give us page by page of most excellent feedback.

Thanks to Beverly Tseng-Freeman, Anne Hsieh, Rob Aseron, and Stephen Wheeler for the tons of user research on social interfaces they conducted while part of the Yahoo! Platform UED team. Their excellent research stands behind many of these recommended patterns.

To Our Essayists

Many thanks to Bryce Glass, our unsung third author, for his expertise on Reputation systems and the reputation patterns, and for writing two essays for us.

To Randy Farmer, for his excellent thinking on Identity from all perspectives and his core set of "open" patterns.

To danah boyd, for encouraging Erin to go foraging through her wonderful thesis document and allowing us to excerpt it in our section on Youth.

To Billie Mandel, for crafting thoughtful guidance for those designing in the Mobile space.

To Stuart French, for his expertise in social knowledge management in the enterprise environment.

To Joshua Porter, for paving the way with his book, *Designing for the Social Web*, and for graciously adding his thoughts to our book.

To Thomas Vander Wal, for thinking about the future in his essay on social metadata.

To Chris Fahey, skeptic, coach, and friend, for his essay distinguishing patterns from cliches.

To Tom Hughes-Croucher, YDN evangelist colleague and deep thinker on social application design, for his thoughts on users' mental models.

To Matt Jones, inspiring pioneer and gifted communicator, for his elaboration on the intriguing palimpsest metaphor he contributed to this body of thought.

To Whitney Hess, vanguard of a new generation of UX designers, for her sensitive insights into the perils and opportunities of the onboarding process.

To Leisa Reichelt, pioneer of open design processes and sharp theorist, for expanding on her ambient intimacy coinage.

To Andrew Hinton, information philosopher, advanced practitioner, and community leader, for his illumination of the problems of context in these new environments.

To Andrius Kuliskaukus and the Minciu Sodas collective, for their contributions to freedom and self-sufficiency around the world, and some crowdsourced thoughts on the value of the public domain as a preferred licensing option.

To Derek Powazek, trailblazer of community-oriented design and communication, for his exploration of people as meaning-making machines.

To Harjeet S. Gulati, who found our project through the wiki, added a wealth of definitions and other useful contributions there, and then consented to contribute his thoughts on knowledge management in the enterprise.

To Gary Burnett, who has been studying and publishing about online community dynamics from an information science perspective, for his findings on the establishment of social norms.

To Shara Kasaric, accomplished professional community moderator, for her deeply useful, hard-won tips about fostering a thriving community online.

To Micah Laaker, colleague and mentor, for his enumeration of 13 types of openness.

To Chris Messina, designer, citizen activist, and catalyst, for his essay pondering Generation Open.

To Robyn Tippins, YDN community manager and skilled blogger, for her insights on the community-building trifecta.

Without the work of the numerous thinkers, designers, builders, and schemers who have been mapping the digital social product space for the past decade or more (cited for further reading throughout the book)—notably, Ward Cunningham, Howard Rheingold, Amy Jo Kim, Dave Winer, Marc Canter, David Weinberger, Gene Smith, Clay Shirky, Mary Hodder, Stewart Butterfield, Edward Vielmetti, Kevin Marks, Tom Coates, Jeremy Keith, Allen Tom, Brian Oberkirch, Liz Lawley, Lane Becker, Susan Mernit, Tara Hunt and many, many others—we could not have written this book. This is decidedly an effort in sense-making and organization, an attempt to give the community at the very least a straw model that tries to wrap its metaphorical arms around the entire landscape of social interaction design.

Part I

What Are Social Patterns?

In the past 15 years, we have watched the proliferation of Internet technology spread across the globe and have been immersed in the creation of tools and interactive experiences to help people navigate their way to information, find other people, and create their own places on the Web. We have seen the rise and fall of the first wave—the dot.com boom and bust—and have experienced firsthand the explosion of Web 2.0 and social media as both designers and participants.

These electronic connections and social tools are changing the way we interact with one another. We believe that these tools can be designed and simplified to help normal people expand their online experiences with others. These social patterns of behavior and the interfaces to support them have emerged and continue to evolve as we find better ways to bring people together.

Social patterns are the components and pieces of interactivity that are the building blocks of social experiences. They are the best practices and principles we have seen emerge from hundreds of sites and applications with social features or focus. They are the emergent interaction patterns that have become the standard way for users to interact with their content and with the people who matter most to them.

Chapter 1

Mommy, What's a Social User Experience Pattern?

> *I have a dream for the Web...and it has two parts. In the first part, the Web becomes a much more powerful means for collaboration between people. I have always imagined the information space as something to which everyone has immediate and intuitive access, and not just to browse, but to create. Furthermore, the dream of people-to-people communication through shared knowledge must be possible for groups of all sizes, interacting electronically with as much ease as they do now in person.*
>
> —Tim Berners-Lee
> *Weaving the Web*, p 157, 1999

A Little Social Backstory...

Social design for interactive digital spaces has been around since the earliest bulletin board systems. The most famous being The Well (1985), which was described by *Wired* magazine in 1997* as "the world's most influential online community" and predated the World Wide Web and browser interfaces by several years.

---

* Hafner, Katie. 1997. "The Epic Saga of The Well: The World's Most Influential Online Community (And It's Not AOL)." *Wired*, 5.05, *http://www.wired.com/wired/archive/5.05/ff_well_pr.html.*

The Well

The Well started in 1985 on a VAX system and a series of modems. Conceived by Stewart Brand and Larry Brilliant, Brand had a simple idea to "take a group of interesting people, give them the means to stay in continuous communication with one another, stand back, and see what happens." He also had the idea that community created online through written dialog could be strengthened through offline, face-to-face meetings, and he set out to combine the two quite successfully.

From the 1997 *Wired* article: "But probably the most important of Brand's early convictions for The Well was that people should take responsibility for what they said. There would be no anonymity; everyone's real name would be available on the system, linked to his or her login. Brand came up with a credo that would, through the years, spark no end of debate: 'You own your own words.' That proviso greeted members each time they logged on. 'I was doing the usual, considering what could go wrong,' he recalls. 'One thing would be people blaming us for what people said on The Well. And the way I figured you get around that was to put the responsibility on the individual.'"

Since the beginning of connected computers, we have tried to have computer-mediated experiences between people. As Clay Shirky notes in a 2004 Salon article, "Online social networks go all the way back to the Plato BBS 40 years ago!"

PLATO

"PLATO (Programmed Logic for Automated Teaching Operations) originated in the early 1960's at the Urbana campus of the University of Illinois. Professor Don Bitzer became interested in using computers for teaching, and with some colleagues founded the Computer-based Education Research Laboratory (CERL).

"The sense of an online community began to emerge on PLATO in 1973–74, as Notes, Talkomatic, 'term-talk', and Personal Notes were introduced in quick succession. People met and got acquainted in Talkomatic, and carried on romances via 'term-talk' and Personal Notes. The release of Group Notes in 1976 gave the community fertile new ground for growth, but by that time it was already well established. The community had been building its own additions to the software infrastructure in the form of multiplayer games and alternative online communications. One such program was Pad, an online bulletin board where people could post graffiti or random musings. Another was Newsreport, a lighthearted online newspaper published periodically by Bruce Parello, aka The Red Sweater."

Excerpted from David R. Woolley's 1994 article "PLATO: The Emergence of Online Community" (http://thinkofit.com/plato/dwplato.htm#community). *An earlier version of this article appeared in the January 1994 issue of* Matrix News.

In the early days of the Web, social experiences were simply called *community* and generally consisted of message boards, groups, list-servs, and virtual worlds. Amy Jo Kim, author and community expert, calls these "place-centric" gathering places. Community features allowed users to talk and interact with one another, and the connection among people was usually based on the topic of interest that drew them to the site in the first place. Communities formed around interests, and relationships evolved over time. There was little distinction between the building of the tools to enable these gatherings and the groups of people who made up the community itself. Bonds were formed in this space but generally didn't exist in the real (offline) world.

The interfaces and interaction design for these types of tools were all over the board—from graphical representations like eWorld (see Figure 1-1) to scary-looking, only for early adopters, text-only BBSs, to the simple forms of AOL chat rooms.

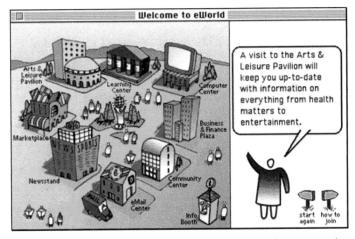

Figure 1-1. *The very graphical interface of eWorld was the next step up from BBSs and was competing with AOL.*

The first example that straddled the line between *community* and what we now call *social networks* was the site SixDegrees.com (1997; see Figure 1-2). SixDegrees showcased connections among people, allowed users to create and manage their personal profiles, and brought people together based on interests and other features. Sound familiar?

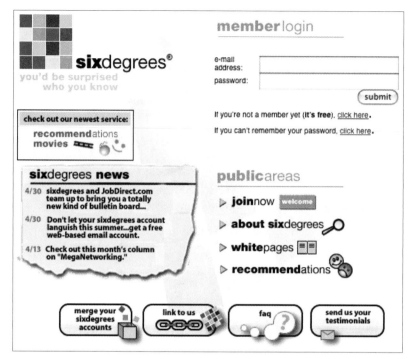

Figure 1-2. *SixDegrees.com was one of the first social networks that connected people and built user profiles.*

Somewhere along the way, though, before the dot-com bust, *community* became a dirty word—most likely because it was overly resource-intensive to build and care for, and no one had quite figured out how to make money from all that work.

With the advent of Web 2.0, and the second wave of websites and applications and the richer experiences they offer—more sophisticated technologies and faster bandwidth for the masses—social networking has taken on a new life. Suddenly, it is all the rage, and every site must have social features. In this phase, social has many more components and options available to users, but still generally means features or sites that allow interaction in real or asynchronous time among users. The tools are more robust, storage space is more ample, and more people are online to participate. The increase in online population is a major driving force for the shift to prioritizing these types of features and sites. There is critical mass now. By 2006, 73% of Americans, 64% of Europeans, and over 50% in the rest of the world were online and participating.

Another key difference between the first cycle of social and now is that the social network—the real relationships with people that we know and care about—is key to the interactions and features. Features are gated based on the degrees of connection between two people. Many of the tools and websites offer features and functions that support existing offline relationships and behaviors. These sites count on each person bringing his personal network into the online experience. The concept of tribes and friends has become more important than ever and has driven the development of many products.

What was ho-hum in 1997 is now the core—for user features as well as opportunities for making money. Additionally, the power of the many, or the wisdom of crowds, is being leveraged to exert some control over content creation and self-moderation processes. Companies are learning that successful social experiences shouldn't and can't be overly controlled. They are learning they can leverage the crowd to do some of the heavy lifting, which in turn spares them some of the costs. User-generated content has helped many businesses and the participating community keep things moderated.

The other factor contributing to the spread of these types of features is the expertise of a new generation of users. These folks have grown up with technology and expect it to help facilitate and mediate all their interactions with friends, colleagues, teachers, and coworkers. They move seamlessly from computer to their mobile device or phone and back, and they want the tools to move with them. They work with technology, they play in technology, they breathe this technology, and it is virtually invisible to them.

The terms *community, social media, and social networking* all describe these kinds of tools and experiences. The terms often are used interchangeably, but they provide different views and facets of the same phenomenon.

In a paper published in the *Journal of Computer-Mediated Communication* in 2007, danah boyd, a noted researcher specializing in social network sites, and Nicole B. Ellison defined social network sites as "web-based services that allow individuals to (1) construct a public or semi-public profile within a bounded system, (2) articulate a list of other users with whom they share a connection, and (3) view and traverse their list of connections and those made by others within the system. The nature and nomenclature of these connections may vary from site to site."

According to Wikipedia, "social media is the use of electronic and Internet tools for the purpose of sharing and discussing information and experiences with other human beings," and it defines social networking as "a service which focuses on building online communities of people who share interests and activities, or who are interested in exploring the interests and activities of others. Most social network services are web based and provide a variety of ways for users to interact, such as e-mail and instant messaging services." Community is defined as the group of people who utilize these environments and tools.

Well, What About That Social Media? Can You Expand on That?

The term *social media* first came on our radar as a way of generalizing what was going on with blogs circa 2002. The combination of blogging with RSS (newsfeeds, feedreaders)—sometimes in the same application (as with Dave Winer's Radio Userland software)—enabled a call-and-response, many-to-many conversational ecosystem to arise, become a bubble, calve into many smaller overlapping and distinct subcommunities, and so on.

In that scenario, the blog posts were the media, but then (as now) much blogging involved linking to sources that themselves might come from the traditional, mainstream media (or *MSM*, as some of the political bloggers tend to call it) or from other independent voices. Many people online realized they were consuming much of their media (news, gossip, video clips, information) through social intermediaries: reading articles when a more prominent blogger linked to them, discovering media fads and memes by following BoingBoing or many other similar trend-tracking sites, and tuning in to the blogs and publications of like-minded people and relying on them to filter the vast, unfathomable information flow for those valuable nuggets of relevancy.

Along the way, the term *social media* began to stand in for Web 2.0, or the Social Web, or social networking, or (now) the experiences epitomized by Facebook and Twitter. Christian called this "the living web" in his last book, *The Power of Many: How the Living Web is Transforming Politics, Business, and Everyday Life* (Wiley). Technorati tried branding it as the "world live web." The idea is that as the Web becomes more *social* (that's the word we've all converged on), there is an element of it that is read-write, that involves people writing and revising and responding to one another, not in a one-to-one or one-to-many fashion, but many-to-many. The problem with using *social media* as a generic term for the entire Internet-enabled social context is that the word "media," already slippery (does it refer to works of creation, or to finding relevant news/media items, or to public chatter and commentary, or all of these things?), starts to add nothing to the phrase, and doesn't really address the social graph.

Most recently, we've seen a proliferation of social media marketing experts and gurus online, and their messages range from the sublime (that marketing can truly be turned inside out as a form of customer service, through Cluetrainful engagement* with customers, i.e., treating them as human beings through ordinary conversations and public responsiveness), to the mundane (as in the early days of the Internet, every local market has its village explainers), to the ridiculous (a glorified version of spam).

The collection of patterns that comprise this book were once labeled "social media patterns," after the social media toolkit that Matt Leacock started at Yahoo!, but as it evolved, it became clear that we were using "social media" to mean "social networking" or "involving the social graph" or just "social," so for clarity's sake, we're using it to refer to "media that is created, filtered, engaged with, and remixed socially."

---

* *The Cluetrain Manifesto (http://www.cluetrain.com/)*

Here's a similar, but slightly more community-oriented definition of social media from Harjeet Gulati:

> *Social Media collectively refers to content (in the form of Text (Blogs, Discussion Forums, Wikis), Voice (Podcasts), or Video (YouTube) that is generated by the community of users for consumption within the same community. In this model, the role of Publisher and Consumer of information is delegated to the community at large. The role of the Channel becomes key in this model even as the degree of control that the community exercises over the content that is displayed within the boundaries of a given system varies. Where the term "media" meant traditional channels like Newspaper, Radio and Television, the advent of the Web in the early nineties accelerated the inclusion of the Web as a medium to reach out to others. The content ownership in traditional media continued to be with the "publishers" of content—the production houses, newspapers, tv channels, and radio stations. Content Owners/Publishers, the Channel and the Consumers were clearly differentiated. As the Web continued to evolve, the term "Social Media" has come to dominate the discussion. Social Media encourages a participative, collective model of content creation, distribution and usage and is more representative of the tastes and inclinations of the community at large.*

We find it most useful to focus on the social objects (which may be media objects, but may also be such things as calendar events) and the activities people can do with them, and with one another, through our social interfaces.

For a further exploration of this term, see also "Social Media in Plain English" (*http://www.youtube.com/watch?v=MpIOClX1jPE*) from Common Craft.

What Do We Mean by Principle, Best Practice, and Patterns?

With the growing expectation of seamless experiences, it is important for designers to see the emerging standards and to understand how one experience of a site and its interactions affects expectations for the next site. By working with standard and emerging best practices, principles, and interaction patterns, the designer takes some of the burden of understanding how the application works off the user, who then can focus on the unique properties of the social experience she is building.

To start, we do define these three things differently. They live along a continuum, from prescriptive (rules you should follow) to assumptions (a basic generalization that is accepted as true) to process (ways to approach thinking about these concepts).

Principle: A Basic Truth, Law, or Assumption

Principles are basic assumptions that have been accepted as true. In interaction design, they can lend guidance for how to approach a design problem, and have been shown to be generally true with respect to a known user experience problem or a set of accepted truths. Principles don't prescribe the solution, though, like an interaction pattern does; instead, they support the rationale behind an interaction design pattern or set of best practices.

Practice (or Best Practice): A Habitual or Customary Action or Way of Doing Something

Best practices are funny things. They are often confused with principles or interaction patterns. They fall along the continuum and are less prescriptive than an interaction pattern solution—at least in our definition. We often include best practices inside an interaction pattern. The *best practice* helps clarify how to approach a design solution, and is generally the most efficient and effective way to solve the problem, although not necessarily the only way.

Pattern: A Model or Original Used As an Archetype

When we developed the Yahoo! Pattern Library, we defined a *pattern* as:

> *Common, successful interaction design components and design solutions for a known problem in a context.*

Patterns are used like building blocks or bricks. They are fundamental components of a user experience and describe interaction processes. They can be combined with other patterns as well as other pieces of interface and content to create an interactive user experience. They are technology and visually agnostic, meaning we do not prescribe particular technological solutions or visual design aesthetics in the patterns. User experience design patterns give guidance to a designer for how to solve a specific problem in a particular context, in a way that has been shown to work over and over again.

The notion of using interaction design patterns in the user experience design process follows the model that computer software programming took when it adopted the concepts and philosophies of Christopher Alexander. Alexander, an architect, wrote the book *A Pattern Language*. In his book he describes a language—a set of rules or patterns for design—for how to design and build cities, buildings, and other human spaces. The approach is repeatable and works at various levels of scale.

Alexander says that "each pattern describes a problem which occurs over and over again in our environment, and then describes the core of the solution to that problem, in such a way that you can use this solution a million times over, without ever doing it the same way twice."

In addition to developing this language of elemental repeatable patterns, he was concerned with the human aspect of building. In a 2008 interview, Alexander says that his ideas "make [homes] work so that people would feel good." This human approach and concern for the person (as user) is part of what has appealed to both software developers and user experience designers.

The idea of building with a pattern language was adopted by the computer software industry in 1987, when Ward Cunningham and Kent Beck began experimenting with the idea of applying patterns to programming. As Ward says, they "looked for a way to write programs that embraced the user, where users felt supported by the computer program, not interrogated by the computer program."

This approach took off, and in 1995 the book *Design Patterns: Elements of Reusable Object-Oriented Software* by Erich Gamma, Richard Helm, Ralph Johnson, and John Vlissides (known as the Gang of Four) was published.

In 1997, Jenifer Tidwell published a collection of user interface patterns for the human-computer interaction (HCI) community based on the premise that capturing the collective wisdom of experienced designers helps educate novice designers and gives the community as a whole a common vocabulary for discussion. She specifically stated that she was attempting to create an Alexandrian-like language for interface designers and the HCI community. The evolution of that site and her work became the book *Designing Interfaces*, published in 2005 by O'Reilly Media.

Several others published collections on the Web, including Martijn van Welie, a long-time proponent of patterns in the interaction design realm, which in turn inspired my (Erin's) team at Yahoo! to publish portions of our internal interaction pattern library to the public in 2006.

I had joined Yahoo! in 2004 to build a pattern library for the ever-growing user experience design team and to create a common vocabulary for the network of sites that Yahoo! produced for its hundreds of millions of global users. We built the library in a collaborative manner, utilizing the most successful, well-researched design solutions as models for each pattern. Designers from across the company contributed patterns, commented and discussed their merits, added new information as technology and users changed, and moderated the quality and lifecycle of each pattern. In 2006, spearheaded by Bill Scott, we were able to go public with our work with a subset of the internal library. The work has been very well received by the interaction design and information architecture community, and has inspired many in their design work. Since 2007, Christian has been further evangelizing the library and bridging the gaps between design and development and open source communities.

The notion of having a suite of reusable building blocks to inform and help designers develop their sites and applications has gained traction within the interaction design community as the demands for web and mobile interfaces have become more complex. When the Web was mostly text, there wasn't a whole lot of variety to how a user interacted with a site, and the toolkit was small. The complexity of client applications was difficult at best to duplicate online. But that was then. Now, whole businesses and industries rely on easy-to-use web-based software to conduct their business. There is more need than ever to have a common language for designers and developers. And as social becomes integrated into every facet of interactive experiences, it is important to put a stake in the ground about just what those pieces should be and how they should and shouldn't behave.

The Importance of Anti-Patterns

The term *anti-patterns* was coined in 1995 by Andrew Koenig in the *C++ Report*, and was inspired by the Gang of Four's book *Design Patterns*.

Koenig defined the term with two variants:

- Those that describe a bad solution to a problem that resulted in a bad situation.

- Those that describe how to get out of a bad situation and how to proceed from there to a good solution.

Anti-patterns became a popular method for understanding bad design solutions in programming with the publication of the book *Anti-Patterns: Refactoring Software, Architectures, and Projects in Crisis* by William Brown et al.

For our purposes, anti-patterns are common mistakes or a bad solution to a common problem. It is sometimes easier to understand how to design successfully by dissecting what not to do. In the world of social experiences, often the anti-patterns have some sort of jarring or malicious side effects.

The anti-patterns we illustrate will point out why the solution seems good and why it turns out to be bad, and then we will discuss refactored alternatives that are more successful or gentler to the user experience.

So, That's All the Little Parts: Now What?

Our approach for the rest of this book is similar to Christopher Alexander's, in that we start with a foundational set of high-level practices that underpin the individual interactions detailed in subsequent chapters.

In each section, we talk about which patterns build on others and how you can combine patterns to create a robust experience. We cross-reference patterns and give examples from the wild where we see examples of these patterns in action.

The social patterns support the entire lifecycle that a user may experience within a site or application, from signing up to actively participating, to building a reputation, to dating or collaborating with friends, to collaborative games and even moderation. We are building a vocabulary and language for social application design in the same spirit as Alexander:

> *We were always looking for the capacity of a pattern language to generate coherence, and that was the most vital test used, again and again, during the process of creating a language. The language was always seen as a whole. We were looking for the extent to which, as a whole, a pattern language would produce a coherent entity.*

Patterns...or Clichés?

Clichés. They're a dime a dozen. Avoid them like the plague, or so we're told.

But are they really that bad? Would we really be better off if, every single time we wanted to say something, we had to start from scratch and think of a whole new way of saying it?

The word *cliché* comes from printing with movable type: typesetters would take a commonly used expression and cast it in a single block called a *cliché*, rather than setting the whole phrase by hand every time. Over time, the term came to be used to describe the words and phrases themselves. For authors who are tempted to use them, clichés can indeed be problematic:

- In a writer's hasty use of a cliché, he may end up saying something he didn't exactly mean.
- By choosing a cliché instead of looking for something new, the author loses an opportunity to surprise and delight the reader with more elegant or thought-provoking words.
- An overly obvious cliché may come across as cheesy and banal: readers will hear the cliché, not the message.

But in normal life, clichés are not only permissible but are, in fact, critical to our everyday communication. Clichés make our messages efficient and more easily understood.

So are design patterns the same as clichés?

In a sense, yes: they're proven, ready-made, and often familiar ways of solving creative problems. And just like with clichés, it's important to recognize when they are useful and relevant... and when they are ill-suited or misleading.

In an interview with the Unbeige blog, designer and author Steven Heller was asked about his design process:

> *Unbeige: What's the first thing you do when you're starting to design something, and you're faced with a blank page/computer screen?*

> *Steven Heller: Pray. Then fall into my bag of clichés and wiggle around.*

It's true: a design pattern, or a cliché, is often just a starting point. It's often the first thing you reach for from your palette of design tools when assembling the rough outlines of a design solution. A writer's quick first draft of an essay or story may include a few hackneyed clichés she will eventually improve, sometimes with the help of an editor. Think of patterns the same way: your first pass at a user experience design may include a few basic patterns that, as initially drawn, feel a little too obvious, almost cliché. But when you view them again in the big picture, you can see where they don't quite work and will require some changes and improvement. A little wiggling around.

Occasionally a basic design pattern will be a perfect fit the first time out. But usually not. You should always think hard about how the pattern itself could be reimagined to suit the particular demands of your product. So go ahead: reinvent the wheel.

—Christopher Fahey,
founding partner at Behavior Design

Further Reading

Anti-Patterns: Refactoring Software, Architectures, and Projects in Crisis, by William Brown, Raphael Malveau, Skip McCormick, and Tom Mowbray, Wiley, 1998

Community Building on the Web: Secret Strategies for Successful Online Communities, by Amy Jo Kim, Peachpit Press, 2000

Design Patterns, by Erich Gamma, Richard Helm, Ralph Johnson, and John M. Vlissides, Addison-Wesley Professional, 1994

Design for Community, by Derek Powazek, Waite Group Press, 2001

Designing for the Social Web, by Joshua Porter, New Riders Press, 2008

Designing Interfaces, by Jenifer Tidwell, O'Reilly Media, Inc., 2005

Groundswell, by Charlene Li and Josh Bernoff, Harvard Business School Press, 2008

A Pattern Language: Towns, Buildings, Construction (Center for Environmental Structure Series), by Christopher Alexander, Oxford University Press, 1977

Social Media in Plain English, *http://www.youtube.com/watch?v=MpIOClX1jPE*

A Timeless Way of Building, by Christopher Alexander, Oxford University Press, 1979

The Virtual Community: Homesteading on the Electronic Frontier, by Howard Rheingold, The MIT Press, 2000

The Well: A Story of Love, Death and Real Life in the Seminal Online Community, by Katie Hafner, Carroll, Graf Publishers, 2001

Chapter 2

Social to the Core

*The Web is more a social creation than a technical one. I designed it for a
social effect—to help people work together—and not as a technical toy.*

—Tim Berners-Lee, *Weaving the Web* (1999)

In *A Timeless Way of Building*, Christopher Alexander explains the purpose of pattern languages in part by saying that they are about imbuing built spaces with "the quality without a name." There is something, often something ineffable, about some architectural spaces that make them inviting, warm, humane, comfortable, healthy, and alive. Analyzing these spaces may tell us that the seating area is built on a good scale or that the lighting helps foster small group conversations, but underlying these granular design decisions are some higher-order principles that can be applied across the board.

Metaphorically, online social spaces operate similarly. A well-designed sign-up flow will have a real, direct impact on whether people feel invited and encouraged to join and capable of doing so. That may be one specific interface you will need to define for your site. But internalizing some higher-level principles first can help you make better design decisions as you get down to the details.

So before delving deeply into all of the specific design decisions you're going to make when creating a new site or application, it can be helpful to take a step back and think about what underlying principles will help make your project successful. Consider the example in Figure 2-1. How can you create a space that invites healthy participation from users, grows organically, and creates value that is greater than the sum of its parts?

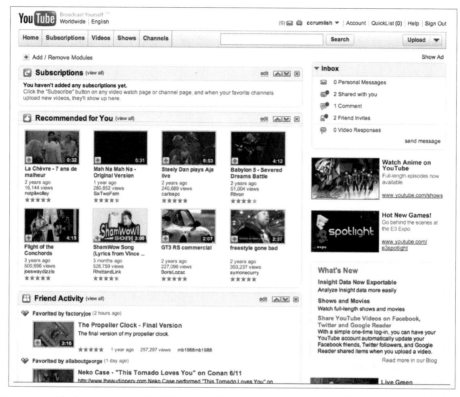

Figure 2-1. *The home page that YouTube created for me automatically after I'd used it for a while (and signed up for an account) employs a number of different strategies to engage my attention, invite my participation, and to try to encourage me to explore some of the more social aspects of the site. Can you identify any social design principles at work here?*

We've identified a few principles that are as close to universal as possible. Most or all successful social websites and apps exhibit these factors. They can help you decide how and when to apply the more tactical design patterns we'll be explaining throughout the rest of this book, too. Before diving into the interconnected language of the design patterns, take a few moments to consider these principles and stow them in the back of your mind. Not only will you find that they cut across and inform many of the behavioral scenarios you're designing for with these patterns, but they will also help you make decisions when you go beyond the comfortable boundaries of past experience.

One common characteristic of social sites is that they must strive to work for everyone (that is to say, everyone in the target audience). They can't be tailored to a specific, narrow niche. But how do you cut across the variations in your user group? You can't please everybody. In fact, user experience design inherently involves trade-offs. So how do you cast as wide a net as possible and include as many people as possible?

Deliberately Leave Things Incomplete

One of the key differences between designing a social environment online and designing a traditional media-style, broadcast-oriented content site is that the design of a social community online cannot be entirely predetermined. Or, rather, let me say that it *should not* be. The denizens of a social site must be given the opportunity to "finish" the design themselves.

This principle finds form in a number of familiar concepts: customization, skinning, user-contributed tags, and the emergent folksonomies they can give rise to.

You might call this part of the process "meta-design." Rather than giving our users a fish, we are giving them a rod, reel, bait, and instructions to teach them how to fish. We design the rules of the system but not all of the outcomes. Some call this *generative design*, as you are designing interfaces that enable your participants to generate their own finished environments.

By designing with this philosophy, we create open space rather than filled-in labyrinths. If we are successful in bringing people to our site, engaging them, and involving them in the life of the community (as will be discussed in the following chapters), then they will make the subsequent choices, individually and collectively, that will determine the more detailed shape of their shared environment.

Now, clearly there are limits. There is a boundary you must find between the parts of your environment that are fundamental (stable, unchanging, and reliable) and those that are malleable. The line by necessity gets drawn in different parts of the architecture depending on the type of site. Think of a fairly simple example: skinning one's own profile page. MySpace permitted a riot of design permutations, creating a carnivalesque atmosphere reminiscent of the homestead on Geocities in the olden days of the Web. Facebook came along and offered you whatever color scheme you liked, as long as you liked a tasteful medley of blue tones. Neither design choice is inherently correct or incorrect, but the choice itself determines a vastly different outcome, potentially setting the tone for your entire social site.

Pave the Cowpaths

A motto often heard from supporters of microformats is "Pave the cowpaths," which means, essentially, look where the paths are already being formed by behavior and then formalize them, rather than creating some sort of idealized path structure that ignores history and tradition and human nature and geometry and ergonomics and common sense. This principle is sometimes applied on campuses, and sometimes a rear-guard "keep off the grass" action is fought instead, to no avail.

In the design of social interfaces, this rubric has two applications. The first is simply to do your ethnographic homework and study some of your potential customers. How do they do what they do today? Yes, of course the thing you want them to do will be better, but is it really entirely different? Can you offer people a way to continue doing most of the things they're comfortable doing today as you introduce new possibilities into their lives, or are you really going to insist on them changing everything at once?

The second application of Pave the Cowpaths comes later in the lifecycle of your site, when you have a user base and it starts doing things you never anticipated. Often the impulse is to stamp out these rogue behaviors and enforce draconian rules requiring only the behaviors you had planned for. This really only make sense if the behaviors you are trying to stamp out are truly destructive or evil. There are many anecdotes about thriving social sites that killed themselves off by legislating against fun and forcing their users into exile to find the activities they had been improvising "incorrectly" in the site they had to leave.

A better plan is to support the behaviors your users are engaged in. Let your users tell you what the best and highest use of your interface may turn out to be. Don't be so arrogant as to assume you know everything about how the social dynamics you've unleashed need to evolve.

Your Users' Mental Models

One of the things I like about computers is their ability to create magic. They provide abilities that no one thought possible and make them a reality. Yet, for many people this is also the biggest source of complaint about computers.

When you drive a car, you probably don't understand the thermodynamics of expanding chains of combusting hydrocarbons happening under the hood. Perhaps you understand the concept that gas expands in the engine block, pushing pistons in sequence, which makes the car go. But, even if you don't, you can still understand that there is a direct correlation between the accelerator and the car moving forward. Of course, most interfaces are not quite this simple, even in cars. If the car won't move, you assess what might have happened. And lo, you've left the parking brake on! With this error dealt with, you are free to go about your driving.

Obviously I'm not going to ask you to model your user interfaces after cars. However, it is interesting that while cars contain significant amounts of complexity (complexity you and I almost certainly don't fully understand), we can still functionally use them and recover the situation when things go wrong. This is because the sequence of events that makes the car work has formed a mental model in our heads. The car goes forward only when it contains fuel, the engine is on, you are not applying the brakes, and you are pressing the accelerator. Since we have this model of how the car works, we are able to troubleshoot when it doesn't behave as we expected.

What is significant about the models we create is how functional they are. They aren't based on the combustion of hydrocarbons or lateral torque. Heck, if there is serious engine trouble, that is still a black box to me, but I know I can call AAA to tow me to a garage. And this, dear friends, is the crux of it: you need to design interfaces that let people recover from their mistakes. The problem you face as the designers of magical boxes rather than cars, however, is that users do not have the same robust mental model of computers that they have for cars. When things go wrong, and they certainly will, your users are lost in a sea of uncertainty.

—continued—

Your Users' Mental Models

So, how do we solve this dilly of a pickle? Let's start with what we know. Users must have a mental model of computers; otherwise, they wouldn't be able to use them at all. However, the scope of this mental model covers, say, user interface widgets and probably some landmark- or list-based navigation. The problem, the thing that makes computers different from cars, is that computers interact differently based on context or conditions outside of our control. Much of this context may not be understood by the user, or may have never been explained. Cars are pretty old technology, and children learn about them in school. By the time we first learn to drive a car, we are expected to have a basic understanding of how it works, however generalized that model is. The same is not true for computers. Computer users are often actively discouraged from learning the underlying principles of what they are doing, and told to focus on the specifics of the interface.

A great example of how this leads to the breakdown of users' mental models is interaction with the Web. The Web is probably one of the least benign environments for a user on his computer, and yet it is arguably the most successful computing platform. When using the Web, there are numerous contextual or circumstantial errors than can occur, but the majority of users have no mental model with which to understand and recover from them. We looked at four possible causes of the gas pedal not accelerating a car, and yet a web page failing to load can have upward of a dozen causes. Since users lack a mental model, the best plan of action is to try and self-diagnose the error and educate the user. The distinction is important. Although it may seem sufficient to tell users that something went wrong and what they can do next, they eventually are going to get into the same state again with the same confusion. Instead, if there was a problem with the DNS, tell them so, and help them understand what DNS is. Maybe you have to use an analogy of a phone book for website numbers that their computer dials, or maybe you can convey the information in a more straight-up way. However you do it, don't just let your users keep failing and becoming frustrated. Instead, give them a mental model that will last them a lifetime as a satisfied customer.

—Tom Hughes-Croucher
Yahoo! Developer Network Evangelist

Strict Versus Fluid Taxonomies

Part of leaving the design unfinished involves determining which elements to nail down and which to leave more free-form. Using Flickr as a sort of canonical thriving social application (as I often will), it's easy to see examples of both design decisions at work. Some elements of Flickr's interface are rigidly defined. These include the object model, the site's master navigation, and the short list of predefined relation types.

The object model provides for people: people have collections of media objects, people can join groups and submit media objects to them, and so on. The site's master navigation has these items at its top level: Home, You, Organize, Contacts, Groups, Explore. The short list of predefined relation types allows for a person to define another person as a contact (this relationship need not be reciprocated to take effect), and optionally to further classify the person as a friend, a family member, or both (see Figure 2-2).

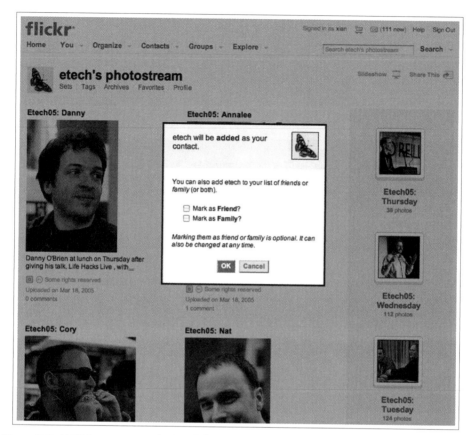

Figure 2-2. *At Flickr, contacts can be friend, family, or both (but that's it).*

I'm not saying these design and information architecture decisions have never changed. Since its launch, Flickr has added a second media type (video), and has refactored its navigation menus without changing the basic philosophy. It has also changed from a free-form connection model that allowed users to define additional relationships to the narrow one it has today (because relatively few users took much advantage of this feature, so it offered limited value for the maintenance required).

This last change backed off from the more fluid taxonomy approach that, where appropriate, can enable users to invent concepts, labels, classifications, and groups in an evolving way that meets their needs without requiring you, as the designer, to fully anticipate every conceivable scenario that your social application might foster and support.

In addition to these "rigid" taxonomy elements, Flickr also gives its users unlimited freedom along some carefully defined axes to invent whatever meaning they need. Examples of this include Flickr's well-known free tagging feature, which enables users to tag their own objects and gives users the option of permitting others to tag them as well (see Figure 2-3).

Figure 2-3. *There's no way the designer of a social application can anticipate every tag a user might want to apply. What controlled vocabulary, for instance, would ever include a tag called "thehairofchrisheilmann"?*

Another free-form taxonomy element inherent in Flickr's design is the unlimited ability to create groups with any conceivable name or purpose. This feature involves a number of patterns we'll discuss presently, including the concept of a group, ridiculously easy group formation, discussions, joining, invitation, and the ability to add media objects to a group's "pool."

Flickr users also invented the concept of an award associated with a group. These often-gaudy images are offered to users in the comments on a particularly relevant image or video and generally accompanied by an invitation to join the associated group (or at the very least to proudly display the award, which, incidentally, then functions as a sort of advertisement for the related group). Many people consider these awards tacky and pushy, but they do represent an innovation invented by users and permitted (but not directly supported) by the Flickr UI.

In this way (with or without awards) groups can function as a browsing "pivot" for users, taking them from the image of a friend to a related group, and then on to other images (see Figures 2-4, 2-5, and 2-6).

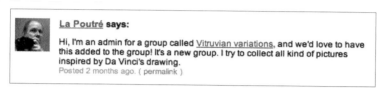

La Poutré says:

Hi, I'm an admin for a group called <u>Vitruvian variations</u>, and we'd love to have this added to the group! It's a new group. I try to collect all kind of pictures inspired by Da Vinci's drawing.
Posted 2 months ago. (permalink)

Figure 2-4. A caricature of Merlin Mann in the style of da Vinci's "Vetruvian Man" prompts an invitation to a group dedicated to just such parodies and variations.

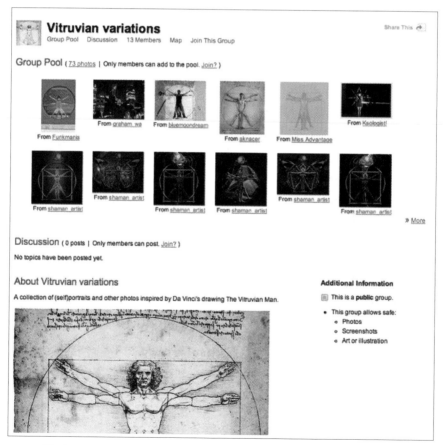

Figure 2-5. The Vitruvian variations group showcases a series of images with a common theme.

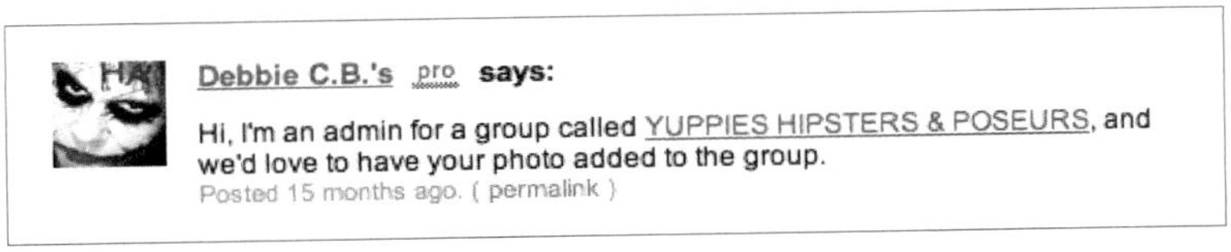

> **Debbie C.B.'s** <u>pro</u> **says:**
>
> Hi, I'm an admin for a group called <u>YUPPIES HIPSTERS & POSEURS</u>, and we'd love to have your photo added to the group.
> Posted 15 months ago. (permalink)

Figure 2-6. Another image in the group then prompts this further invitation that appears to facetiously parody the whole "Hi, I'm an administrator for a group called…" social interaction.

Palimpsest

In a talk that Matt "blackbeltjones" Jones gave at Adaptive Path's MX week in 2008, he recommended the metaphor of the palimpsest (*http://www.slideshare.net/blackbeltjones/battle-for-the-planet-of-the-apes-a-perspective-on-social-software-and-social-networks/56*) as a "model for social tools," while speaking of Dopplr, a social network for frequent travelers:

> *Our content itself gets smarter as it aggregates our thoughts about it.…. I think the palimpsest as a model for social tools is a powerful one.*

> *Of course they originated from the scarcity of media, something we don't exactly suffer [from]. But thinking about the medium as something that accretes messages in the way they did helps me.*

> *I also just like saying it. Palimpsest!*

We like saying it, too!

Literally, a *palimpsest* is a manuscript (this being an ancient term, it might be papyrus or parchment) that has been overwritten at least once, with the earlier text only partially erased and obscured. Thus the layers of the preceding meaning are still slightly visible through or "behind" the most current layer. The word has also been used as a metaphor to describe any place that reveals its own history.

Kenneth G. Wilson defined it in *The Columbia Guide to Standard American English* as "a piece of writing that has been erased one or more times and written over, so that it is layers deep. It then provides a metaphor for complicated reading or deciphering or simply for penetrating to truth through layers of matter overlying it. The metaphor is not so much about mystery or age as it is about layers of meaning."

OK, so what does it mean, then? Well, it means providing your users with ways to annotate, add meaning, add metadata, reformat, recreate, and change the environment you've designed for them, while still leaving traces of the earlier contexts.

Flickr Commons, shown in Figure 2-7, is a great example of this, also ~~stolen~~ borrowed from Matt.

Figure 2-7. *The Commons at Flickr provides a way for members of the community to annotate (by adding tags or comments to) photos from various museums and libraries (starting with the Library of Congress), thus adding successive layers of meaning to the digitized artifacts from these collections.*

Toward the Digital Palimpsest

The historical form of the palimpsest as a model for social tools is a powerful one.

Of course, it originated from the scarcity of media, when shortages of writing material meant continual reuse. This is something we don't exactly suffer from. Nevertheless, thinking about the Web through the lens of this ancient medium raises interesting points for me. Doing so points to a future where our content itself gets smarter as it aggregates our thoughts about it.

Layering of information on information—metadata—is of course nothing new. But the participative nature of doing so is.

—continued—

Toward the Digital Palimpsest

As recent publications by Clay Shirky and David Weinberger point out, everybody is annotating everything with everything else. Also, advances in mobile and locative technology point to the turning of the world around us into a palimpsest.

So what can we learn from the ancient analogue form of the palimpsest and its affordances?

For instance, look at maps from the collection of the National Maritime Museum, Greenwich, near my home, where successive explorers annotated new opportunities, theories, and obstacles on the same document taken on several expeditions over the course of several years.

From this, we could make the analogy that a successful digital palimpsest would require a permanent URL, which could be passed around and around without fear of fragmenting the knowledge accreting. Of course, there are not just positive lessons to be taken from the form. It takes a very liberal view of knowledge to say that everything that accretes on the palimpsest has the same value.

Those who examine historical versions of these palimpsests find something both in the form and the content, each layered over the other through tens or hundreds of years. Often the most valuable information is seen as worthless only a very short period of time later and written over, lost until modern conservation techniques can rediscover it.

The digital palimpsest inhabits a publish-everything, filter-later world, where we follow the dictums of one of the fathers of the Internet, John Postel: be conservative about what you put out and be liberal about what you accept. Understanding and filtering are key skills in reading palimpsests, both physical and ancient or modern and digital.

Work by Martin Wattenberg and Fernanda Viégas, including the beautiful and useful history flow (*http://www.research.ibm.com/visual/projects/history_flow/*), which depicts change over time within Wikipedia, points to the role information visualization will play in decoding our future palimpsests.

Recent announcements from Google on its "Wave" technology point to the substrate of the Web becoming one of real-time collaboration in the creation of content and meaning. That this is done through accretion of messages and media, rather than the publishing of pages, indicates that Google Wave may be the first full, real-time instantiation of the digital palimpsest.

And in the future it won't just be *everybody* annotating everything. *Everything* will be annotating everything, too.

Physical sensors will account for 20% of nonvideo Internet traffic by 2012, or so industry analyst Gartner predicts. Nonhuman chatter—the sense-memory of billions of things—will join the thoughts of millions of people.

Our environments, the objects within them, and ourselves will become palimpsests for us to participate in creating.

—Matt Jones, Design Principal at Schulze & Webb Ltd.,
and cofounder of Dopplr.com

Social but Not Social Only

Throughout this book, we will at times introduce patterns and principles whose domain is not limited to the realm of social applications. That's OK. There has always been a social undercurrent to the Internet, inherent in the fact that it has always offered a connection among people. For most of us, before we had Internet access, our computers were more like filing cabinets than telephones. They weren't communication devices, at least not in any direct way. (A typewriter may enable you to write a letter, but it doesn't deliver the letter to your correspondent.)

When personal computers became more readily networked and ultimately the "cloud" of the Internet, the experience of getting in front of a screen and typing on a keyboard (and later perhaps talking into a mic and staring into a camera) all became potentially social rather than solipsistic.

Thus a number of the patterns and principles in this book, such as the next set of patterns in this chapter, might be considered good advice for most contemporary web development projects, but they are particularly applicable to sites with a social dimension. (And, of course, that's also becoming a greater and greater percentage of the sites out there over time.)

Talk Like a Person!

(I was originally going to call this section "Speak in Human Voice" but then I decided to follow my own advice. I mean, really, who talks that way? "Talk like a person!" I think is closer to the mark.)

When many of us started putting together personal sites, art projects, and other creative or informal objects starting in the 1990s, the air of informality online was palpable. But when business came online a bit later in the decade, many of the first business-oriented websites reproduced the remote, inanimate, almost robotic corporate voice you tend to find in annual reports and catalog copy.

Even there, the more savvy enterprises appreciated the value of communicating to potential customers in a human voice. The corporation has always been a mask that disguises the human nature of the people who do the actual work of the business. Revealing the humanity of the people at the other end of the wire has a softening and welcoming effect.

Sure, there are still times where great formality and even perhaps distance are useful, but in an age when authority emerges from collaboration rather than being handed down from on high, the remote, formal, stylized tone of printed communications is continually in the process of giving way to a more natural, conversational tone. Abby Kirigin of TipJoy says, "I think it is important to note that conversational speech also takes you off the pedestal—and there is good and bad associated with that. You exchange some authority for a much better bond with your users. Overall that's great, I love it. Yet there is a time and a place to be authoritative. I've seen some people react negatively when they go to TOS and privacy pages that don't have what they perceive to be enough authoritative, legal statements. (There's a fine line here.)"

Of course it's easy to say "talk like a person," but what kind of person? Well, how about the type of person you hope will get involved with your site? Model the sort of tone and personality you're aiming to recruit.

This is all the more true in the context of social sites. If a website does not communicate from the get-go that it is populated, and written by, ordinary human beings, how will people ever feel comfortable there? The antiseptic air of a hospital or the bureaucratic formality of the Department of Motor Vehicles is no environment for fostering connections, relationships, or collaboration.

Bear in mind as well that the writing on your site or in your application is a key part of the user interface. Call it web copy, nomenclature, and labels if you like, but it's as much a part of the UI as the buttons, windows, and sliders.

So, communicate with your site participants in a human voice. But how? Getting this wrong is often creepy, verging on ghoulish, like an aging divorcee with love beads on at a love-in. The bottom line is *authenticity*. Would you really say that? Can you read it out loud without cringing? Does it *sound* like your kind of people?

This looks like a job for some patterns.

Conversation

The easiest way to talk like a person (in the user interface copy of your site or application) is to adopt a conversational tone (Figure 2-8).

- **Don't upload content that is illegal or prohibited.**
  If we find you doing that, your account will be deleted and we'll take appropriate action, which may include reporting you to the authorities.

- **Don't vent your frustrations, rant, or bore the brains out of other members.**
  Flickr is not a venue for you to harass, abuse, impersonate, or intimidate others. If we receive a valid complaint about your conduct, we'll send you a warning or terminate your account.

- **Don't be creepy.**
  You know the guy. Don't be that guy.

Figure 2-8. *Use the language of contemporary speech, not that of textbooks, tax forms, or street signs.*

What

People reading impersonal text on a screen will remain disengaged.

Use when

Use this pattern when writing copy for a social site, including instructions, errors, and other messages coming from the system itself and addressed to the reader, visitor, or member.

How

Resist the urge to write like a grad student or a bureaucrat. Ask yourself if that's really how you talk. Read any copy out loud, and strike out anything that feels awkward to say. Try speaking the text out loud to another person to see how it feels in your mouth, hear how it sounds aloud, and observe how the other person responds.

Despite what your English teacher may have told you, it's OK to use contractions, to split infinitives, and even to start sentences with conjunctions. Just make sure it feels natural.

Special cases

Be careful to avoid obscure slang unless you have already established confidence in the minds of your users to the extent that they are willing to rely on context and gist to follow your meaning.

Don't mistake being cute for being real.

Why

A conversational tone provides an opportunity for your site's visitor to respond as if really being spoken to by another person. This receptive state of mind permits the reader to enter into a dialogue with the site and reinforces the feeling that the site is made by people and not machines.

Examples

Flickr's terms of service epitomize this plainspoken approach, particularly the "Don't be that guy" comment.

Self-Deprecating Error Message

Error messages should always put the blame squarely on the shoulders of the site's owners and not on those of the visitor (Figure 2-9).

Figure 2-9. *Self-deprecating or just cute?*

What

Error messages written in a negative or even neutral tone can sound accusatory, suggesting that the visitor has misread instructions, filled out a form incorrectly, or otherwise screwed up. Being blamed for an error by a computer is off-putting.

Use when

Use this pattern when writing the copy for error messages at your site. You were planning to write those messages, right? You weren't going to forget about them (yielding helpful dialog boxes that say something like "Error 41"), right? You weren't going to expect your engineers to write them (yielding helpful dialog boxes that say something like "Error 41: Error 41 has occurred"), were you?

How

Writing in a *conversational tone*, explain to the extent possible what has gone wrong, why, and what to do next, if anything. Be sure to express the error in terms of a failure on the part of the system. Even if the cause of the error is the user's failure to comply with an instruction, assume that the instructions were unclear or that the entry form didn't provide sufficient guidance.

Don't blame the user for the error. Take the blame, apologize, and move forward.

Special cases

Saying "Oops" is one way to mimic a very human way of noticing a problem and taking responsibility at the same time. However, as Bill Cosby once joked, you never want to hear your surgeon say "Oops." It's equally true that for sites dealing with sensitive personal information or circumstances (such as, for example, medical or financial contexts), a more formal tone may be appropriate to avoid the appearance of flippancy. Even in a formal or sensitive situation, it's equally important to avoid blaming the victim when a problem occurs.

Examples

GetSatisfaction.com takes responsibility ("We couldn't find it") when a search turns up no results (Figure 2-10).

Figure 2-10. *Get Satisfaction doesn't make the user feel bad when a search fails.*

Likewise, Twitter takes the blame for a failed search, makes light of the problem with a LOLcat image, and offers some links to help the user proceed.

Ask Questions

One of the most common structures for a human conversation or dialogue is the format of question and answer (Figure 2-11). Since the days of the oldest mailing lists, Usenet, and Gopher, frequently asked question lists (FAQs) have sought to answer a person's questions with either the collected wisdom of the community or the answers from some authority.

Figure 2-11. *Twitter asks you a question to get you started.*

People naturally have questions and ask them, either silently while seeking an answer or directly if they perceive an opportunity to do so (in an inviting interface or in the context of a welcoming group of helpful, experienced community members).

But this pattern is about how you, as the voice of your site, should ask questions of your users.

What

It's very easy to arrive at a page or context online and not be sure what to do, how to proceed, what to say, what to type. A blank space can be very intimidating. (You should have seen my flopsweat when I started writing this chapter.)

An empty or silent page can leave the site visitor unsure of how to proceed.

Use when

Use this pattern when writing explanatory copy, help text, and labels on potential but currently unpopulated features in the user's interface.

How

Ask questions. Pose suggestions in the form of inviting questions. Write copy in an inquisitive way so that the site visitor feels compelled to reply with an answer.

Why

Questions invite responses, and asking them is a way of inviting participation.

Examples

Twitter asks you, "What are you doing?" Some people get hung up on whether or not to take this literally, but the point is that Twitter asked, it prompted. It's starting the conversation. It's inviting you to respond.

Your Versus My

Site developers frequently argue about how to label a user's own customized elements or collected objects to distinguish them from generic site content or objects belonging to other users of the site (Figure 2-12).

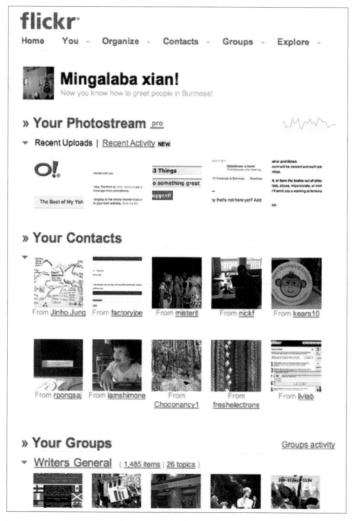

Figure 2-12. *Flickr refers to "your stuff," not "my stuff."*

There are two schools of thought on this, which can be called "Your" and "My." The names of some popular sites hint at this dilemma: My Yahoo, MySpace, YouTube.

Labeling stuff with "My" imitates the point of view of the user. It is as if the user has printed out labels and stuck them to various objects: My Lunch, My Desk, My Red Stapler. Except the user hasn't done this; you (the site) did it for her.

Labeling stuff with "Your" instead reinforces the conversational dialogue. It is how another human being might address you when talking about your stuff. Even with MySpace, people say things like "I saw what you put on your MySpace."

What

The possessive pronoun used to personalize or customize content on a site can reinforce either a social or solipsistic state of mind, depending on whether it's expressed in the second or first person.

Use when

Use this pattern when labeling objects belonging to or chosen by the individual user.

How

Use "Your" to label personal objects in social sites.

Open questions

Chris Fahey, a founder of the Behavior design firm, cautions that the choice between Your and My may depend on your brand:

> *This is, to me, something where a strong creative vision (brand identity, voice, audience relationship with the brand) can wildly trump any theoretical logical or usability goodness. A brand that has a personality that sounds like the product is a person, or speaks on behalf of a group of real people (like Flickr, which even says Hello to you), it makes sense to say "Your." But for brands that position themselves as an almost cybernetic extension of your personal infospace (like MySpace or Windows), "me" and "my" might actually make sense. In fact, consistency is probably the paramount rule here.*

Another approach that somewhat sidesteps the polarity of Your versus My is to use the person's name. Bill Scott, the lead UI Engineer at Netflix (and a renowned patternista himself) tells me that at Netflix they avoid "Your," preferring "Bill's recommendations." Their rationale is that it communicates the personalization (the same way "your" and "my" are supposed to), and it also clarifies that "it is you and not your kid (when using multiple profiles in a household)." But then again, for most people Netflix may be more of a personal utility than a social environment.

Objects labeled "My" on behalf of a user by the system give the feeling of an impersonal, if helpful, robotic valet or assistant, generically identifying items as if by proxy. This mode of nomenclature works just fine for private, individual environments. If a site has the feel of a bathroom cabinet or sock drawer, then calling items My Toothpaste or My Socks suits the solipsistic environment just fine.

However, in a social site, we want to avoid the call of introversion and instead encourage our participants to open themselves up to the possibility of conversation, both with their codenizens of the site and with the site (or rather the people "behind" the site) itself. Hence, we use "Your" to engage the social mind in a dialogue. A human being, even perhaps a live assistant or valet, might say, "I bought you your favorite toothpaste," or "Here are your socks."

Flickr refers to all of the user's objects as "Your."

The canonical asocial anti-pattern is perhaps Yahoo!'s My Yahoo site, where everything is labeled as "My," the site's name has My in it (MySpace falls prey to the same thinking, by the way), and the site's initials are even MY (Figure 2-13).

Figure 2-13. *My Yahoo provides users with a personal, customized experience, but one that has not, up to now, been social, and the labeling comports with that.*

No Joking Around

It's often been said that sarcasm and irony don't translate well into email (or ASCII communication in general). Hence the proliferation of smilies and other emoticons to soften the impact of stark words or cue the reader that the writer might have been kidding around and not intending to give offense.

By the same token, it's nearly impossible to tell jokes in user interface copy because a sense of humor is a unique thing in each person. What strikes one as funny might strike another as vulgar, inappropriate, boring, or tedious, and if the site has an international audience, differences in culture only exacerbate the potential problems.

Resist the urge to tell jokes or to be facetious in your interface copy.

What

People appreciate humor and ice-breaking witticisms, but unserious text in an interface is as likely to confuse people as amuse them.

Use when

Apply this pattern when tempted to put jokes in your interface.

How

Strike out any out-and-out jokes. This is not say that you can't be witty or make sly allusions to shared cultural references. But very few people can tell a joke well, especially to an invisible audience.

Special cases

A niche site catering to a community with a well-worn stock of traditional witticisms can probably offer jokes in that same vein safely without the risk of alienating or confusing potential site members.

Why

Because humor strikes so many people in different ways and because it's nearly impossible to anticipate exactly who will end up reading interface copy, it's best to eliminate outright jokes to avoid giving offense or creating unnecessary friction.

Let your users tell each other their own jokes.

Don't Break Email!

If you're using email as a broadcast medium—to send reminders or notifications, for example—and not enabling people to reply to the messages they receive, that's lame. There's no reason why you can't handle replies properly, forwarding them as further notifications to the correct recipients. This balances your interest in hosting and facilitating communication among members, and between your service and your customers, with your users' interest in being able to respond to email messages using their existing habits and customs.

For example, at one time email messages sent from 37 Signals' Basecamp product were one-way only, labeled with a warning message to the tune of "do not reply." It got wise, though, and as long as you reply above a certain line, it takes your reply and adds it to the comment thread on Basecamp (Figure 2-14), which serves its interests (keeping the conversation on the site) and yours (being able to hit Reply like a normal human being).

Figure 2-14. *It's quite possible to use email as a reengagement and contact medium for your application without frustrating your users when they rely on their experience and attempt to respond to email messages, just to drive more clicks on your pages.*

Be Open

Another broad principle I'd like to plant now in the back of your mind is that of openness. Being open is all the rage these days, but it means many things to many people. It can mean radical transparency, the use of open source software, exposing platform hooks, crowdsourcing, and more. In Chapter 17, we'll discuss several approaches to openness that we believe are essential to the effective design and development of social environments online, but for now just keep in mind the question "how could this interface be improved if we made it more open?" while designing your experiences.

Learn from Games

We'll talk a little bit later about the fascinating intersection between game design and social design that's opening up new possibilities for social experiences in game environments and introducing playful elements to social interfaces. An application doesn't have to literally be a game or be presented as a game to employ many of the same design techniques that make games fun to play.

It's no coincidence that Ludicorp's first product was something called Game Neverending (its second was Flickr, which owes at least some of its success to the almost addictive game-like quality of its user interfaces).

Even in the enterprise, interfaces don't have to be dry and tedious. Think about how to delight your users and encourage them to engage with one another.

Games are among the oldest "social interfaces." The rules and tokens of a game provide a set of affordances and an environment in which people interact. In fact, people will make up their own games with whatever elements they find handy. Many of the "memes" that spread on sites like LiveJournal, blogs, MySpace, and Facebook ("Which Buffy Character Are You?", "37 Things You Didn't Know About My Cat," or "iPod Shuffle Ouija") utilize built-in posting, commenting, and polling features, which isn't to say that you couldn't encourage your users to invent games for one another by giving them generative tools with which to do so.

Cargo Cult Anti-Pattern

The original cargo cults were people overawed by more advanced technology (in this case World War II–era aviation artifacts) who began imitating the forms of what they saw (wooden radio towers, torch-lit runways, counterfeit uniforms) in hopes of bringing the benefit ("cargo") that they had witnessed flowing from these same rituals and objects in the past. In their worst misapplication, design patterns can lapse into a sort of cargo cult, in which past structures and layouts and flows are imitated and reproduced with no real understanding of how or why they worked in their original context. A superficial but ubiquitous example of this is the proliferation of startups whose domain names featured a common word with a schwa vowel dropped from the final syllable, as if it was the spelling of Flickr that made it so successful (see Figures 2-15 and 2-16).

Figure 2-15. *Flickr still has its original slogan (or something rather close), whereas Zooomr has dropped its very similar one.*

Figure 2-16. *Zooomr imitated the way Flickr dropped the schwa vowel from the end of its source word. Its tagline was once also very close to Flickr's tagline, and much of the source markup was remarkably similar as well. Imitation is the sincerest form of flattery, they say, but it helps if you understand what you're imitating and why.*

Respect the Ethical Dimension

When you are designing experiences for people, or designing frameworks within which people will create their own experiences, there is always an ethical dimension.

What commitments are you making explicitly or implying when you open your doors for business?

Are you promising to keep people safe, to keep their information secure, to respect their privacy?

Are you willing to bend ethical rules to cheat your way through the cold-start problem and rapidly build your social graph? Balzac once wrote, "The secret of great wealth with no obvious source is some forgotten crime, forgotten because it was done neatly." Many successful social sites today founded themselves on an original sin, perhaps a spammy viral invitation model or unapproved abuse of new users' address books. Some companies never lived down the taint, and others seem to have passed some unspoken statute of limitations.

You'll find that some of the forces that must be balanced to apply many of these patterns involve ethical dilemmas. Is opt-out good enough? Is this disclosure adequate? Is it your responsibility to stop the bullying?

Throughout this book, we'll call out ethical factors when we see them, and encourage you in general to keep an eye out for them yourselves.

Further Reading

"Are We Building a Better Internet?" on page 476

"Cargo Cult Software Engineering," by Steve McConnell, *http://www.stevemcconnell.com/ieeesoftware/eic10.htm?*

Grasping Social Patterns, by Christian Crumlish, *http://www.slideshare.net/xian/grasping-social-patterns*

Jargon File entry on Cargo Cult Programming, *http://www.jargon.net/jargonfile/c/cargocultprogramming.html*

"Me vs. You (vs. i)," *http://www.graphpaper.com/2007/08-17_me-vs-you-vs-i* (Chris Fahey's Graphpaper blog)

"Rule 1," by Dave Winer, *http://archive.scripting.com/2002/09/29#rule1?*

"User vs. You," *http://www.graphpaper.com/2007/08-02_user-vs-you* (Chris Fahey's Graphpaper blog

Wikipedia entry on Cargo Cult Programming, *http://en.wikipedia.org/wiki/Cargo_cult_programming*

"You vs. I," *http://www.graphpaper.com/2007/08-11_you-vs-i* (Chris Fahey's Graphpaper blog)

"Your Web Application as a Text Adventure," *http://2007.sxsw.com/blogs/podcasts.php/2007/05/31/your_web_application_as_a_text_adventure?* (Michael Buffington, podcast from South by Southwest 2007)

Part II

I Am Somebody

The notion of *self*, something long discussed and debated by philosophers, psychologists, and scientists, is now part of the discussion in the user experience design world.

In the social space online, people can declare explicit attributes about themselves and build a rich profile for others to view. Balanced against the reputation a person builds through his actions and words, this profile can give others a sense of who he is. Just by being involved, engaged, and inclusive, people can build a portrait of the self and an identity within the system, which others can then interact with.

The next few chapters discuss in depth the patterns and considerations for providing the framework within which a person can engage with a service, build his identity (real or otherwise), assert himself so others can connect and interact with him, and develop a rich reputation that is built out of his activity within the system.

Chapter 3

You're Invited!

The table was a large one, but the three were all crowded together at one corner of it: "No room! No room!" they cried out when they saw Alice coming. "There's plenty of room!" said Alice indignantly, and she sat down in a large arm-chair at one end of the table.

"Have some wine," the March Hare said in an encouraging tone.

Alice looked all round the table, but there was nothing on it but tea. "I don't see any wine," she remarked.

"There isn't any," said the March Hare.

"Then it wasn't very civil of you to offer it," said Alice angrily.

"It wasn't very civil of you to sit down without being invited," said the March Hare.

"I didn't know it was your table," said Alice; "it's laid for a great many more than three."

"Your hair wants cutting," said the Hatter. He had been looking at Alice for some time with great curiosity, and this was his first speech.

"You should learn not to make personal remarks," Alice said with some severity; "it's very rude."

— Lewis Carroll, "A Mad Tea Party," Chapter VII,
Alice in Wonderland

Engagement

I recently held a party to celebrate my birthday. In planning the party, I needed to decide who was invited as well as the theme and events of the party itself. I had limited time to plan, and since this was a personal celebration, I wanted it limited to friends and family—I didn't necessarily want to have a blowout party and invite everyone I have ever known. When I had confirmed the invite list, I sent out invitations. A couple of times between initially planning and the actual party, I sent out reminder updates to increase the anticipation of the event.

Once the night of the party arrived, I spent my time greeting people as they entered my home and then mixing through the crowd to make sure people felt welcome and that they were having a good time. As host, it was part of my responsibility to check in, to mingle, to make sure the house was welcoming, and to keep the food and drinks stocked.

Starting a site that is social or has social components is not really that different from planning and hosting a party. You need to think about who's invited, whether they can invite other people, and what is going to happen once they are there. Once people come to the site, you need to greet them and welcome them in a friendly manner, and make them feel like they are important and have value to add to the community. If they don't know the others there, then you need to make introductions or make it easy for people to introduce themselves. At that point, they need to feel as if they can mingle and have interesting conversations, even if they hadn't known one another before arriving.

Don't forget the cold-start issue, either. Early adopters like to come in and poke around, test the waters. They will show up and sign up for every new thing as it comes along. Like the homesteaders of old, they come in, lay the groundwork of a community, and either stay to become old-timers or move on if it's not to their liking. Preparing for these types of users often goes beyond the simple interactions of signing up and has implications in how you welcome your users, how and when you encourage them to bring their friends along, and how easy that process is to set up.

The first steps in the process of encouraging people to come in and participate set the tone of their whole experience. How you follow up and welcome your users can make their first impressions favorable or not. People will share their first impressions with others, and that can affect the growth of your site and your brand if they are not favorable.

Think about the processes you have in place to allow your users to participate and become engaged in your community. How complex or easy does your registration need to be? What barriers are you willing to put in place between your site and what your users want to do? What barriers can you remove? What's the bare minimum to get started? How much personal information is stored, and what privacy controls do you need to have in place to help people feel secure about their activity and contributions?

How will you engage early adopters, who may be incredibly influential in spreading the word about your service? Will you have a private or open beta? What's the value of one over the other? Are there levels of engagement, a lifecycle that users go through where features are progressively disclosed? How do you re engage users who may be spending less time on your site than when they were newly engaged?

This collection of patterns addresses these questions with best practices for how to handle many of the options that affect the user's entrée to a community, his overall participation lifecycle, and privacy options.

Sign-up or Registration

A user wants to access parts of a site or application that require creating or saving personal information. A user wants to contribute content to the site's community and have it attributed and saved for later. (See Figures 3-1 and 3-2.)

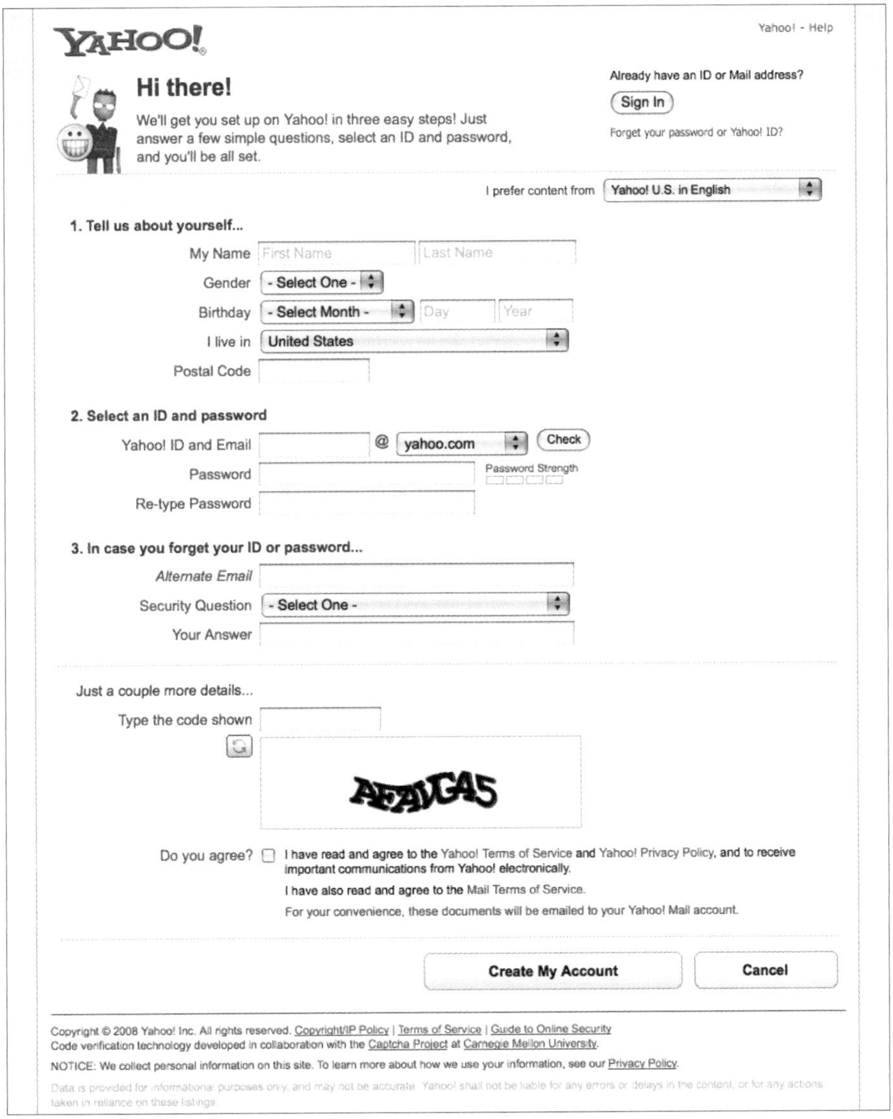

Figure 3-1. *The Yahoo.com registration screen collects enough information to provide value and security.*

Figure 3-2. *Tumblr registration is an example of barebones data collection just to get the user started.*

Use when

Use this pattern when:

- Features require leaving personal or private information, and privacy and security are a concern.

- Financial transactions require remembering billing, shipping, and transaction information.

- A user wants to participate—leaving comments, blogging, posting to message boards, posting photos, building a personal network—and this participation needs to be attributed and/or associated with the user for purposes of building community or reputation, or building up a personal profile or knowledge base.

How

- Collect the bare minimum of information needed that still allows your user to participate in the site. This is often an email address—used as the login—and a password. Consider whether or not registration is even needed (see Figure 3-3).

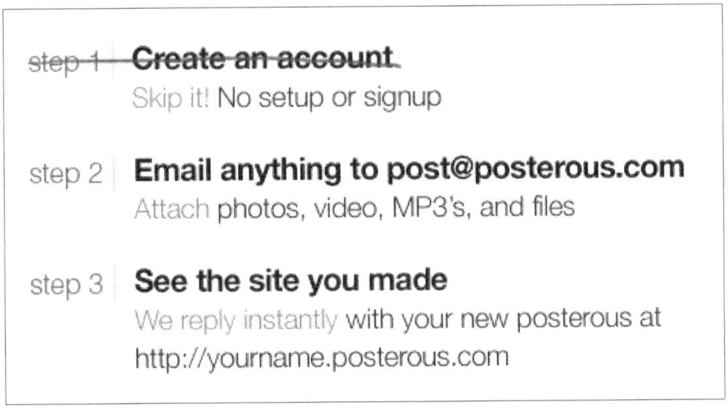

step 1   ~~Create an account~~
         Skip it! No setup or signup

step 2   **Email anything to post@posterous.com**
         Attach photos, video, MP3's, and files

step 3   **See the site you made**
         We reply instantly with your new posterous at
         http://yourname.posterous.com

Figure 3-3. *posterous.com doesn't require a sign-up before using. The act of sending an email through the service creates an account automatically tied to the user's email address and name.*

- Collect other information only as necessary for a compelling experience. Ask your-self if the data you are about to collect can be requested in another part of the site at another time.

- Provide explanations about what each piece of information requested will provide in terms of user benefits. For example:

  - Zip code or other location information provides location-relevant restaurants and stores.

  - Mobile phone number allows delivery of content to phone and delivery of con-tent from phone to a web-based account.

- Require registration at the last possible moment in the users' process of exploring the site, such as when they want to save a video they have created.

- After registration, deliver the users back to the task they were in before they were sidetracked. If they were coming from a tour or exploration process, put them in the most logical spot that encourages them to get started.

- Avoid gradual engagement solutions that simply distribute the various input fields in a sign-up form across multiple pages. It's a good possibility that this will reduce efficiency and not delight anyone.[*]

- Allow the creation of a unique identifier by allowing the use of an email address, which is a unique piece of data and can be verified with the user.

---

[*] *Web Form Design* by Luke Wroblewski. Rosenfeld Media, Brooklyn, NY, 2008; page 206.

- Don't force the user to try and create a unique name that isn't an email address. Unless she is an early adopter on your site, the odds that the name (often her first name) she wants is available gets smaller over time (as in Figure 3-4). At best, this will only annoy your users, and at worst cause site abandonment and ill will.

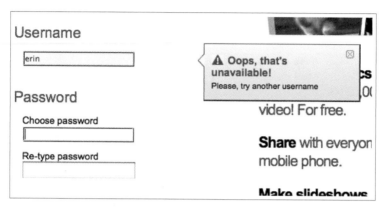

Figure 3-4. *Sign-up error message on PhotoBucket. This error was generated because the namespace is full. The user would have more success if she were allowed to use her email address, which is already a unique identifier.*

- Allow use of a nonunique nickname to reflect back to the user and for communication between the system and user.

- Clearly label what elements are required for a username and password. Are capital letters and numbers required? Are alternate characters not allowed? A minimum of 6 characters or a maximum of 15? Say so up front, and don't wait to present this information in an error message. Jared Spool calls this designing defensively. Clearly stating expectations up front will prevent interruptions and ensure a more successful sign-up experience.

- Provide feedback as the user fills out the form, as in Figure 3-5. Examples include a checkbox as a field is filled out correctly (e.g., a fully realized email address) or a password strength meter to indicate the security potential of a password.

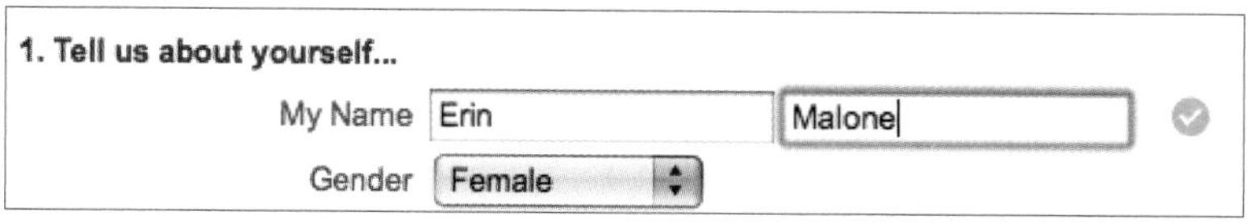

Figure 3-5. *Yahoo!'s registration form shows green checks when sections are correctly filled out.*

- Provide inline, contextual error messages that validate dates and data formation or check on username availability before the Submit button is pressed (see Figure 3-6). This will allay user irritation and result in less drop-off in completions.

1. Tell us about yourself...

My Name	Erin	Malone
Gender	- Select One -	
⚠ Birthday	August	5 2010 ◀ Are you really from the future?
I live in	United States	
Postal Code		

Figure 3-6. *Yahoo!'s registration form provides inline error messaging when something is not right with the field entry. In this case, the user put a future date into the field. The error message uses humor to let the user know that this entry is not acceptable.*

- Make sure the level of security required for the password matches the level of security required for the data the user will be creating or saving. Saving a recipe is very different from paying a bill at a bank. The expectations for site security and the type of password used are very different. Adjust accordingly.

- Include a captcha if absolutely necessary. Captchas are used to "prove" that the person registering for the service is a person and not a robot. Unfortunately, nefarious people have figured out how to get around this by using cheap labor to read captchas and create accounts for the purposes of sending spam and other types of attacks. Captchas also require a workaround for accessibility and are often hard to read, so make absolutely sure you require this extra work from your users.

- Consider skipping the entire registration form and allow users to sign up with OpenID (*http://openid.net/what/*), OAuth (*http://oauth.net*), or Facebook Connect (*http://developers.facebook.com/connect.php*).

Why

Registration is often an interruption for users when they are in the middle of some other process. It's a known and accepted evil when personal data or user-generated content needs to be stored, but that doesn't mean sites should take advantage of the interruption to collect a life story and the user's firstborn. (See Figure 3-7.)

Figure 3-7. *Sign-up screen from Twitter.*

Users will give what they believe is necessary in exchange for a good experience. If more information than a unique identifier and password is needed, it is important to be very clear why that information is necessary and what value it will bring to the user. Registration is a barter with users, and they will abandon the process and your site if the value isn't clearly articulated or seen as high enough.

Accessibility

The sign-in form should easily navigable via the keyboard, with the Submit button triggered by the Return key.

Related patterns

"Sign In" on page 51

"Sign-In Continuity" on page 54

"Sign Out" on page 56

"Terms of Service" on page 252

As seen on

Tumblr (*http://www.tumblr.com*)

Twitter (*http://www.twitter.com*)

Yahoo! (*http://www.yahoo.com*)

Yelp (*http://www.yelp.com*)

Sign In

What

The user wants to access her personalized information or an application that is stored on the host site (Figure 3-8).

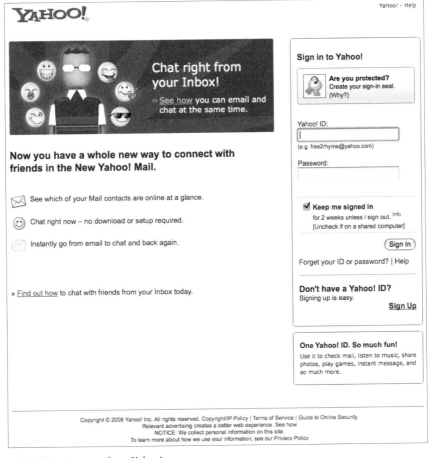

Figure 3-8. *Sign-in screen from Yahoo!.*

Use this pattern when:

- Personal data needs to be stored or when there is customization or personalization unique to the particular user.

- The site is a repository for user-generated content and the submissions or files need to be identified and/or managed by the author.

- There are security or privacy concerns and the user's data needs to be protected.

Don't require the user to sign in if it isn't really necessary. Just because you want to know who is on your site doesn't mean that's a good reason to put up the barrier to your users.

- Provide a clearly labeled Sign In button, as in Figure 3-9. Don't use the label Login. Remember you are speaking like a real person.

Figure 3-9. *Sign-in module from Twitter.com.*

- Provide an input field for the username.
  - This should be a unique identifier. Many sites use an email address (Figure 3-10) to alleviate the namespace problem that will happen as a site scales.

Figure 3-10. *Sign-in widget from Dopplr.com.*

  - To avoid unnecessary errors, clearly label what type of username is required for the field (Figure 3-11). Many users often utilize a variety of login names, will forget which one is used, and can end up locked out, frustrated, or abandoning the site.

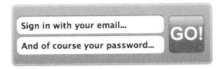

Figure 3-11. *Sign-in widget from Centerd.com.*

- Provide an input field for the password.

- Provide a clear way to retrieve the username if it is forgotten.

- Provide a clear way to retrieve the password if it is forgotten.

- If appropriate, allow the user to stay signed in to the site for an extended amount of time. This is often presented with a checkbox and text that clearly lets the user know how long he will stay signed in. Don't forget to set the right expectations of what will be remembered. Is it the name and password, or just the name only? Be clear.

- Once signed in, the site should reflect back in some way that the user is signed in. This is often presented by showing the user's name (login or nickname) and a Sign Out option.

- Provide a way to sign out once signed in.

- If the user does not have an account, provide easy access to signing up for the site, without distracting the user who just wants to sign in.

- Delay the sign-in requirement until the last possible moment—when the user needs access to private information or needs to save data.

- Options such as "Keep me signed in for 2 weeks" or "Remember me on this computer" should be opt-in. If the user's computer is shared, this protects against accidentally allowing another person into the account.

Why

Having users sign in to your site allows them to save information and content for later use. Registered and signed-in users are more valuable to your business, as you will generally have more information about them (both direct information, and indirect information gleaned through their behavior and interactions).

Requiring users to sign in to do certain tasks—leaving comments, posting photos or videos, participating in a conversation—forces them to be responsible for their participation. They build up a reputation and a body of work, and others know who they are by their actions and participation.

Accessibility

The sign-in form should easily navigable via the keyboard, with the sign-in button being triggered by the Return key.

Related patterns

"Sign-In Continuity" on page 54

"Sign-up or Registration" on page 45

"Sign Out" on page 56

As seen on

Amazon.com (*http://www.amazon.com*)

Facebook (*http://www.facebook.com*)

Google Reader (*http://google.com/reader*)

LinkedIn (*http://www.linkedin.com*)

Photobucket (*http://www.photobucket.com*)

TripIt (*http://www.tripit.com*)

Twitter (*http://www.twitter.com*)

Yahoo! (*http://www.yahoo.com*)

YouTube (*http://www.youtube.com*)

Sign-In Continuity

What

A user who has an account but is not currently signed in wants to participate by contributing something.

Use when

Use this pattern when authentication is required for participation in a community. Forms of participation include (but are not limited to) comments, votes, ratings, tags, posts to blogs or forums, and so on.

How

- When the user attempts to comment (or take similar action), remind her of the need to sign in first and deliver her to the sign-in flow.

- When the user has successfully signed in, return her to the context she was in when she was about to comment or take similar action (Figure 3-12).

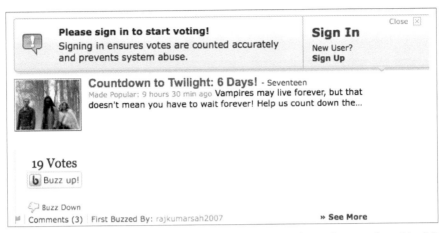

Figure 3-12. *Yahoo! Buzz prompts for sign-in only when needed, and once the user is logged in, delivers her back to her original task.*

- When handling the submission of information, preserve any data that has been entered prior to the login procedure.

Why

It's important that the sign-in requirement does not present an undue barrier to participation for the user.

Special cases

If security concerns (such as cross-site scripting issues, and possible cross-domain issues) require an interruption in flow or even that the user be returned to a home page, then at least insert an alert message with a clear call to action to resume the moment of participation.

This message might include a link to the last known location, a pre populated form, or a message indicating a redirect in *x* seconds.

Related patterns

"Sign In" on page 51

"Sign Out" on page 56

"Sign-up or Registration" on page 45

As seen on

Kayak (*http://www.kayak.com*)

Yahoo! Buzz (*http://buzz.yahoo.com*)

Sign Out

The user wants to sign out of the system, to end a session, or become anonymous (Figure 3-13).

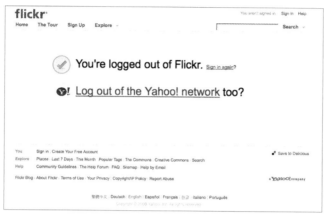

Figure 3-13. *Sign-out screen on flickr.com.*

Use this pattern when:

- A user wants to end his session.

- A user wants to become anonymous.

- A user is on a public computer and needs to preserve privacy and security of his personal data and contributions.

- The user has signed out and you want to continue his relationship with your site. For example, you want to give him ideas for where to go next and information about new features.

- Consider providing a landing page that clearly indicates that the user is no longer signed in.

- Offer clear options for features to explore, even if he is signed out, or for when he returns.

- Provide the ability to easily sign back in.

- Keep the page light in terms of content and performance size in order to mitigate frustration and end the session on a positive experience.

Why

Once a user signs out of a service, it isn't clear what his next intentions are. Sites often will throw a user back to the home page once he is signed out, but this can be overwhelming and doesn't always clearly indicate whether the logout process succeeded.

Providing a Sign Out landing page that clearly indicates the logout's success will let the user know that he has been successful.

This page is also an opportunity for communication about new or unexplored features as part of a reengagement strategy (see the pattern "Reengagement" on page 75).

Related patterns

"Reengagement" on page 75

"Sign In" on page 51

As seen on

Flickr (*http://www.flickr.com*)

The Usage Lifecycle

The usage lifecycle is a simple idea, made up of several steps that illustrate a general progression people go through when using software.

First, people hear about software in some way, perhaps from a colleague or friend. After that, they decide to give it a try and sign up or register for it. Then, they go through the crucial step of using it for the first time. Finally, they fall into a pattern of ongoing use (or not using it at all).

By looking at your software in terms of the usage lifecycle, we recognize that each step in the lifecycle has very particular design challenges that we can focus our efforts on.

For example, people who have heard about software often have questions about it. What are the questions people ask about your software? Are you listening and writing them down, embedding them on your website and within your application, and preempting new customers who will undoubtedly have the same questions? Or, alternatively, is there a way to short-circuit the sign-up process, a notorious part of the lifecycle? Can we get people using the software before they sign up for it?

The usage lifecycle isn't rocket science, but a good framework to keep in mind throughout design. It can help you design contextual help within your application or help you put together materials for enabling people to learn about and get started using your software.

If we're lucky, people will move through this lifecycle relatively quickly and with confidence. If that happens, they'll be much more likely to share their enthusiasm with others. This is the ultimate goal: a virtuous cycle of sharing.

—Josh Porter, Bokardo Design and author of
Designing for the Social Web

Invitations

Invitations, both sending and acting upon them once received, are core to the viral nature of social web experiences.

Receive Invitation

A user receives an invitation from a friend or connection to join a site (Figure 3-14).

Figure 3-14. *Invitation to join Twine.com.*

Use when

Use this pattern when:

- The user experience is enhanced by building a network of user connections.
- Growth of the service is dependent on friends of friends.
- You want to supplement traditional user acquisition with user-based referrals.

How

- The invitation should have personal messaging from the sender.
- The sender should be clearly identified to the recipient.
- The benefits of joining and participating should be clearly articulated to the recipient.
- A very clear "Call to Action" button or link should be available for the recipient to easily step right into the site to try it out.

Why

Having a formal invitation in place for your users to send to their friends allows you to combine a controlled marketing message from your site with a personal message from the user. This process also guarantees a consistent call-to-action for viral growth.

Related patterns

"Send Invitation" on page 59

Send Invitation

What

A user sends an invitation to a friend or group of friends asking them to join in a site experience (Figure 3-15).

Figure 3-15. *"Invite by email" screen on Twitter.*

Use this pattern when:

- The user experience is enhanced by having a network of connections.
- Growth of the service is dependent on friends of friends.
- You want to supplement traditional user acquisition with user-based referrals.
- A user has participated in the site enough to have formed an opinion of its value and can then recommend it to a friend.

Don't use this pattern right after registration, when the user hasn't actually participated in the site. When presenting the option to invite others, do so after enough interaction with your site that the user actually knows what she is referring.

- Use an in-context email form.
- Provide the user with a sample message that showcases the benefits of joining the service.
- Make the prefilled content editable, and allow the user to personalize the invitation.
- Allow users to invite others via access to their address books.

- Provide a mechanism that allows users to send copies of the message to themselves.
- Provide a mechanism to bring contacts and email addresses over from other social services. Use a standard accepted technology, such as OAuth and OpenID, rather than the password anti-pattern (see "The Password Anti-Pattern", next).
- Don't force a user to invite others to the site before she has had a chance to try out the features.
- Do make it easy for a new user to find the "invite friends" link.
- Don't spam a user's address book or contact list from other sites.

Special cases

If the use of the site and its features is heavily dependent on a group of people interacting, then the need to allow a user to bring friends along, through invitations or bulk registering, will override the recommendation of encouraging use before inviting friends.

Why

Allowing users to invite their friends to your site is part of the viral nature of a social site. Providing tools and system interactions that allow your users to be good netizens will enhance the overall experience and your site's reputation in the long run.

Related patterns

"Receive Invitation" on page 58

As seen on

Twitter (*http://www.twitter.com*)

The Password Anti-Pattern

Just what is the password anti-pattern? And why is this an issue? On many social sites, to combat the cold-start situation where a user joins and has no friends, the site might ask a person to find his friends on the site by comparing known data pulled in from another service (such as the user's online address book). The site may ask the user to open up access to all his various online address books so that it can match names and email addresses to current customers and then offer the new user a list of friends on the service for the purposes of making connections (see Figure 3-16).

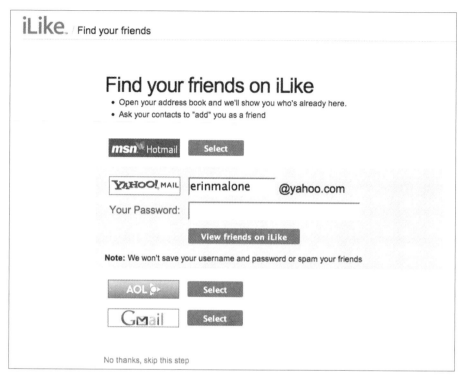

Figure 3-16. *Password anti-pattern as seen on iLike.com.*

Sites implement this because it's easy. The problem with this interaction is that the site is asking the user to supply a username and password for another service. Many sites never intend to do anything beyond that one-time data grab and promise not to use the name and password for anything but that, but there is really no way for a user to trust the site or know that the site owners are telling the truth. The end goal of this solution is to make it easy and painless for a person to find his friends and become more quickly engaged. Unfortunately, there are phishing scammers and account hackers who have created sites or services that "appear" trustworthy, but are really just grabbing a user's account for nefarious purposes. Additionally, this practice violates the terms of service for many of the sites that are being accessed.

The password anti-pattern teaches users to give their login credentials away to a stranger and sets them up to be more easily phished across the Internet. People get used to the practice and eventually don't think twice about giving this information to a new site in exchange for some cool new promise.

A safer alternative is to use services such as OAuth, OpenID, or Facebook Connect to officially authorize access to the user's data on the other site.

OAuth is "[a]n open protocol to allow secure API authorization in a simple and standard method from desktop and web applications." In other words, it is an open technology that allows sites to access a user's data in a safe way that doesn't require the user to throw names and passwords all over the Internet. The actual access happens on the third-party site where the data is stored and under its control. AOL, Yahoo!, and Google have all agreed to support OAuth, so there should be no reason to perpetuate this anti-pattern in the coming years. Additionally, OAuth is a core component to the OpenSocial API, which is being developed and supported by many companies creating social software.

Flickr implemented a similar authorization scheme a while ago, in which any third party that wants access to a user's photos requires a user to come through to Flickr to "authorize" the gateway and transfer of data. FriendFeed calls its solution RemoteKey, which "is a kind of password that you can give to third-party applications and websites to let them interact with FriendFeed on your behalf." RemoteKey offers a limited set of actions to safeguard the user's account. Twitter has recently implemented OAuth for account access, which will in turn stop the account hackers that have been popping up right and left around the Twitter ecosystem.

Ultimately, users should have access to their data and should be allowed to bring it from one site to another—whether it's their connections, their social graph, or their contributed data, such as photos or videos. Social sites, which need connections to enhance the user's experience, should adopt safe authentication interactions that both allow users to access their data *and* protect them by teaching better Net behavior for keeping their passwords safe.

Authorize

The user wants to participate on a site without starting from scratch. She would like to bring her data and files over from another site, as shown in Figures 3-17, 3-18, and 3-19.

Figure 3-17. *An authorization screen on Facebook lets the Flickr application access Facebook profile information.*

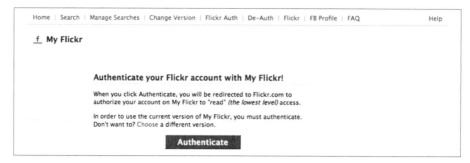

Figure 3-18. *An authentication screen from the My Flickr Facebook application gives the user the option to let the application read from her flickr.com account.*

Figure 3-19. *Flickr's authorization screen giving third-party read access to data in the Flickr account. Allowing the access lets Flickr pictures from my stream show up in a Facebook application on my profile.*

Use when

Use this pattern when:

- Features on your site are enhanced or expanded by accessing data and files from another site (Site A in the upcoming example).

- User-generated content or data on your site has the potential to enhance or enable other sites that your users may be participating in (Site B in the upcoming example).

How

Successful authentication requires cooperation from two sites: one with features and functionality enhanced by a user's data (Site A) and the other with that user's data and/or files to share (Site B).

Site A

- Before automatically using the Password Anti-Pattern (see "The Password Anti-Pattern" on page 61) to access a user's data, check to see whether the other site is using OAuth. If so, tap into that protocol to facilitate the data transaction.

- Site A should ask the user what data she would like to access.

- Show possible choices, such as flickr.com, photobucket.com, smugmug.com, etc. for photos, or Yahoo! Address Book, Plaxo.com, Google, etc. for contacts.

- Once the user selects the site where her data lives, Site A should send the user to that site to grant access.

- Information about how the data will be used should be presented on Site A.

Site B

- Use the open authentication protocol, OAuth, to facilitate the authorization process.

- Site A will send its user to Site B. The user signs in to his account, and Site B should present a screen that asks if the user really wants to share the data with Site A.

- Upon agreement, the user is sent back to Site A, and the data is now available in that experience.

- Information about how Site A will use the permissions granted should be clearly presented to the user on Site B.

- Allow the user to cancel the authorization at any point.

- Provide an easy way for the user to revoke permissions from Site A.

Why

Using an authorization flow and protocol such as OAuth allows a user to give access among sites without exposing her username and password. This process is the preferred method of allowing data-sharing, rather than using the Password Anti-Pattern.

Related patterns

"The Password Anti-Pattern" on page 61

As seen on

Facebook (*http://www.facebook.com*)

Flickr (*http://www.flickr.com*)

Private Beta

What

A user is eager to try out a site even before it's fully ready for the general public.

Use when

Use this pattern when:

- You want a limited group of users to help you test and popularize your first release (Figure 3-20).

Figure 3-20. *twine.com shows its beta status in the upper-left corner. The sign-up form on the home page states that the product is still in beta, that it's adding members every day by invitation only, and that signing up requests an invitation but does not necessarily sign the user up for the product at this time.*

- You want to allow a small user list the opportunity to invite *N* new users to grow your site virally, but in a controlled fashion.

How

- Clearly indicate that the site is in private beta.
- Offer a list of features and benefits or a tour of the product to let the user know what he is signing up for.
- When requiring a user to sign up to receive information about the beta or an invitation to join at the next release:
  - Provide an email address field for sign-up.
  - Provide a username field for sign-up.
  - Show a confirmation page letting the user know that the sign-up request was received, and indicate a timeframe for when he might expect a response or invitation to join the site.
  - Send a confirmation email to the address provided, to verify the address and remind the user that he signed up to receive an invitation to join the beta at a future date.
- When allowing users to invite a limited number of others to the private beta:
  - Clearly indicate how many invitations the user gets in total.
  - Keep a count of how many invitations the user has sent out or has left from the total, and put this in a visible location.
  - Allow the user to add a custom message to the invitation.
  - Clearly articulate feature highlights and benefits to the potential invitee.

Why

A private beta can give you the opportunity to test-drive social features with a small group of people before opening the doors to the public. Starting off in a private beta also allows you to seed areas of the site with friends and family in order to avoid the cold-start issue. Additionally, the exclusivity of a private beta can encourage hype and desire for the service, and increase the requests for accounts.

Special cases

It used to be that beta was a period of time when real users would be asked to try the site out—to find bugs at a larger scale that might not have shown up with smaller test groups—and then the product would move quickly to General Availability (GA) release, where the public at large would have access.

In today's world of Web 2.0 and the ability to quickly launch web applications, we are seeing more and more sites slap the beta flag on the site and then never remove it. (See Figures 3-21, 3-22, and 3-23.)

Figure 3-21. *Gmail has been in beta since 2004.*

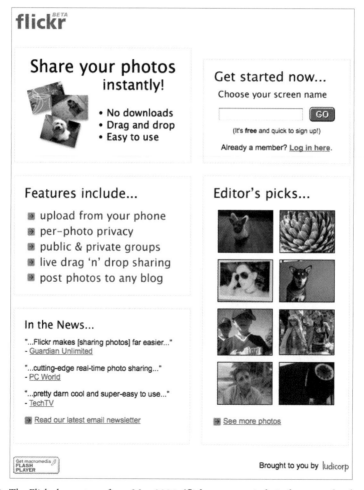

Figure 3-22. *The Flickr home page from May 2004. (flickr.com was in beta for a couple of years.)*

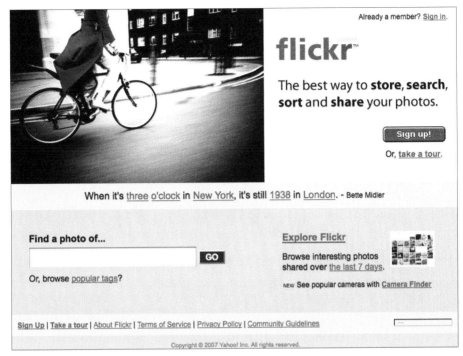

Figure 3-23. *The Flickr home page from January 2007. (flickr.com briefly moved into "gamma" in early 2007/late 2006 and for a while afterward put "loves you" where "beta" and "gamma" had been.)*

This generally does a disservice to users and to the process of software development. Beta has certain implications about quality and the site's point in the lifecycle of development. Keeping the beta flag for a lengthy period of time tells your users that the site is buggy and that you may not be spending time working through bugs to a full GA release. After a while, that message implies that you don't care to improve the site, which could have the adverse effect of driving users away—because if you don't care, then why should they?

As seen on

Flickr (*http://www.flickr.com*)

Gmail (*http://mail.google.com*)

Onboarding

What is onboarding, and why is it important?

Most companies think that getting people to sign up is the ultimate challenge, but what about getting them oriented to your site and actually using it? That process of helping people get started is called **onboarding**, and it's crucial that you give it the attention it deserves.

When left to their own devices in a new space without any sense of direction or purpose, many users can feel lost, overwhelmed, and confused about what they're supposed to be doing there. The user might have arrived at your site from a link in an article, an organic search result, or on the recommendation of a friend. In essence, the user is taking a leap of faith that she will be able to achieve something on your site, and it's your responsibility to shake her hand and show her the ropes when she gets there.

They say you don't get a second chance to make a first impression, and on the Web it's truer than ever. If you don't capture the attention of new visitors from the moment they arrive and guide them on their initial journey through the site, they won't learn that the benefit you provide outweighs the cost—their time and effort to participate—and as a result, won't stick around very long. Worse, they'll tell their friends not to bother visiting, either.

Onboarding is the process by which you can help users overcome the cold-start problem—a blank profile, an unfamiliar interface, a general feeling of "what the heck do I do next?" Many websites force users to start from square one and build up content (and value) over time. Social apps in particular are prone to this because so much of their usefulness is derived from person-to-person interaction and user-generated content.

The term *onboarding* comes from the field of human resources and the common practice of new hire orientation. In that context, the steps in the process are often referred to as *accommodate*, *assimilate*, and *accelerate*—all of which apply quite nicely to how new users ought to be treated in order to bring them into the fold.

Accommodating your users means giving them the tools they want and need to use your site to their benefit. Assimilating means helping the user to absorb the culture of the site and, in a sense, come to resemble the existing users. And accelerating generally applies to delivering on the value proposition better and faster.

Oftentimes, the true value of your product or service becomes apparent only after significant use—perhaps because the user needs a sizable social network to really reap the benefits, or because continued activity on the site ultimately leads to something, like better recommendations. But don't make the mistake of assuming that your users will stick with you that long. You need to help them get there as quickly and painlessly as possible in order to make your case.

Designing the onboarding process for your site is most commonly limited to a first-time use scenario: from the moment just after a user has signed up until the end of his first session. There are certainly extended approaches you can take to consider the user's needs during subsequent visits until he is exhibiting a desired behavior on the site, but exert caution, lest you be seen as too heavy-handed or pushy. Typically, once a user understands the lay of the land, he wants to be left alone to explore.

—continued—

Onboarding

A prime example of great onboarding

One of the best and most often-cited examples of an onboarding process is on Tumblr.com. Tumblr proudly calls itself the easiest way to blog and goes to great lengths to prove its point. The sign-up process itself is dead simple—just a single form to provide an email address, password, and desired URL. Once the user confirms her credentials by logging in, she is presented with the main interface and blogging tool, but most of the page is dimly lit. Her attention is directed to the toolbar, and a large bubble tells her exactly what to do next: "Create your first post!". In actuality, there are a dozen things she could do from here, but the guide is making a decision for her. By limiting the user's focus, Tumblr ensures that she is significantly less overwhelmed by the options at this point, while simultaneously being trained on the primary purpose of the product—to create content.

As the user mouses over each of the post options, only the subtitle changes: "try writing about something you did today"; "try linking to a cool website you like." The language is clear and concise, the value inherent to the directive, and the user begins to conceptualize the variety of things she can achieve with the product despite the very simple interaction that is required.

At any point in the process the user can "x-out"—close the large bubble and exit to the main interface—without further interruption, but the copy and visualizations are compelling enough to urge her forward.

Once the user posts something, the next step in the onboarding process is to customize the blog. Now everything on the screen is dim except for the location of the Customize link. Not only is the user being taught about the ability to customize, she's also learning where to access the functionality later on when she needs it again. Now that the user knows how to post content and customize her blog, the last step in the onboarding process is to "Follow some cool people!". One of the biggest differentiators for Tumblr is its highly active community, but until a new user is connected to several other bloggers, she might not truly comprehend its magnitude. Tumblr overcomes this by encouraging users to find their friends early on, in a variety of methods. A user can scan for contacts in an existing email address book, or follow people under Staff Picks, Music, or Art and Artists. By observing the usage patterns of these popular and highly active users, new users will most quickly understand how to use Tumblr to their advantage, nearly guaranteeing more frequent use of the site.

Other variations on onboarding

Onboarding can sidestep the sign-up process entirely. TripIt, a travel itinerary and planner site, allows users to simply forward the site a recent travel confirmation email and TripIt takes care of the rest. By sucking in all of this content automatically, TripIt removes any effort new users have to put into the first-time experience and can almost immediately present the site's value. They do have a sign-up process (just an email and password), but it is not required to see their tools in action. This strikingly reduces the barrier to entry and is still rare enough to make a user sit up and take notice.

When it originally launched last year, Yahoo!'s Shine, a website for women, had an interesting take on first-time use. Though it is no longer live, Shine's onboarding process wasn't directed at recent registrants, but instead was directed at first-time visitors to the site to help orient them to its variety of features. On a user's first visit, a "Welcome to Shine" layer appeared in the center of the page. It said, "Shine features the best writers and bloggers in women's publishing. Plus, connect with likeminded women, share stories and more. Take a ten-second tour to see more."

—continued—

Onboarding

By clicking the single call to action, a Continue button, the user was moved all around the page, with the browser auto-scrolling accordingly. It was a three-step process that also used the familiar bubble pointing at the functionality on the page with a short description of its purpose. It highlighted access to Yahoo! Mail in the sidebar, a recent activity stream of user-submitted content, and a quick-access headline list at the very bottom of the page. In the last bubble was a Get Started link that ended the onboarding process and scrolled the user all the way back up to the top of the page.

Suffice it to say, there are a variety of ways to handle a new user orientation. The user's mindset and the site's business goals, brand identity, and value proposition must all be taken into account. After all, this is the first impression, and you know what they say about those.

—Whitney Hess, *http://whitneyhess.com/blog/*

Welcome Area

What

A user registers for a new service and needs to have a sense of what can be done at the site and how to get started (Figure 3-24).

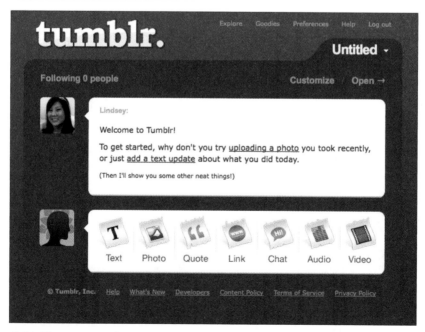

Figure 3-24. *The new user welcome area on tumblr.com with a greeting from Lindsey.*

Use this pattern when:

- A new user first accesses your site.
- You want to acquaint the user with important or useful features.

- Provide the new user with a warm and gracious welcome to your site and services. This can be a special welcome screen right after registering for the service or a special email highlighting features, as in Figure 3-25. Consider sending a welcome email in addition to the start screen so the user has a quick reference of features.

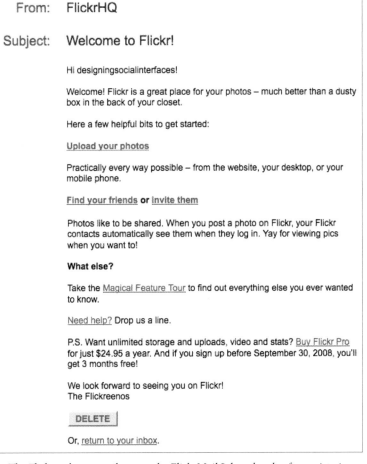

Figure 3-25. *The Flickr welcome mail sent to the FlickrMail Inbox shortly after registering.*

- Allow the user to easily move off of the welcome area and into the full features of the site.

- Treat your new users as you would guests in your home. If possible, welcome them personally and check in periodically (without being annoying).

- Use the welcome area to highlight the choices a user can make to get started on the service and what he might do first, as shown in Figure 3-26.

Figure 3-26. *As the new user starts to engage in the site, Tumblr presents encouraging messages and prompts to try another feature.*

- Consider offering tours of key scenarios from the Welcome Area, but don't force the user to go through them.

- Don't overwhelm the user with a lot of pop-over bubbles or other intrusive interface elements.

- Don't dumb down the site language just because the user is new to your site. Keep your welcome language friendly and clear. Don't assume that the new user is an Internet novice, but don't assume he is an Internet expert, either.

Why

Providing a welcome area or start space is akin to orientation for a new job or college, or giving your friends a tour of your home the first time they visit. The more welcoming you are (in a light-handed fashion, of course), the more your users will feel comfortable and *want* to spend time on your site.

Related patterns

"Reengagement" on page 75

As seen on

Flickr (*http://www.flickr.com*)

Tumblr (*http://www.tumblr.com*)

Reengagement

What

A user participates in your community and then stops or forgets about your offerings. (See Figures 3-27 and 3-28.)

Figure 3-27. *Dogster.com sends out a graphically formatted newsletter to users on a periodic basis. The mail promotes a new or timely feature on the site and calls attention to other areas that may not have been explored recently.*

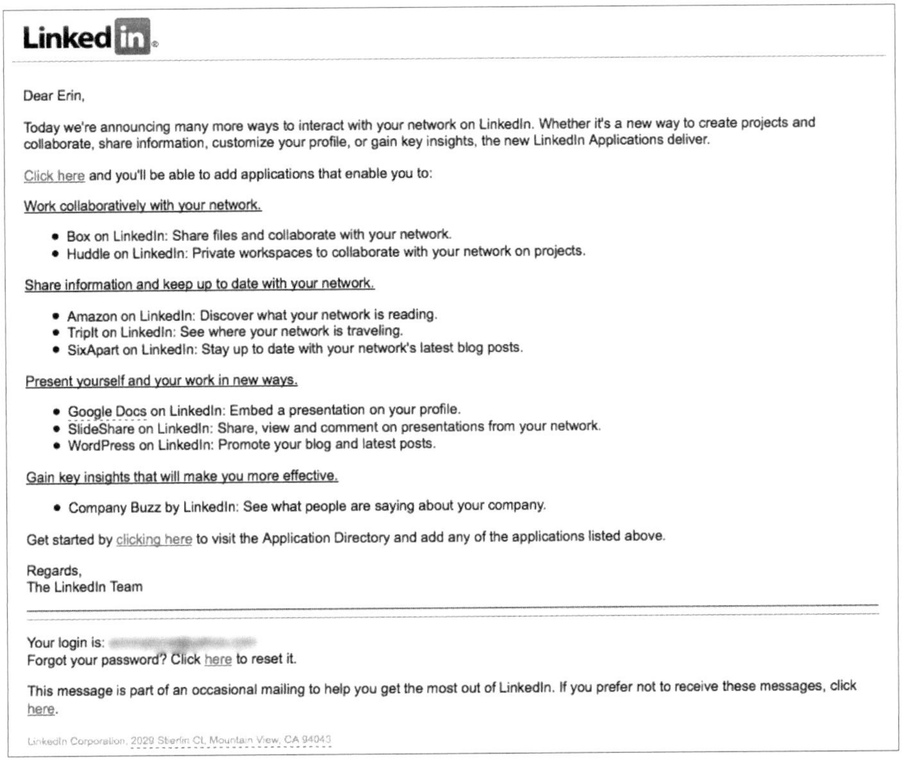

LinkedIn

Dear Erin,

Today we're announcing many more ways to interact with your network on LinkedIn. Whether it's a new way to create projects and collaborate, share information, customize your profile, or gain key insights, the new LinkedIn Applications deliver.

Click here and you'll be able to add applications that enable you to:

Work collaboratively with your network.

- Box on LinkedIn: Share files and collaborate with your network.
- Huddle on LinkedIn: Private workspaces to collaborate with your network on projects.

Share information and keep up to date with your network.

- Amazon on LinkedIn: Discover what your network is reading.
- TripIt on LinkedIn: See where your network is traveling.
- SixApart on LinkedIn: Stay up to date with your network's latest blog posts.

Present yourself and your work in new ways.

- Google Docs on LinkedIn: Embed a presentation on your profile.
- SlideShare on LinkedIn: Share, view and comment on presentations from your network.
- WordPress on LinkedIn: Promote your blog and latest posts.

Gain key insights that will make you more effective.

- Company Buzz by LinkedIn: See what people are saying about your company.

Get started by clicking here to visit the Application Directory and add any of the applications listed above.

Regards,
The LinkedIn Team

Your login is:
Forgot your password? Click here to reset it.

This message is part of an occasional mailing to help you get the most out of LinkedIn. If you prefer not to receive these messages, click here.

LinkedIn Corporation, 2029 Stierlin Ct, Mountain View, CA 94043

Figure 3-28. *LinkedIn.com sends out text announcements promoting new features. The mail also reminds the user of his login and contains a prompt for resetting the password in case it is forgotten. Forgotten usernames and passwords are often a deterrent to revisiting a site.*

Use when

Use this pattern when:

- You want to entice users back to your site.
- You want to inform users of new features.

How

- Allow your users to opt in to email correspondence from your site when they initially sign up.
- Plan an ongoing schedule for outgoing email.
- Emails should highlight key features and/or new features (see Figure 3-29).

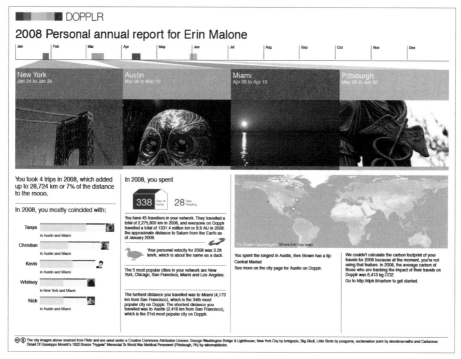

Figure 3-29. *Dopplr sends out an annual report at the end of the year recapping your trips, comparing your travel to others in your network, and giving an overview of your carbon footprint. The report was such an unexpected and pleasant surprise, people were talking about it for days, and it definitely encouraged reengagement for those who had forgotten to use the service.*

- If your user hasn't been to your site for some amount of time, send email that entices him back to the site, but only if he agreed to receive email. If the site has features that are based on relationships, share a piece of public data from the user's friends to let him know what he is missing.

- Develop a set of rules for how long a user must be absent before you send a reengagement email.

- The email should contain a very clear call to action.

- There should be a limited amount of messages included in each email.

- Don't send too many emails too often, or you will have the reverse effect: keeping the user away from your site.

Why

It goes without saying that you want to create a compelling service that your users will return to day after day. But there are times when you want to let users know about new features or new ways of using the service in order to reenergize them or remind them of why they signed up in the first place.

Reengagement of your users should be an ongoing effort. In most cases, reengagement efforts are done through email campaigns sent out on a regular basis. Emails are usually varied and highlight features or recent activities by the user's network on the site. Surprising and fun messages, such as Dopplr's annual report (Figure 3-29), can have the extra benefit of word-of-mouth discussion driving people back to the service.

Related patterns

"Welcome Area" on page 72

Further Reading

"8 More Design Mistakes with Account Sign-in," by Jared M. Spool, *http://www.uie.com/articles/account_design_mistakes_part2/*

"Account Sign-in: 8 Design Mistakes to Avoid," by Jared M. Spool, *http://www.uie.com/articles/account_design_mistakes/*

"Design for Sign Up: How to Motivate People To Sign Up For Your Web App," by Joshua Porter, *http://www.peachpit.com/articles/article.aspx?p=1216150*

Information about Facebook Connect, *http://developers.facebook.com/connect.php*

Information about OAuth, *http://oauth.net/*

Web Form Design: Filling in the Blank, by Luke Wroblewski, Rosenfeld Media, May 2008

"What is OpenID?", *http://openid.net/what/*

Chapter 4

Where's the Rest of Me?

We all perform. It's what we do for each other all the time, deliberately or unintentionally. It's a way of telling about ourselves in the hope of being recognized as what we'd like to be.

—Richard Avedon

The core around which social sites revolve is people—who they are, how you know them, what they are contributing. People and their presentations of self and their contributions make for a rich and intertwined community. Without understanding who you are, your friends won't know you. Potential connections won't trust what you say or be encouraged to connect to you. You won't be able to recognize your friends in the crowd of participants, and you won't necessarily trust new people if you don't have some way of formulating a picture of who they are.

The work that goes into defining themselves, and into building connections, is often a significant hurdle for users who want to try a new site. And having a well-established identity and network on one site is a huge deterrent for switching to other sites. Help your users by automating as much as possible; aggregating activity like comments or reviews, and presenting user status streams of connections, creates a rich and interesting default without requiring much work from your users.

There is a growing belief that a person's identity belongs to him and not to the software or service in which the data has been created. The proliferation of socially enabled sites that do not interoperate means people must recreate themselves at each and every site they go to. In some cases, this isn't an issue, since the context of the community often dictates what persona to present. But for many users, the facets of themselves they would like to present to others just isn't that different from site to site.

The open standards community is working to create a technical solution that allows users to authenticate anywhere with a single name and password. Often called the *identity solution*, this particular part of the puzzle is limited to authentication—how the system knows a person—and does not encompass the rich data set that describes a person's identity and by which other people come to know that person.

The collection of patterns in this chapter addresses the various interfaces that present personal and activity information about a person to others. They make up the components that might be considered a user's brand: the image that he projects to others that then creates a perception of him. This includes the profile, the personalization of that profile, how a user's contributions are attributed to him and what control is available for that, the avatar, what information is private, where a user can manage all these pieces of information, and the personal dashboard, where a person see what's happening across his network of connections. The profile should be mixed together with attribution presentation, contact cards, and other public information to create a personal and rich people-centric experience.

The profile and the presentation of a person, whether automated through activity or customized by the individual, allows you to know someone and gives your users the opportunity to express whichever side of themselves they are comfortable sharing with the world.

Identity

User identity and the ability to control its presentation is a core element of building a social website. The ability to create and manage an identity within the context of the site is the foundation upon which the rest—contributions, relationships, reputations—is built. It's about people and who they portray themselves to be.

When thinking about these topics, be aware that providing the ability for users to define their names is just step one in helping them craft their identities. As discussed in "Sign-up or Registration" on page 45, allowing the user to create a nickname (rather than be saddled with some horrid identifier he got because the namespace was full) is one of the best design decisions you can make. Wouldn't you rather be known as "jack of all design" rather than "jack089"?

There are several other items that make up an identity for the user. These include "Profile", "Avatars", "Reflectors", and "Attribution". Associated with these patterns are a user's reputation and his connections.

When deciding what to pull together, know that you don't need every piece, and that you can start with some elements and add others as needed.

Here are some points to consider across all the patterns in this chapter:

- Let your users be expressive where it matters. Profiles on MySpace are extremely expressive and reflect its younger user base (Figure 4-1), whereas profiles on LinkedIn are not customizable and reflect the professional nature of the interactions (Figure 4-2).

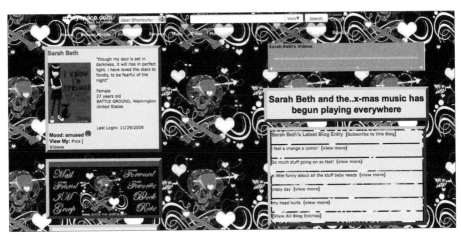

Figure 4-1. *Customized MySpace profile.*

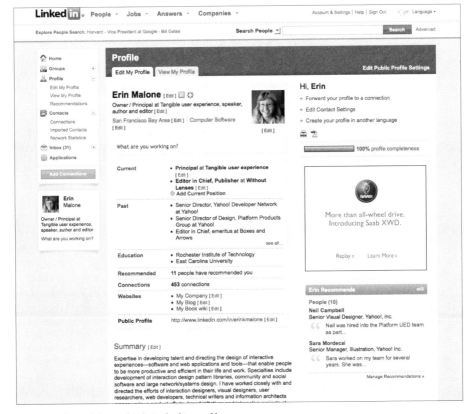

Figure 4-2. *One of the author's LinkedIn profiles.*

- Give users control over how to present themselves. Users should own their actions and have a reputation attached to their identities, but the option to stay anonymous should be offered in some instances.

- Let your users decide who sees what parts of their profiles (Figure 4-3). Give enough control and permissioned access. Do my friends see my birth date, or does everyone? If it's everyone, be prepared for a lot of fake data.

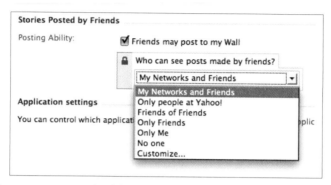

Figure 4-3. *Privacy settings on Facebook for parts of a profile.*

- Be clear on reflecting back to users what they see as editors/owners versus how others see them. The dating sites have this idea down to a science, but on many other websites, who sees what isn't clearly articulated.

- Having robust identity solutions won't alleviate sock puppets (see "Sock Puppets" on page 305) and alternate identities that people may create.

Tripartite Identity Pattern

One of the most misunderstood patterns in social media design is that of user identity management. Product designers often confuse the many different roles required by various user identifiers. This confusion is compounded by using older online services, such as Yahoo!, eBay, and America Online, as canonical references. These services established their identity models based on engineering-centric requirements long before we had a more subtle understanding of user requirements for social media. By conjoining the requirements of engineering (establishing sessions, retrieving database records, etc.) with the user's requirements of recognizability and self-expression, many older identity models actually discourage user participation. For example, Yahoo! found that users consistently listed that the fear of spammers farming their email address was their number one reason for abandoning the creation of user-created content, such as restaurant reviews and message board postings. This ultimately led to a very expensive and radical reengineering of the Yahoo identity model, which has been underway since 2006.

Consistently I've found that a tripartite identity model best fits most online services and should be forward-compatible with current identity-sharing methods and future proposals.

—continued—

Tripartite Identity Pattern

The three components of user identity are: the *account* identifier, the *login* identifier, and the *public* identifier.

Account identifier (DB Key)

From an engineering point of view, there is always one database key—one way to access a user's record and one way to refer to them in cookies and potentially in URLs. In a real sense, the account identifier is the closest thing the company has to a user. It must be unique and permanent. Typically this is represented by a very large random number and is not under the user's control in any way. In fact, from the user's point of view, this identifier should be invisible or at the very least inert; there should be no inherent public capabilities associated with this identifier. For example, it should not be an email address, accepted as a login name, or displayed as a public name or as a status in an instant messenger address.

Login identifier(s) (Session Authentication)

Login identifiers are necessary to create valid sessions associated with an account identifier. Logins are the user's method of granting access to his privileged information on the service. Typically, these are represented by unique and validated name/password pairs. Note that the service need not generate its own unique namespace for login identifiers, but may adopt identifiers from other providers. For example, many services accept email addresses as login identifiers, usually after verifying that the user is in control of that address. Increasingly, more sophisticated capability-based identities are accepted, such as OpenID and Facebook Connect, which provide login credentials without constantly asking for a name and password.

By separating the login identifier from the account identifier, it is much easier to allow the user to customize his login as the situation changes. Since the account identifier need never change, data migration issues are mitigated. Likewise, separating the login identifier from public identifiers protects the user from those who would crack their accounts. Finally, a service could provide the opportunity to attach multiple different login identifiers to a single account, thus allowing the service to aggregate information gathered from multiple identity suppliers.

Public identifier(s) (Social Identity)

Unlike the technically required account and login identifiers, the public identifier represents how the user wishes to be perceived by other users on the service. Think of it like clothing or the name people know you by. By definition, it does not possess the technical requirement to be 100% unique. There are many John Smiths of the world, thousands of them on Amazon.com, hundreds of them write reviews, and everything seems to work out fine.

Online, a user's public identifier is usually a compound object: a photo, a nickname, and perhaps age, gender, and location. It provides sufficient information for any viewer to quickly interpret personal context. Public identifiers are usually linked to a detailed user profile, where further identity differentiation is available: "Is this the same John Smith from New York who also wrote the review of *The Great Gatsby* that I like so much?" or "Is this the Mary Jones I went to college with?"

A sufficiently diverse service such as Yahoo! may wish to offer multiple public identifiers when a specific context requires it. For example, when playing wild-west poker, a user may wish to present the public identity of a rough-and-tumble outlaw or a saloon girl without having that imagery associated with his or her movie reviews.

—Randy Farmer, Social Media Strategist, MSB Associates

Profile

The profile is one of the core pieces of a social offering. It becomes the face of the user in your system. Profiles can be an expressive place for users to create a "voice" or "image" of how they wish to be seen in the context of your site, and depending on the nature of your site, can be a hub around which relationships and activities revolve. Profiles are often an aggregate representation of all the activity of a user and her friends on your site.

What

Users want a central, public location to display all the relevant content and information about themselves to others—both those they know and those they don't (Figure 4-4).

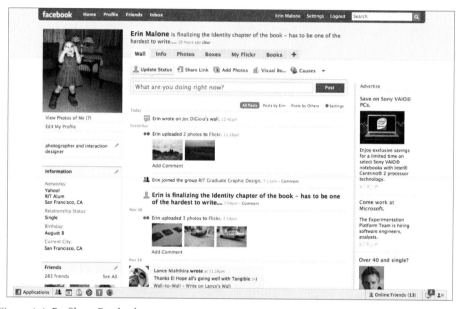

Figure 4-4. *Profile on Facebook.*

Use when

Use this pattern when:

- Your site encourages a lot of user-generated content and you want one place to show a specific user's contribution.

- Your site encourages relationship building.

- You want to allow users to look up another user to learn more about her.

- You want to allow users to express their personalities.

- To allow users to share information about themselves with others.

- You want to present a user's activity stream (such as status alerts) from site and/or Internet activity.

How

Core profile

- Allow the user to customize his display name or provide a nickname option.

- Yahoo! profiles require a first and last name, but also allow a display name, which can be a handle, a nickname, or the user's name. It's his choice. The full name is shared with connections, which then disambiguates whom a person may be, especially if his associated image is an icon or an avatar.

- Don't make the display name the same as the user login. Doing this gives phishers and other nefarious persons half of a user's login information. You should provide a safe place for people to connect, and guarding their login and personal information is critical.

- Allow users to select which items they want seen by the public and which they want to keep private or just between "friends" (Figure 4-5).

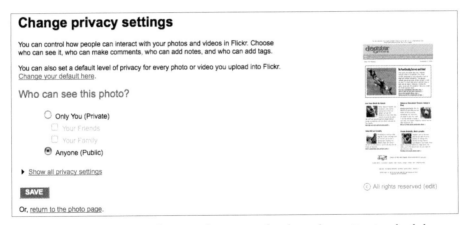

Figure 4-5. *Flickr allows users to designate what gets seen by whom when an item is uploaded.*

- Allow users the opportunity to customize portions of the profile. The profile is a form of self-expression. MySpace profiles represent one extreme of this, as they allow users to totally visually customize their profiles. LinkedIn and Facebook profiles are much more rigid in their customization, restricting it to text, an image, and the user's activity to differentiate and define a person's personality.

- Don't force the user to publicly display all her information.

- Collect only the amount of information necessary for meaningful relationships or community activities. Don't force the user to fill in all fields or data sections in order for the profile to be displayed.

- Allow the user to upload one or more images of herself.

- Provide a view into the profile as a user's network will see it.

- Provide a view into the profile as the public—not connections—will see it.

Profile preferences and updating

- Profile preferences should be readily available to the user who owns the profile. If the user is logged in, present a large, easy-to-find link to edit the profile.

- One of the tough decisions to make is whether any elements of the profile are tied to the account and not editable. For example, on a Yahoo! profile, items presented in the user's contact card, username, gender, age, and location are optional but some of these items are also collected in registration. The two (Yahoo!'s profile and registration data) are not connected, so the profile can be an expressive reflection of the person.

- The data fields selected for the profile should be individually editable, with as many elements as possible pulled in automatically (if applicable). Data for the profile is often gathered by presenting a series of questions and then filling out a series of forms and free-text fields.

- Collect information for the profile data entries through site activity if possible.

- Always allow the user to go back and change information later, but don't force profile completion if this is unnecessary to the core site experience.

- Encourage profile completion by giving users clues that indicate how complete their profiles are or by using defaults (like a default avatar) that encourages customization, but don't force completion if it isn't necessary for a good user experience.

- If possible, allow the user to migrate profile content, a profile image, nickname, and core personal information from other services using the OpenSocial API.

- Use WYSIWYG + lightweight edit links (Figure 4-6).

Figure 4-6. *Facebook has light edit controls, seen only by the profile owner, on each module of the profile.*

- Wherever applicable, the profile page displayed to the user should be as close as possible to what the consumers of the profile will see. The owner of the profile should be able to get an accurate sense of what the consumers of the profile will see without the need to preview the profile.

- The differences between the consumer's view and the owner's view are typically limited to additional "Edit" links that point to forms for updating content.

- Profiles that include a lot of permissioned content might include permissions indicators for denoting public versus permissioned versus private content. Robust profiles also might include controls for inline editing, as well as drag-and-drop handles that appear on hover.

- When the owner of the profile selects a link to his profile, load the profile page in Edit mode, not Preview mode.

- Don't overload the profile page with content management options for the content owner.

- Do provide a separate "control panel" for the owner to manage his content.

- Do provide a separate Updates/Status Consumption Environment so the owner of the relationships can keep tabs on the content generated by related people.

Private information

- Some of the information that may be collected in an account profile is private. Emerging open APIs such as the Yahoo! Social API (*http://developer.yahoo.com/social/*) and the Portable Contacts (*http://portablecontacts.net/draft-spec.html*) spec encourage data items such as phone numbers, real birthdays, and addresses to be collected for use in services like address books or invitation services, where a user actually knows the person viewing the information. (See Figure 4-7.)

Figure 4-7. *Personal information collected on Plaxo.*

- Make sure that information tied to the account, such as passwords, password retrieval questions, credit card information, and other financial and personal information, stays in a private area accessible only to the account holder.

- Keep private information in an Account area, separated from the Profile display.

- Offer the option to make private information public to only those people in the closest circles of connections, such as family or close friends (Figures 4-8 and 4-9).

Figure 4-8. *Privacy settings in Facebook. Each data item in the Contact Information section of the profile has extremely granular settings.*

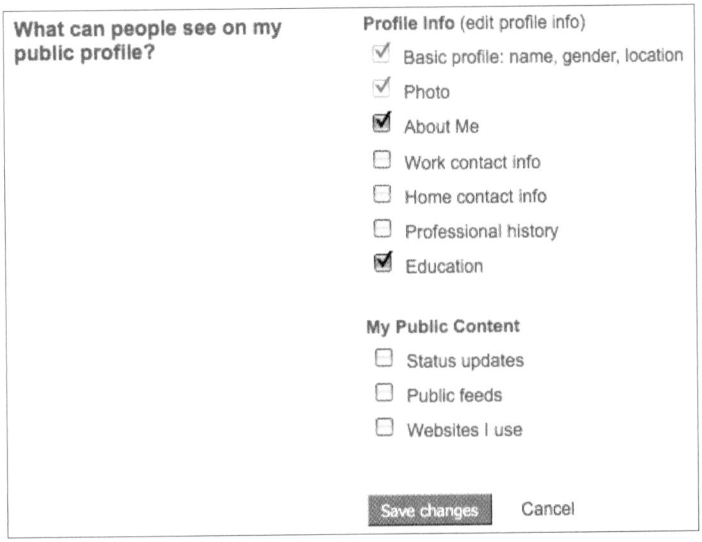

Figure 4-9. *Privacy settings in Plaxo let the user select areas of the profile to keep private while other areas can be shared.*

Profile decorating

Sites that revolve around the profile, such as Cyworld (Figure 4-10) and MySpace (Figure 4-11), encourage profile decorating as part of the profile owner's personal expression. These sites appeal to a youth market, and the process of decorating, changing looks, and adding and exchanging graphical items—such as wallpaper, stickers, props, or furniture—is part of the user's expression of her personality. This is akin to a teenager plastering posters on the walls of her room. Self-expression is a key component of the experience and has a direct impact on the perception of the creator, as much as any other type of content she might upload.

Figure 4-10. *Profile on Cyworld allows users to add colors, backgrounds, and interactive minirooms, which can be filled with avatars of friends as well as purchased props and furniture.*

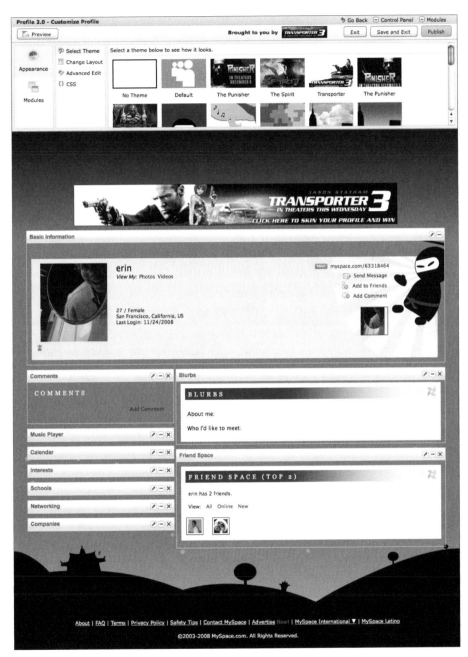

Figure 4-11. *Customized MySpace profile with simple customization tools.*

- Contrast this to more task-oriented sites like LinkedIn or Facebook, where the content and interactions among people are considered primary and the interface exists to house these. When developing a profile system, think about what is important to your users, their goals on your site, and how important the profile and self-expression may be in that context.

- To encourage adoption, offer easily applied skins and layout options.

- Offer add-ons such as stickers, mini-avatars, furniture, or props for expanded expression opportunities.

- Allow advanced users to do more customization, such as CSS and HTML.

- Allow different content modules or applications to be added on an à la carte basis.

Profile claiming

- Some sites may automatically create a bare-bones profile for a person and then allow that user to claim ownership of it.

- An unverified or unclaimed profile may exist for a user through several methods (comment contribution, a friend's invitation, etc.).

- Users leaving anonymous comments or other anonymous content may want to eventually claim ownership of that content to build their reputations as contributors.

- Users may have skeletal profiles made for them when their friends join the site and invite them to participate.

- Allow an invited user or owner of anonymous content to easily claim his profile or aggregated content. Dropping an encoded cookie is one way to allow later retrieval of anonymous content.

- Verification of some data string (such as a verified email address) can pair a premade profile with the intended user.

- Regardless of the technical method for allowing this, make sure it's easy, unobtrusive, and not creepy. A couple of years ago, Yahoo! released a profile experiment called Mash, where users could make profiles for their friends and then invite them to come claim the profile. Many people didn't understand why there was already content on "their" profile page and why people other than themselves could edit it. It was a fun experiment if you "got it," but confusing and creepy for everyone else.

Faceted identity

Users are quite skilled at slicing their identities up depending on the context of interaction. For example, who you are in your family is different than the slice of yourself you present at the office. Online it's no different. See Figures 4-12, 4-13, and 4-14.

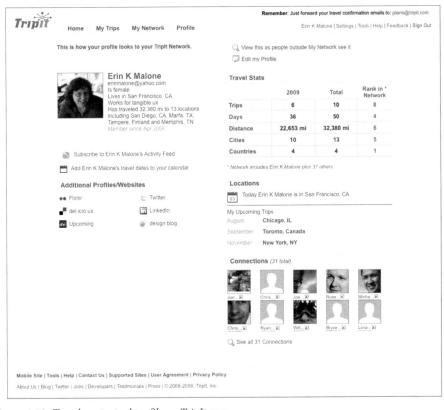

Figure 4-12. *Travel-contextual profile on TripIt.com.*

Figure 4-13. *Books-contextual profile on goodreads.com.*

Figure 4-14. *Local-contextual profile on Yelp.com.*

- Consider the context of your experience and cater the profile to it.

- Whenever possible, keep the core user identity information consistent—username, gender, location—through the use of a central design solution. All other information should be collected or automatically aggregated based on the activities of the site.

- Sites like Facebook have addressed the various interests of its users through the addition of applications. Many of these applications are presented as separate tabs in the profile and offer a glimpse into facets of the person (Figure 4-15).

Figure 4-15. *Sectional tabs on Facebook give an indication of a user's interests.*

Recommendations

Use the emerging common profile/identity fields as defined in the OpenSocial spec (*http://code.google.com/apis/opensocial/docs/0.8/reference/#opensocial.Person.Field_field_summary*), the Portable Contacts spec (*http://portablecontacts.net/draft-spec.html*), or Yahoo!'s Social Platform API (*http://developer.yahoo.com/social/rest_api_guide/social_dir_api.html*). Select the data items that are meaningful to your context and disregard the rest, but be consistent in the field labels and how the information is stored. This will ensure future portability for your users and will allow you to import data from other sources when a user joins. The goal is to let the user bring her data (where applicable) with her around the Internet, rather than forcing her to rebuild a profile every time she signs up for something new.

Considerations

The type of information collected and presented shapes a picture of the user and sets a tone for your site. For example, LinkedIn collects professional information about current and past work experience (Figure 4-16). Profiles are supplemented by the addition of recommendations from other users and applications from third-party developers.

Figure 4-16. *LinkedIn's profile focuses on job experience and professional expertise.*

Facebook has a series of free-form fields but also a robust section of past school atten-
dance (Figure 4-17). Since Facebook started as a university social network, this is appropriate. It has since expanded its profile to also include work experience and applications
from third-party developers.

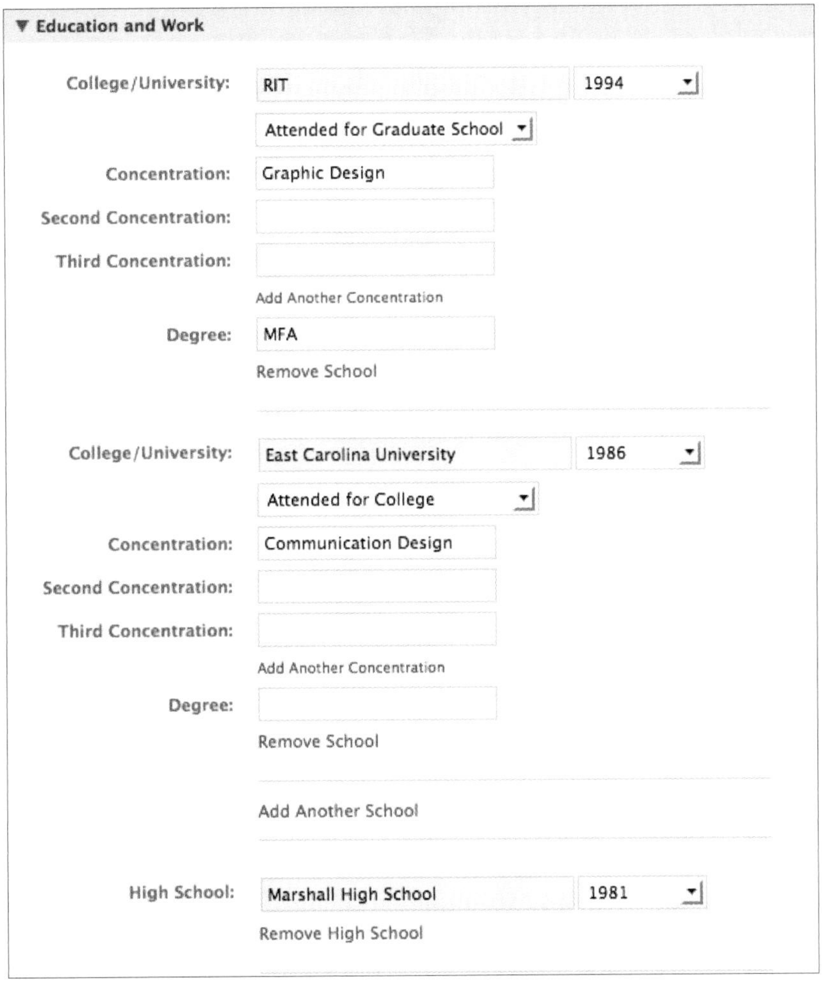

Figure 4-17. *Facebook has a robust area for collecting school information. School affiliation is one of
the ways that Facebook creates networks of people with similar backgrounds.*

Networks such as Orkut, Friendster, and MySpace revolve around the profile and cater
to a youthful audience, so the information collected centers on marital status, types of
relationships the user is seeking, and interests such as music and video.

Each of these social networks uses specific profile data to give users an idea of its social
emphasis and the community that exists on the site.

Open questions

As the various entities put forward open standards for the profile and a user's identity, making a decision about which protocol to adopt becomes increasingly important. Most of the large players in the space have adopted and are participating in the OpenSocial standard. Following this standard, or being compatible with it, will make your users' data more accessible to them in the long run.

Making a decision to go against the emerging standards might be interesting to you in the short term, but may have negative ramifications in the long run as more and more users of services demand the ability to carry their data back and forth between sites.

Why

A central profile for your service is the hub around which relationships and other activities can revolve. Carefully selecting the data fields that make sense for your site will ensure that the profile has meaningful context to your users. Providing customizing features will encourage personalization and ownership of the profile and the site, which in turn supports longer-term usage.

Related patterns

"Attribution" on page 113

"Identity Cards or Contact Cards" on page 111

As seen on

Facebook (*http://www.facebook.com*)

MySpace (*http://www.myspace.com*)

Plaxo (*http://www.plaxo.com*)

Yahoo! (*http://www.yahoo.com*)

Testimonials (or Personal Recommendations)

Testimonials are endorsements and can provide information about a person or about aspects of the person's interests or skills (Figure 4-18). This can help round out a profile and provide alternative perspectives.

Figure 4-18. *Testimonials in Flickr are presented in the profile and can help shape the perception of that person.*

What

A person is interested in what others think about him or his work and wants others to see this as supporting his own information and skillset.

Use this pattern when:

- You want to allow users to provide endorsements for other people in their networks.

- You want to share information from other people about a person in his profile.

- Provide a module in the profile for presentation of testimonials.

- Allow people from the user's network to write a testimonial or recommendation for the user.

- Present a clear call to action when a person is viewing a profile that is not her own. Both Flickr and LinkedIn provide links to the main body of the profile in a secondary column of information.

- Consider allowing the testimonial writer to select how she knows this person (Figure 4-19).

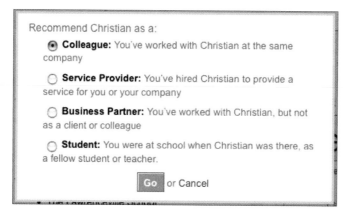

Figure 4-19. *LinkedIn asks how the writer knows the person in order to give context to the recommendation.*

- Allow the person being written about to approve the testimonial or recommendation before it is published. After all, the profile belongs to the user, and he should be in control of the content presented.

- Clearly articulate to the writer that the recommendation will have to be approved before being published (Figure 4-20). This will deter people who want to be nasty or rude or who are trying to spam the profile.

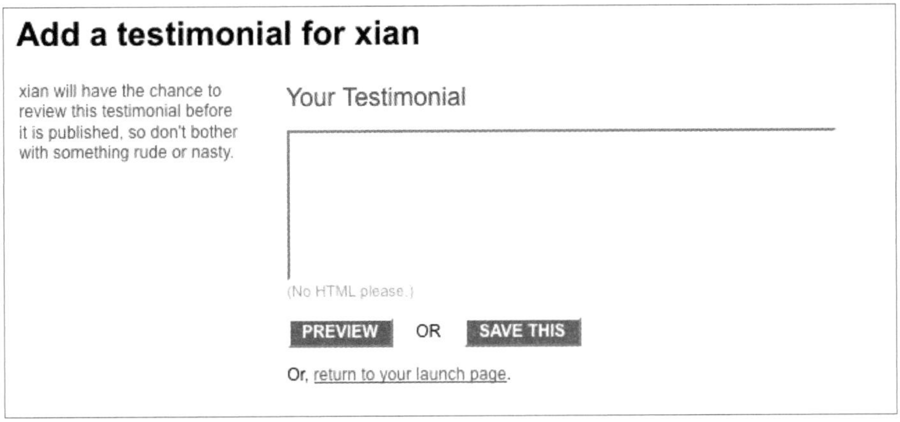

Add a testimonial for xian

xian will have the chance to review this testimonial before it is published, so don't bother with something rude or nasty.

Your Testimonial

(No HTML please.)

PREVIEW   OR   SAVE THIS

Or, return to your launch page.

Figure 4-20. *Flickr lets the writer know that the person will review the testimonial before it is published.*

- Provide attribution for the testimonial or recommendation and link that back to the writer's own profile. This will help lend credibility to the recommendation.

- Consider presenting on the user's profile the recommendations that she has written for others (Figure 4-21).

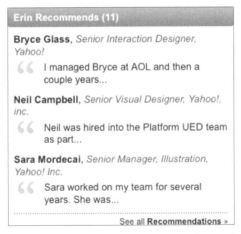

Erin Recommends (11)

Bryce Glass, *Senior Interaction Designer, Yahoo!*
" I managed Bryce at AOL and then a couple years...

Neil Campbell, *Senior Visual Designer, Yahoo!, inc.*
" Neil was hired into the Platform UED team as part...

Sara Mordecai, *Senior Manager, Illustration, Yahoo! Inc.*
" Sara worked on my team for several years. She was...

See all **Recommendations »**

Figure 4-21. *LinkedIn shows viewers of a profile a list of recommendations this person has written for others in her network.*

- Consider presenting on the user's dashboard (see "Personal Dashboard" on page 104) a block or module showing recent recommendations or testimonials written by people in the user's network (Figure 4-22). This could also be presented in an activity stream (see "Activity Streams" on page 135).

> **RECOMMENDATIONS** (2)
>
> **Lisa Colvin recommends Joanna Bitter, PMP**, "Over the course of the multiple projects that Joanna managed in the time we worked together, I found..." Read more »
>
> **Lisa Colvin recommends Yana R**, "Yana has been an extremely detail-oriented, proactive and intelligent partner in all of the projects..." Read more »

Figure 4-22. *Recommendation activity on the network in LinkedIn.*

Why

Letting users provide an endorsement for people in their network allows them to share positive information about that person in a more permanent and meaningful way than a comment or more temporary flag of approval. For professional-leaning sites, such as LinkedIn, recommendations provide profile viewers with information about the person from a variety of perspectives, which can help in making hiring or business decisions.

As seen on

Flickr (*http://www.flickr.com*)

LinkedIn (*http://www.linkedin.com*)

Personal Dashboard

What

The user wants to check in and see status updates from her friends, current activity from her network, comments from friends on recent posts, and other happenings from across her network (Figure 4-23).

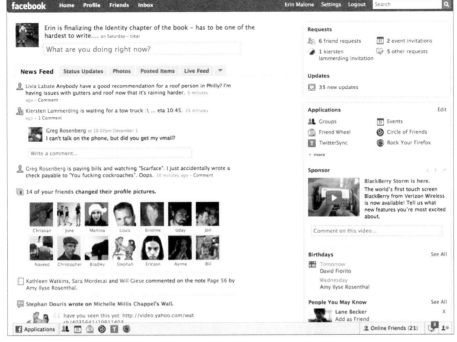

Figure 4-23. *Once a user is logged in, the home page is a personal dashboard, providing access to recent activity from friends and most other site features.*

Use when

Use this pattern when:

- The experience of the site revolves around the activities of people and their networks, regardless of whether the activity takes place on the network.

- You want a companion to the public profile.

- You want to encourage repeat usage.

How

- Provide access to other features and applications from the dashboard (Figure 4-24).

Figure 4-24. *Flickr's signed-in home page shows recent activity around photos (my recent uploads, my comments, and conversation around photos), uploads from my contacts, access to my stats, recent uploads from the groups I am part of, and at the bottom of the page, a collection of images that Flickr thinks I might be interested in.*

- Allow users to select what elements they want displayed in their dashboards. Give them a reason to come back repeatedly.

- Don't hide important social aspects to make room for editorial or advertising. The site Upcoming moved "Friends Events" off the home page in a recent redesign to make room for "Popular Events," which are now shown by default (Figure 4-25). "Friends Events" are a click away and much less discoverable than before. This change, while exposing more events for the user, seriously damaged the viral nature of the site.

Figure 4-25. *Upcoming started out as a site to track your events and those of your friends. The current home page relegates my events to a small sidebar and now hides My Friends events under a tab.*

- Allow users to supplement their network's onsite activity updates with RSS feeds of other activity from other sites.

- Provide the ability to create a status update directly in the dashboard if status is an important part of the site.

- Provide easy access to the profiles of people in the user's network.

- Provide easy access to the user's own profile for review and editing.

Why

The Personal Dashboard is the companion to the profile. The dashboard should contain information and access to activities that the user wants to participate in on an ongoing basis. From the dashboard, she should be able to click into her friends' profiles to get more information about them and their interests. For sites like Facebook, Friendfeed, and even the redesigned Flickr, the dashboard is the user's version of the home page for the site and revolves around recent activity of all kinds.

Related patterns

"Profile" on page 86

As seen on

Facebook (*http://www.facebook.com*)

Flickr (*http://www.flickr.com*)

Friendfeed (*http://www.friendfeed.com*)

Reflectors

What

A user needs to know what public identity he is participating under when creating content.

A user needs to be able to edit the public identity he is participating under when viewing his profile or creating content (Figure 4-26).

Figure 4-26. *A simple identity reflector lets the user know how others will see the attribution on a piece of content.*

Use when

- Use wherever a user may participate and need a persistent way to get to her public profile.
- Use when a user is about to participate and wants to change the display of her attribution.

How

- Reflect the user's current public identity back to him.
- Present a link to view the public profile (if any) for the current context. If a contextual profile is not applicable, present a link to the user's primary public profile.
- Limit the identity information to the display name and display image. There is no need to show age, gender, location, or contextual identity information back to the owner/user. Save that data for the public view.

Editing the display name (using an AJAX overlay)

- Provide an easy way to change the display of how the user will be seen (Figure 4-27).

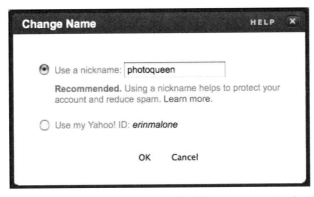

Figure 4-27. *Simple overlay allows the user to change the display name associated with the content about to be created.*

- To reduce identity theft and spam, encourage the use of a display name that does not expose an authentication ID or email address.

- Provide the means to post in a "publicly anonymous" way to reduce the need for additional, separate identities.

- In contexts that require it, allow a user to post using an alternate, separate identity.

- Place the control at the bottom of a content submission form so that users focus first on their contributions (and not on whether they need to change their identities).

Editing the display image (using an AJAX overlay)

- Present a link that gives the user the ability to edit and change out his display image (Figure 4-28).

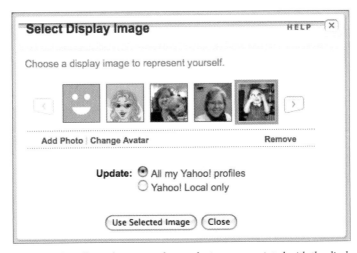

Figure 4-28. *Simple overlay allows the user to change the image associated with the display name.*

- Present a window that displays the set of images belonging to the user. Use a floating window to keep the user in context.

- Allow the user to select one of his existing images (or avatar) or let him add a new image (Figure 4-29).

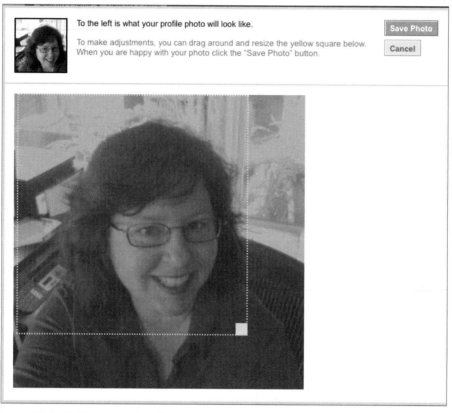

Figure 4-29. *LinkedIn has an inline photo cropper overlay that allows users to adjust the placement of the image within the square presentation.*

- On sites with multiple contexts (Yahoo!, for example), let the user decide whether the new image should be used in all contexts or just the current context.

Why

Reflecting back the name and image a user is currently associated with allows control over that person's identity. There may be specific nicknames or a preferred identity in certain contexts that a person wants to use. Allowing the user to see how she will be seen gives peace of mind as well as a sense of control and ownership on the site, which in turn encourages more participation.

Related patterns

"Identity Cards or Contact Cards", described next

"Profile" on page 86

Sources

Based on the work of Matt Leacock, Sara Berg, and the Yahoo! Social Platform team

As seen on

Yahoo! Local (*http://local.yahoo.com*)

Identity Cards or Contact Cards

What

A user needs to get more information about another participant in an online community without interrupting his current task. The needed information might include identity information (to aid in recognition and to help the user relate to the participant) or reputation information (to help the user make decisions regarding trust). (See Figures 4-30 and 4-31.)

Figure 4-30. *Contact card as used on Yahoo!.*

Figure 4-31. *Contact card as used on FriendFeed.*

Use this pattern when:

- A user's display image or display name is shown.

- Additional information about the participants is desired (in context) without adding clutter to the screen.

- Open a small panel when the user hovers over a target's display name or image.

- Present a larger version of the user's display image, the user's full display name, and other pertinent information the target chooses to share with the community (real name, age, gender, location).

- Present a Relationship Reflector. Yahoo! indicates whether a user is one of your connections. Flickr shares whether the person is a contact or a friend (Figure 4-32). FriendFeed indicates whether you subscribe to that person's status feeds.

Figure 4-32. *Flickr indicates relationship status in the overlay, activated by clicking the arrow next to the user's avatar.*

- Allow the ability to subscribe to, follow, connect to, unsubscribe, or block the user from this panel.

- Optionally extend the previously described ability with contextual identity information, such as reputation information or links to new participation in the current context.

- Identity cards or badges allow the user to interact with another participant in an on-line community in a predictable way and in context.

- They provide the means to reduce identity-related clutter on the screen.

- When ID cards are used, Presence Indicators, Reputation Emblems, and Relationship Reflectors can be tucked away but easily accessible. Truncated nicknames can be expanded. Block links can be made less salient. Small or tiny (and often illegible) display images can be shown at a more recognizable size to better humanize an online community and increase positive participation.

Related patterns

"Attribution" on page 113

"Profile" on page 86

"Reflectors" on page 108

Sources

Based on the work of Matt Leacock, Sara Berg, and the Yahoo! Social Platform Yahoo! Profiles (*http://profiles.yahoo.com*)

Friendfeed (*http://www.friendfeed.com*)

Flickr (*http://www.flickr.com*)

Attribution

What

A content consumer needs to understand the source of a contribution, and the source of a contribution needs to receive proper credit for his post (Figure 4-33). A user needs to assign her public identity when contributing content or joining an online community.

Figure 4-33. *Attribution for the review is presented to the left of the content on Yelp.*

Use when contributing content, joining a community, or editing a public profile.

For the content consumer

- List the author's display name and display image (if space and performance permits) in close proximity to the title (or summary) of the post.

- Link the display name and display image to the most contextually relevant user profile. If a contextual profile is not available, link the name and image to the user's primary profile.

For the content creator

- Reflect back the user's current public identity and give her the ability to update it prior to submitting content or joining a community.

"Identity Cards or Contact Cards" on page 111

"Reflectors" on page 108

Sources

Based on the work of Matt Leacock, Sara Berg, and the Yahoo! Social Platform team

As seen on

Flickr (*http://www.flickr.com*)

Yahoo Local (*http://local.yahoo.com*)

Yelp (*http://www.yelp.com*)

Avatars

Avatar is both a generic name for a visual representation of a user online and a product name for animated/cartoon or 3D renderings and drawings that represent a user online. In the December 2, 2008 issue of the *New York Observer*, Gillian Reagan writes:

> *Profile pictures—or avatars, in online parlance—show people at our thinnest, handsomest, most fun (some call these our best 'MySpace angles'). But increasingly—as more than half the country use social media regularly, according to marketing research firm IDC—the entertainment value of these sites is segueing into something more serious; social networks can help snag a job interview, a date or even the No. 1 spot in the Oval Office. And as the sites get more important in our professional lives, so does the avatar. It's the image that sums up who we are online.*

What

A user wants to have a visual representation of himself as part of his online identity (Figure 4-34).

Erin Malone

photoqueen

Female · in denial

"working on my social design book!"

Change Photo · Edit Profile

Figure 4-34. *Profile identity card on Yahoo! showing an avatar as a visual identifier.*

Use when

Use this pattern when the user wants to have a visual associated with her identity.

How

- Allow the user to upload any kind of image as an avatar. This can be a small portrait, an icon, or an illustration that the user believes represents him.

- Allow the ability to upload a larger image—100×100 pixels—and automatically resize for smaller uses. Many services use an image that is 48×48 pixels inline, but a larger image—60×60 pixels or 100×100 pixels—may be used on the profile (Figure 4-35). Resize the image for use in buddy lists and instant messenger lists. These are often much smaller than what is used on the Web.

Figure 4-35. *Avatars used on MyBlogLog. The larger image is a reflector back to the user, and the smaller images indicate other visitors to the profile.*

- Avatars (the illustrated representations) allow for a degree of anonymity (Figure 4-36), but do reduce the perceived credibility of the poster in many cases.

Figure 4-36. *Cartoon-style avatar as used on Yahoo! Games.*

Default image

- If the user has not designated a display image for the current context, use a "Not Pictured" image as the default avatar (Figure 4-37). This will encourage the user to customize so that he has an identity that is unique from other users.

Figure 4-37. *"Not Pictured" icons as used on MyBlogLog, Flickr, Twitter, Yelp, and Facebook.*

Multiple avatars

- Allow the user to upload multiple avatars and to change the presentation through the edit capabilities on the profile or identity card in context of use. (See "Editing the display image (using an AJAX overlay)" in "Reflectors" on page 108.)

- Yahoo!'s identity cards and reflectors allow users to upload multiple images. The instant messenger software Adium allows the user to select the current image from up to 10 recent icons (Figure 4-38). In most cases, when users want to change their avatars, they upload another image and overwrite the previous one.

Figure 4-38. *Adium allows the user to select his image from the 10 most recently used images.*

- Consider allowing multiple images to be uploaded and stored for later selection.

Mood expressions

- Allow users to attach a special status message or emoticon to supplement their avatars by indicating a particular mood (Figure 4-39).

Figure 4-39. *Mood expression attached to a profile image on a Cyworld profile.*

- Consider when to use mood expressions versus a status message associated with the profile image.

Why

Allowing users to upload images encourages them to build up real identities. The avatar or image allows users to associate a likeness and a reputation with the person.

Related patterns

"Identity Cards or Contact Cards" on page 111

"Reflectors" on page 108

As seen on

Adium (*http://www.adiumx.com*)

Cyworld (*http://www.cyworld.com*)

Yahoo! (*http://profiles.yahoo.com*)

Further Reading

"Anonymity and Online Community: Identity Matters," by John M. Grohol, *http://www. alistapart.com/articles/identitymatters*

Communities of Practice: Learning, Meaning, and Identity, by Etienne Wenger, Cambridge University Press, 1999

"Faceted Id/entity: Managing representation in a digital world," by danah boyd (MS thesis), *http://smg.media.mit.edu/papers/danah/danahThesis.pdf*

Google's Portable Contacts API, *http://code.google.com/apis/contacts/docs/poco/1.0/ developers_guide.html*

"Identity and Deception in the Virtual Community," by Judith S. Donath, *http://smg. media.mit.edu/people/judith/Identity/IdentityDeception.html*

"Identity and Identification in a Networked World," by Tim Schneider and Michael Zimmer, *http://www.uic.edu/htbin/cgiwrap/bin/ojs/index.php/fm/article/view/1417/1335*

Memory, Identity, Community: The Idea of Narrative in the Human Sciences (SUNY Series in the Philosophy of the Social Sciences), by Lewis P. Hinchman, State University of New York Press, 1997

Portable Contacts Spec, *http://portablecontacts.net/*

The Saturated Self: Dilemmas of Identity in Contemporary Life, by Kenneth Gergen, Basic Books, 2000

Storylines: Craftartists' Narratives of Identity, by Elliot G. Mishler, Harvard University Press, 2004

"Superstar Avatars," by Gillian Reagan, *http://www.observer.com/2008/o2/ superstar-avatars?page=0%2C0*

Yahoo!'s Open Social API, *http://developer.yahoo.com/social/*

Chapter 5

We Are Here! We Are Here! We Are Here!

It's impossible to move, to live, to operate at any level without leaving traces,
bits, seemingly meaningless fragments of personal information.
—William Gibson

How do you know someone's present? In class, they used to call roll and each person would respond with "here" or "yo" (it was the 1970s) or even "present." Usually you can just look around. But how about when someone is standing behind you and he clears his throat, not because he's feeling hoarse but as a way of letting you know he's standing there so he won't startle you. In the real world we are tuned to all sort of indications of who is present (either in the immediate moment or the recent stretch of time) and who is absent. If you see an unmown lawn, it may mean no one's been home for a while, or it may mean that the homeowner is an iconoclast at war with the neighborhood association, but if you notice a pile of uncollected newspapers on the stoop, that's a pretty good sign of absence. Likewise, if the curtains are open and they were closed earlier or a light is on that was dark before, that's another sign that someone's there.

Graffiti showing a nose peeking above a wall with the legend "Kilroy was here" may also tell you that someone has been by, perhaps recently.

In his fantastic anthropology weblog, This Blog Sits At (*http://www.cultureby.com/ trilogy/2007/12/status-casting.html*), Grant McCracken has written about statuscasting (broadcasting your status; we'll get to that soon) as "phatic" communication:

> *When we status-cast, we're a little like animals. As I argued in my post on the "puzzle of exhaust data" I suggested that one way to think about exhaust data was to treat it as phatic communication. (In humans and other animals, phatic communication consists of non-verbal gestures and small, sub-linguistic noises. Murmurs, shouts, groans, all of these are phatic.) We can say that tiny posts on Twitter are phatic, too. You may not care that I am "feeding my cat." But knowing this tells you I exist, my location, my condition, my, er, status. Twitter data are not "exhaust data" precisely because they serve this locational purpose.*

In an earlier blog post, he discusses how static messages "stack nicely":

> *The phatic messages "stack" nicely, each message presupposing and building on its predecessor. These messages are: 1. I exist. 2. I'm ok. 3. You exist. 4. You're ok. 5. The channel is open. 6. The network exists. 7. The network is active. 8. The network is flowing. When I use Twitter or Facebook to say that I am entertaining my cat, no one, I'm pretty, sure gives a good God damn that I am entertaining my cat. But they are reminded that they have someone called Grant McCracken who exists in their network. This is not nothing. Facebook sustains social knowledge and networks that begin in conferences and then fade almost immediately until a couple of months later we have a hard time attaching a face to that business card still banging around in our briefcase. A "newsflash" about my cat helps keep the network node called Grant McCracken from blinking out.*

So, while we may not be able to be fully present across all sensory channels when we're physically remote (hence the concept of "telepresence" or "online presence"), we do have a growing set of tools and traditions for simulating or modeling presence in the online world (Figure 5-1). For many of us, the first encounter with these sorts of presence indicators occurs in instant message or other real-time communication applications.

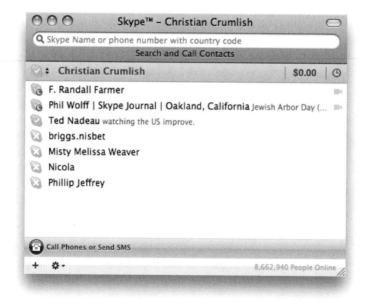

Figure 5-1. *What are the tools that enable remote or partial presence (not just indicators of availability but mindfulness, attention, and responsiveness)?*

Taken together, these various modes of remote presence contribute to what is now often called the real-time web (or the living web, or the live web): the aspect of online social behavior that is updated constantly as each individual takes an action and a record of it is shared with some public listening in (or found soon thereafter via social search).

A Brief History of Online Presence

Talking about presence online can be confusing, as the term has been applied to a spectrum of meanings, including at least these three:

1. There's the old concept of a presence as a persistent "place" online where a business or project can be found—a sort of euphemism for a website (e.g., "We need an online presence," "We need to improve our online presence"). This was often said in a keeping-up-with-the-Joneses sense at the turn of the millennium. (This sense is largely handled by the identity patterns discussed in Chapter 3.)

2. The human equivalent of this is the interesting bit, since it relates to the sense in which a blog, for instance, can create an ongoing sense of a person, and its state of currency can help create the sense that the blogger is actively "present" in that space and can be found there.

3. Next, there is presence in the sense that instant messenger (IM) and Twitter theorists discuss it. IM programs have an online presence indicator that conveys to the whole world or to a user's connections (or to those from whom the user is not hiding) that one is currently online and available for communication; this is *present* not in a physical sense but in an availability sense. This is synchronous, real-time presence, to be distinguished from the asynchronous sense of #1 and #2. Here we also get statuscasting (so, beyond "Available," there start to be free-form choices—often with limited character counts—for indicating what we're doing or how we're feeling at the moment), and thus the phatic communication others have written about: at times "meaningless" bits of communication designed more to signal presence, connection, and attention (as in Figure 5-2).

Figure 5-2. *Some statuscasting may seem trivial. It can sometimes be the equivalent of (nonverbal) phatic communication, the sounds and grunts of acknowledgment we make to remind one another that we exist. Somehow, though, my mental image of Cecily making peanut brittle makes me feel that I know her a little better than I did before.*

We're mainly talking about sense #3 in this book, and to a lesser extent #2. To bring this back down to earth a bit from the realm of philosophy, we can say that presence is a prerequisite for real-time (or minimal-lag) communication, and that it can itself be used as a medium for phatic communication.

The Future of Presence

In his Telepocalypse blog (*http://www.telepocalypse.net/archives/000636.html*), Martin Geddes writes:

> *It is very easy when talking about presence to get sucked into thinking about IM icons, and the messaging of comings and going using protocols like SIMPLE. But go take a look at the work of Media Lab Europe in Dublin. They have flower pots that bloom according to the availability of your special other. Tables that remember what was on them. Then there are the haptic (touchy feely) instant messages, the time-smeared entrance lobby webcam, and so on. Presence isn't just about smiley icons.*

Presence Actions and Facets

The primary principle to bear in mind when designing presence interfaces is to maximize opportunities for your users to declare themselves present to one another (similar to leaving footprints or other human traces). Practically speaking, this breaks down into a few actions that the user or system can take:

- Publishing presence information
- Displaying current presence status
- Displaying a timeline of recent presence items
- Maintaining a history (partial or complete) of past presence declarations
- Providing users with a way to subscribe to presence updates
- Providing users with a way to filter presence updates

There are also a number of different aspects or facets of presence that may be included in an update, including but not necessarily limited to the following:

- Status, as in availability
- Status, as in current activity
- Mood
- Environment
- Location
- Device Status (on/off)
- Other (system-, device-, or user-defined facets)

Finally, there's the public with whom your availability, status, mood, location, and so on are shared, referred to in the instant-messenger context as your "buddy list."

Availability is the bottom line for online presence (Figure 5-3). If you're available, that's fairly straightforward. It means, ostensibly, that it's acceptable to contact you (interrupt you) in real time. Unavailability can take several flavors (away, busy, idle). These facets originated in the context of messenger and chat applications, but they map fairly consistently to other persistent presence indicators.

Figure 5-3. *Perhaps the most fundamental bit of presence information is available versus unavailable.*

Richer options for status are possible (beyond simply available or not). Many applications with presence features enable the user to either manually enter a status update (generally, what she's currently doing) or have some application or object update her status automatically. Status information usually can be layered on top of availability information (Figure 5-4).

Figure 5-4. *Beyond indication availability, a presence status update might also indicate what activity the user is currently engaged in.*

A mood selector, such as the one shown in Figure 5-5, enables the user to indicate how she currently feels (something otherwise rather difficult to discern through cold mechanical interfaces). Beware of trying to supply a complete taxonomy of human emotions. Chances are, you'll overcomplicate things.

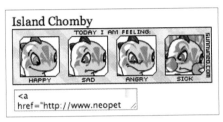

Figure 5-5. *A mood vocabulary can be free-form or based on a controlled list. Neopets offers four standard moods: happy, sad, angry, and sick.*

Identifying your current location, either to other people or to applications, enables geographical information, such as proximity and physical availability, to come into play. (See Chapter 16.) Location information may be entered manually or detected automatically using services such as GPS, mobile phone cell towers, or by polling an geographical information broker service such as Yahoo!'s Fire Eagle platform (*http://fireeagle.yahoo. com*). Twitter has evolved a folk syntax for location using "L:" as a prefix, followed by latitude and longitude information or place names, but it doesn't seem to be widely adopted. Twitter lists the user's location as part of his profile, implying a more static, longstanding answer, although some Twitter applications gather current geo information, usually from the inputting device, and use it to update the user's location field. This mismatch between a static, non archived, no-history-having profile item (perfect for "location of birth") and an ongoing stream of status updates (perfect for "where I am now" snapshots) today yields an unsatisfying experience, but one that is no doubt a business opportunity for someone.

Availability

The interface pattern for managing and displaying availability may also be referred to as "online presence indicators" (OPIs). They provide a way for users to display to other people (either the public or their contacts, depending on the rules of the system) when they are available for contact and when they are not (Figure 5-6).

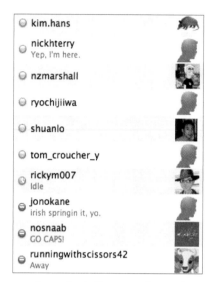

Figure 5-6. *A small set of icons can be used to indicate at a glance who is available, who is idle, and who is away. The interface may optionally sort the listed people by availability, as in this Yahoo! Messenger window.*

What

Users need to see who else is online, available, and open to contact.

Use when

Here are four typical use cases for online presence indicators:

- A person wants to determine whether his friend is online.
- A person wants to see who is available for contact.
- A person wants to see whether his friend is available for communication.
- A person wants to show his contacts that he is busy.

How

Allow users to visually identify themselves in one of three possible states: "Available," "Busy," or "Offline," explained further in the following table. Additionally, if technically feasible, the client can identify the user as "Idle" if she is away from the computer for a set period of time.

Available	The user is signed in and available for contact. If the Busy and Idle states are unavailable, the OPI defaults to this state, more broadly defined as the Online state. An application may permit the user to reveal availability manually, or it may be set to display "Available" whenever the user signs in.

Busy	The user is signed in, but has declared herself as Busy. "Busy" refers to two separate contexts that, in turn, relate to the diametrically opposed impetuses for IMing: focused intent and serendipity. One refers to actual busy-ness, requesting that others abide by those associated social mores (e.g., if a user sees someone set to "Do Not Disturb", he knows that person is contactable, but will contact her only when necessary). The other refers to a form of explicit idle-ness that explains a user's potential delay in response, which otherwise may not be adequately conveyed by the Idle state described next (e.g., "Stepped Out", "Not at My Desk", "Out to Lunch"). Setting your status as Busy bears no functional significance, and serves only as a social announcement. It is represented by the international "No Entry" sign, as shown in Figure 5-6.
Idle	The user is signed in, but the client observes that no keyboard or mouse activity has happened within a set period of time (the Windows client for Yahoo! Messenger defaults to 15 minutes). The user has the option to override this setting, thereby always appearing as either Available or Busy.
Offline	The user is not signed in, or has signed in as "Invisible."

Adopt a set of consistent icons for these three (or four, including "Idle") states. Studies show that stoplight colors (red, green, amber) don't map well to these choices, even though they are widely used among IM applications. This is mainly because while "Available" can be easily mapped to "Go" (green), three of the states (Busy, Offline, and Idle) are all equivalent to "Stop" (red), and none of them map particularly well to "Slow Down/Proceed with Caution" (amber).

Stealth Mode

An automated system that is too transparent or honest may put users into awkward situations, such as when they wish to be available to some, but not all, of their contacts. Therefore, you might find it useful to provide a stealth mode (Figure 5-7), the ability to sign in as "Invisible" and hence not reveal oneself automatically on connecting to the application.

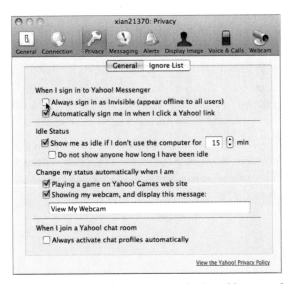

Figure 5-7. *You may offer your users (as Yahoo! Messenger does) stealth options that can disguise the user's true availability as a way of managing attention and interruption and selectively determining who sees the user as present.*

Yahoo! Messenger, for example, enables a granular selectivity by which you can appear Invisible only to specific people, using this procedure:

1. The user clicks his contact's name while pressing the Control (Ctrl) key to highlight the contact. This automatically opens a pop-up menu.

2. The user selects Stealth Settings.

3. The user clicks Permanently Offline.

This contact will thereafter never see you as online unless you change this setting. To remind the user, the contact appears in italics on the user's Messenger List. (Messenger offers a similar feature for whole groups.)

Why

Revealing availability is the fundamental building block of online presence. Providing your users with dead-easy ways to do this fosters the sense of presence and availability that helps a social system feel inhabited by real people with realistic comings and goings.

Open questions

What's the overall value of being online if users can still receive offline messages? What's the overall value of being busy if there's no direct consequence, other than serving as a visual note to others?

Example: Yahoo! OPIs

Yahoo! employs online presence indicators in a variety of contexts—in Messenger clients, across other Yahoo! properties, and outside the network (in the form of "badges"). For a user, they primarily communicate two concepts: whether that user is signed in to the Messenger service, and whether other users are signed in to the Mesenger service.

Online presence indicators are a foundation of the Messenger product: all IM experiences across OSes and devices must represent "online" and "offline" contacts in a manner that is visually consistent across clients, but still tailored to the clients' individual aesthetics.

As shown in Figure 5-8, the disc indicating that the user is online and available is yellow (not green). The disc indicating offline or unavailable is gray. This originally was derived from the Yahoo! smiley icon, but has been rationalized as symbolizing the sun and the moon, day and night, being awake versus being asleep.

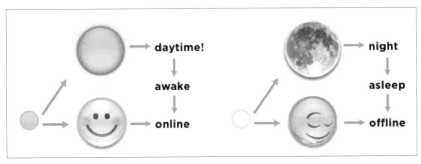

Figure 5-8. *Yahoo!'s visual system for OPI aims to emphasize the binary nature of being online versus being offline. Using the stoplight metaphor introduces ambiguities around Busy (red) and Offline (gray), and introduces a false notion of Idle (yellow) as an intermediary state between Available and Busy. Yahoo!'s discs are also intended to be interchangeable with the smileys as appropriate, and might well represent a visual metaphor that is more universal.*

Sources

Much of this pattern is derived from the work of Matte Sheinker at Yahoo!.

Mood

Online communication is notoriously impoverished compared with face-to-face presence (at least when there's no video camera or smell-o-vision pheromone exchange mechanism). Just as emoticons (sideways smiley faces and other glyphs) evolved as a way of cueing emotions and breaking through some of the brittleness of text-only dialogue, mood indicators can give users a way of signaling their emotional state to each other, and give more flavor to communication (Figure 5-9).

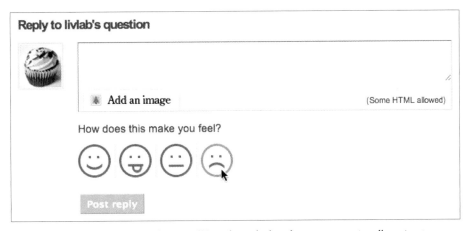

Figure 5-9. *GetSatisfaction provides a small list of moods that the user can optionally assign to a comment. The interface isn't designed for presence, but it does attempt to capture how the user feels at the time of commenting.*

Environment

An indication of what music the user is currently listening to is the most common environment report in presence updates. This can be used to give the flavor of the person's environment, and doubles as a potential talking point. A "what I'm listening to" field or the use of a status field for this purpose can be filled in manually by the user, or an application can be set to read what music is currently playing from the operating system or device (Figure 5-10). The process of uploading this information to an ongoing stream is referred to as "scrobbling" (as popularized by Last.fm).

Figure 5-10. *An application can automatically detect the current song playing in an application such as iTunes and assign its identifying information as the user's current status. Often, a musical note symbol serves as a clue to the user's friends that the information wasn't entered manually and is in fact song data.*

Buddy List

The user wants a distinct list of people she knows (friends, coworkers, family) to communicate with in real time (Figure 5-11).

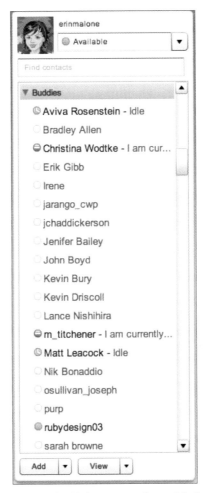

Figure 5-11. *Yahoo! Instant Messenger's buddy list. Icons indicate if the buddy is online, offline, idle, or away.*

Use when

Use this pattern when offering just-in-time communications, such as instant messaging.

How

- The buddy list is a list of people a user wants to keep track of.
- Indicate which users are currently online (see "Presence Actions and Facets" on page 125).
- Indicate which users are offline.
- Indicate when a user is online but may be busy and not taking messages.
- Consider indicating when a user is idle, which often indicates that the user is not at the computer or is engaged in another task.
- Allow users to organize their buddies into meaningful groupings, such as friends, family, golf buddies, work peeps, etc.
- Consider allowing the creation of on-the-fly group chats through the selection of multiple people in a buddy list.
- Consider storing messages sent to a buddy for later retrieval, if the message is sent when he is no longer online.
- Enhance recognition by allowing the user to add nicknames or friendly names to his view of the buddy list.
- Enhance recognition and user expression by presenting the buddy's name or nickname with her avatar (Figure 5-12).

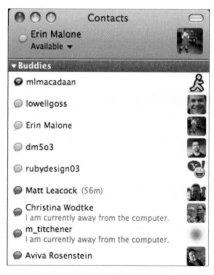

Figure 5-12. *Buddy list showing avatars to help disambiguate buddies.*

Why

Real-time communications and the buddy list to support them add an immediate and real-life component to what are often asynchronous online experiences.

Related patterns

"Adding Friends" on page 361

"Many Publics" on page 228

"Private Conversation" on page 298

As seen on

Adium (*http://adium.im/*)

AIM (*http://www.aim.com/*)

Skype (*http://www.skype.com/*)

Yahoo! Messenger (*http://messenger.yahoo.com/*)

Activity Streams

When status updates first emerged in the context of instant messenger programs, they were inherently fleeting, temporally tied to the immediate moment and then discarded. It really doesn't make that much sense to keep an infinite log of Available, Busy, Idle, Offline, and so on for the life of the user or the application. But as other status-capturing interfaces have evolved, the idea of at least maintaining a stream of recent history and then possibly mixing status reports with other snapshots of online activity has taken hold as a way of displaying presence.

There is still an element of the ephemeral in this. You'd rarely thumb through days and days of old status updates to find what a specific person was doing or thinking or listening to at some arbitrary point in the past (at least if you're not a stalker). However, there's really nothing to stop these sorts of feeds of personal status updates from being stored, permalinked, catalogued, indexed, made searchable, and so on, even if presence affordances are geared more naturally toward the present moment and the recent past.

You'll need to think about persistence of old status updates. Are you committing to keeping them findable forever, or just for the last few days? Will you give your users a way to download or archive status data, or even transport it to another system? These cumulative activity updates can paint a persistent portrait of a person online.

You can view a person's activity stream as the sum total of observable behaviors he is engaging with online or within your system. (At Yahoo! we call this a person's "vitality" online.) This may include status updates, but it may also include any number of other recordable activities that can be captured via RSS feeds or by polling or scraping activity feeds across a wide variety of services. This may also be a mix of services within your system or network, or may combine services across the public Internet.

An activity stream (or feed) may therefore consist of an aggregation of updates and activities that together can create a much richer sense of what the user has been doing, thinking about, and saying in the recent past (Figure 5-13).

Figure 5-13. *When aggregating actions and behaviors across a number of different services, an activity stream of vitality updates can paint a more well-rounded picture of a person's day or recent activities for his followers.*

Services that aggregate activity streams online include Facebook, Friendfeed, MyBlogLog, and Yahoo! Profiles.

When presenting an activity stream to your users, consider whether to offer a single type of update (such as status messages) or a mixture of multiple forms of activity (links, posted media, songs listened to, and so on). If mingling multiple types of activity, think about how your users may want to isolate a single context.

Statuscasting

Statuscasting is the custom of broadcasting an ongoing stream of status updates to the public or to a set of contacts or followers. Similar in concept to IM status updates, statuscasting incorporates the idea of the ongoing feed that can be browsed into the past. It does not necessarily indicate availability at any given point, but does imply it, in the sense that if you see a recent status update from a friend, you might conclude that she is available for contact.

There may be some value in cross-feeding status updates from one system to another. Twitter users, for example, can have their status updates on Twitter become their status messages in their IM clients (or vice versa). Likewise, posts to Twitter might be broadcast into another service, such as Facebook or Friendfeed or Yahoo! Updates. Be careful how you enable this kind of connection, however, as the original context may be stripped away, and the updates may not make sense or work well in the new context. For example, Away, Idle, and Available are 80% or more of all IM statuses.

Statuscasting tools such as Twitter (Figure 5-14) lend themselves to inventive variations and uses. If you give people a box to type into and a button to press, they will discover their own uses for it.

Figure 5-14. *Twitter famously asks the user to answer the question "What are you doing?" in 140 characters or less. Although usage has evolved to the point that many Twitter users rarely address that question, a stream of status updates nonetheless paints a picture of their moment-to-moment thoughts and experiences. Nestled between my many shout-outs to other Twitter users are a few items that report in a matter-of-fact way what I was doing that day.*

In addition to displaying a single person's statuscast feed, it's common to provide a way to see a collection of people (everybody or just the user's friends) and their most recent updates. These kinds of interfaces may benefit from offering the user an easy way to filter or sort, especially when one person is dominating the combined feed with a stream of constant updates.

Microblogging

What

Microblogging allows users to create short posts. These are often aggregated into a stream and can consist of text, pictures, or video.

Services such as Twitter and Yammer (for enterprise applications) constrain users to 140 characters. The constraint grew out of a primary use case of text messaging limits of 160 characters. Twitter wanted to be able to include the username, so the message limit was set to 140 characters (Figure 5-15). People's posts flow into the stream based on time and have a more ephemeral nature than blogging. Most people use microblogging to alert others to what they are doing at that moment or to ask short questions or announce whereabouts.

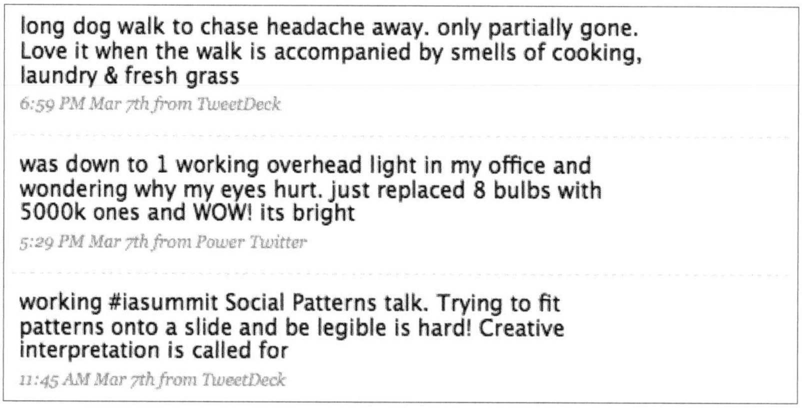

long dog walk to chase headache away. only partially gone.
Love it when the walk is accompanied by smells of cooking,
laundry & fresh grass
6:59 PM Mar 7th from TweetDeck

was down to 1 working overhead light in my office and
wondering why my eyes hurt. just replaced 8 bulbs with
5000k ones and WOW! its bright
5:29 PM Mar 7th from Power Twitter

working #iasummit Social Patterns talk. Trying to fit
patterns onto a slide and be legible is hard! Creative
interpretation is called for
11:45 AM Mar 7th from TweetDeck

Figure 5-15. *Short messages limited to 140 characters are how microblogging is defined on Twitter.*

Ecosystems of other functionality have sprung up around the microblogging phenomenon that allow users to aggregate their own posts onto their blog sites, search for specific threads of conversations, post onto other services (e.g., Twitter posts appearing on Facebook), and group people together around specific topics of conversation.

- Use as a light alternative to blogging.
- Use when you want to allow conversations and real-time updates but don't need the synchronous conversations of instant messaging.

- The basic interface for microblogging is a text field, with a clearly marked character count limit and a Submit button. For alternatives to text (such as video and photos), clearly indicate the size and time limits.
- Provide a method for viewing once posted. Both an author view and a community view should be available.

Sometimes all you need to do is say a few words or share a short thought. Microblogging addresses that need without the heavy-duty interface or overhead of blogs.

"Blogs: Ownership" on page 245

"Comments" on page 278

"Private Conversation" on page 298

"Public Conversation" on page 296

"Statuscasting" on page 137

12 Seconds (*http://12seconds.tv/*)

Twitter (*http://www.twitter.com*)

Yammer (*https://www.yammer.com/*)

Updates

Updates provide people with mini stories about what their connections and others are doing on the Net (Figure 5-16). People can also consume mini stories on topics they are interested in.

Figure 5-16. *Here, a mixed stream of updates from friends can serve as a serendipitous feed showing numerous people engaged in various activities.*

What

Users want to see what their friends have been doing presented in a convenient format. Additionally, applications derive an advertising benefit from being able to share with the public or a controlled audience what their users have been doing. These updates can serve as reminders to other users about what is possible within the system.

Updates can be produced and consumed in nearly every imaginable context: across a single application or network, across the Web, on mobile devices, and so on. Vitality can be displayed in a context-sensitive manner, presenting information that is relevant to what a user is currently consuming. For example, in a general context, such as Yahoo!'s Front Page, users will get a more global, aggregated vitality view consisting of updates on their connections' activities from across Yahoo!. In a more focused context, such as Yahoo! Fantasy Sports, the vitality items shown are limited to what their connections do specifically in Sports and on topics related to the content they are currently viewing in Sports. This context sensitivity ensures that users see updates from the people they care about— their connections—and on topics they are interested in.

Updates aim to provide users with delightful, personally relevant, timely content that engages them, helps them connect with others and participate in one another's lives, and encourages their participation in the service.

To accomplish this, create syndicated digests of user activity from content-producing sources and third-party sites and applications, and make them available to content-consuming properties and other sites.

A sophisticated vitality system will learn about the user's preferences by tracking click-through, so if the items in the stream start with a "good enough" guess, they can improve through iterative refinement of the weighted algorithm that selects items. The experience for an ordinary user, then, is to be shown updates presented more or less as "stuff we think you'd want to see based on who you are and where you are on the site."

Updates tend to follow the form of subject, verb, and object, with an optional indirect option, as discussed in Chris Messina's presentation on open activity streams (*http://www.slideshare.net/factoryjoe/activity-streams-presentation*).

Updates Opt-in Disclosure

One ethical issue that arises when launching or maintaining a vitality service is that users need to be fully informed and affirmatively opted-in to having their activities tracked and published in various locations on the Web. At the same time, especially when launching such a service, one wants to avoid "scaring off" the customers with overtly legalistic boilerplate warnings. You must walk a fine line in trying to encourage participation without deceiving or antagonizing your users.

When users contribute content to sites that produce updates, an opt-in disclosure informs them in context that their content will be shared with other users (Figure 5-17). The disclosure interface can be presented in line or as a modal overlay.

Figure 5-17. *Notify your users that their actions are being recorded and sent to an update stream, and give them a way of opting out, or you risk potential backlash.*

When Facebook first launched its Beacon service, which published reports on the user's Feed about activities taking place elsewhere, it did not disclose this functionality or obtain opt-ins. Consequently, users revolted and accused the service of, among other things, "ruining Christmas" by inadvertently showing the purchase of gifts at online stores such as Amazon to the gifts' intended recipients.

What

Users who contribute content need to be informed that summary posts of their content (known as "updates") will be shared beyond the site on which they are creating it. Additionally, users need to be given the opportunity to control the sharing settings (who the content will be shared with) in the system prior to publishing their content.

Use when

Use this pattern when users are contributing content on your site that will be distributed as updates via a vitality system. For example, when users review a TV show on Yahoo! TV, they are presented with a textual in line disclosure to inform them of distribution via Vitality. The in line disclosure is used for in-depth contributions, such as writing reviews, comments, etc., and this disclosure appears every time a user contributes content. The modal overlay (pop-up) disclosure is used for quick contributions (ratings, buzzing, etc.) and appears every time, unless users check the provided box that says, "Don't show this message again."

How

For user-generated content that prompts users for an in-depth contribution, such as writing reviews, comments, blog posts, etc., provide an in-line disclosure and a link to manage sharing settings.

For user-generated content that prompts users for quick contributions, such as rating, voting up, and so on, a modal overlay (pop-up) may display a confirmation message (for the content they just created), a disclosure message about sharing, a link to manage sharing, a "Don't show this message again" option to prevent the overlay in this context in the future, and an OK button to dismiss the overlay.

Why

It is important to offer full disclosure to users about where their content will appear and who it will be shared with.

Sources

This pattern is derived from the work of Barry Crane and the Yahoo! Social platform team.

Managing Incoming Updates

As users start to rely on a feed of updates for news of their friends' doings online and clues to interesting bookmarked or recommended items, it is important to give them tools for fine-tuning the feed. Some refinement comes from the ability to add or remove sources (following or friending versus leaving or unfriending), but finer-grained options can involve the ability to ask for more or less of a certain type of content or items from a specific person.

To avoid cluttering up an interface with a row of icons or widgets attached to every single update in a feed, it is more elegant to supply a small, discreet icon for triggering a context menu, and even make that icon invisible until the user accidentally discovers it on hover (Figure 5-18).

Figure 5-18. *If I want more items from my friend Greg in my Facebook feed, I can point to the current item, and when the Options icon appears, I can click on it to pop up a context menu.*

Additional responsive choices for managing items (such as reporting abusive content) can be offered on the same menu, since the triggering item is so compact.

In an aggregated feed, it can be easy to lose track of items as they are rapidly supplanted by newer updates, so offering your users a way to filter the feed to only show items from a single source or to hide one or more sources can enable them to cut through the noise (Figure 5-19).

Figure 5-19. *Friendfeed offers a row of icons that the user can click to isolate one single source of updates from the aggregated vitality feed he is viewing.*

Lifestreams

Aggregated vitality is sometimes referred to as *lifestreaming*, but others reserve that term for the sort of updates feed that incorporates items from "the real world" (as opposed to just online behaviors). In the long run, this distinction is bound to break down, but currently there is some value to preserving it, as we begin to see devices for capturing stimuli from the user's surroundings in an ambient way and automatically uploading them to a service where they can be viewed and consumed publicly by friends or followers.

Examples of this include Blogging in Motion (*http://blogginginmotion.com/*), the winning hack at Yahoo! Open Hack Day 2006 (Figure 5-20).

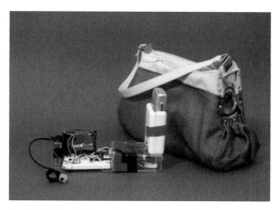

Figure 5-20. *The Blogging in Motion hack combines a camera phone, a purse, a pedometer, a GPS parser called ZoneTag, and a Flickr account to enable automated regular live photoblogging of the life of the person carrying the purse.*

Perhaps coincidentally, Yahoo!'s next Open Hack Day, in 2008, also featured a lifestreaming hack, called Purple Pedals (*http://purplepedals.com*; see Figure 5-21).

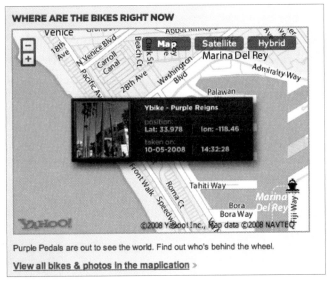

Figure 5-21. *The Purple Pedals GPS-Flickr Bikes automatically take pictures, tag them with geolocation, and upload them to Flickr (much like the Blogging in Motion purse).*

Keep Company

Technology can be cold and impersonal. When the concept of a "ghost in the machine" first arose, it was used to deride Descartes mind-body dualism, ridiculing the idea that the body is a simple meaty mechanism and the spirit is some ghostly presence that imbues it with humanity. Dualism has fallen out of fashion in philosophical circles, but the truth is that in today's online social systems, there is a fundamental duality baked right in. The machinery connects us, but without the human presences (the ghosts), it is simply a tangle of wires and electronic impulses.

In the real world, we like to know that there are other people around, coming and going, adding to the life of a place. An abandoned building is scary, but one that has signs of life can be much warmer and more welcoming. There are a number of ways to communicate this sense of life in a social interface.

Ambient Intimacy

Ambient intimacy is about being able to keep in touch with people with a level of regularity and intimacy that you wouldn't usually have access to, because time and space conspire to make it impossible.

Ambient describes the lightness, the atmospheric, non directional, and distributed nature of the communication. These are communications that are one to many: they're not quite broadcast and yet not exactly conversational. They flood over a somewhat defined space. Within that space is intimacy—the closeness, familiarity, and warmth that this kind of communication can create. There is an ever-present network of friends available wherever you can access the Internet—or even just send a text message.

Flickr lets me see what friends are eating for lunch, how they've redecorated their bedroom, and their latest haircut. Twitter tells me when they're hungry, what technology is currently frustrating them, who they're having drinks with tonight.

Who cares? Who wants this level of detail? Isn't this all just annoying noise? There are certainly many people who think this, but they tend to be not so noisy themselves. It seems to me that there are lots of people for whom being social is very much a "real-life" activity, and technology is just about getting stuff done.

There are a lot of us, though, who find great value in this ongoing noise. It helps us get to know people who would otherwise be just acquaintances. It makes us feel closer to people we care for but in whose lives we're not able to participate as closely as we'd like.

Knowing these details creates intimacy. (It also saves a lot of time when you finally do get to catch up with these people in real life!) It's not so much about meaning; it's just about being in touch.

As Ian Curry at Frog Design writes:

> It's basically blogging reduced to what the Russian linguist Mikhail Bakhtin called "the phatic function." Like saying "what's up?" as you pass someone in the hall when you have no intention of finding out what is actually up, the phatic function is communication simply to indicate that communication can occur. It made me think of the light, low-content text message circles Mizuko Ito described existing among Japanese teens - it's not so important what gets said as that it's nice to stay in contact with people. These light exchanges typify the kind of communication that arises among people who are saturated with other forms of communication.

—continued—

Ambient Intimacy

This is not an effect or an activity that is new or that is inherently connected to new social tools. Much the same was observed in a Japanese ethnographic research study into the use of camera phones by young people undertaken by Mizuko Ito and Daisuke Okabe, who found the following:

> [M]essaging can be a way of maintaining ongoing background awareness of others, and of keeping multiple channels of communication open…many of the messages we saw exchanged…included messages that informants described as 'insignificant' or 'not urgent'. Some examples of messages in this category are communications such as 'I'm just walking up the hill now', 'I'm tired', 'I guess I'll take a bath now', 'just bought a new pair of shoes', 'groan, I just work up with a hangover' or 'the episode today totally sucked, didn't it?'

On its own, a Twitter or a Facebook status update may seem trivial and meaningless, but to examine an update in isolation is to miss the point of the social system that is at play here. These apparently trivial updates are really critical to maintaining connection with a network of often loose ties. This network can give rich social rewards to those who participate; however, more and more participants are finding that the rewards extend beyond just being social and discovering that the connectedness and serendipity of ambient intimacy can bring great professional gains as well.

These days, ambient intimacy plays many roles in my life: it has stopped me from missing an important international flight and helped me keep sane whilst at home with a small baby. It is my outsourced tech support resource, my recommendation engine, my news filter. Twitter lets me virtually attend conferences I can't get to but am interested in. But most valuable of all, it has allowed me to create, maintain, and even build professional and personal relationships with people in my field whose work I admire and from whom I have been able to learn and develop as a professional.

So, although the question may be "what are you doing?" and perhaps you don't really care, know that there is much more going on here than just a status update. It's a whole new way of being connected, and its power shouldn't be underestimated.

—Leisa Reichelt,
User Experience Consultant, Disambiguity Ltd.

Signs of Life

The easiest way to communicate to your returning visitors the liveliness of your social environment is to present them on login with a summary of recent activities, ideally those of people they're connected to. For new users it may still be worthwhile to show them examples of recent activities, perhaps anonymizing the identities of the users to preserve their privacy. This is what LinkedIn does, and it doubles as a reminder to the user of the range of activities she can engage in within the service (Figure 5-22).

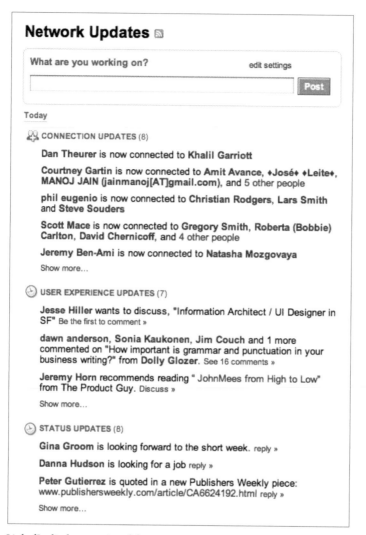

Figure 5-22. *LinkedIn displays a series of clusters reporting on recent activities in the user's network, giving a sense of the health and, yes, vitality of the network.*

Similarly, when you log back into a project on Basecamp, it shows you not only which users are participating in the project, but whether any of them are currently online, or how long it's been since they visited (Figure 5-23). (See also "Reengagement" on page 75.)

People on this project

IAI Board

Christian Crumlish
You are logged in right now

Paul Goodson
Latest activity about 5 hours ago

Melissa Weaver
Latest activity 11 days ago

Stacy Surla
Latest activity 26 days ago

Jorge Arango
Hasn't logged in recently

Figure 5-23. *Basecamp tells you not only who else is involved in the current project but whether those users are currently logged in and, if not, how long it's been since they dropped by.*

User Gallery

Another technique for signaling the transient presence of other visitors is MyBlogLog's faceroll widget (Figure 5-24), which shows recent visitors to a blog or site (from opted-in users of MyBlogLog), which can give the current visitor a sense that he has company while reading the blog, especially if he recognizes some of the faces or names.

Yahoo! designer Bryce Glass once said:

> *MyBlogLog is interesting in this regard, because it establishes my presence at a particular location (a web page) at a specific time. Before Y! acquired MyBlogLog, we had an internal (Hackday-inspired) version of this running... you could put a simple JavaScript insert on any page on the intranet that would display a widget showing the last **n** employees who'd visited the page. Though ultimately killed by legal [over privacy concerns], it was extremely useful for establishing peoples' presence "at" your design document, product requirements document, etc. (Did the team really review your spec? How recently? Who were the holdouts?)*

Recent Visitors

View Reader Community
Join this Community
(provided by MyBlogLog)

Figure 5-24. *There's a fine line between the immediate present and a longer-term historical view. Showing recent visitors, as MyBlogLog's faceroll badge does, gives your latest visitor a sense of which users have been visiting lately and who they're keeping company with, even if people hardly ever comment.*

Who's Here Now?

Perhaps the most immediate interface technique for keeping the current user company is to show her who else is currently logged in to the site (Figure 5-25). Although they may be physically remote, in a sense they are sharing the user's current experience by co-browsing the site.

ARTISTS CURRENTLY ONLINE

145 members
283 guests

Curious which members are on RateMyDrawings right now? The following list shows you RateMyDrawings members that are currently logged in. **Why not see if they're in the** DrawChat room. Users with more drawings appear larger.

MEMBERS: ONLINE NOW

Samobor (68) hmmcKBC25 (0) cute_neko_girl (7) blackbird666999 (106) Iskeanime16 (18)

Random-ness-ness (21) Cross_my_heart (1) kagomeisarose410 (8) natballjr (361) becky_741 (10)

Pikapachirisu (67) tiger72 (18) pinkie (29) RedSkull (21) TAYI0R (38) Rosaria (6) wwefan144 (0)

invadershilo (1) leahb11 (73) TheWhiteWolf222 (0) ShirianekiZ (6) RumikoClover23 (96) foulxplay (1)

Tiger (193) RikoJasmine (34) Zuiyon (46) noircouer (9) rawrmeowrawr (0) xAnime_Catx (23)

Kyashi (33) VictoriaRocks (15) Shia93 (10) thephilosipher (0) vinno (23) david1004 (0)

wildmustangluver (37) Babz86 (0) Golpiko (0) santaury (1) Deadley_GothWolf (25) Rapid (16) mellokun (5)

nervaeda (24) babysoxxx316 (13) Sozo (4) divaagarwal (29) silvercat101 (28) KawinaUzumaki (8)

smileycentralme (0) goatlivver (12) MrWISH (0) zxzxmatheus (9) xxcrystle_cat (8) sylleth (47) kitakun (74)

ZhouCGMP (11) Popelpix (1) Eggy (21) allan2134 (0) magicjuli (0) camino-neo (0) Hana13 (28)

AngelicBetrayal (52) jackfrost (18) Arabian_Horse999 (19) dragonflame2 (261) epq (86)

pinkbeach232 (140) Livin4today (23) iSax (9) sinyrfan78 (0) Batteries (4) sk8terkid264 (34)

Sienna Mollihan (49) bluecottoncandy (61) chichi_jackstar (42) Dave_28 (59)

dontcall11 (73) art_attack (203) jsnyder132 (69) Japan98 (2) squirril-sama (115)

Figure 5-25. *RateMyDrawings.com indicates who else is logged in to the site and gives you a way to select that person to see his contributions.*

Similarly, Facebook now shows you which of your "friends" are currently online (Figure 5-26).

Figure 5-26. *Once Facebook launched its own instant messenger service, its Online Friends feature came full circle, essentially replicating the fundamental "availability" presence pattern.*

Further Reading

Activity Streams, *http://activitystrea.ms/* (extension to the Atom spec)

Google Wave, *http://wave.google.com/* (combines email, public conversation, chat, and wiki patterns to create a performative collaborative space with elements of presence)

Telepocalypse blog, *http://www.telepocalypse.net/*

This Blog Sits At, *http://www.cultureby.com/*

Chapter 6

Would You Buy a Used Car from This Person?

*What is reputation? It's the general opinion (judgment) (more techni-
cally, a social evaluation) of (and by) the public (or a group or a person)
toward an entity (person, a group of people, or an organization or brand or
object)—as distinct and different from the background (others)—concerning
the likelihood of the entity to behave in a certain way in the future [under
certain circumstances]. It is a ubiquitous, spontaneous and highly efficient
mechanism of social control.*

—Ted Nadeau, Reputation 2.0
(http://www.slideshare.net/ted.nadeau/sxsw-2007-reputation-20)

Remember how you felt before the first day at a new school? Maybe it was frightening, the fear of the unknown, a new social environment with invisible rules and, for better or worse, a clean slate. Maybe it was exciting, a chance to reinvent yourself. Until it turns out your enemy from summer camp arrived just before you, talking behind your back and tainting your reputation before you even had a chance to make your first impression. This has never happened to you? Maybe I'm flashing back to high school.

Reputation online is another one of those social problem spaces that models the real world, connects to the real world, and in some ways simply extends the real world. One's reputation online may not be precisely the same thing as one's "real world" reputation, but the principles are similar. Reputation is largely a matter of context. Are you known to be a certain way in your family, another among your fellow congregants, a third on the dance floor, a fourth on the mailing list, and yet another to total strangers via Google?

Including reputation metrics and services in your social interface is somewhat less ambitious than trying to measure people's real-world reputations or even trying to capture their online, virtual reputations. You can simply focus on the communities you are fostering in your application, the values you are trying to instill in the environment, the behaviors you wish to encourage, and the types of people you wish to engage ever more deeply in your social environment.

Still, this is no small task, and a large part of it is determining the sorts of reputation patterns you wish to apply, as they all come with consequences and side effects. (Implementing a reputation platform is also an ambitious engineering task, beyond the scope of this book, but ably described in O'Reilly's forthcoming *Building Web Reputation Systems* by F. Randall Farmer and Bryce Glass.)

Reputation Influences Behavior

A person participating in a social structure expects to develop a reputation and hopes for insight into the reputations of others, but each designed model of participation and reputation embodies its own set of biases and incentive structures. Balancing these forces determines in large measure the success or failure of a social system.

Note that we are talking here about "people reputation" and not "object reputation." We're talking "she's really helpful," not "huge appetizers but too much salt."

When we published a bunch of this chapter's patterns in the Yahoo! Design Pattern library, some people questioned whether what we're talking about here is really reputation, or if reputation is something less easily measurable, a conclusion drawn in the minds of the individuals taking in the behaviors and published metrics about one another. Philosophically, this is an interesting distinction, but in the interest of defining a solvable set of design problems, we will leave direct mind control out of the discussion and instead focus on models of reputation that can be calculated and displayed by an application interface.

Fundamentally, a reputation system involves tracking desirable behavior and then recognizing it publicly. So, any well-designed reputation system is going to start with an inventory of desirable behaviors. Do you want to make sure people try out a certain feature, or strive for higher-quality contributions, or log endless hours responding to others? Just as managers say, "You can't manage what you can't measure," the same applies to reputation. You can't acknowledge what you aren't tracking.

When defining desirable behaviors, be sure to think about the individuals, the groups, and the site itself.

Note that a functioning reputation system requires stable, persistent identities (as discussed in Chapter 3).

Note also that the source of the following patterns is the Yahoo! Design Pattern library, based primarily on the work of Bryce Glass, Randy Farmer, and Yvonne French.

Competitive Spectrum

First, determine how competitive or cooperative a culture you wish to cultivate on your site. This determination will help you select the appropriate reputation patterns to apply. What kind of community are you building? Tough or nurturing? What role do you want reputation to play there? Hard-edged and unforgiving, gentle and caring, or somewhere in between?

What

When a new or existing community requires a reputation system, the designer must pay careful attention to the degree of *competitiveness* the community ought to exhibit. Haphazardly introducing competitive incentives into noncompetitive contexts can create problems and may cause a schism within the community.

Use when

Use this pattern when choosing the type of reputation system to design for a community.

How

The chart in Figure 6-1 attempts to describe a community in terms of its "competitiveness"— a broad term, but used here to describe a combination of things: the *individual goals* of community members, and to what degree those goals coexist peacefully or conflict; the *actions* that community members engage in, and to what degree those actions may impinge on the experiences of other community members; and to what degree *person-to-person* comparisons or contests are desired.

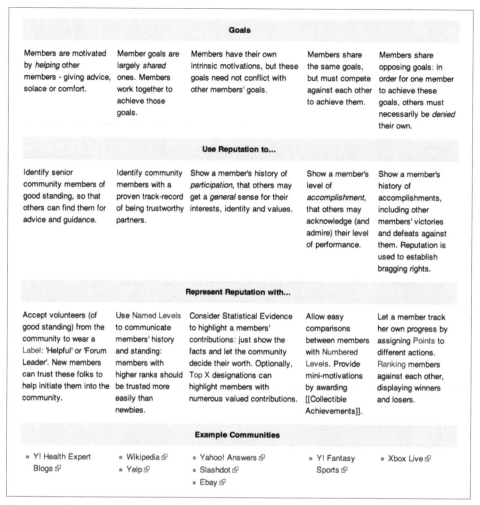

Goals

Members are motivated by *helping* other members - giving advice, solace or comfort.	Member goals are largely *shared* ones. Members work together to achieve those goals.	Members have their own intrinsic motivations, but these goals need not conflict with other members' goals.	Members share the same goals, but must compete against each other to achieve them.	Members share opposing goals: in order for one member to achieve these goals, others must necessarily be *denied* their own.

Use Reputation to...

Identify senior community members of good standing, so that others can find them for advice and guidance.	Identify community members with a proven track-record of being trustworthy partners.	Show a member's history of *participation*, that others may get a *general* sense for their interests, identity and values.	Show a member's level of *accomplishment*, that others may acknowledge (and admire) their level of performance.	Show a member's history of accomplishments, including other members' victories and defeats against them. Reputation is used to establish bragging rights.

Represent Reputation with...

Accept volunteers (of good standing) from the community to wear a Label: 'Helpful' or 'Forum Leader'. New members can trust these folks to help initiate them into the community.	Use Named Levels to communicate members' history and standing: members with higher ranks should be trusted more easily than newbies.	Consider Statistical Evidence to highlight a members' contributions: just show the facts and let the community decide their worth. Optionally, Top X designations can highlight members with numerous valued contributions.	Allow easy comparisons between members with Numbered Levels. Provide mini-motivations by awarding [[Collectible Achievements]].	Let a member track her own progress by assigning Points to different actions. Ranking members against each other, displaying winners and losers.

Example Communities

• Y! Health Expert Blogs 🔗	• Wikipedia 🔗 • Yelp 🔗	• Yahoo! Answers 🔗 • Slashdot 🔗 • Ebay 🔗	• Y! Fantasy Sports 🔗	• Xbox Live 🔗

Figure 6-1. *The Competitiveness Spectrum helps you choose reputation patterns appropriate to the tone and culture of your community.*

This "Competitiveness Spectrum" is admittedly subjective, and it would not be surprising to find many examples where this model does not hold up exactly as illustrated. The trick is to have *any* kind of framework to start from, not to have a definitive and comprehensive model.

Depending on the relative level of competitiveness present in your community, we'll recommend appropriate reputation patterns.

Why

- In Metrics for Healthy Communities (*http://www.horsepigcow.com/2007/10/03/metrics-for-healthy-communities/*), Tara Hunt attempts to describe the health of a community. One measure is the balance between competition and collaboration.

- In his (wonderfully titled) post "I Love My Chicken Wire Mommy" (*http://benbrown.com/says/2007/10/29/i-love-my-chicken-wire-mommy/*), Ben Brown talks about Consumating.com's "ill-fated point system" and the effects that it wreaked upon the community spirit.

Levels

Clearly defined levels of accomplishment provide an explicit measurement of reputation, capturing and sharing an empirical assessment of the individual's reputation in the social structure. Levels are typically named or numbered. Named levels generally have an explicit rank order (as in Figure 6-2), so in a sense both variations can be viewed as numbered levels.

Figure 6-2. *One form of reputation is a ranking system that characterizes your level of experience or accomplishment.*

Named Levels

What

Participants in a community need some way to gauge their own personal development within that community: how far they've progressed, or how deeply they've interacted with the community or its offerings. Additionally, these same measures can be used to compare members, to understand who has more or less experience in the community (as long as a high degree of comparability is not desired).

Use when

You want to enable consumers to discover and identify high-quality contributors. The community is competitive, but not highly competitive. Although named levels can have a competitive edge to them (my Wookie beats your Jawa!), they are perceived as less competitive than some other patterns (e.g., "Rankings", "Points", "Numbered Levels"), perhaps because they are less empirical in nature. You want to enable your users to track their individual growth in the community, and suggest ways that they may attain the next level in the hierarchy.

How

Define a family of reputations on a progressive continuum. Each level that is achieved is higher than the one before it. Levels are given unique names, which can give them a fun and approachable quality. Quick comparisons between levels, however, become slightly more difficult.

Recommendations

Consider a generic, but universally understandable, set of names for your property. For example, Gold, Silver, and Bronze levels are generally well understood. These might be appropriate in sports contexts, or, more generally, any context where clarity and understanding of the level hierarchy are more important than fun, context-specific names. Or consider thematically named levels, using a fun and "natural" set of names that enhances the experience. (For example, a *Star Wars* community might leverage the names of creatures or concepts from that universe.) You may consider adding levels at the upper end of the scale, in cases where a significant number of users have already achieved the highest possible level. It is not recommended, however, that you add "interstitial" levels, or levels between already existing ones. In general, add levels sparingly, if at all: you risk losing the trust of the community with too many or when you make arbitrary-seeming changes to your reputation system.

Cautions

Selecting a good set of thematically appropriate names may be more difficult than it seems. Don't expect your users to intuitively know that one name indicates a more senior level than any other. In our *Star Wars* example, "Jedi" trumps "Padawan," but does "Bounty Hunter" win over "Podracer"? Also, the more specific to a context your chosen names are, the greater the risk that you'll alienate or confuse a visitor who's not yet attuned to that community. Avoid even slightly offensive names for levels (e.g., "Music Hotshot!" or "Photo Flyguy!"). These may be learnable with appropriate supporting material, but remember that reputations are also a form of self-expression, and odds are good that a sizable portion of your community won't want to be identified with frivolous, insulting, or just goofy-sounding labels. Ambiguous level names like these tested very poorly with some of our users.

- Yahoo! Music's Ratings Level reputation uses a simple named level system (supported by a type of points system, wherein the act of rating a track earns you one point).

- Yahoo! EuroSport Message Boards employ a simple Gold/Silver/Bronze naming system to reward quality contributors on a particular message board.

- Blizzard's *World of Warcraft* uses named levels to communicate reputation among clans (Figure 6-3). This naming system effectively communicates the hierarchy of levels (for example, "Honored" is obviously better than "Hated").

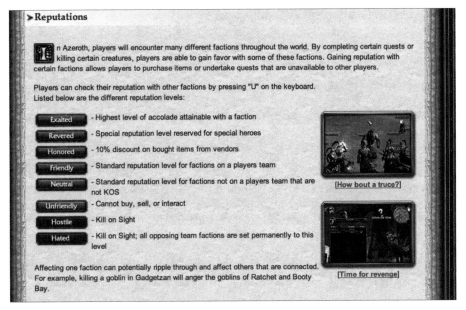

Figure 6-3. *World of Warcraft's named levels correspond to clear affinities and antagonisms.*

"Profile" on page 86

Numbered Levels

Implicit within a named level system of ranks is a linear order of the levels. This means that all levels are inherently numerical or can be represented numerically (Figure 6-4). A design decision you have to make is whether you want to expose the numbers in the interface or leave them hidden.

Figure 6-4. *While less engaging, explicitly numbered levels make comparisons between people dead simple.*

What

Participants in a community need some way to gauge their own personal development within that community: how far they've progressed, or how deeply they've interacted with the community or its offerings. Additionally, these same measures can be used to compare members, to understand who has more or less experience in the community.

Use when

You want to enable your users to track their individual growth in the community. A large (or open-ended) number of levels is desirable. For example, *World of Warcraft* currently allows users to advance to Level 70. You also want to enable easy comparisons between users. (At a glance, Level 1 is more junior than Level 5.) You're trying to encourage a more competitive community spirit.

How

Establish a family of reputations on a progressive continuum. Each level achieved is higher than the one before it. Levels are referred to by their number, which makes comparisons between levels very straightforward and easy to do. (Numbered levels, however, can be perceived as cold and impersonal.)

Recommendations

In most cases, numbered level systems should go no higher than 10 or so. A strong point of these systems is that they can be added to at a later date with minimal fuss. If, for example, too great a percentage of your community starts to achieve the upper limits of the system (see the upcoming "Exclusivity" section), consider "opening up" new higher levels for top achievers to attain. (Don't do this too frequently, though, or the community members may perceive that you're just dangling an unattainable carrot in front of them.)

Cautions

In user testing, we've seen some strong reactions to numbered levels from folks who make associations with "being graded" or assessed. Others noted that numbers just "seem impersonal and kinda cold." Be careful about noting lower-leveled users in information-dense contexts such as lists, because there will be many of them. For example, in a search results page showing user-generated content, don't fill a table column by noting all of the Level 1 and 2 contributors. Instead, consider calling out only the most remarkable level-holders in the community ("Level 10 Contributor!").

Exclusivity

Exclusivity in the Numbered Levels pattern relates to the distribution of reputations across the available levels. Ideally, from the high end of the register to the low, your numbered levels should follow a power-law distribution. (For a good general discussion of power laws in a social web context, see Clay Shirky's "Power Laws, Weblogs, and Inequality" at *http://www.shirky.com/writings/powerlaw_weblog.html*.)

Examples

World of Warcraft tracks an individual's progress via a numbered level (Figure 6-5).

Region	Level Range	PvP Status	Note
Elwynn Forest	1-10	Alliance	Human Starting
Eversong Forest	1-10	Horde	Blood Elf Starting
Dun Morogh	1-10	Alliance	Dwarf/Gnome Starting
Tirisfal Glades	1-10	Horde	Undead Starting
Ghostlands	10-20	Horde	Blood Elf Favored
Loch Modan	10-20	Alliance	Dwarf Favored
Silverpine Forest	10-20	Horde	Undead Favored
Westfall	10-20	Alliance	Human Favored
Redridge Mountains	15-25	Contested	Alliance Favored
Duskwood	18-30	Contested	Alliance Favored
Hillsbrad Foothills	20-30	Contested	
Wetlands	20-30	Contested	Alliance Favored
Alterac Mountains	30-40	Contested	
Arathi Highlands	30-40	Contested	
Stranglethorn Vale	30-45	Contested	
Badlands	35-45	Contested	
Swamp of Sorrows	35-45	Contested	Horde Favored
The Hinterlands	45-50	Contested	
Searing Gorge	43-50	Contested	
The Blasted Lands	45-55	Contested	
Burning Steppes	50-58	Contested	
Western Plaguelands	51-58	Contested	
Eastern Plaguelands	53-60	Contested	
Deadwind Pass	55-60	Contested	
Isle of Quel'Danas	70	Contested	

Eastern Kingdoms

Figure 6-5. *In this chart, the upper limit is Level 70, but it's subject to change as new expansion packs are introduced. New "regions" in the game are only available to players of certain levels.*

Yahoo! Answers employs a sort of "belt and suspenders and lederhosen" approach to reputation, using points, numbered levels, and labels (Figures 6-6 and 6-7).

Figure 6-6. *Yahoo! Answers displays a contributor's numbered level prominently on her user card.*

Levels

Levels are another way to keep track of how active you (and others) have been. The more points you accumulate, the higher your level. Yahoo! Answers recognizes your level achievements with our special brand of thank you's!

And finally, as you attain higher levels, you'll also be able to contribute more to Yahoo! Answers - you can ask, answer, vote and rate more frequently.

Level	Points	Questions	Answers	Comments	Stars	Ratings	Votes
7	25,000+		*unlimited*		100	unlimited	100
6	10,000 - 24,999		*unlimited*		100	unlimited	100
5	5,000 - 9,999		* unlimited *		100	unlimited	80
4	2,500 - 4,999	20	80	40	100	unlimited	80
3	1,000 - 2,499	15	60	30	100	unlimited	60
2	250 - 999	10	40	20	100	unlimited	40
1	1 - 249	5	20	10	10	0	20

*All limitations are per day

Figure 6-7. *Yahoo! Answers explains its system of levels, how levels are tied to points, and the benefits "unlocked" at higher levels.*

Labels

Not all reputation designations are linear or ordinal. They don't all constitute ranks or steps on a ladder. You can offer labels to reward achievements, participation in activities, or other qualitative measurements of status (Figure 6-8).

Figure 6-8. *Labels help identify special people in your community.*

What

Community members need to identify other, "special" members of the community who have distinguished themselves in some way. Perhaps they've excelled at one particular skill that the community values; perhaps they are official representatives for the community or an affiliated organization; perhaps they have volunteered to be a helpful resource for others in the community.

You have identified some desirable behaviors for your community that you'd like to promote. You want to allow users to volunteer for a "role" or responsibility within the community. You need a reputation to reflect that a user has been vetted or validated, either by your organization or a trusted third party. The community's culture can occupy any point along the Competitiveness Spectrum.

Define one or more families of reputations that are not sequential in nature. Each reputation is crafted to identify and reward particular behaviors or qualities within a community. Labels are helpful for consumers in identifying more-experienced contributors who possess these qualities (e.g., "Helpful" guides or "Elite" reviewers). These labels are not particularly useful for comparing one reputation-holder to another.

Reputation holders may accrue more than one "Identifying Label" at a time. These labels may also require a user to apply for or accept the reputation before it is publicly displayed.

37Signals awards badges to commenters on its Signal vs. Noise blog (Figure 6-9): "Comments posted on SvN that are off-topic, blatantly inflammatory, or otherwise inappropriate or vapid may either be removed or be slapped with the Troll cap," whereas the Royalty Crown is used to "show off 'royal' comments within a thread."

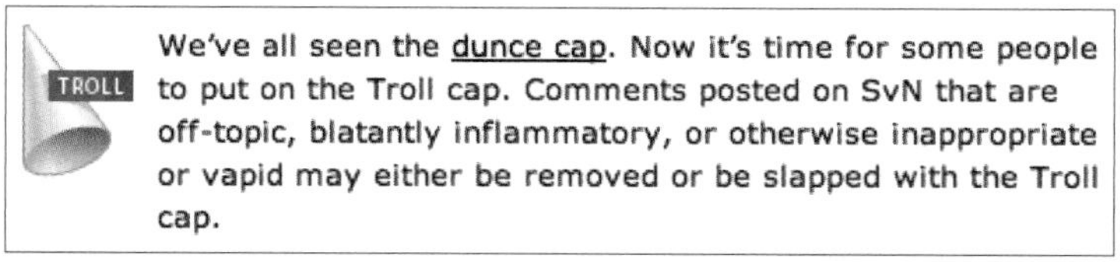

We've all seen the <u>dunce cap</u>. Now it's time for some people to put on the Troll cap. Comments posted on SvN that are off-topic, blatantly inflammatory, or otherwise inappropriate or vapid may either be removed or be slapped with the Troll cap.

Figure 6-9. *The Troll cap doesn't show up often in Signal vs. Noise comment threads, but the threat of it may well have a deterrent effect.*

At Get Satisfaction, users who can prove they are employed by the company being discussed are identified with an Official Rep label and the word "Employee" on their avatar (Figure 6-10).

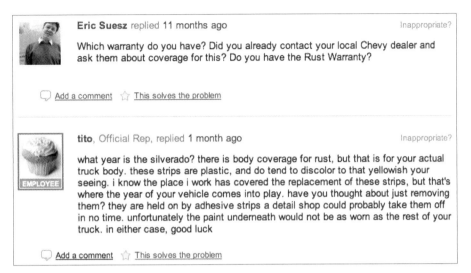

Figure 6-10. *The Employee badge on tito's avatar (Get Satisfaction gives you a cupcake by default) and the words "Official Rep" after his name in the byline work together to label him as someone authorized to speak for Chevrolet.*

Yahoo! Answers awards a Top Contributor badge to "someone in the Answers community who, through their participation on Answers, has shown that they are knowledgeable in a particular category" (Figure 6-11).

Figure 6-11. *Omega Mistress Bekki is not only a Level 7 contributor with 76,642 points but has also earned the label of "Top Contributor" with respect to a specific domain of knowledge (in this case, Physics).*

Related patterns

"Avatars" on page 115

"Identity Cards or Contact Cards" on page 111

"Profile" on page 86

Awards

Awards, given by the host community or from one peer to another and displayed on a profile or user card, can help identify worthy community members and provide incentives for positive behavior.

Collectible Achievements

Some participants in communities respond to opportunities to earn or win awards that can be collected and displayed to other community members.

What

How can you encourage your participants to engage more deeply, strive to accomplish great things (whether cooperatively or competitively), or, for that matter, show up at a focus group? How can your members show off their accomplishments to one another, preen, and earn respect?

Use when

You want to leverage users' compulsive natures. They may seem silly or trivial, but collectible achievements can have an addictive quality when done right, and may compel your users to explore parts of your offering that otherwise might not appeal to them. You want to encourage the community to try out all aspects of your offering. For instance, if you'd like to encourage more trades in a fantasy sports context, consider rewarding users with an achievement upon the completion of his 10th successful trade. ("Successful" is key here; make sure to introduce and enforce some notion of quality in the achievement.)

How

Provide some boon or reward to users for attaining certain goals within the community. Make them a consistent family, or program, of collectibles. Enhance their fun appeal by fetishizing them in some way: develop attractive trophies, icons, or "gamepieces" to represent each achievement, and allow users to save them and put them on display. Provide a healthy mix of difficulties: make some achievements very easy and quick (low-hanging fruit) while ensuring that others require time and effort to conquer, and perhaps "unlock" new achievements as easier ones are accomplished.

Recommendations

Achievements, like most reputation mechanisms, should encourage quality participation over mere repetitious activity. So, don't reward a user's "20th game played." Rather, you should reward "20 wins in one season." It may be useful to develop a number of "first-time" achievements (e.g., "First Review posted," "First Recipe Written," "First Comment

Received"). Make these achievements worth less than others that are more difficult, and don't continue to reward the same behavior. These "first" achievements are useful for encouraging people to try new and novel features, but don't reward them for gaming those features repeatedly. List the available achievements for your product, so that users will know which ones are available to them. Also, indicate the ones they've achieved already. Keep some achievements "locked" or grayed-out until their display has been earned. Collectible achievements should not be confused with points, although you could intermix the two (for example, award a certain number of points for each achievement earned).

Exclusivity

Feel free to be fairly generous with collectible achievements; every member of your community should have easy access to some. But also keep some rarer achievements in short supply, and make those more difficult to obtain.

Temporality

Yelp describes its Elite Squad as "our way of recognizing some of our most active and influential members, both on and off the site." Note that Elite status is also temporal in nature, and is earned on a yearly basis (Figure 6-12).

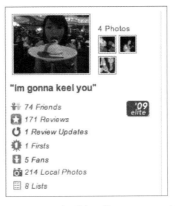

Figure 6-12. *In addition to peer-to-peer awards, Yelp offers a temporal Elite status.*

Examples

The Xbox Live service awards achievements to players for completing very specific actions within games (Figure 6-13).

Figure 6-13. *Each Halo 3 Achievement awarded has a specific point value.*

Yahoo! Fantasy Sports awards collectible trophies for various sports (Figure 6-14).

Figure 6-14. *These awards are temporal in nature, and are awarded for a specific season of play. A "Trophy Case" on the player's profile keeps the achievements on display.*

Related pattern

"Profile" on page 86

Peer-to-Peer Awards

The state does not need to maintain a monopoly on the ability to hand out medals. Let the chamber of commerce and the Elks have their own awards. Let the tyke make a World's Greatest Granddad coffee mug on the pottery wheel. Enabling your users to share compliments by bestowing awards on one another offers another opportunity for social "grooming" behavior and the reinforcement of weak ties (giving someone a prize is less of a commitment than inviting him into your private group, for example).

What

People enjoy giving and receiving compliments and will use existing message board and guestbook features for this purpose in a pinch, but the whole system can benefit if these kinds of gestures are enabled and supported more formally.

Use when

Use when you're trying to foster more collaborative and cooperative peer-to-peer relationships.

How

- In the context of participatory activities (such as posting content, giving feedback, writing reviews, etc.) and in the context of a user's profile, provide an interface through which a fellow site member can select a type of award and then customize it by either adding a note or otherwise decorating or labeling it.

- Optionally, permit the recipient of the award to approve it before it is displayed.

- Display the award in a gallery on the recipient's profile.

Recommendations

Although you may be tempted to offer an ever-longer list of award categories or types, experiment with a smaller, more focused list of roughly five to seven categories, to avoid overwhelming your users with too many arbitrary options.

Users may feel obligated to reciprocate awards, and although there's nothing inherently wrong with mutual backscratching, indiscriminate award-giving can feel like a form of spam if it creates a sense of obligation in the recipient. Provide your users with guidelines and establish forgiving social norms (for instance, that there really is no expectation of reciprocation) to mitigate some of the social behavior patterns that will otherwise assert themselves if unchecked.

Yelp compliments are a kind of award that any user can give to another to be displayed on the recipient's profile and user card (Figure 6-15).

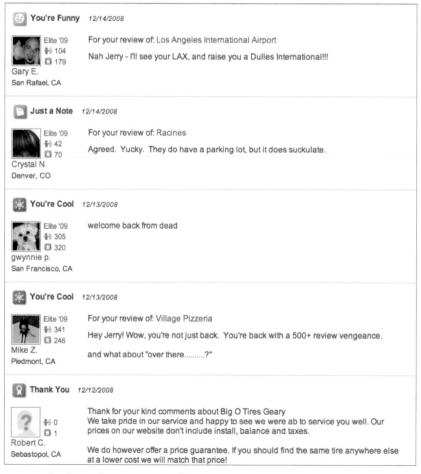

Figure 6-15. *Yelp offers perhaps too many different categories for its Compliments, but users seem comfortable choosing among them.*

On Yahoo!'s intranet, we have a system called Backyard Bravos, through which we can spontaneously award one another prizes from about five categories. Hovering on the award displays a detailed note in a tool tip (Figure 6-16).

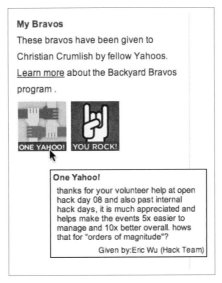

Figure 6-16. *Here I immodestly brandish my One Yahoo! award from coworker Eric Wu (next to the You Rock! award that my summer intern may have felt obligated to place like a polished apple on my desk).*

Related patterns

"Give Gift" on page 223

"Profile" on page 86

"Testimonials (or Personal Recommendations)" on page 100

Rankings

Rankings, like levels, enable clear comparisons. Unlike levels, rankings are oriented toward listing the highest, the top, and the best in each category. Rankings are measured in terms of accumulated points. As with numbered levels, points may be displayed explicitly or kept hidden as a driver of position.

Points

Points provide an almost infinitely scaleable process for comparing people based on their accumulated scores.

What

In some communities, participants want a tangible measurement of their accomplishments for personal satisfaction and to make comparisons with other competitors.

Use when

Use this pattern when the community is *highly competitive*, and the activities that users engage in are competitive in nature (e.g., player-versus-player contests or coaching a fantasy football team).

Points are generally discouraged in social sites, except in cases where the fundamental, primary *purpose* of the community is competition, such as fantasy sports or games.

Specifically, don't use this pattern when:

- The activities that users engage in are *not* competitive in nature (e.g., writing recipes or sharing photos).

- The awarding of points might demean or *devalue* the activity that they're meant to reward. By pinning an arbitrary incentive value to an activity, you may unintentionally replace a user's satisfying, intrinsic motivation with a petty, extrinsic one.

How

Maintain and display a cumulative count of the number of points that a user has earned within a community. The points generally come from performing one of a number of activities on the site.

Points are best awarded to congratulate *performance* rather than merely to acknowledge *activity*.

You may also want to account for *social points*, driven by actions that others in the community take toward a community member. When possible, these social points should reflect a measure of quality (e.g., giving a "thumbs up" rating to a well-written comment) rather than a generic or rote activity (e.g., awarding a number of points for each friend added in a social network).

Recommendations

Consider points as a *supplement* to some other reputation pattern, where the points themselves are not the primary indicator of reputation. Rather, they just give users a sense for their levels of achievement and indicate progress toward the next reputation milestone (for example, "Dwalin is a Level 8 Dwarf (342)").

Points should reward *performance* (e.g., winning a game against an opponent) rather than *activity* (e.g., 10 points for every message posted). Points that reward activity may lead users to perform that activity again and again with no regard for the quality of their contributions. The gaming world even has a term for this: grinding (*http://en.wikipedia.org/wiki/Grind_(gaming)*).

In some communities, participants want a tangible measurement of their accomplishments for personal satisfaction and to make comparisons with other competitors.

One exception to the performance recommendation: points may be a useful reward of activity *the first time* a user performs an action (e.g., "You completed your profile! Here are 20 points"). These "first time" awards are hard to game, and can encourage users to explore new areas of your offering.

Examples

Yahoo! Answers (Figure 6-17) awards points to users for a variety of actions (*http://answers.yahoo.com/info/scoring_system;_ylt=AqAAJlkazAoSjM8PHj5tvVbpy6IX;_ylv=3*).

Points Table

Action	Points
Begin participating on Yahoo! Answers	One Time: 100
Ask a question	-5
Choose a best answer for your question	3
No Best Answer was selected by voters on your question	Points Returned: 5
Answer a question	2
Deleting an answer	-2
Log in to Yahoo! Answers	Once daily: 1
Vote for a best answer	1
Vote for No best answer	0
Have your answer selected as the best answer	10
Receive a "thumbs-up" rating on a best answer that you wrote (up to 50 thumbs-up are counted)	1 per "thumbs-up"

Figure 6-17. The Yahoo! Answers points system is carefully calibrated to nudge users toward greater engagement.

Xbox Live's GamerScore (*http://en.wikipedia.org/wiki/Xbox_Live#Gamerscore*) is a measure that corresponds to the number of points accumulated by an XBox Live player.

eBay's Feedback Score (*http://pages.ebay.com/help/feedback/feedback-scores.html*) is based on the number of successful transactions that a seller or buyer has completed.

See OMGPOP.com (formerly the dating site iminlikewithyou.com) for examples of how to use reputation, levels, and points to keep people playing.

Leaderboard

In highly competitive communities, a leaderboard can spur on ever-fiercer efforts to reach the top.

In highly competitive communities that use a ranking system, users may want to know who are the very best performers in a category, or overall.

Use this pattern when:

- The community is highly competitive, and the activities that users engage in are competitive in nature (e.g., player-versus-player contests or coaching a fantasy football team).

- You want to enable player-to-player comparisons, or permit users to definitively settle "Who is better?" arguments.

Don't use this pattern when the activities that users engage in are *not* competitive in nature (e.g., writing recipes or sharing photos).

Display user rankings in leaderboards. A *leaderboard* is a list showing a fixed number of top competitors, ranked by score from highest to lowest.

On the Yahoo! network, ranking and leaderboards are generally discouraged, except in cases where the fundamental, primary *purpose* of the community is competition, as with fantasy sports or games.

Provide multiple views of a leaderboard, including all-time standings (overall rankings) and weekly or daily standings (latest movers in the community). Typically, the all-time view will be more stable (sometimes downright stagnant), so consider making the "latest movers" view the default one for the leaderboard.

Also consider the easy ability to *filter* a leaderboard—perhaps showing only a user and her contacts or friends and their relative standings, without the extra noise of the larger community.

In "Is Harriet Klausner for real?" (*http://bokardo.com/archives/is-harriet-klausner-for-real/*), Joshua Porter discusses Amazon's #1 Reviewer and her *phenomenal* (unbelievable?) review rate that averages seven books a day in an apparent effort to stay at the top of the reviewer leaderboards:

Klausner is apparently trying to game the system so she keeps her position. In a world where building social tools like this is becoming more common every day, Klausner is diluting the value of her reviews just for personal gain. While nobody is going to get too upset over less-than-helpful reviews, the larger, longer effect is that if she's merely writing them to keep her spot, she's not writing them for the right reason. Amazon's social design should incentivize her to write valuable reviews, not allow her to write them without value.

So, remember, any number you track and display, any metric, becomes a score. People will treat them as points and work to accumulate them, and some people will game the system, seeking the numerical reward over whatever the "spirit" of the service is.

Leaderboards Considered Harmful

It's still too early to speak in absolutes about the design of social media sites, but one fact *is* becoming abundantly clear: ranking the members of your community—and pitting them one-against-the-other in a competitive fashion—is typically a bad idea. Like the fabled *djinni* of yore, leaderboards on your site promise riches (comparisons! incentives! user engagement!!) but often lead to undesired consequences.

So why do we use them? The typical thought process goes something like this: there's an activity on your site that you'd like to promote; a number of people engaged in that activity who should be recognized; and a whole buncha *other* people who need a kick in the pants to jump in. Leaderboards seem like the perfect solution. Active contributors will get their recognition: placement at the top of the ranks. The also-rans will find incentive: to emulate leaders and climb the boards.

And that activity you're trying to promote? Usage should *swell* with all those earnest, motivated users plugging away, right? It's the classic win-win-win scenario! In practice, employing this pattern has rarely been this straightforward. Here are but a few reasons why leaderboards are hard to get right.

What do you measure?

Many leaderboards make the mistake of basing standings *only on what is easy to measure.* Unfortunately, what's easy to measure oftentimes tells you nothing at all about what is *good*. Leaderboards tend to fare well in very competitive contexts, because there's a convenient correlation between measurability and quality. (It's called "performance"—number of wins versus losses within overall attempts.)

But how do you measure *quality* in a user-generated video community? Or a site for ratings and reviews? It should have very little to do with the quantities of simple activity that a person generates (the number of times an action is repeated, a comment is given, or a review is posted). But these types of things—discrete, countable, and objective—are exactly what leaderboards excel at.

—continued—

Leaderboards Considered Harmful

Whatever you *do* measure will be taken way too seriously

Even if you succeed in leavening your leaderboard with metrics for quality (perhaps you weigh community votes or count "send-to-a-friend" actions), be aware that—because the leaderboard singles these factors out for praise and reward—your community will hold these things in high esteem as well. Leaderboards have this amazing "Code of Hammurabi" effect on community values: what's written becomes the law of the land. And you'll likely notice this effect in the things that people do—and *won't* do—on your site. So tread carefully. Are you really that much smarter than your community that you alone should dictate the makeup of its character?

If it *looks* like a leaderboard, and *quacks* like a leaderboard...

Even sites that don't display overt leaderboards may veer too closely into the "comparative statistics" realm. Consider Twitter and its prominent display of community members' stats (Figure 6-18).

Figure 6-18. *How else will you know if you're winning?*

The problem doesn't lie with the *existence* of the stats, but perhaps in the prominence of their display. It gives Twitter the appearance of a community that values popularity and the sheer size of your social network. Is it any wonder, then, that a whole host of community-created leaderboards have sprung up to allow just such comparisons? Twitterholic, Twitterank, Favrd, and a whole host of others are the natural extension of this value-by-numbers approach.

Leaderboards are powerful and capricious

In the earliest days of Orkut (Google's also-ran entry into social networking), the property managers featured a harmless little widget at the top of the site: a country-counter, showing members' geographical origins. Cute, right? Harmless, certainly. Google had no way of knowing, however, that the *entire population of Brazil* would make it a point of national pride to push their country to the top of that list! Brazilian blogger Naitze Teng writes: "Communities dedicated to raising the number of Brazilians on Orkut were following the numbers closely, planning gatherings and flash mobs to coincide with the inevitable. When it was reported that Brazilians had outnumbered Americans registered on Orkut, parties...were thrown in celebration" (*http://www.popmatters.com/columns/teng/060629.shtml*).

—continued—

Leaderboards Considered Harmful

Today, Brazil maintains its number one position on Orkut (51% of Orkut users are Brazilian as of this writing, and the U.S. and India are tied for a distant second with 17% apiece; see *http://www.orkut.com/Main#MembersAll.aspx)*. Orkut is—basically—a Brazilian social network. Which is not a bad "problem" for Google to have, but is probably never an outcome it would have expected from such a simple, small, and insignificant thing as a leaderboard widget.

Cui bono?

This may be the most insidious artifact of a leaderboard community: the very presence of a leaderboard *changes the community dynamic* and calls into question the motivations of *everyone* for any action he or she might take! If that sounds a bit extreme, consider Twitter: friend counts and followers have become the coins of that realm, and when I get a notification of a new follower…? Well, I'm more apt to believe that it's just someone fishing around for a reciprocal "follow." Sad, but true. And this is a site that *itself has never officially featured a leaderboard.* Twitter merely made the statistics known and provided an API to get at them, and in doing so, it may have let the djinni out of the bottle.

—Bryce Glass, coauthor,
Building Web Reputation Systems
(*http://buildingreputation.com*)

Examples

Yahoo! Answers updates its leaderboard weekly, and ranks its community by all-time and weekly leaders (Figure 6-19).

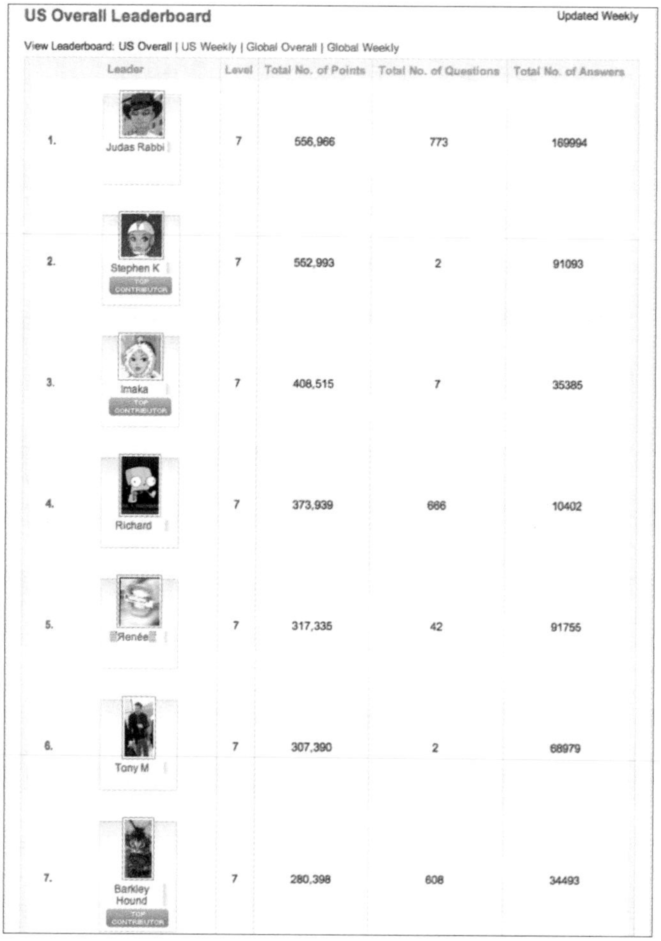

US Overall Leaderboard — Updated Weekly

View Leaderboard: US Overall | US Weekly | Global Overall | Global Weekly

	Leader	Level	Total No. of Points	Total No. of Questions	Total No. of Answers
1.	Judas Rabbi	7	556,966	773	169994
2.	Stephen K (TOP CONTRIBUTOR)	7	552,993	2	91093
3.	Imaka (TOP CONTRIBUTOR)	7	408,515	7	35385
4.	Richard	7	373,939	666	10402
5.	Renée	7	317,335	42	91755
6.	Tony M	7	307,390	2	68979
7.	Barkley Hound (TOP CONTRIBUTOR)	7	280,398	608	34493

Figure 6-19. *The Yahoo! Answers US Overall Leaderboard recognizes people who have answered a mind-boggling number of questions.*

Top X

One way to cast the net of rewards more widely in a ranking system is to identify people as belonging to the Top 10, Top 25, Top 50, Top 100, and so on. This provides a sort of logarithmic ranking scale, which is less specific than "being number one" but still offers comparative awards to top performers (Figure 6-20). The music charts in the old-school record industry work this way (Top 10 hit!, America's Top 40!, in the Top 100 "with a bullet!").

Figure 6-20. *If you can't be number one, maybe you can get into the top 100.*

Participants in some communities welcome the challenge of striving to enter the top tier of competitors.

You want to encourage top contributors to continue to provide high-quality content (and continue to serve as examples of valued community behaviors to the rest of the community). You want to motivate heavy (but not yet *top*) contributors to increase the quality and frequency of their contributions.

Don't use this pattern when:

- Introducing an "elite" designation could produce an unwanted community divide (for example, in a community whose spirit is more about collaboration or nurturing its members).

- The context for the reputation would be unclear. For example "Top 10 Shopper" on Y! Shopping is confusing, and doesn't provide any useful interpretation, but "Top 10 Reviewer in Books" is better: it's more specific and lets consumers know this person's area of experience.

Group contributors numerically into "buckets" of performance, and acknowledge top performers for their superior achievements. Top 10, 50, and 100 are some commonly used groupings. Consider providing some additional award for the number one contributor in the community: an especially ornate badge, or even a blog announcement on those rare occasions when the top slot changes hands.

The exclusivity (basically "how many of these should be awarded?") of this reputation type is somewhat self-explanatory: there would be *10* community members in the Top 10, and *90* more within the Top 100. Consider, however, the upper threshold that you're prepared to reward. You may want to go no higher than a Top 100 designation, for example, regardless of the actual size of your community. In comparative studies, we've heard several users state that "Top 1,000" badges are silly, or seem frivolous. ("They're just givin' 'em away" is a typical reaction.)

Examples

Amazon's Top Reviewers (*http://www.amazon.com/gp/customer-reviews/top-reviewers. html*) program is long-standing and much emulated. In its original incarnation, however, questions abounded about the motivations (and ethics; see *http://www.slate.com/ id/2182002/pagenum/all/*) of contributors at the highest levels of the leaderboard. Amazon ultimately responded by changing the rules for the list, and maintaining a smaller nod to the "classic" leaderboard rankings (Figure 6-21).

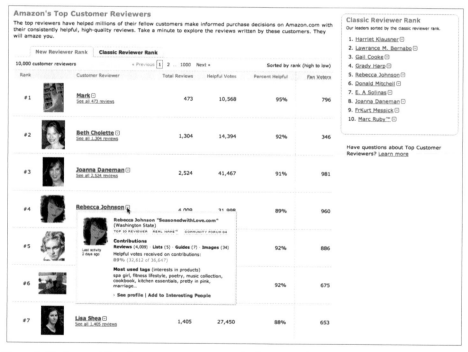

Figure 6-21. *Amazon's list of top customer reviewers displays a number of criteria used to determine the displayed rank. Hovering on a reviewer's icon pulls up a user card, in this case showing some labels, including the Top 10 Reviewer honor.*

The FBI's 10 Most Wanted List (*http://www.fbi.gov/wanted/topten/fugitives/fugitives.htm*; Figure 6-22) almost never came to be. When it was suggested, J. Edgar Hoover was worried that criminals would be motivated to commit more spectacular crimes! It has been a long-running and successful program, however.

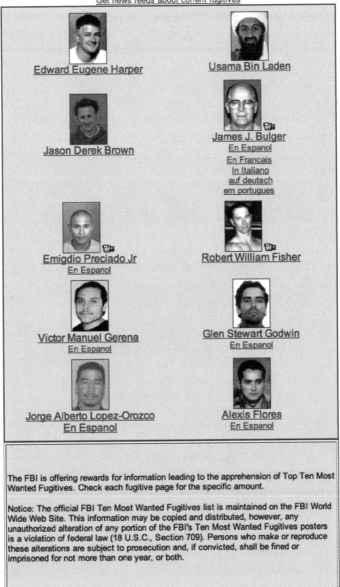

Figure 6-22. *The FBI's top 10 list of infamous fugitives can help clarify your thinking about how incentives work for a Top X list.*

Tools for Monitoring Reputation

Finally, it's worth noting that if you are going to impose a reputation system on your users, then you owe it to them to provide clear information about the standards they are being judged by, the criteria for ranking, and their current standing in any system (as well as prospects for upcoming recognition). In the wider world of the Internet, users are becoming more aware of the need for monitoring their reputation as exposed by search engines, incoming links, evidence of participation in social networks (including ill-advised college-party photos on Facebook that may need to be scrubbed once you "befriend" your boss there), and so on.

It's too early to make strong assertions about tools for monitoring reputation and visibility online. Some sort of dashboard for doing this would be welcome, no doubt. In the meantime, pay attention to the sorts of tools and systems people employ now to cobble together their own reputation-monitoring solutions. These may include automating ego-searches and then subscribing to RSS feeds of the results to notify the user of recent mentions found via Google, Technorati, Twitter, Facebook, or who knows where else.

I'm using just such a jerry-rigged system right now to listen for discussion about social patterns, social interfaces, this book, its associated wiki, and related conversations (Figure 6-23).

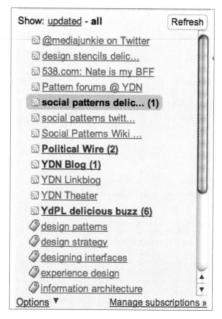

Figure 6-23. *I'm pushing a bunch of custom RSS feeds into my newsreader to stay on top of discussions about me or this book project.*

Also pay attention to third-party services such as Spock and RapLeaf that attempt to track and monitor reputation and trust relationships (Figure 6-24).

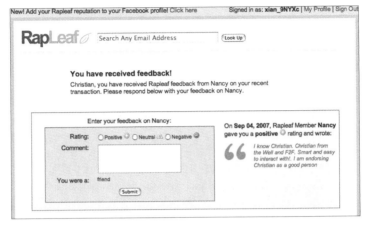

Figure 6-24. *A well-regarded standalone reputation maintenance service could be used as a utility and plugged into your social platform if you don't wish to develop your own custom solution. RapLeaf is vying to be a trusted reputation provider, but there is no clear gold-standard winner in this space yet.*

Friend Ranking

Another emerging pattern that can't yet be viewed as a demonstrable success is a game-driven approach to inviting your users to compare their friends across a variety of axes (Figure 6-25).

Figure 6-25. *Being asked to compare your friends and acquaintances (who may themselves come from widely differing facets of your life) can feel rather awkward. It can just as easily become a compelling game-like experience, conceptually descended from the HotOrNot-type services that appeared in the 1990s.*

Telling people they've just been compared is one way to lure them into participating in your data-gathering process. One common practice appears to be notifying people only when they *win* a comparison (Figure 6-26).

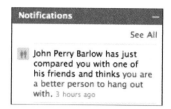

Figure 6-26. *I guess JP Barlow had a great time with me that one evening in Albuquerque, or perhaps he has never spent any quality hang time at all with whomever he compared me to.*

By itself, a widget that asks people to compare friends doesn't get you much, but if you can accumulate a data store with a rich web of crowdsourced comparisons, then you can start calculating some, well, rankings, and publish or display them in an attempt to spur further engagement with your service.

Reputation interfaces like the one shown in Figure 6-27 present the known issues of leaderboards, and more broadly demonstrate the way social networks cluster around highly connected "hub" people who then end up getting recommended to everyone or singled out in a power law–driven, self-perpetuating trend.

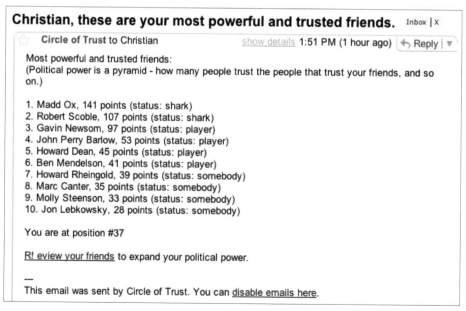

Figure 6-27. *Another friend-ranking tool powered by Facebook notified me by email of the Top 10 most trusted (and by extension, it reasons, most powerful) friends in my network.*

Further Reading

"I Love My Chicken Wire Mommy," by Ben Brown,
http://benbrown.com/says/2007/10/29/i-love-my-chicken-wire-mommy/

"Is Harriet Klausner for real?," by Joshua Porter, *http://bokardo.com/archives/is-harriet-klausner-for-real/*

"Metrics for Healthy Communities," by Tara Hunt,
http://www.horsepigcow.com/2007/10/03/metrics-for-healthy-communities/

Part III

Objects of My Desire

People congregate and participate on social sites for reasons that are as varied and wide as the interests of all the people participating. Most people are drawn to a site based on their particular interests, in hopes of learning more or meeting others like themselves. They may be looking for information, or they may have information to share. They have a passion—such as making handcrafted jewelry or taking landscape photographs—and at some point, they will want to share that with other people.

As a social site designer, you should begin by defining the type of activity that you want to encourage in your space. Do you want people to collect or share? Are you interested in user contributions, such as comments or reviews, or curated information that you control? Or do you want to create a framework around a specialized type of user-generated object that will then be the center of a social ecosystem, such as photos, or items for sale, or PowerPoint presentations?

Some of the earliest social networking sites to gain traction (SixDegrees, Friendster) ran into a "now what?" wall. After a user had signed up, filled out a profile, found friends, and made connections, there wasn't really much of anything to do there. The sites lacked a model of a social object, without which there are no activities besides trying to create a scale model of one's own real-life social graph.

Once you have a handle on the type of activity you want to foster and its associated sub-activities, it is important to define the type of social object around which this activity will revolve. It will also be important to define who is responsible for providing the social object—the site or its users.

The term "social object" first surfaced in a blog post by Jyri Engeström on April 13, 2005. Jyri, cofounder of jaiku and now a product manager at Google, wrote:

> *Social networks consist of people who are connected by a shared object. That's why many sociologists, especially activity theorists, actor-network theorists and post-ANT people prefer to talk about "socio-material networks," or just "activities" or "practices" (as I do) instead of social networks.... Flickr, for example, has turned photos into objects of sociality. On del.icio.us the objects are the URLs. EVDB, Upcoming.org, and evnt focus on events as objects.*

The concept has been further refined to encourage site builders to define the nouns and the verbs of the site, the verbs being what people do with the social objects the site is built around. These can be things like play, read, view, share, collect, display, comment on, annotate, etc. You get the idea. Social is then further layered into the site by making objects shareable, which we'll cover in detail in Chapter 8.

JP Rangaswami posits this metaphor about social objects:

> You can have a conversation without a social object. You cannot have a social object without a conversation. It is the conversation that makes the object "social."

> Conversations grow around social objects, much like pearls grow around microscopic dust. Social objects are about growth, they are "live."

> If you try and "inject" a social object into a conversation, then what you get, at best, is a cultured pearl. That's what mass media did. Mass media tried to farm conversations. And created cultured pearls. Social objects are natural, not artificial.

> A successful social object is one that has layer upon layer of conversation created around it; as the number of participants increases, social objects enjoy network effects. Social objects are about participation and participants.

When designing your social interfaces, ask yourself what social objects belong in the architecture and how you are going to support them. What activities are you going to make possible that enable people to engage with one another around these social objects? The patterns in the next several chapters address activities and behaviors that revolve around a social object, as well as patterns to provide a framework for creating or delivering user-generated social objects.

Chapter 7

Hunters Gather

Collecting can be a way of achieving personal identity and a nurturing hobby to make one feel good, safe and loved. Collecting can provide a method of predictability and bring a sense of security to one's life. When people collect they have a sense of belonging to something, days look brighter and they feel more important.

—Sheldon S. Greenberg

Collecting

One of the inherent human activities is collecting. Whether it's photographs to remind one of an experience, or physical objects, such as stamps, books, or figurines of owls, most people collect something. This behavior has translated easily into online spaces.

People will share what they find or have collected, and, like a trophy case in the home, they will display those collections for others to see, envy, and borrow. Eventually they have conversations around them.

Collecting can be divided into a few related activities: Saving, marking Favorites, Tagging, and Displaying. Saving and Favorites are similar in that the user action involves saving a URL or visual pointer to an item on a website. The difference lies in whether the host site (the repository) is also the owner of the content being saved. Favorites are generally markers for content on the site hosting the item, whereas Saving involves being able to save anything from anywhere to a third-party site or widget. An additional distinction that may be made between Saving and Favoriting is how integral the collection is to the site. In many cases, Favorites are an associated action but not the core activity: think SlideShare or Flickr, where Favorites allow users to mark things they especially like from across the site and collect them in their profiles, but the core activity is posting and sharing photos or presentations. To continue this definition, Saving might be the core activity of the service, such as Delicious or EverNote, where the entire service revolves around saving pointers to things of interest from across the Internet.

A companion tool to Collecting is Tagging. Tagging gives people tools for organizing their collections and aids in findability when the person wants to locate a specific object in his collection at a later date.

Displaying takes that collection—whether it's a group of favorites or items saved—and offers a framework to display to others.

Saving

What

A user wants to save an item for later viewing, sharing, or discussion (Figure 7-1).

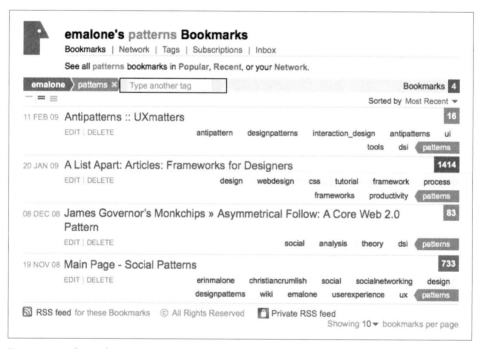

Figure 7-1. *Delicious lets users save bookmarks that are then accessible from anywhere and shareable with others.*

Use when

- Use to enable people to save websites, pages, clippings, photos, videos, or other items in an online environment.

- Use to allow people to show off, share, or collaborate around a collection of online items.

- Provide an easy way for users to save an item of interest.
- Provide a toolbar link or other add-ons that can be added to the browser (Figure 7-2).

Figure 7-2. *Delicious offers add-ons to the browser chrome for easier saving.*

- Allow the user to add tags, a description, or other metadata to the saved item.
- Associate the saved item with the user's name and account.
- When saving, allow the user to specify whether the item is public or private.
- If other people have saved the item before, offer the associated tags as options.
- Indicate how many people have saved the item.
- Consider allowing people to form groups around items or collections of items.
- Provide an easy way to add an item to a group at the time of the initial save.

When presenting the collection to the owner:

- Present public and private items.
- Allow the owner to delete or edit information about the item.
- Present the collection in reverse chronological order.
- Allow items to be filtered by tag.
- Allow items to be filtered by date, month, and year.
- Allow items to be filtered alphabetically.
- Allow items to be filtered by type (e.g., website, web page, photo, video, clipping of text, audio clips).

When presenting the collection to others:

- Allow public items to be presented to anyone.
- Present items in reverse chronological order.
- Allow items to be filtered by tag.
- Allow items to be filtered by date, month, and year.
- Allow items to be filtered alphabetically.

- Allow items to be filtered by type (e.g., website, web page, photo, video, clipping of text, audio clips).

When saving web pages, there are two options:

Saving a pointer to the original item

> When saving a pointer, it points to the most recent public version of the item (Figure 7-3). This may be different than what the user intended to save if there have been updates or changes to the original page. Additionally, there is also the potential for the item to be deleted or moved, in which case the pointer link will no longer work.

Figure 7-3. *Evernote saves a variety of media. When saving web pages, it saves a copy of the page and then offers the user a pointer to the page on the live Internet.*

Saving a copy of the original item

> When saving a copy of the original item, the user is guaranteed to always have access to the item she wanted to save. But, if the user saved a URL to a site such as a blog or a news site, the page saved will not be in sync with the original site the next time that site is updated.

Clearly indicate which method is being used. When saving a copy, offer a link or pointer to the original "live" item.

"Displaying" on page 196

"Favorites" on page 193

Delicious (*http://www.delicious.com*)

Evernote (*http://ma.gnolia.com/*)

GoodReads (*http://www.goodreads.com/*)

LibraryThing (*http://www.librarything.com/*)

Stumble Upon (*http://www.stumbleupon.com*)

Favorites

The concept of Favorites has been around since the early days of AOL. It's only recently, with the active pursuit of user participation, that the idea of favoriting an item to be stored on the source website has become commonplace.

A user wants to mark an item (person, place, or thing) as a preferred object (Figures 7-4, 7-5, and 7-6).

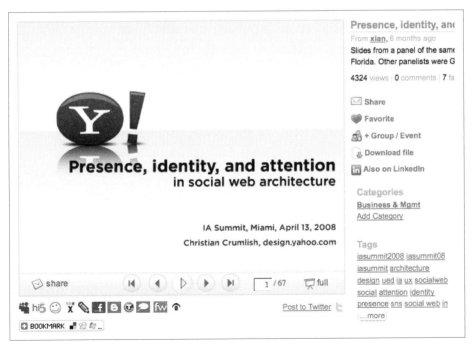

Figure 7-4. *SlideShare groups the Favorite call to action with other tools. Favorites are indicated with the heart icon, which was first popularized by AOL.*

Figure 7-5. *The iconography and text label prior to marking the item as a favorite on flickr.com. Flickr uses the star icon as part of the Favorite call to action.*

Figure 7-6. *The icon for making an item a Fave is in close proximity to the photo on flickr.com. Once the user has made the item a favorite, the icon changes color, indicating it is now a Fave.*

Use when

- Use this pattern when you want to let a user create his own list of preferred items.

- Use this approach instead of requiring a user to bookmark the item's page.

How

- Allow users to create a list of favorite objects on your site.

- Provide a "Favorite this" link in close proximity to each object. When an object is selected, consider allowing users to add tags, their own description, or other metadata that will help them recall the item later.

- Allow favorited items to be browsed and searched by keyword or tag (Figure 7-7).

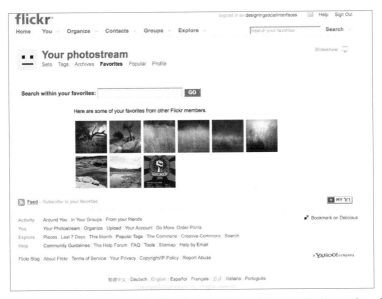

Figure 7-7. *A Favorites collection on Flickr. The photos are browsable as a collection and can be searched or viewed as a slideshow.*

- Collect favorited items together on their own page for easy access. Associate the collected favorited items with the user's profile or identity.

- Consider allowing users to share their collections of favorited items with their friends and connections (see "Collecting" on page 189 and "Displaying" on page 196).

- Don't associate favorites with people, as that may lead to negative community behavior.

- Allow the object creator to see who has "favorited" one of his items.

Why

Allowing users to interact with the content on your site supports a sense of ownership by the community and encourages cross-user conversation and interaction, and Favorites is a simple way to do this.

Related patterns

"Displaying" on page 196

"Send/Share Widget" on page 212

As seen on

Flickr (*http://www.flickr.com*)

SlideShare (*http://www.slideshare.net*)

YouTube (*http://www.youtube.com*)

Displaying

What

The user has created a collection and wants to display it to other people (Figure 7-8).

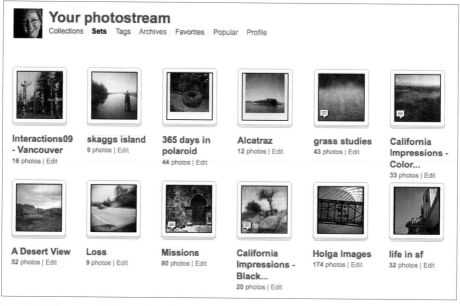

Figure 7-8. *Photos on Flickr can be collected into sets for viewing.*

Use when

- Use this pattern to offer opportunities for people to create collections.
- Use this pattern to allow users to show off their collections outside of the collection's original location.

How

- Allow users to create modules or badges that display a portion of their collection (Figure 7-9).

Figure 7-9. *User-generated content sites such as SlideShare allow content creators to make a badge and display their contributions on their own websites.*

- Provide users with a URL or embed tag for the collection display that can be added as a module or widget to their personal sites or blogs.

- Consider creating widgets to display collections on the major social networks, such as MySpace and Facebook, and sites like Yahoo!.

- Allow the user to select a subset of items to display. Consider limiting the item count, or filter by a tag or date range.

- Items displayed should link back to the originating site. If the item is a URL, link the tags or other metadata back to the parent site (the provider of the widget).

Why

People spend a lot of time collecting, curating, and managing their collections. Once these collections are created and curated, owners usually want to display and share their collections with others.

When connections and friends comment or rate these collections, or even just view the display, the owner's effort is validated. Additionally, she may be seen as an expert in the area of interest, which enhances her reputation, thereby increasing her likelihood of doing more collecting.

Related patterns

"Hosted Modules" on page 450

As seen on

Delicious (*http://delicious.com*)

Facebook (*http://facebook.com*)

Flickr (*http://www.flickr.com*)

SlideShare (*http://www.slideshare.net*)

Add/Subscribe

What

A person wants to subscribe to someone else's content and read it in an environment of the user's own choosing rather than at the source site (Figure 7-10).

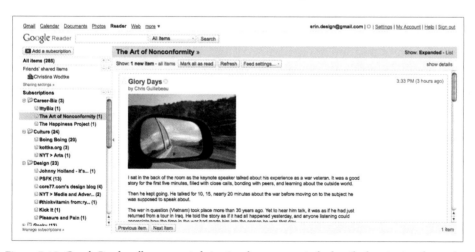

Figure 7-10. Google Reader allows users to bring in a large amount of subscribed content and organize it in the way that makes sense to them.

- Use the pattern to allow users to consume content wherever they want.

- Use this pattern to allow content to be brought in from other sources to "mix it up" and provide a more customized experience.

- When presenting dynamic content, like regular blog posts, forums, or photo and activity streams, provide a call to action for subscribing (Figure 7-11).

Figure 7-11. *Flickr allows users to subscribe to a person's photostream.*

- Use the standard RSS/Subscribe icon.

- When the user selects Add or Subscribe, present options for where she can consume the feed (Figure 7-12).

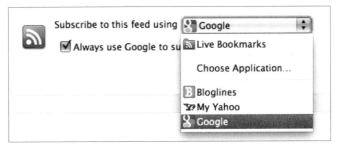

Figure 7-12. *A variety of sources for consuming a subscription should be offered to the user after she selects the RSS or Subscribe link.*

- Present the URL for the feed, which allows users to cut and paste it into their favorite feed readers.

- Additionally, offer a range of choices for automatically adding the feed to a list of reader services, such as My Yahoo! or Google Reader.

Allowing users to consume content where they want encourages readership. Forcing the user to consume only at your source imparts a rigid, monolithic attitude and ultimately may drive readers away.

Related patterns

"Collecting" on page 189

"Favorites" on page 193

As seen on

Delicious (*http://www.delicious.com*)

Flickr (*http://www.flickr.com*)

Google Reader (*http://reader.google.com*)

The New York Times (*http://www.nytimes.com*)

Yahoo! (*http://www.yahoo.com*)

Tagging

What

A user wants to attach his own keyword or set of keywords to an object for organization and later retrieval (Figure 7-13).

Figure 7-13. *Photo on flickr.com with tags.*

Use this pattern:

- When a user is collecting a large amount of unstructured data, such as photos.

- When a user wants to manage a large collection of items, such as books.

- To blend user-generated labels and keywords with structured metadata.

- Allow users to add their own tags to an object (Figure 7-14).

Figure 7-14. *The inline "Add a Tag" mechanism for an object on flickr.com.*

- Allow users to delete tags they have associated with an object. This allows for deletion of duplicates or misspellings.

- Provide very clear instructions for how to separate distinct tags. There are two methods currently popular across the Web right now: comma-delimited and space-delimited (Figures 7-15 and 7-16). Either of these can be used, but be consistent and very clear about which should be used. There is nothing more frustrating than thinking the delimiter is a comma and entering a multiword tag, only to have it separated out into multiple tags, thereby changing the meaning or intent of the tag because the site used spaces.

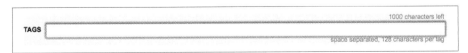

Figure 7-15. *Delicious labels the tag field with a note indicating that tags should be space-separated rather than comma-separated.*

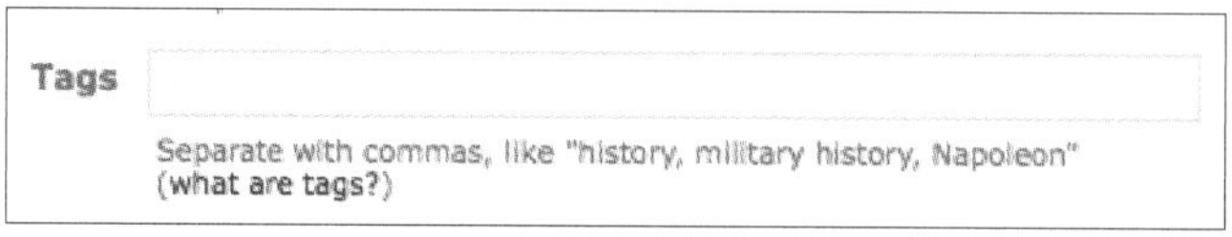

Figure 7-16. *LibraryThing.com indicates that tags need to be separated with a comma rather than a space and gives an example.*

- For more robust social engagement, allow connections and/or friends to tag objects in a collection.

- Don't be afraid to mix a controlled vocabulary (defined by the site architects) and user-generated tags.

Recommendations

Adding tagging to objects as a product feature should offer a benefit to the user. Do the tags help her find and manage her collection? Do the tags tighten the circle of community? Tagging as a user activity is more successful when there is a payoff to the users and their friends.

Provide tag hints if the item being tagged is a public item (a news article, a bookmark). Delicious.com shares recommended tags or previous tags associated with the object so that the user can select from these or simply add to the collective tag set for the object.

Tags and the ability to add a tag mechanism should be in close proximity to the object being tagged.

Open questions

Whether to use a comma or a space as the delimiter is still an outstanding question across the Web, and a standard solution has not emerged. It is unlikely that one will prevail over the other, as both are pervasive and have roots to traditional database delimiters, which allow several options.

Related patterns

"Find with Tags" on page 203

"Tag Cloud" on page 204

As seen on

Amazon (*http://www.amazon.com*)

Delicious (*http://delicious.com*)

Flickr (*http://www.flickr.com*)

LibraryThing (*http://www.librarything.com*)

Find with Tags

A user wants to find a specific object (photo, bookmark, book, article, etc.) through searching or browsing (Figure 7-17).

Figure 7-17. *Search box with "Tags only" selected on Flickr.*

Use when there is a large collection of objects to sort through or manipulate.

- Allow a keyword search through the tag database.
- Allow the user to browse through a list of tags.
- Once an object is found, display all the associated tags and allow the user to pivot off one of these other tags to create another search based on the new tag as keyword (Figure 7-18).

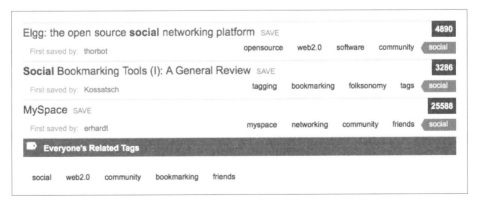

Figure 7-18. *Search results on Delicious. Each item shows the searched-for tag highlighted in grey. The other tags for the item are also shown, as are everyone's related tags, allowing for an easy pivot into another search.*

- Allow combinations of words to be searched together.

Recommendations

Objects that have tags associated with them should be findable through a search and browse mechanism using the associated tags.

Why

For large collections of assets, mechanisms for searching for a specific object should be part of the findability philosophy of the site. Searching through tags and using tags as a finding aid lets users employ their own words from their mental models of the item for later retrieval.

Related patterns

"Tag Cloud" on page 204

"Tagging" on page 200

As seen on

Delicious (*http://delicious.com*)

Flickr (*http://www.flickr.com*)

LibraryThing (*http://www.librarything.com*)

Tag Cloud

What

A user wants to know which tags are associated with an object, a site, or a person, and which tags are used most often (Figure 7-19).

Figure 7-19. *Most popular tags on Amazon.com.*

Use this pattern when:

- You want to present all of the tags associated with a site.

- You want to present the most popular tags on a site.

- You want to present all the tags associated with a person's identity.

- You need a browsing mechanism for item retrieval.

Present tags in an easily learned format.

Many sites present tags alphabetically and then enlarge the tags proportionally based on popularity. This presentation is popular but not always easily understood by users, and it can take up a lot of real estate in the interface (Figure 7-20).

Figure 7-20. *Example of a portion of an alphabetical tag cloud from a My Authors list on LibraryThing. The list is quite long and unruly.*

If using proportionally sized tags based on popularity, define the sizing algorithm to reflect a sense of what's popular rather than the real distribution of the tags (Figure 7-21). Using real distribution would yield huge differences in sizes and would be unwieldy without giving the user more meaningful information from which to draw conclusions.

2002 2003 2004 2005 2006 2007 2008 35mm 4x5 alviso ansel april aquarium art asa400 asia backyard baltimore bapc bayareaphotographerscollective beach bernalheights biking birthday blackandwhite bw california cameraphone canada cat cats cellphone chloe christmas construction desert designers dog eliot emalone erin erinmalone family familyphotos festival fiestaonthehill film filmisnotdead flower gallery garden gaypride2007 gayprideparade germanshepherd gltbprideparade2006 goldengatepark grass groups hardlystrictlybluegrass holga hongkong house hp5 ia iasummit iasummit06 iasummit2003 iasummit2006 iasummit2007 ilford ilivehere ishootfilm kittens kodak kualalumpur landscape lasvegas loss malaysia malone marinagreen marsh miami missions mobile montreal mountains music newmexico newyork nokia ocean october old oldfamilyphotos opening oregon pangkorisland parade party pencam photographers photography photoshoot pinhole polaroid portland portraits prideparade prideparade2007sanfrancisco reception remodel roadtrip rocks sanantonio sand sanfrancisco sanjose sculpture sf sfpride sfpride2007 sheila shozu snow sonyericsson spanish street texas tnt travel tree trees type52 type59 type79 ued vancouver virginia water whitemountains willowglen yahoo yahoos yellow yosemite zero45 zeroimage zeroimage45 zoneplate

All Your Tags

- See all your tags in a big list here, from which you can perform a number of handy management-type tricks. (This page only shows your 150 most popular tags.)
- You can search through multiple tags, for example, to find photos and videos tagged with 'christmas' *and* 'party'.

Figure 7-21. *Flickr shows only the top 150 most popular tags in my personal tag cloud. I can see all tags in a big list on another page, but with thousands of tags, it is not very useful.*

Open questions

The usefulness of a tag cloud is still under debate. Tag clouds look neat and make a nice graphical element, but the nuances of the sizing differences are often lost on the average user. If the item or the site has a lot of tags, then the cloud becomes less usable than a site or object with fewer tags. Consider a site like Flickr, which has millions of tags but has organized their presentation by dividing them into its "Explore" area for public tags and a "Your Tags" area, which presents a subset of the most used tags for a particular person's items. In both cases, they present a small subset of the total.

Additionally, some sites display the different sized tags to represent some editorial emphasis or other data instead of popularity or implied ranking. The lack of a standard meaning behind the tag cloud presentation makes it difficult for end users to know what to expect or to predict the inherent meaning in the visualization of the tag cloud.

The other design problem is how to handle a tag cloud with too few tags or a handful of tags with only one or two that are used a lot. In that case, designers should consider whether a tag cloud is useful and should even be part of the presentation.

Using the tag cloud presentation, popularized by Flickr, is a good way to show users a visual representation of the popular concepts within a person's objects or the site. A tag cloud encourages browsing and exploration in an alternative way from the site's standard navigation and supports serendipitous discovery.

Related patterns

"Find with Tags" on page 203

"Tagging" on page 200

As seen on

Amazon (*http://www.amazon.com*)

Flickr (*http://flickr.com*)

LibraryThing (*http://www.librarything.com*)

Further Reading

"Analysis: The Psychology Behind Item Collecting And Achievement Hoarding," by Kris Graft, *http://www.gamasutra.com/php-bin/news_index.php?story=23724*

"A Passion For Stuff: 'Collections Of Nothing,'"
http://www.npr.org/templates/story/story.php?storyId=98828345
and *http://www.designobserver.com/archives/entry.html?id=38781*

Tagging: People-powered Metadata for the Social Web, by Gene Smith, New Riders Press, 2008

"Why some social network services work and others don't Or: the case for object-centered sociality," by Jyri Engstrom, April 13, 2005,
http://www.zengestrom.com/blog/2005/04/why_some_social.html

Chapter 8

Share and Share Alike

Friendship marks a life even more deeply than love. Love risks degenerating into obsession, friendship is never anything but sharing.

—Elie Wiesel

Sharing means that more than one person can see, have, do, talk about, or otherwise relate to the same thing, possibly at the same time. In the real world, sharing means allowing someone else to have access to or control over an object that you currently own or control, and involves a degree of sacrifice. Electronic things made of bits can be replicated or reflected with almost no friction, as compared with real objects.

This may mean sharing is generally easier in a virtual space (than, say, in kindergarten, when giving up the G.I. Joe meant losing control over his adventures), but therefore also less meaningful (or less likely to teach us to play well together, as when we learned that we could plan what G.I. Joe would do next *together*).

Organic "Word of Mouth"

Count me among those not fully comfortable with the word "viral" as a way of describing successful runaway distribution. I understand that it's the common term marketers and entrepreneurs have learned and are comfortable using, and I don't want to impose a "correct" lingo on things, but I agree with those who suggest that viral growth isn't the ideal metaphor for healthy, sustainable positive expansion. (It seems one trope away from concepts like metastasis.)

Call it what you will, though, a primary motivation for enabling and encouraging sharing among your users is so that good ideas, compelling objects, and interesting activities can spread like wildfire. At best, this benefits the creators of the objects as well as those who enjoy participating in the spreading phenomenon.

So how do we encourage sharing, or even simply enable it? Well, there are already a number of well-established interface elements for doing so.

Tools for Sharing

Some conventions have emerged for providing readers with tools for sharing whatever they're currently experiencing on the Web or in your application. These tools may be used for several of the patterns in this set, so I'll describe them here first.

Bookmarklet

What

A *bookmarklet* is a small computer application, usually written in JavaScript, and stored as the URL of a bookmark in a web browser or as a hyperlink on a web page. Bookmarklets are designed to add one-click functionality to a browser or web page. When clicked, a bookmarklet performs some function, one of a wide variety such as a search query or data extraction. The term is a combination of the terms "bookmark" and "applet" (see Figure 8-1).

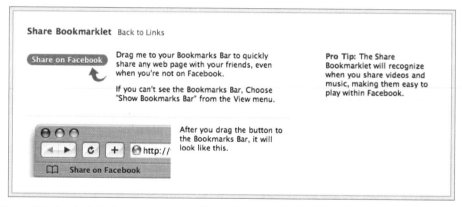

Figure 8-1. *Facebook invites its users to install a bookmarklet for sharing content on their site from around the Web.*

Use when

Bookmarklets work well for dedicated users already in the habit of sharing and looking for more convenient ways to do so, but they may also work for recruiting new sharers, if well presented (otherwise, first-time use of a bookmarklet tends to be rather nonintuitive).

How

The executing script has access to the current page, which it may inspect and change.

"Installation of a bookmarklet" can be performed by creating a new bookmark and pasting the code into the URL destination field, but more often you provide the user with a link and encourage him to "drag" it onto his bookmarks toolbar.

Extensible browser plug-ins, such as the Delicious add-on for Firefox, represent a more sophisticated approach to the bookmarklet concept (Figure 8-2).

Figure 8-2. *The Delicious add-on for Firefox is like a bookmarklet on steroids.*

One problem with bookmarklets is that they can't be keyboard-accessible (with shortcuts), but they can be made to run on any browser and can even be self-updating.

Why

Bookmarklets make sharing easier, thus reducing the friction for the user and facilitating more activity on the network.

As seen on

Delicious (*http://delicious.com/*)

Facebook (*http://www.facebook.com*)

TwitThis (*http://twitthis.com/*)

Most blog software (such as Blogger, Movable Type, and so on)

Send/Share Widget

A *sharing widget* is a small graphical element placed within the markup of a hypertext file that enables users to share content and information resources with the community, in conjunction with a third-party site or social networking application platform such as Facebook or MySpace.

For instance, the "Share This" widget shown in Figure 8-3 enables the user to share the content of a page (or a component of a page) with friends on social networking sites such as MySpace and Facebook. In doing this, the widget (or gadget, as widgets are sometimes referred to) acts as a bridge between the content of a given site and the backend application platforms supported by the widget, abstracting out the complexity of the application platform from the user application.

Figure 8-3. *A small button labeled "Share This" or similar can expand to display a selection for sharing choices in a widget.*

Provide a sharing widget in contexts where the user may wish to directly send a pointer, invite someone to view something, or add a copy of, or a reference to, something to a shared or public space he owns or has access to.

For direct sending, a user might just as well opt to copy and paste a link into an ordinary email message. This meets the user's needs and benefits the community, but the behavior will not be trackable by the system, and thus the system won't be able to learn from this. It's important not to hinder the user, but be aware that if the sharing widget doesn't provide any utility beyond traditional email, then there's little reason for users to adopt it. (With users who aren't technically savvy, however, saving them from having to manipulate URLs and other computer-istic text strings may be value enough to warrant use of the widget.)

By far, the primary form of sharing is direct sending. Secondary forms of sharing (such as IM, SMS/text message, Facebook, etc.), when included, should be secondary within the sharing drop-down.

When users are logged in, you can prepopulate the sharing form with their information and give them contact-list or address-book access with autocomplete in the recipient field of the form.

How

- Provide a button or link labeled Share or Send or something similar.
- When the user invokes the button, display an overlay form with sending and sharing options, which can behave as individual "tabbed" areas in the form. Optionally include other object utilities, such as "print" in this same context (Figure 8-4).

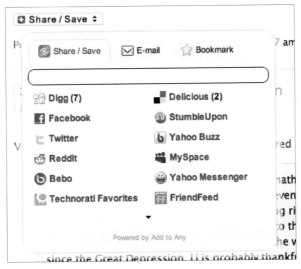

Figure 8-4. AddToAny offers an extensible Share This widget for embedding on sites.

Users have come to expect these sorts of conveniences for grabbing and sharing content. Remember, everyone is overwhelmed with information and reminders to revisit or share information. If users can send or share content on impulse with immediate gratification, it is much more likely they will take the action and learn to expect to be able to do so (Figure 8-5).

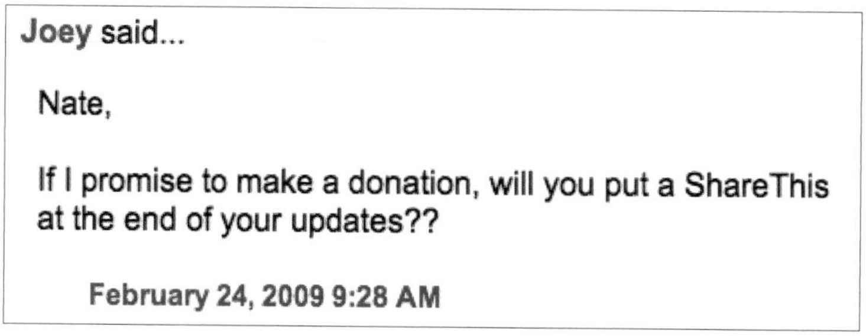

> **Joey said...**
>
> Nate,
>
> **If I promise to make a donation, will you put a ShareThis at the end of your updates??**
>
> **February 24, 2009 9:28 AM**

Figure 8-5. *A reader of Nate Silver's Fivethirtyeight.com blog asks him to add a sharing widget to his blog template.*

As a designer of social experiences, you have several potential avenues for employing a Share This widget:

- You can design and make your own widget, and use it throughout your service and/ or encourage others to adopt it, thus driving at least some traffic back to your service.

- You can publish icons, methods, and APIs for adding your service to existing or incumbent widgets (see Chapter 17).

- You can embrace someone else's widget if you simply want to incorporate its functionality and aren't using sharing to drive direct participation in your own network or application.

Internationalization

Different bookmarking and media-sharing applications are popular or dominant in different regions. You can plan ahead for localization when designing a sharing widget by supporting modular swapping in and out of third-party services.

Known issues

As the number of platforms for sharing proliferates, the idea of displaying an array of icons for destinations won't scale.

Why

Incorporating a Send/Share widget into the template or the browser's chrome when presenting content or applications, or providing such a widget for others to incorporate into their own interfaces, can help facilitate sharing and interaction on your network. You also can provide this functionality to your users through third-party bookmarking and media-sharing services.

Related patterns

"Send This" on page 216

As seen on

Facebook (*http://www.facebook.com/*)

Flickr (*http://www.flickr.com/*)

Google Reader (*http://www.google.com/reader/*)

Most blog and zine sites everywhere

Activity Streams

Activity Streams (see Chapter 5) are a third interface for sharing, but in this case they are the passive way a user's activities—including posting, bookmarking, sharing, and commenting on things—can be displayed in an ongoing Vitality feed.

Private Sharing

When information resources or digital assets are shared directly with a single user or a named group of users, it can be referred to as Private Sharing, although it may be a matter of sharing with one of "Many Publics".

While not necessarily a one-to-one relationship (as a user may send the same thing to a list of people), the experience is perceived as direct and point-to-point. This is in contrast with "Public Sharing", which feels more akin to hanging something up in a common space, such as a corkboard in a break room at work: it may be seen by others who are included in that specific limited public, but no single person has been explicitly invited to look.

Direct ("private") sharing, however, does imply a direct invitation and may feel more personal. It's important that a social interface have a clear strategy about how to present private sharing versus public sharing. If a user is notified or invited to see or do something as though the invitation were personal and direct when in fact it was a blast to a large, semifiltered list of buddies, this can lead to miscommunication and missed opportunities. If Howard Dean really invited me to play a word game with him on Facebook, I'd be flattered and inclined to make some time to do so, but if what really happened is that he (or his intern) accidentally invited everyone on his contact list after installing an application with perhaps a misleading interface, then I am in for a disappointment.

The true common patterns for direct sharing are "Send This" and "Casual Privacy". The former is analogous to an email message containing a link to a public resource with an optional message, such as "Check out this article I read in *USA Today*." The latter is similar but involves inviting a person to see one's own posted object or collection, and frequently follows the Public Sharing pattern as a secondary, promotional step.

See also "Collecting" on page 189 and "Displaying" on page 196.

Send This

What

A user wants to share an object (pointer, media, or application) with one or more people (Figure 8-6). The application is involved in the sharing in order to indicate who is sharing what with whom, and how often.

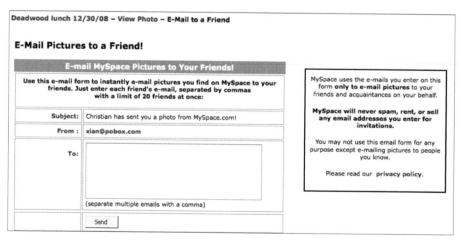

Figure 8-6. *Direct sending at MySpace.*

Use when

Use when displaying content, resources, or applications on your site or elsewhere. When the user is logged in, you may provide an easier process by pre populating her sender information and offering access to her contact list.

Enable people to spontaneously share content or objects they find by sending them to a friend or posting them to a shared, personal, or public space. Provide a consistent Share This widget on each page or associate one with each granular object (pointers, media, applications).

Sending can be enabled for logged-out users with an encouragement to log in to gain access to contacts, or it can be enabled only for logged-in users, in which case it may be an incentive to sign up or a barrier to participation (Figure 8-7).

Figure 8-7. *Sign-in can be a barrier to email, or an upsell, or entirely optional. The New York Times is experimenting with sponsorship of the article tools as a way of monetizing the behaviors around its content.*

When the user invokes the sharing link, provide—in a pop up or overlay if possible—the minimal interface needed to facilitate rapid sending or posting. Offer autocomplete selection from an address book or a set of contacts if possible.

Consider including a text field for adding a personal note, although most people will skip this, and some may even be slowed down by it. One approach is to include a link that, if invoked, expands the optional text field, as Flickr's widget does.

Any interface that mimics (or hooks into) email can be misused for spam. If using CAPTCHA, consider supporting audio CAPTCHA to provide better accessibility. Sophisticated users may likewise be reluctant to use a one-off sending method that won't be tracked or archived in their personal mail system.

A Send This option on a useful and ubiquitous Send/Share widget can provide your users with a convenient and familiar method for sharing more content, objects, and applications with one another. If they opt to execute their direct sharing through your widget, you can learn from the behavioral patterns and optimize your interfaces and offerings.

Related patterns

"Don't Break Email!" on page 35

"Faceted identity" on page 95

"One-way following (aka asynchronous following)" on page 364

"Profile" on page 86

"Updates" on page 139

As seen on

Flickr (*http://www.flickr.com/*)

The New York Times (*http://nytimes.com/*)

The Onion (*http://www.theonion.com/*)

Yahoo! (*http://www.yahoo.com/*)

Casual Privacy

What

When people post content or discover it online, they sometimes like to invite other people to view it (Figure 8-8). This can be done with a Send This interface, but in some cases the resource isn't inherently viewable to anyone without an explicit invitation.

Figure 8-8. *After uploading an image to Facebook, you can invite someone to view it at a custom URL.*

Use when

Provide users with an invitation option after they have posted content, uploaded resources, or installed an application.

They aren't really needed for public resources that can be shared easily with a bookmarklet or Share This widget.

How

Generate a unique custom link for the content, and give users an option to copy and paste it into an ordinary email message or to send it automatically with a Send This interface.

Why

A custom link that gives limited access to a direct recipient using Casual Privacy enables fluid sharing within a system of overlapping publics. This relieves the sender from creating formal groups, configuring privacy settings, and granting explicit privileges.

Provide a form of temporary or limited access for the recipient of the custom link (Figure 8-9).

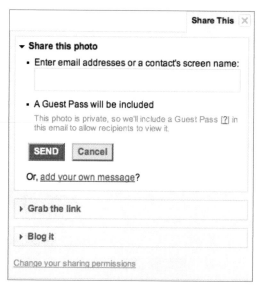

Figure 8-9. *When a member attempts to send a link for a photo (or video) to a person who does not inherently have permission to view it, either because it's private or because it's viewable only by members of a group (in Flickr's case, friend or family) that the person does not belong to, Flickr automatically generates a Guest Pass.*

Optionally provide boilerplate invitation copy that the user may customize.

If the recipient follows the offered link back to your site, remind him once there that he is a guest and may be seeing content not otherwise viewable (Figure 8-10).

> You're surfing around Flickr on a Guest Pass to see xian's photostream and "test-of-privacy".

Figure 8-10. *Flickr appends a reminder message to the page accessed via the custom link as well as to any subsequent pages the recipient visits.*

Related patterns

"Many Publics" on page 228

Sources

Kellan Elliott-McCrea's "Casual Privacy" talk at Web 2.0 Expo SF 2008, *http://www.web2expo.com/webexsf2008/public/schedule/detail/1826*

Kellan Elliott-McCrea's "Casual Privacy" slides from Ignite Web 2.0 Expo, *http://www.slideshare.net/kellan/casual-privacy-ignite-web20-expo*

As seen on

Facebook (*http://www.facebook.com/*)

Flickr (*http://www.flickr.com/*)

Share Application

What

A user who enjoys an application may want to share it with friends, particularly if it is collaborative or game-like in any way (Figure 8-11).

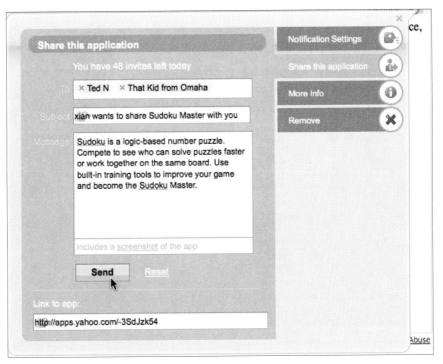

Figure 8-11. *Sharing an application is much like sharing any other object, but it does require that the recipient install the app.*

Use when

When hosting or providing a platform for applications, incorporate a sharing flow in order to facilitate organic distribution of popular applications.

- Incorporate a Send/Share widget into the chrome of your application canvas. Enable users to choose recipients from among their contacts (Figure 8-12).

Figure 8-12. *Sending someone an application means asking her to install it, so she has to trust you if she's going to do it.*

- Notify recipients of the invitation and ask them to install the application. Post vitality updates to announce when a new application is installed.

Why

One of the appeals of social media is the phenomenon of supercharged word-of-mouth growth patterns through easy peer-to-peer sharing and distribution of applications.

As seen on

Facebook (*http://www.facebook.com/*)

iGoogle (*http://www.google.com/ig*)

MySpace (*http://www.myspace.com/*)

Yahoo! (*http://www.yahoo.com/*)

Give Gift

What

Users seem to enjoy opportunities to make friendly gestures to one another, especially when those gifts can appear as a tangible, persistent decoration in personal or shared spaces (Figure 8-13).

Figure 8-13. *Public or visible gift giving is a testament to love or friendship.*

Use when

Use this pattern in friendship- and romance-oriented social environments where visual displays of affection are welcome.

How

Provide an inherent gift-giving feature or enable third-party application developers to do so through APIs for messaging between contacts and the ability to display objects on a profile.

If building an intrinsic gift-giving interface, add a Give Gift command to the list of actions a member can perform when viewing the profile or user card of another member, and/or provide a unique starting point for gift giving on the profile (Figure 8-14).

Figure 8-14. *Facebook profiles feature a gift box where a visitor can initiate the gift-giving process.*

Display the gift choices (Figures 8-15 and 8-16).

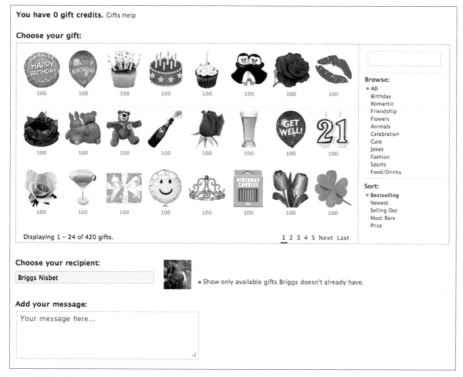

Figure 8-15. *Choosing a gift. What's my budget?*

Figure 8-16. *This box of chocolates is only available until sold out, with only half a million left.*

Optionally, give the sender a range of choices about how public the display of the gift and optional accompanying message should be (Figure 8-17). Who should see them (friends, everybody?), and where (on the profile, in the activity stream, elsewhere?), and who can read the note?

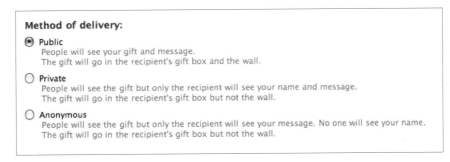

Figure 8-17. *Facebook offers three degrees of publicness or the option of privacy for gifts.*

Optionally, charge your users to send a gift (Figure 8-18). (Weigh the revenue benefit against the degree of frictionlessness you are counting on to establish this behavior.)

Figure 8-18. *Facebook charges real money for its virtual gifts.*

As Abby Kirigin of TipJoy put it when reviewing an earlier draft of this chapter:

> *The introduction of scarcity provides value and is meaningful to the recipient (as in "oh you cared enough to buy me one of those rare rose virtual gifts"). Social networks in Asia are showing huge successes in virtual goods payments and provide a solid model for the Western world as the reliance on monetization through advertising falls out of favor.*

Notify the sender when the giving has been successfully accomplished (Figure 8-19).

Figure 8-19. *Success!*

Give the recipient the option of accepting (and thus displaying on his profile) or reject-ing the gift. If a gift is rejected, do not explicitly notify the sender. If the gift is accepted, display it on the user's profile and/or in his activity stream, according to the rules of your gift system and the choices the sender and receiver made (Figure 8-20).

Figure 8-20. *I chose the most public option so my gift appears on B's wall, as well as in her gift box.*

Special cases

Optionally enable gift giving between strangers, but consider the risk of spam and stalking.

Think about whether you want to charge for virtual gifts and potentially find a revenue source there, promote free gift giving, or explore other forms of scarcity.

Why

Virtual gifts provide at minimum the equivalent of a Phatic Poke, a small positive gesture between two people. If displayed on a profile they may also represent a reminder of the friendship. Micropayments for virtual gifts could represent one of several revenue streams for a social application with a sufficiently engaged community. Services for delivering real gifts would extend the goodwill of a positive interaction beyond the confines of the virtual space and would have straightforward monetization opportunities.

Related patterns

"Peer-to-Peer Awards" on page 169

"Profile" on page 86

"Nudging" on page 301

As seen on

Facebook (*http://www.facebook.com/*)

NeoPets (*http://www.neopets.com/*)

Public Sharing

While we sometimes prefer the phrase Direct Sharing over Private Sharing (partly in recognition of the fact that nothing contributed to an internetworked data system is ultimately "private" in any meaningful, dependable way), for the sake of clarity, we are trying to be consistent about contrasting private and public facets of many of these social interactions. Still, rather than viewing things through the lens of the age-old public/private dichotomy, it may be more fruitful to think in terms of many overlapping public spaces, some of which are more public than others.

In any given system, there may be a range of sharing possibilities, from objects that are freely viewable to any passersby, to items restricted to viewing only by (logged-in, authenticated) members of the community, to those that can be seen only by those either included in a formal group or explicitly invited.

We consider any kind of sharing that isn't directed at an individual or a specific, defined list of individuals to be public sharing. This form of sharing can be active, as when a user affirmatively posts content or information to a site for viewing and commenting by friends, followers, fans, family, the general public, or any other such audience. It can also be passive, as when activities are tracked and reported on an ongoing basis, generating update notices to friends or items in activity streams without requiring that the user consciously and deliberately share the activity or object.

Many Publics

As danah boyd wrote in her PhD thesis, "Taken Out of Context":

> *Networked publics are publics that are restructured by networked technologies. As such, they are simultaneously (1) the space constructed through networked technologies and (2) the imagined community that emerges as a result of the intersection of people, technology, and practice. Social network sites like MySpace and Facebook are networked publics, just like parks and other outdoor spaces can be understood as publics. Collections of people connected through networked technologies like "the blogosphere" are publics, just like those connected by geography or identity are.... The concept of networked publics is slippery because the concept of "publics" is messy. The term "public" is contested, has multiple meanings, and is used across disciplines to signal different concepts. During my interviews, I found that teens also struggle to define this term and rely on multiple meanings to approach a definition from different angles. When used descriptively, "public" is often in opposition to the equally slippery concept "private" to signal potential access.*

When designing a social application of any kind, you must immediately grapple with the perspectives of—at the very least—two publics. One is the "whole world" that will have some way of glimpsing your site, if only to see the high walls of your private garden. The other is the networked public you hope to cultivate, composed of the body of all of your site's members and participants. Most likely there will be more than two. The outside world may itself have subpublics that view your site in different ways. More importantly, as your members meet one another and organize themselves into groups around common interests, there will start to be multiple networked publics within (or, really, facilitated by) your system.

Thus, when your users engage in Public Sharing through your application, this may mean they are sharing objects with the whole world (as when someone posts content to an ordinary blog), or with the entire membership of your site, or with some other designated public they relate to through your site.

Any interface for One-Time Sharing (see "Share This" on page 232) or Ongoing Sharing should therefore provide choices to the user about who will be allowed to see the social objects she is sharing.

Alternatively, those choices may be baked into the rules of the system, so, for example, when choosing to share an object at Facebook, one choice is to add it to your profile (Figure 8-21).

Figure 8-21. *When an object is shared by posting it to one's profile, the rules for who can see it are inherited from the rules of the profile and the account, not set manually at the point of sharing.*

The Rising Importance of Context Management

There was a time when we could be fairly certain where we were at any given time. Just looking at our surroundings would let us know if we were in a public park or a quiet library, a dance hall or a funeral parlor. And our actions and conversations could easily adapt to these contexts: in a library, we'd know not to yell "heads up" and toss a football, and we'd know to avoid doing the hustle during someone's eulogy.

But as more and more of our lives are lived via the Web, and the contexts we inhabit are increasingly made of digits rather than atoms, our long-held assumptions about reality are dissolving under our typing-and-texting fingertips.

A pre-Web example of this problem is something most people have experienced: accidentally emailing with "Reply All" rather than "Reply." Most email applications make it brutally easy to click Reply All by accident. In the physical world in which we evolved, the difference between a private conversation and a public one required more physical effort and provided more sensory clues. But in an email application, there's almost no difference: the buttons are usually identical and only a few pixels apart.

You'd think we would have learned something from our embarrassments with email, but newer applications aren't much of an improvement. Twitter, for example, allows basically the same mistake if you use "@" instead of "d." Not only that, but you have to put a space after the *d*. Twitter users, by the time of this writing, are used to seeing at least a few of these errors made by their friends every week, usually followed by another tweet explaining that was a "mis-tweet" or cursing the *d* versus @ convention.

—continued—

The Rising Importance of Context Management

At least with those applications, it's basically a binary choice for a single piece of data: one message goes either to one or multiple recipients, and the contexts are straightforward and relatively transparent. But on many popular social network platforms, the problem becomes exponentially more complicated.

Because of its history, Facebook is an especially good example. Facebook started as a social web application with a built-in context: undergraduates at Harvard. Soon it expanded to other colleges and universities, but its contextual architecture continued to be based on school affiliation. The power of designing for a shared real-world context allowed Facebook's structure to assume a lot about its users: they would have a lot in common, including their ages, college culture, and circles of friends.

Facebook's context provided a safe haven for college students to express themselves with their peers in all their immature, formative glory. For the first time, a generation of late-teens unwittingly documented their transition to adulthood in a published format. But it was OK, because anybody on Facebook with them was "there" only because they were already "there" at their college, at that time.

But then, in 2006 when Facebook opened its virtual doors to anyone 13 or over with an email address, everything changed. Graduates who were now starting their careers found their middle-aged coworkers asking to be friends on Facebook. I recall some of my younger office friends reeling at the thought that their cube mates and managers might see their photos or read their embarrassing teenage rants "out of context."

The Facebook example serves a discussion of context well because it's probably the largest virtual place to have ever so suddenly unhinged itself from its physical place. Its inhabitants, who could previously afford an assumed mental model of "this web place corresponds to the physical place where I spent my college years" found themselves in a radically different place. A contextual shift that would have required massive physical effort in the physical world was accomplished with a few lines of code and the flip of a switch.

Not that there wasn't warning. The folks who run Facebook had announced the change was coming. So why weren't more people ready? In part because such a reality shift doesn't have much precedent: few people were used to thinking about the implications of such a change. But also because the platform didn't provide any tools for managing the context conversion.

This lack of tools for managing multiple contexts is behind some of the biggest complaints about Facebook and social network platforms (such as MySpace and LinkedIn). For Facebook, long-time residents realized they would like to still keep up their immature and embarrassing memories from college to share just with their college friends, just like before; they wanted to preserve that context in its own space. But Facebook provided no capabilities for segmenting the experience. It was all or nothing, for every "friend" you added. And then, when Facebook launched its News feed—showing all your activities to your friends, and those of your friends to you—users rebelled, in part because they hadn't been given adequate tools for managing the contexts where their information might appear. This is to say nothing of the disastrous launch of Facebook's "Beacon" service, where all users were opted in by default to share information about their purchases on other affiliated sites.

—continued—

The Rising Importance of Context Management

On MySpace, the early bugbear was the threat of predator activity and the lack of privacy. Again, the platform was built with the assumption that users were fine with collapsing their contexts into one space, where everything was viewable by every "friend" added. And on LinkedIn, users have often complained the platform doesn't allow them to keep legitimate peer connections separate from others, such as recruiters.

Not all platforms have made these mistakes. The Flickr photo site has long distinguished between Family and Friends, Private and Public. LiveJournal, a pioneering social platform, has provided robust permissions controls to its users for years, allowing creation of many different user-and-group combinations.

However, there's still an important missing feature, one that should be considered for all social platforms as they add new context-creation abilities: it's either impossible or difficult for users to review their profiles and posts from others' points of view.

Giving users the ability to create new contexts is a great step, but they also need the ability to easily simulate each user-category's experience of their space. If a user creates a "coworkers" group and tries to carefully expose only their professional information, there's no straightforward way to view his own space using that filter. With the Reply All problem described earlier, we at least get a chance to proofread our message before hitting the button. But most social platforms don't even give us that ability.

This function—perhaps call it "View as Different User Type"—is just one example of a whole class of design patterns we still need for managing the mind-bending complexity we've created for ourselves on the Web. There are certainly others waiting to be explored. For example, what if we had more than just one way to say "no, thank you" to an invitation or request, depending on the type of person requesting? Or a way to send a friendly explanatory note with your refusal, thereby adding context to an otherwise cold interaction? Or what about the option to simply turn off whole portions of site functionality for some groups and not others? Maybe I'd love to get zombie-throwing-game invitations from my relatives, but not from people I haven't seen since middle school?

In the rush to allow everyone to do everything online, designers often forget that some of the limitations of physical life are actually helpful, comforting, and even necessary. We're social species, but we're also a nesting species, given to having our little nook in the tribal cave. Maybe we should take a step back and think of these patterns not unlike their originator, Mr. Alexander, did: how have people lived and interacted successfully over many generations? What can we learn from the best of those structures, even in the structureless clouds of cyberspace? Ideally, the result would be the best of both worlds: architectures that fit our ingrained assumptions about the world, while giving us the magical ability to link across divides that were impossible to cross before.

—Andrew Hinton, inkblurt.com

Share This

What

User wants to share an object (pointer, media, or application) with one or more people. The application wants to be involved in the sharing in order to learn who is sharing what with whom, and how often (Figure 8-22).

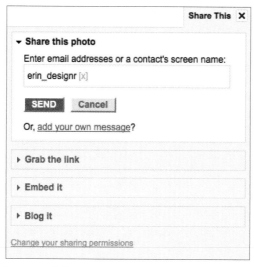

Figure 8-22. *One-time sharing at Flickr.*

Use when

Use when displaying content, resources, or applications on your site or elsewhere.

How

Enable people to spontaneously share content or objects they find by sending them to a friend or posting them to a shared, personal, or public space. Provide a consistent Share This widget on each page, or associate one with each granular object (pointers, media, applications).

When the user invokes the sharing link, provide—in a pop up or overlay if possible—the minimal interface needed to facilitate rapid posting. Optionally include a Send This invitation to explicitly choose recipients to be notified of the posting.

While the initial gesture of sharing is consistent, there are actually multiple architectures of sharing that can be made available to the user, most notably:

- Social Bookmarking

- Uploading to the Cloud
- Embedding
- Ongoing Sharing

Why

Providing a one-time Public Sharing option in a ubiquitous Share This widget can provide your users with a convenient and familiar method for sharing more content and objects and applications with one another. If they opt to execute their public sharing through your widget, you can learn from the behavioral patterns and optimize your interfaces and offerings.

Related patterns

"Activity Streams" on page 135

"Faceted identity" on page 95

"One-way following (aka asynchronous following)" on page 364

"Profile" on page 86

"Updates" on page 139

As seen on

Flickr (*http://www.flickr.com/*)

The New York Times (*http://nytimes.com/*)

The Onion (*http://www.theonion.com/*)

Yahoo! (*http://www.yahoo.com/*)

Social Bookmarking

Social bookmarking is a way for a community of users to collectively organize hyperlinks to web-based knowledge resources in a community-managed list. Social bookmarking uses keywords and metadata to organize these resources instead of utilizing a conventional hierarchical folder organization. Retrieval of this information from such systems is based on keyword search.

Social bookmarking is thus a form of One-Time Sharing for gathering pointers, generally in the form of title, link, description (the same canonical form used for early blogging and RSS).

Social bookmarking thrives thanks to the convenience of a bookmarklet, which moves the action of bookmarking socially into the same part of the interface (the "browser chrome") where old-school (solipsistic) bookmarking was always done (see Figure 8-23).

Figure 8-23. A bit o' JavaScript is all it takes to make a humble bookmark into a mighty social bookmarking bookmarklet.

Whether invoked via a bookmarklet or Share This widget, the social bookmarking interface can guide the person posting the pointer toward capturing and reviewing the title and description metadata for the bookmark (see Figure 8-24).

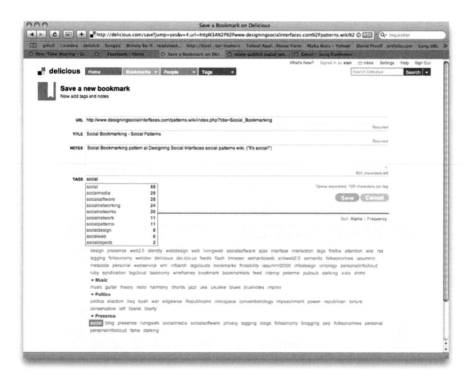

Figure 8-24. A bookmarklet may present anything from a brief pop-up confirmation dialog box to a full-page presentation of nuanced options.

Uploading to the Cloud

Photos, files, videos, documents, and many other kinds of social objects are uploaded, posted to, and hosted by social applications "in the cloud." Without getting into the technology of grid computing or service level, uptime, redundancy, security, and backups, we'll just talk about the cloud in a more intuitive sense, as the place "out there" where we're increasingly leaving our email inboxes, our photographs, our financial information, and more.

Where social bookmarking deals with sharing pointers to objects, uploading to the cloud means sharing the objects themselves, by contributing digital copies to the site's repository. The terminology for this from the user point of view may be share, post, add, upload, or even bookmark or send. Flickr talks about uploading photos and, now, videos. Facebook has an Add Photos button and a Photos tab with a button labeled "+Create a New Photo Album."

Uploaders typically hook into the user's system interface for browsing and selecting files (as used by an ordinary Open dialog box) when presented in a browser or application interface. They can also be standalone client applications, which you may develop or which you may encourage third-party developers to create by publishing and facilitating the use of your APIs (Figure 8-25).

Figure 8-25. *The latest version of iPhoto now contains a native Flickr exporter (uploader), but even with earlier versions of iPhoto you could purchase an affordable plug-in called FlickrExport for iPhoto to upload one or more photos to Flickr directly from within the iPhoto application.*

Embedding

Users like to be able to collect and display media objects (such as videos, images, and even slideshows) as well as badges and applications on their profiles, blogs, and activity streams (Figure 8-26).

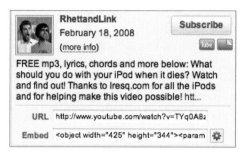

Figure 8-26. *Supporting the use of embed codes for rich media and applications can enable organic growth and runaway memes.*

Embedding works best when displaying media or other objects that can be distributed freely.

Generate an embed code. An *embed code* is a snippet of markup that a user can copy and paste directly into a blog entry template, MySpace page, or other social space for sharing that the user controls (Figure 8-27).

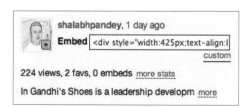

Figure 8-27. *Copying and pasting text strings is definitely an interaction flow that could be improved upon, but it's the state of the art today for flexible embedding.*

You may need to supply unique variations on the code to support variant hosting environments or to make the process simpler. SlideShare, for example, offers a generic embed code for most situations and a different code for embedding slideshows in WordPress blogs (Figure 8-28).

Figure 8-28. *SlideShare offers a custom embed code for WordPress bloggers.*

Consider giving your users the option of customizing the size, color palette, and presentation of the embedded object. Both SlideShare and YouTube, for example, enable the user to opt out of the display of related objects—slideshows and videos, respectively (Figure 8-29).

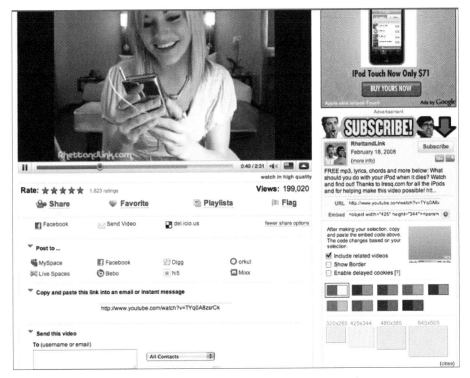

Figure 8-29. *YouTube supports customization of the embedded object, within limits.*

When possible, gather statistics about the number of times an object has been embedded, where, and how often it's been viewed or accessed through embeds (Figure 8-30).

More Info

Visible to everyone
Embedding is allowed
Secret URL is disabled
Edit privacy settings

© All Rights Reserved.

Total Views 6842
       6341 on SlideShare
       501 from embeds
Comments 4
Favorites 9
Downloads 109

Most viewed embeds
289 views on http://radar.oreilly.com
95 views on http://developer.yahoo.net
86 views on http://xianlandia.com
7 views on http://x-pollen.com
7 views on http://developer.yahoo.com
more

Also on LinkedIn
Uploaded via SlideShare

Figure 8-30. *When possible, share embedding statistics by posting them alongside the object in its native habitat, as SlideShare does here.*

Why

Users like to share and display content. The easier you make it for them to do so, the more likely they will. Embedding also has strong potential for organic spread, as it enables rapid duplication and redistribution. It is widely thought that YouTube obtained much of its early phenomenal growth from the fact that its videos could be embedded easily on MySpace pages.

Related patterns

"Badging" on page 446

"Displaying" on page 196

Google Docs (*http://docs.google.com/*)

Scribd (*http://www.scribd.com/*)

SlideShare (*http://www.slideshare.net/*)

Vimeo (*http://vimeo.com/*)

YouTube (*http://www.youtube.com/*)

Ongoing Sharing

Ongoing sharing may also be described as passive sharing. It refers to any process through which participants may initially opt in to enable their activities to be tracked and posted as updates to Activity Streams.

Whenever I log in to Flickr or Vimeo or SlideShare, one of the things I see right away are recent uploads from my contacts (Figure 8-31).

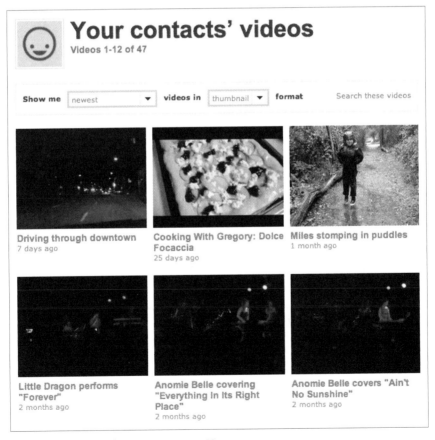

Figure 8-31. *Recent videos from my contacts on Vimeo.*

Different from directly sharing content with individuals or even actively sharing it with different-sized publics, ongoing sharing is a less conscious but more pervasive form of sharing, discussed at length in "Updates" on page 139.

It's a good idea to occasionally remind people that they're sharing information passively in an ongoing way, to protect them from the inadvertent indiscretions that can follow from forgetting who's watching them (Figure 8-32).

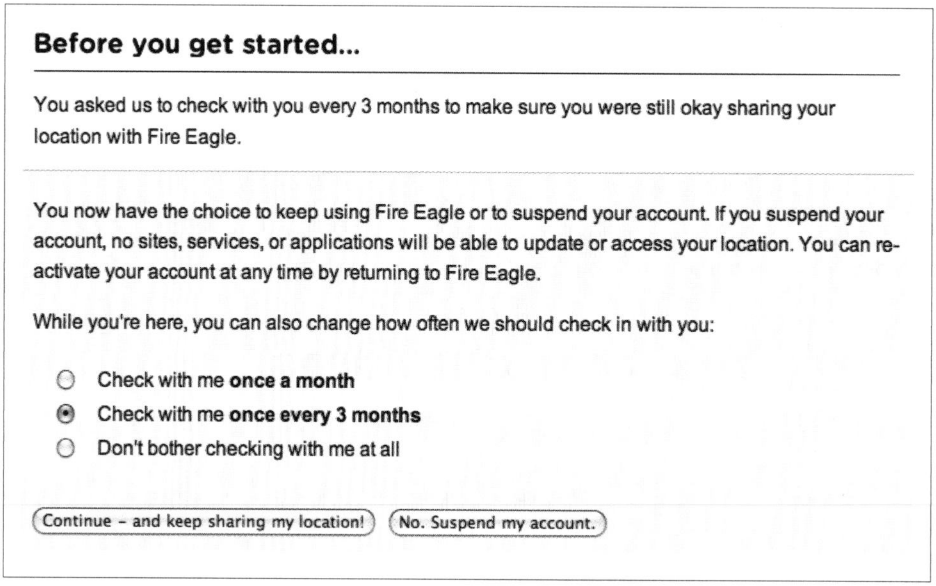

Figure 8-32. *It's easy to forget you authorized an auto-stalking tool! (So Fire Eagle takes special care to remind users and give them every opportunity to stop sharing.)*

Further Reading

Kellan Elliott-McCrea's "Casual Privacy" talk at Web 2.0 Expo SF 2008, *http://www.web2expo.com/webexsf2008/public/schedule/detail/1826*

Kellan Elliott-McCrea's "Casual Privacy" slides from Ignite Web 2.0 Expo, *http://www.slideshare.net/kellan/casual-privacy-ignite-web20-expo*

Tip a Friend, *http://ui-patterns.com/pattern/TipAFriend* (see negative comments and suggestions that it's an anti-pattern)

Chapter 9

The Megalophone

It is in vain to say human beings ought to be satisfied with tranquillity: they must have action; and they will make it if they cannot find it.

—Charlotte Brontë

Keeping up with friends is the viral part of what keeps the social web growing, but it is the sites with intense activity around a topic that keep people coming back over and over again, and this activity often provides the core around which these communities are built. It's the there, there.

Destinations where people are contributing and conversing about something are often harder to define and design, because the structure and the content are defined and created by the users. This is the place where people stand on their soap boxes and inspire dialogues and arguments, and it is the place where private conversations, secrets, and intense debates can happen around subjects people are intensely passionate about.

The key is to design flexible frameworks and spaces for people to define their own sense of place. Blogs have been successful over the years because the tools out there allowed users to customize everything—the look, how often to publish, how long or short a post, how many authors or categories—while still displaying a standard suite of meta information. Pretty much everything is open, and because of that the variety of blogs and uses of blogging software are as varied as the number of people out there.

There are some emergent display patterns for blogs, forums, email, chat, and instant messages, and following these enables users to understand the type of content and the implied expectations of behavior relating to it.

Team up one or more of these broadcasting patterns with patterns such as "Sign-up or Registration" (Chapter 3), "Identity" (Chapter 4), "Identity Cards or Contact Cards" (Chapter 4), "Reputation Influences Behavior" (Chapter 6), "Ratings (Stars or 1–5)" (Chapter 10), "Comments" (Chapter 10), and "Adding Friends" (Chapter 14), to fully round out these tools.

Broadcasting

The patterns in this section give people the tools to broadcast in a one-to-many form through methods such as blogs and microblogs. Posting photos, videos, and podcasts also falls in this category and is often associated with Microblogging and Activity Streams (Chapter 5). In addition, publishing tools like licenses, rights, and Terms of Service (which cover the contracts between your site and the user who is broadcasting, and between the user and his audience of readers) are covered in detail.

Blogs: Presentation

What

A user wants to read commentary and view events, images, and videos on a regular basis by a particular author (Figure 9-1).

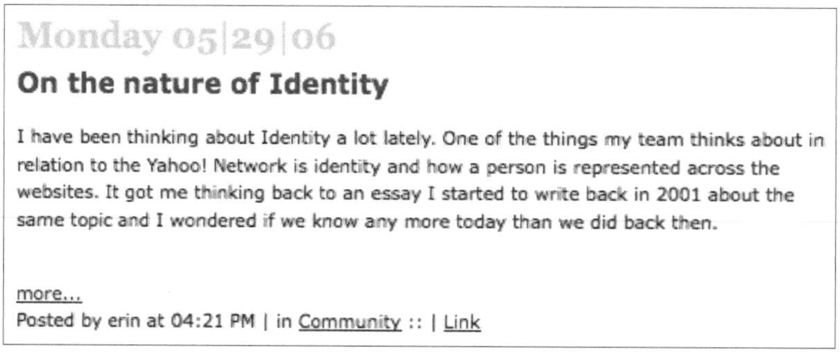

Monday 05|29|06

On the nature of Identity

I have been thinking about Identity a lot lately. One of the things my team thinks about in relation to the Yahoo! Network is identity and how a person is represented across the websites. It got me thinking back to an essay I started to write back in 2001 about the same topic and I wondered if we know any more today than we did back then.

more...
Posted by erin at 04:21 PM | in Community :: | Link

Figure 9-1. *Blog post from Design Writings.*

Use when

- Use this pattern to bring a more casual level of commentary to readers as a complement to more formal editorial content.

- Combine this pattern with "Comments" on page 278 and "Tagging" on page 200 to encourage reader participation and conversations.

- Combine this pattern with "Hosted Modules" on page 450 to encourage the readership community members to interact.

Blogs have been around long enough to have settled into both a common format for individual posts and aggregation of the posts. Despite the advanced capabilities of common blogging software, readers have come to recognize blogs by their presentation pattern.

Posts

The individual blog post should contain these fundamentals:

- Title or headline.
- Content (this is the main content of the posting).
- Short description. This can be an abstract extracted from the main content post, or a separate field can be provided to allow the author to write a separate abstract.
- Datestamp.
- Timestamp.
- Author attribution. This is especially important if your site has multiple blog authors (see "Attribution" on page 113).
- Tags or keywords. Allow the author to pretag the post.
- Comments. Most blogs have an option that allows readers to leave comments on a post. When comments are enabled, the number of comments for the post should be displayed and should be linked to the comments. The Comment link is the call to action linking to the comment form.

  When comments are enabled, there should also be tools available for managing spam. A common option is holding comments for review, which allows the moderator or blog owner to delete spam before approving comments for publication. Recent years have seen the creation of antispam technology such as Akismet, which provides an API to developers that prefilters spam.

- Permalink. This is the permanent link for the posting that will allow someone to bookmark the entry or blog about it.

Presentation of posts

- Present posts in reverse chronology.
- Allow the option for presenting posts on an index page with a title and short description for each that links off to the full post.
- Provide the ability to have a single page for each individual post.
- Provide the ability for a user to navigate backward and forward from one post to the next. Clearly indicate whether the user is going back in time.

- Archive past posts. Allow archiving by date, tag, keyword, or category (Figures 9-2 and 9-3).

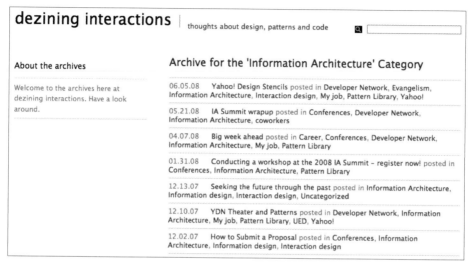

Figure 9-2. *Archive by category. Posts are presented in reverse chronological order.*

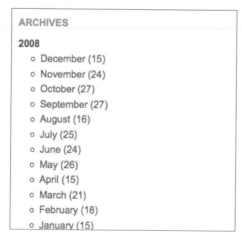

Figure 9-3. *Archives by date on Yahoo! Developer Network. Each month has an indication of how many posts were published.*

- Provide a search capability that searches titles, content, and tags.
- Allow users to subscribe to an RSS feed of the blog. Consider allowing users to subscribe to a specific category or tag.

- Provide an About area or page for author information. Information about the author lends credibility to the blog.

- Unless the blog is private, allow posts to be crawled by search engines.

Why

Blogs have been around for many years now and are a core part of both personal and corporate websites. They allow informal announcements and commentary on topics of interest to the authors. Blogs that have comments and tagging enabled allow sites to build a two-way relationship with their readers.

Related patterns

"Lifestreams" on page 144

"Statuscasting" on page 137

As seen on

Blogger (*http://www.blogger.com*)

Dezining interactions (*http://www.emdezine.com/dezininginteractions*)

Six Apart (*http://sixapart.com*)

Wake Up (*http://xianlandia.com*)

WordPress (*http://www.wordpress.com*)

Yahoo! Developer Network (*http://developer.yahoo.com*)

Blogs: Ownership

What

A user wants to write commentary and post events, images, and videos on a regular basis (Figure 9-4).

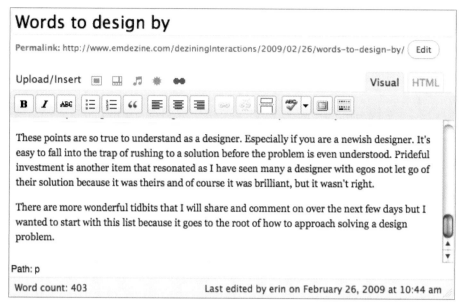

Figure 9-4. *WordPress offers rich tools for the blogging author.*

Use this pattern to create the framework that allows users to publish text, links, images, and/or video on a regular basis.

- Provide the author with the capability to record his thoughts, commentary, interesting links, photos, and other material.

- Allow the user to customize the template of the blog presentation.

- Provide a field for a title.

- Provide a large enough text entry for the body of the blog post. Consider rich-text editing tools to allow the author to format a post without having to know HTML.

- Allow the author to preview before publishing.

- Allow the author to add tags or categories before publishing.

- Consider allowing the author to schedule the publication of the blog posting into the future (Figure 9-5). This allows an author to write a series of posts at one time and then have those posts autopublish on a predetermined schedule.

Figure 9-5. *WordPress offers the ability to schedule publication into the future, in addition to the instant publish capability.*

- Allow the author to bring in other modules of relevant content and material from other places. This might be badges from photo or link collection sites or a network of relevant relationships.

- Provide the ability to upload and post photos and videos as well as text.

- Give authors a dashboard to view all previous posts with a clear ability to edit (Figure 9-6).

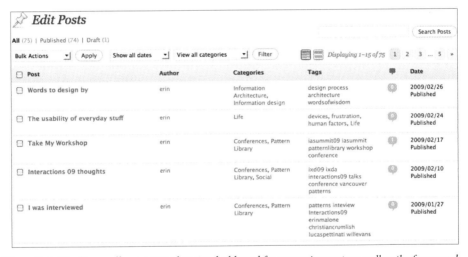

Figure 9-6. *WordPress offers a comprehensive dashboard for managing posts as well as the framework for the blog.*

- Allow authors to go back into older posts and edit or update them. Consider providing an automatic mechanism for indicating on the main page and in the index and archives list that the post has been updated without moving the post in the time stream.

- Allow authors to delete posts.

- Give authors the ability to turn comments on and off for each post.

- Provide authors with tools for moderating comments and comment spam (Figure 9-7).

- Allow the blog owner to add authors.

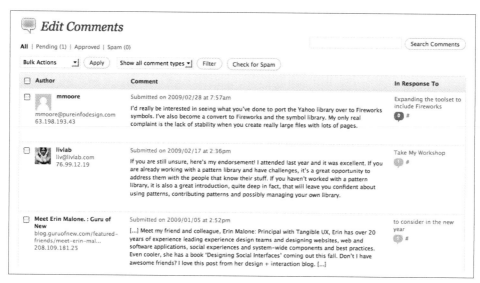

Figure 9-7. *WordPress allows the blog owner to preview comments before they are posted.*

Light blogging tools can make blogging easier. More sophisticated and powerful tools put the ownership of managing the system (as well as the output) on the author. People will gravitate to the level of tool that is appropriate—whether it's a hosted service, an embedded tool in a social network, or a fully owned piece of software sitting on the user's server. Regardless, there is a base set of functionality that is now expected in blogging tools.

Giving people rich tools to share their thoughts and viewpoints is powerful. Even if only five people read it, everyone has something to say, and for every person saying something, there are a few who will listen and respond.

Related patterns

"Blogs: Presentation" on page 242

"Lifestreams" on page 144

"Statuscasting" on page 137

As seen on

Blogger (*http://www.blogger.com/*)

Six Apart (*http://sixapart.com*)

WordPress (*http://www.wordpress.com*)

Microblogging

Microblogging allows users to create short posts, and this type of blogging has surfaced in services such as Twitter, Yammer, and even on Facebook's home page. These are often aggregated into a stream and can consist of text, pictures, or video (see "Microblogging" on page 138 for full details).

Publishing

As people move into the role of content creator and publisher, it is important to make sure they understand the range of rights and licenses that might restrict their publishing activities. This next suite of patterns covers areas such as the Terms of Service under which people contribute and participate on some sites, and discusses copyright and the Creative Commons licenses content creators can grant others who may want to use their content.

Lifecycle

What

A person wants to know when something happened (Figure 9-8).

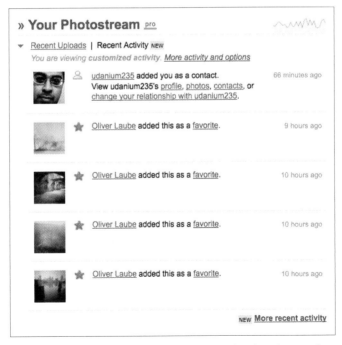

Figure 9-8. *Flickr shows recent activity to users and timestamps for when the event happened.*

- Use to give users an indication of when an item, a thought, or a conversation was added to the site.

- Use to distinguish a flow between two people.

- Use to indicate the freshness of an item, especially if highlighted.

- Indicate in the metadata of the item—photo, blog post, forum post, or an item in a conversation environment such as IM or Twitter—a time- and/or datestamp (Figure 9-9).

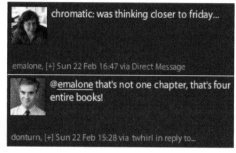

Figure 9-9. *TweetDeck, a Twitter client, stamps tweets with the date, time, type of tweet (reply, direct message), and how the tweet was sent.*

- Allow users to filter items by date.

- Allow users to search or browse by date. For blog posts, provide an archive by month and year in addition to categories or tags.

Freshness

Show items by newest item first as a default (Figure 9-10).

Some sites, such as Twitter, show followers by the date the user was first followed. This is not necessarily the best organization for this type of data. This may be interesting information, but makes it difficult to easily find a specific person. There are no filters available to resort the follower list by alphabet, which would be more useful when looking for a specific person to message.

Think about whether it makes sense to sort the information or post type by date as a default.

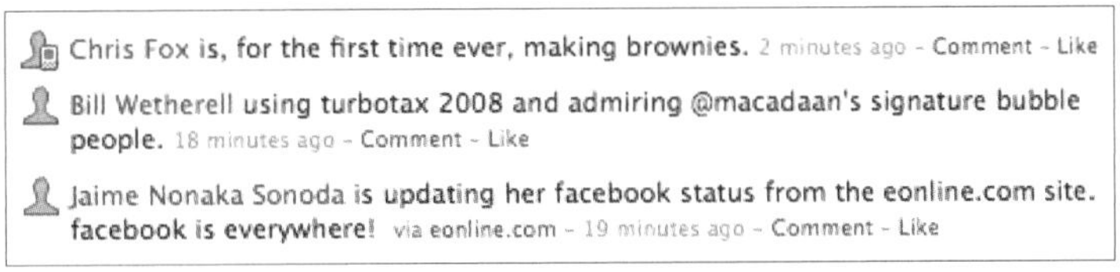

> Chris Fox is, for the first time ever, making brownies. 2 minutes ago – Comment – Like
>
> Bill Wetherell using turbotax 2008 and admiring @macadaan's signature bubble people. 18 minutes ago – Comment – Like
>
> Jaime Nonaka Sonoda is updating her facebook status from the eonline.com site. facebook is everywhere! via eonline.com – 19 minutes ago – Comment – Like

Figure 9-10. *The Facebook news feed orders items by newest first.*

Vitality

Use a vitality or activity stream to showcase an active community. This can be a good incentive for encouraging participation (see "Activity Streams" on page 135).

Related patterns

"Activity Streams" on page 135

"Mobile" on page 432

As seen on

Facebook (*http://www.facebook.com*)

Flickr (*http://www.flickr.com*)

Twitter (*http://www.twitter.com*)

Rights

Before asking people to work together, work for you, or assign work to one another, it's best to choose a model for how rights are going to be handled. It's a matter of some ethical urgency to delineate and preserve people's individual rights as well as to create a framework of rights that fosters a climate of creativity and additive collaboration. It's equally important to educate participants so that they fully understand what rights they retain, what rights they give up, and what rights they must respect before rolling up their sleeves and getting to work (Figure 9-11).

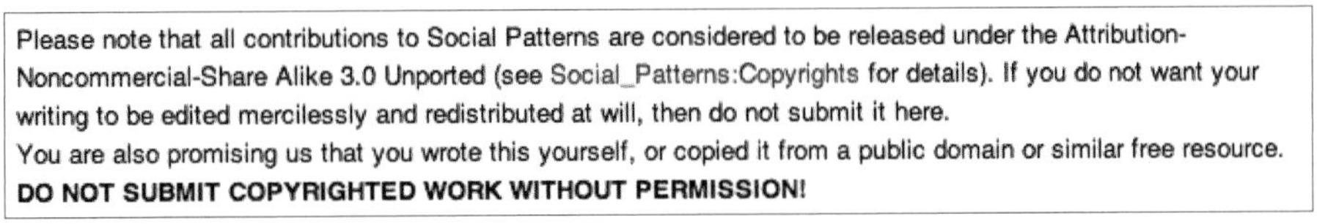

> Please note that all contributions to Social Patterns are considered to be released under the Attribution-Noncommercial-Share Alike 3.0 Unported (see Social_Patterns:Copyrights for details). If you do not want your writing to be edited mercilessly and redistributed at will, then do not submit it here.
> You are also promising us that you wrote this yourself, or copied it from a public domain or similar free resource.
> **DO NOT SUBMIT COPYRIGHTED WORK WITHOUT PERMISSION!**

Figure 9-11. *This notice informs contributors to the wiki companion of this book how their contributions will be handled, but whenever someone becomes an active participant, we also contact that person directly to make sure he or she knows the drill.*

When inviting people to contribute content to your website, ask them to verify that they have the right to do so before they become active contributors.

See "Terms of Service" on page 252 for advice on how to inform participants and to learn about the different license models you might consider for contributed content.

Terms of Service

What

A Terms of Service Agreement provides a legal framework for the use and dissemination of "information services" and intellectual property assets provided on a website. (See Figure 9-12.)

Figure 9-12. *Pressing the primary button constitutes agreement to the legal terms.*

Every website can be construed as a provider of "information services" to the consumers of this information, whether it is visitors or registered members. Although it is not necessary to have a Terms of Service Agreement on a website, it serves as a legal safeguard that establishes roles and responsibility for creation, use, and redistribution/dissemination of intellectual property in the event of a dispute or legal action.

When a form includes a checkbox for the user to indicate agreement to the Terms of Service (TOS), the user often doesn't notice the checkbox and is confronted with an error message and a demand to read and agree to them before completing the form. There's no reason to place the user in this position, where she may feel affronted merely because she did not notice a checkbox.

Use when

- Use this pattern in check-out flows and sign-up forms (Figure 9-13).

Figure 9-13. *The prompt for agreement to the Terms of Service is best when integrated closely into the sign-up (or check-out) flow.*

- Use this pattern when allowing users to create original content that will be publicly hosted on your service.

How

- Consent to the agreement is expressed in the call-to-action button ("Agree and Continue").

- The form offers an option to exit without agreeing ("Cancel" or "Don't Agree/Cancel Order").

- A statement makes it clear that submitting the form constitutes agreement to the terms ("By clicking you agree...").

- The TOS text is available via a clearly labeled hypertext link ("Terms of Service").

- The TOS copy is supplied in a printable format.

Internationalization

In different international regions, laws may require a separate checkbox or an interstitial that forces the user to see the TOS before continuing.

The goal of this pattern is to make the experience of completing the form better for the user and to avoid interrupting her or making her feel as though she has made an error.

Combining the agreement with the call-to-action button and clearly labeling the option offers a streamlined experience in the natural flow of filling out the form. The experience is somewhat analogous to signing a document.

It is important to offer an option to exit (cancel) the form without making the agreement, giving the user an escape hatch and making her consent to the terms meaningful, given that she had an alternate choice available.

Linking to the TOS provides direct access to the legal copy but avoids cluttering the page with either a large amount of verbiage or an embedded text box or iframe.

The language preceding the buttons clearly explains that clicking means agreeing, so the legal force of the agreement is clear.

Offering a printable TOS is a best practice that enables the user to keep a copy of what she agreed to (or an opportunity to show it to a legal expert before agreeing).

These five elements of the pattern work in tandem. Removing any one defeats the purpose of the pattern.

Finally, this pattern represents a best practice in the industry, and is used by companies for whom check-out flows are core experiences (such as PayPal).

"Terms of Service" in the Yahoo! Pattern Library, *http://developer.yahoo.com/ypatterns/ social/people/engagement/tos.html*

eBay (*http://ebay.com*)

PayPal (*http://paypal.com*)

Yahoo! HotJobs advertiser interface (*http://hotjobs.yahoo.com/*)

Licenses

The licensing regime you offer your users (whether it's a single type of license or a range of options) may have a profound effect on the sorts of collaborations that can ensue. If people are unsure about their legal rights, worried about losing their rights, or (worse yet) afraid of being charged with infringing on the rights of others, ordinary risk-aversion will tend to decrease the amount of participation.

There are ethical implications for any system of licenses, but the considerations are many. We don't necessarily suggest that you follow any specific regime, but here are some of the most common in use online:

Public Domain
> The most liberal. Some content eventually will enter the public domain, even when originally given a tighter license.

Creative Commons
> A nuanced range of choices designed to give options encouraging reuse.

Copyleft
> An un-copyright regime invented by hackers.

Copyright
> Traditional government-enforced copyright, which has become imbalanced in favor of original creators and against the public domain.

Public Domain

Public Domain licensing is the most liberal available (Figure 9-14).

Figure 9-14. *Public Domain licensing is the most liberal available.*

From Wikipedia:

> *The public domain is a range of abstract materials—commonly referred to as intellectual property—which are not owned or controlled by anyone. The term indicates that these materials are therefore "public property", and available for anyone to use for any purpose. The public domain can be defined in contrast to several forms of intellectual property; the public domain in contrast to copyrighted works is different from the public domain in contrast to trademarks or patented works. Furthermore, the laws of various countries define the scope of the public domain differently, making it necessary to specify which jurisdiction's public domain is being discussed.*

From Wikipedia's article on public domain licensing at Wikipedia itself:

> *For all practical purposes on Wikipedia, the public domain comprises copyright-free works: anyone can use them in any way and for any purpose. Proper attribution to the author or source of a work, even if it is in the public domain, is still required to avoid plagiarism.*
>
> *The public domain is generally defined (e.g., by the U.S. Copyright Office) as the sum of works that are not copyrighted, i.e., that were not eligible for copyright in the first place, or whose copyright has expired.*
>
> *However, there is no such thing as the public domain on the Internet. International treaties, like the Berne Convention, are not self-executing and do not supersede local law. There is no globally valid "International Copyright Law" that would take precedence over local laws. Instead, signatory countries of the Berne Convention have adapted their laws to comply with the minimum standards set forth by the treaty, often with stronger provisions than required. Whether or not something is copyright-free in some country depends on the laws of individual countries.*
>
> *Wikipedia, and the Wikimedia Foundation, its legal body, are based in Florida, United States. Although legislation is sometimes unclear about which laws are to apply on the Internet, the primary law relevant for Wikipedia is that of the United States. For re-users of Wikipedia content, it is the laws of their respective countries.*
>
> *In the U.S., any work published before January 1, 1923 anywhere in the world is in the public domain. Other countries are not bound to that 1923 date, though.*

If you can get all your stakeholders (from the owner of the site to the participants) to agree to place as much content as possible in the public domain, or to make public domain licensing the default for collaborative content, then you will enable the greatest possible reuse and remixing of your community's content, with the consequence being a giving up of control over how the content may be used or altered by others.

Creative Commons offers a public domain option (see "Creative Commons" on page 260).

The Logic of the Global Brain

Imagine the bandwidth-rich and the bandwidth-poor learning from each other. People online and on-the-ground interact through a set of roles. We may imagine neurons in the brain (an abstract setting) interacting with neurons in a hand or foot (a concrete setting).

This is what the "global brain" is for!

Charles (not his real name) casually referred to a time when he had helped Tom Ochuko find information that was urgently needed. It is a true "good news story" that deserves to be more widely known, both for its own sake and as an example of ICT being used for informal learning. The Internet was used to teach a practical skill that helped save the lives of children in Nyanza, Kenya, when cholera threatened.

This is what happened. In 2008, Tom Ochuko wrote an email from Kenya, explaining that sickness was following the rains; children were getting sick; the river, normally a source of livelihood, had become a killer; and homes and crops had been washed away. The area had already suffered post-election violence. Now it was threatened with cholera.

Tom is an active member of an online community, Minciu Sodas (MS). He is a community activist with particular concern for deaf people. He was also active in the Pyramid of Peace initiative (post-election turmoil response) in 2008. When he needed help, he emailed his friends in the Holistic Helping group in Minciu Sodas. He explained the situation, and that there was a need to provide sanitation—but how? He needed advice from people who were good at constructing toilets.

This was his email:

> *http://groups.yahoo.com/group/holistichelping/message/3028*

> *"Dear Sam,Ken ,Dan,Chelimo,Janet,Maria and all. Its has been reported that-Nyanza is worse now..I Have experienced it now. The children have long stomach runs..with complain in the chest,River Nyando our source of livelihood has become akiller. We cant get nrea any more while the homes are already washed away..with no crops..we cant just live to see this come every year. To begin with we must comstruct toilets..are there peoplwewho are just good in this. Designing,and making. Our ground is loose..and needs abetter structured toilets for every home. Mosquitoes are also breeding,SAM EXPERINCED THIS WHILE HE VISITED ME. The deafimpact children..require nets,Tabs..and Even water containers to keep ..good health and hygine. WE can atlength dicuss this kisumu..is already affected as at now no running water and all are warned taht unless something is done ..Chilera is number two to election vilolence. What are your vies SAM HOW IS MbITA..sOME ARE ADMITTED AT THE HOSPITAL FROM MBITA. Lets comunicate and get alsting solution. TOM OCHUKA"*

> *—continued—*

The Logic of the Global Brain

Fortunately, Charles, one of Tom's online friends, saw the request for information. He searched the Internet and came up with a relevant link. It was to a "Water_Aid_Video" by Adam Hart Davies, on how to build a pit latrine. The key element is simply a piece of plastic drainpipe. The video shows how to cut, heat, and bend the drainpipe, and construct the pit latrine. Tom got the information and acted on it. The health of the children improved.

I asked Charles to give me more details of exactly what happened, so he sent me an email, which he also copied to the Minciu Sodas wiki at *http://www.worknets.org/wiki.cgi?PitLatrine*. It tells how Tom got the information he needed, built the latrine, and improved the health of the children. It was funded locally, so the only thing that came in from the outside was information.

This is not a high-profile story. There was no publicity, no involvement from politicians or large NGOs, no planning and targets and budgets. It was practical local community action.

I am studying how ICT can enable learning, and to me this is a wonderful example of genuine, informal distance learning on-demand. It is far removed from traditional course-based distance learning, which is the main model that many people seem to have. This was something immediate and focused. It was serious, project-based learning, which was needed to solve a pressing problem.

This example is a collaborative approach to learning that has only become possible thanks to the Internet. It is an approach where people who know one another through online communities are ready to share needs and resources and help one another to solve problems, using video and the Internet. It is a kind of e-learning that is radically different from what many people normally think of as e-learning (i.e., traditional, formal, course-based, accredited learning, with a subject expert leading the learning).

There was no subject expert in the group, no one who had the knowledge that Tom needed. The information was on the Internet, but the Internet on its own was not sufficient. Tom has little Internet access and had no realistic chance of finding the information that he needed for himself. The extra was the transnational community of friends. Someone who was bandwidth-poor was supported by someone (in the bandwidth-rich UK) who was more easily able to go online and search for useful information. An intermediary helped to download the information from the Internet in Kenya. It was put onto a CD so that Tom could learn from it offline and share the information.

The thing that strikes me repeatedly about informal Internet-mediated learning is the way that it dramatically increases the number of contacts that you can ask for help. There is new hope for those of us who don't belong in a university, don't start off knowing people locally who are well informed about things that interest us, and don't have any kind of "old school tie network." Anyone who can get on the Internet and ask questions has a chance of finding new contacts. Discussion and answers are available "with a little help from our friends." There is even hope for bandwidth-poor people like Tom if they know people who will help them. Thanks to the Internet, it is worth asking questions, because there is a good chance that someone can help to find an answer.

Imagine a future where teams of volunteers support learning the way that Charles does. (Being a volunteer on such a team would be an interesting and satisfying experience for anyone who enjoys learning new things and meeting new people online.) As the story of Tom and Charles demonstrates, there are exciting and wonderful opportunities for collaborative learning, thanks to the Internet.

—continued—

The Logic of the Global Brain

This may appear to be the story of two people, but actually there are several roles involved:

- Experiencers of the real need: the people who were getting sick.
- Local leader: Tom Ochuka, who wanted to address the need.
- Connector: Tom Ochuka, who himself brought this issue online, and an intermediary who downloaded the video for him.
- Facilitator: Janet Feldman, who leads the online venue where Tom asked for help.
- Researcher: Charles, who took it upon himself to find an answer.
- Publisher: Water Aid, which works for safe water for the world's poor.
- Champion: Adam Hart Davies, who created the video that Water Aid published.
- Presenter: Tom Ochuka, who spread the knowledge locally.
- Documentor: Charles, who wrote up his answer on the Worknets wiki.
- Investigator: Pamela McLean, who noticed the importance of this example.

A crucial role was played by the facilitator, and this role is often the least visible. Facilitators enable people of different cultures to work comfortably together and foster long-term relationships that don't automatically come to people of different cultures. Janet Feldman's working group Holistic Helping is part of Minciu Sodas, a wider online laboratory and network of "independent thinkers" that depends on many patterns to create an environment that brings together and holds together very different people:

- Activity is organized around mature "independent thinkers" such as Janet Feldman, and their deepest value in life. Janet's is "holistic helping": helping in all directions at once, as when responding to the HIV/AIDS challenge in Africa. These are working groups (Yahoo! groups) because email allows a wide range of people to participate, including those with marginal Internet access.
- Overlap of people and cross-pollination of content is encouraged among groups.
- Participants are encouraged to write about what they don't know and would like to know (rather than what they already know), and to write about what they would like to achieve.
- A special effort is made to reach out and sign up new participants and to respond to those who ask for help, but especially those who overcome challenges of poverty, language, and technology to participate.
- The description of the venues and the footers of the letters make clear that all content sent to the group is in the "Public Domain except as noted otherwise," which encourages reuse; encourages people to write seriously and to be proactive, using their own best judgment to help others; and also filters out selfish, destructive people, who by their nature don't want to lose control of anything or be held accountable for their actions.

Perhaps the most important thing to understand is that this story is exceptional and not even the purpose of Minciu Sodas. This very practical example of e-learning is incidental to the continual efforts to bring together the widest variety of people to help one another grow as independent thinkers.

—Andrius Kulikauskas (of Minciu Sodas)
and Pamela McLean (of Dadamac), based on her original post at
http://learnbydoinguk.blogspot.com/2009/01/tom-ricardo-and-life-saving-learning.html
and *http://www.worknets.org/wiki.cgi?PitLatrine*

Sources

Creative Commons public domain dedication, *http://creativecommons.org/licenses/ publicdomain/*

Ethical Public Domain, *http://ethicalpublicdomain.ning.com/*

Public Domain Information Project (royalty-free music), *http://www.pdinfo.com/index. php*

When U.S. Works Pass into the Public Domain, *http://www.unc.edu/~unclng/public-d.htm*

Wikipedia: Public domain, *http://en.wikipedia.org/wiki/Wikipedia:Public_domain*

Creative Commons

Creative Commons licenses were created to foster creative collaboration and encourage people to opt for the loosest possible restrictions while balancing that against any rights they feel they absolutely must retain (Figure 9-15). Creative Commons licenses address four conditions that may be applied:

Attribution
> Others may copy, distribute, display, and perform your copyrighted work and derivative works based on it as long as they give you credit the way you request. For example, patterns in the Yahoo! Design Pattern Library require attribution only.

Share Alike
> Others may distribute derived works based on yours, but only if they use the identical license terms.

Noncommercial
> Others may copy, distribute, display, and perform your work and derivative works based on it, but only for noncommercial purposes.

No Derivative Works
> Others may copy, distribute, display, and perform only verbatim copies of your work.

Figure 9-15. *Creative Commons licenses are composed from different combinations of four basic conditions.*

Creative Commons licenses

Based on those four conditions, there are six non–public domain CC licenses you can choose from or offer as choices for your users:

Attribution

This license lets others distribute, remix, tweak, and build upon your work, even commercially, as long as they credit you for the original creation. This is the most accommodating of licenses offered, in terms of what others can do with your works licensed under Attribution.

Attribution Share Alike

This license lets others remix, tweak, and build upon your work even for commercial reasons, as long as they credit you and license their new creations under the identical terms. This license is often compared to open source software licenses. All new works based on yours will carry the same license, so any derivatives will also allow commercial use.

Attribution No Derivatives

This license allows for redistribution, commercial and noncommercial, as long as it is passed along unchanged and in whole, with credit to you.

Attribution Noncommercial

This license lets others remix, tweak, and build upon your work noncommercially, and although their new works must also acknowledge you and be noncommercial, they don't have to license their derivative works on the same terms.

Attribution Noncommercial Share Alike

This license lets others remix, tweak, and build upon your work noncommercially, as long as they credit you and license their new creations under the identical terms. Others can download and redistribute your work just like the Attribution Non-Commercial No Derivatives license, but they can also translate, make remixes, and produce new stories based on your work. All new work based on yours will carry the same license, so any derivatives will also be noncommercial in nature.

Attribution Noncommercial No Derivatives

This license is the most restrictive of the six main licenses, allowing only redistribution. This license is often called the "free advertising" license because it allows others to download your works and share them with others as long as they mention you and link back to you, but they can't change them in any way or use them commercially.

Sources

Portions of this entry are adapted from content at the Creative Commons website (*http://creativecommons.org*), published under the Creative Commons Attribution License.

Copyleft

Copyleft is a play on the word "copyright" to describe the practice of using copyright law to remove restrictions on distributing copies and modified versions of a work for others and requiring that the same freedoms be preserved in modified versions (Figure 9-16).

Figure 9-16. *Copyleft arose as a strong counter to the dominant copyright regimes.*

Copyleft is a form of licensing and can be used to modify copyrights for works such as computer software, documents, music, and art. In general, copyright law allows an author to prohibit others from reproducing, adapting, or distributing copies of the author's work. In contrast, an author may, through a copyleft licensing scheme, give every person who receives a copy of a work permission to reproduce, adapt, or distribute the work as long as any resulting copies or adaptations are also bound by the same copyleft license. A widely used and originating copyleft license is the GNU General Public License. Similar licenses are available through Creative Commons Share Alike.

Copyleft licenses are sometimes referred to as *viral copyright licenses*, because any works derived from a copyleft work must themselves be copyleft when distributed.

Copyleft is considered "strong" when its provisions can be imposed on derived works, and weak when not all derived works inherit the copyleft license.

Sources

Gratis vs. Libre, *http://en.wikipedia.org/wiki/Gratis_versus_libre*

What is Copyleft?, Free Software Foundation, *http://www.fsf.org/licensing/essays/copyleft. html*

Copyright

Copyright is a form of intellectual property that gives the creator of an original work exclusive rights for a certain time period after which time the work is said to enter the public domain (see "Public Domain" on page 255). These rights include publication, distribution, and adaptation. Copyright covers published and unpublished literary, scientific, and artistic works, whatever the form of expression, provided that such works are fixed in a tangible or material form.

"Copyright" literally means the right to copy.

Internationally, copyright has been somewhat standardized, lasting between 50 to 100 years from the author's death, or a finite period for anonymous or corporate authorship, but there are no "international copyrights" that enable you to protect your work throughout the world (Figure 9-17).

Figure 9-17. *Copyright laws vary from country to country, but have their history in trying to balance the rights of creators against those of the wider community, in the interests of preserving cultural legacy.*

Most countries are signatories of the Berne Convention and the Universal Copyright Convention (UCC), which allow you to protect your works in countries of which you are not a citizen or national. The 1886 Berne Convention first established recognition of copyrights among sovereign nations, rather than merely bilaterally. Under the Berne Convention, copyrights for creative works do not have to be asserted or declared, as they are automatically in force at creation.

"Fair use" is a doctrine in United States copyright law that allows limited use of copyrighted material without requiring permission from the rights holders, such as use for scholarship or review.

Sources

Copyright entry at Wikipedia, *http://en.wikipedia.org/wiki/Copyright*

U.S. Copyright Office, *http://www.copyright.gov/*

What is Copyright Protection?, *http://www.whatiscopyright.org/*

Further Reading

Blog Design Solutions, by David Powers, Phil Sherry, Andy Budd, Simon Collison, John Oxton, Richard Rutter, Chris J. Davis, and Michael Heilemann; friends of ED, 2006

Copyright FAQ, *http://www.copyright.gov/help/faq/*

More about Creative Commons, *http://creativecommons.org/*

"My 140conf Talk: Twitter as Publishing," by Tim O'Reilly, O'Reilly Radar

Chapter 10

Long-Time Listener, First-Time Caller

> *Flatter me, and I may not believe you. Criticize me, and I may not like you.*
> *Ignore me, and I may not forgive you. Encourage me, and I will not forget*
> *you. Love me, and I may be forced to love you.*
>
> —William Arthur Ward

Soliciting Feedback

Soliciting feedback from people, no matter the form, is one of the easiest ways to engage your community. After all, everyone has an opinion. Giving feedback is also considered one of the lowest barriers to entry for user engagement and is often the first step on the ladder of user participation.

User ratings are potentially the easiest item to add to a site to gather user opinions and can start a user down the participation road. Additionally, as you build up the engine around ratings, the information can be used to understand your users and create more value for them through recommendations (see "Recommendations" on page 340) and other socially driven features. Amazon has been quite successful at this, using purchasing behavior and ratings to infer which new products might be interesting to the purchaser.

Finally, leaving comments (which is the first step in having a user-to-user conversation about an item), giving feedback, and reviewing an item are all activities that will potentially grab your user for longer-term activity. Each of these encourages registration and repeat visitation. These patterns can be combined with one of the rating styles and tagging to create a robust suite of user opinion around original or user-generated content.

Vote to Promote

What

The user wants to promote a particular piece of content in a community pool of submissions. This promotion takes the form of a vote for that item, and items with more votes rise in the rankings to be displayed with more prominence (Figure 10-1).

Figure 10-1. *Yahoo! Buzz uses a button labeled "Buzz up!" to promote items in popularity.*

Use when

Use this pattern when:

- Users in the community have the ability to submit content to a "pool" of resources.

- Some democratic form of judgment is needed, to allow the community to compare the subjective quality of one submission to another.

- A sizeable-enough community is required. Ideally, popular submissions in the pool should receive significantly more votes (dozens, hundreds?) than unpopular ones, in order to make comparisons meaningful.

How

Provide a voting mechanism, attached to each candidate item in the community pool. Clicking this mechanism counts as a vote in favor of that item's promotion:

- User gets only one vote per item.

- Display a user's vote back to him, so he can tell what he's voted for.

- Users may change their votes after they are cast.

Highlight popular items:

- Display them on the property's main page.

- Display them first in search results.

- Prominently display the number of votes that an item has received.

Try to ensure that users are voting on items that they have actually consumed (read, watched, listened to):

- On article pages, place vote controls after the article.
- Consider withholding the vote mechanism on high-level listing pages. Make readers click down to an article page before voting.
- Provide a standalone voting mechanism that third-party publishers can include on destination sites.

Items with fewer votes are not punished for their lack of popularity; they merely fall into obscurity, and disappear into the long tail of the popularity-ranked pool.

You may want to consider a moderation control that lets the community decide to remove an item altogether, but don't make this control prominent. The emphasis for this pattern is on promoting the good, not punishing the bad. You should downplay the down-vote.

Why

This pattern has come to popularity recently (most notably on the link-popularity sites Digg, Reddit, and Newsvine, among others). Such systems for collective choice are a good way to promote community participation, and provide a low-cost means for surfacing popular content. Note, however, that popular content does not necessarily equate to quality content, so no promises of content quality should be made.

Special considerations

Community voting systems do present a number of challenges, but particularly the possibility that members of the community may try to game the system, out of any number of motivations:

Malice
Perhaps against another member of the community and that member's contributions

Gain
To realize some reward, monetary or otherwise, from influencing the placement of certain items in the pool

An overarching agenda
Always promoting certain viewpoints or political statements, with little regard for the actual quality of the content being voted for

There are a number of ways to attempt to safeguard against this type of abuse, though nothing can stop gaming altogether. Here are some ways to minimize or hinder abusers in their efforts:

- Vote for things, not people. In keeping with Yahoo!'s general strategy, don't offer users the ability to directly vote on another user: their looks, their likeability, intelligence, or anything else. It's OK for the community to vote on a person's contributions, but not on the quality of her character.

- Consider rate-limiting of votes:
    - Allow the user only a certain number of votes within a given time period.
    - Limit the number of times (or the rate at which) a user votes down a particular user's content (to prevent ad-hominem attacks).

- Weigh other factors besides just the number of votes. Digg, for instance, does not calculate its Digg-score solely on the number of votes a submission receives. Its algorithm also considers "story source (is it a blog repost, or the original story?), user history, traffic levels of the category the story falls under, and user reports." It updates this algorithm frequently. Consider keeping the exact algorithm a secret from the community, or discuss the factored inputs only in general terms.

- If relationship information is available, consider weighting user votes accordingly. Perhaps prohibit users with formal relationships from voting for each other's submissions.

This is currently a popular pattern on the Web, but it is important to consider the contexts in which we use it. Very active and popular communities (Digg is an excellent example) that enable community voting can also engender a certain negativity of spirit (mean comments, opinionated cliques, group attacks on "outlier" viewpoints).

Related patterns

"Ratings (Stars or 1–5)" on page 274

"Reviews" on page 280

"Thumbs Up/Down Ratings" on page 269

Sources

Yahoo!'s Platform design team, the Yahoo! Pattern Library

As seen on

Digg (*http://www.digg.com*)

Yahoo! Buzz (*http://buzz.yahoo.com*)

Thumbs Up/Down Ratings

What

A user wants to express a like/dislike (love/hate) type of opinion about an object (person, place, or thing) he is consuming, reading, or experiencing (Figure 10-2).

Figure 10-2. *Pandora lets users rate songs with a thumbs-up/-down style of rating.*

Use when

- Use when you want to provide the ability to quickly grab a user's opinion on an object.
- Use as an easy, fun way to begin engaging users in the community.
- Use when polarized opinions are more appropriate for the experience than degrees of opinion.

How

Dos and don'ts

Do consider thumb ratings when opinions about a rated asset will tend to be strongly polarized. For example, if you can state the question simply as, "Did you like this, or did you not?", then thumbs may be appropriate. If it seems more natural to state the question as, "How much did you like this?", then star ratings are probably more appropriate. Do consider using thumb ratings for developing personalized recommendations.

For example, Pandora uses declared music interests to create a personalized playlist of songs that are similar in style, and then uses the thumbs-up rating on a song to add more songs like this to the music stream and a thumbs down to remove that song from the music stream (Figures 10-3 and 10-4).

Figure 10-3. *Thumbs-up action on Pandora.*

Figure 10-4. *Thumbs-down action on Pandora.*

The benefit of rating is expressed to the user by instantly stopping the play of the song and giving feedback that Pandora will never play that song again on that station (Figure 10-5).

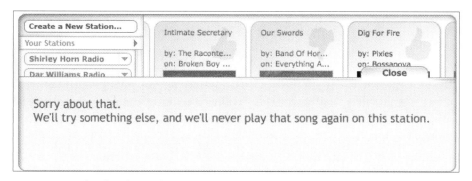

Figure 10-5. *Pandora lets the user know what a thumbs-down action means.*

Don't consider thumbs for rating multiple facets of an asset. For example, don't provide multiple thumbs widgets for a product review intended to register a user's satisfaction with that product's price, quality, design, and features. Generally, thumbs should be associated with an asset in a one-to-one relationship: one asset gets one thumb up or down. (After all, Emperor Nero would never let a gladiator's arm survive but put his leg to death! Think of thumbs as "all or nothing.")

Do use thumb ratings when a fun, lightweight ratings mechanism is desired. The context for these ratings should be appropriately fun and light-hearted as well.

Don't use thumb ratings when you want to provide qualitative data comparisons between assets. For example, in a long listing of DVDs available for rental, you may want to permit sorting of the list by rating. If you provide thumb ratings, this sort would have very little practical utility for the user. Instead, you should consider a scalar, 5-star rating style.

Recommendations

- Place the thumb rating widget in close proximity to the asset being rated (Figure 10-6).

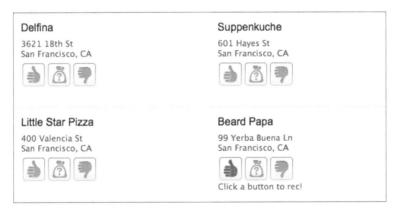

Figure 10-6. *GoodRec places the thumbs-up/-down mechanism right under the name and location of the restaurant.*

- Make sure the rating widget is secondary in prominence to the primary call to action, unless rating is the primary task (Figure 10-7). For example, in a shopping context, it is probably appropriate to keep "Add to Cart" for an item as the predominant call to action, with "Rate This" being less noticeable.

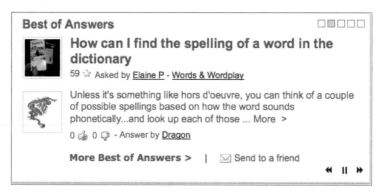

Figure 10-7. *Reading the Question and Answer and clicking through to read all the answers or add an answer are the primary actions on Yahoo! Answers. Thumbs-up/-down rating is lower in the visual hierarchy through size and placement.*

- Be consistent in the treatment of the imagery used for thumbs across the site (or group of sites if applicable).

- Indicate to the user whether or not he has previously rated the item.

- If possible, refresh the widget inline as a user votes and clearly indicate what was selected.

- Allow the user to change his vote at any time.

- Present community consensus tallies as whole numbers rather than percentages for simplicity and ease of understanding.

- Consider highlighting items that have reached a certain level of positive votes over a long amount of time from a large amount of people.

- Be cautious about promoting the lowest-rated or least-favored items, as the negativity can appear insensitive or rude.

Considerations

Vote counts: Why not percentages?

Percentage comparisons between two or more rated items are problematic, due to response liquidity: when there are few ratings (as there will be, initially, for any rated item), small differences of opinion can yield big perceived differences in rating.

For example, if two out of three users give Movie A a thumbs down, it appears that community consensus is 66% negative, which is technically accurate, but may not represent an accurate picture of the tastes of the larger community. Really, two out of three votes just doesn't count for much.

However, if 666 out of 1,000 users slam Movie B (expressed as a percentage, also 66%), then that probably is a significant indicator of the larger community's opinion about that item.

When viewing Movie A alongside Movie B in a feature on "Hot Movies Opening This Weekend," it's misleading to represent their approval ratios as percentages. Better to just give our users the numbers (how many positive, how many negative, and how many overall) and let them figure it out.

Note that this is not the ideal situation, which is why we recommend that any context that relies on heavy data comparisons (e.g., the ability to sort, filter, or promote content based on ratings) may not be an appropriate use of thumb-style ratings.

Also note that this "liquidity problem" is not unique to thumb ratings. It is, in fact, a well-known factor in economics (*http://en.wikipedia.org/wiki/Liquidity*).

Thumbs up only

Use a thumbs-up-only type rating only when you don't want negative ratings to appear insensitive or inappropriate, such as rating a person.

A thumbs-up, positive-only variation may be contextually appropriate for the assets that you want people to rate. If you strongly suspect that opinions about a type of asset will concentrate toward the positive pole of opinion (consistently), then offer them only that option.

A thumbs-up-only option allows users to easily participate with a "Me, too" or "I agree" opinion.

A thumbs-up, positive-only variation may be more culturally appropriate to present. In some cultures it is deemed less-than-appropriate to express a strong negative opinion about something. (And remember, thumb ratings are recommended for contexts in which opinions are strongly polarized.) For these locales, it may be preferable to provide positive-only opinions, and just let the absence of a rating connote a negative opinion.

International considerations

The concept of thumb ratings can be problematic for some locales.

First, the symbolism of an extended and raised thumb is problematic: in some locales, it is considered an insult; in other locales, representations of any body part (especially disembodied ones) are considered offensive; and, finally, some locales will just not "get it."

Second, the very notion of a binary, black-or-white, love-it-or-hate-it ratings system may not be a natural fit for some cultures. Many locales have stated a preference for "shades of gray" in a polarized scale. (Note this is subtly different from star ratings, which imply "I like it exactly this much.")

Third, in some areas it is considered rude to criticize things openly. In this instance, consider the thumbs-up-only variation.

Why

The benefit to other users with thumbs-up/-down style ratings is that these ratings, when assessed in aggregate, can quickly give a sense of the community's opinion of a rated object. They may also be helpful for drawing quick qualitative comparisons between like items (this is better than that), but this is of secondary importance with this rating type.

Related patterns

"Ratings (Stars or 1–5)" on page 274

"Vote to Promote" on page 266

Sources

From the work of Bryce Glass and the Yahoo! Social Platform team

As seen on

Pandora (*http://www.pandora.com*)

TiVo (*http://www.tivo.com/*)

Yahoo! Answers (*http://answers.yahoo.com*)

Ratings (Stars or 1–5)

What

A user wants to quickly leave her opinion on an object, with minimal interruption to any other task flow she is involved in (Figure 10-8).

Figure 10-8. *Rating widget on Yahoo! Local.*

Use when

- Use this pattern when the user wants to leave an opinion quickly.
- Use in combination with reviews for a richer experience.
- Use to quickly tap into the existing "community" of a product.
- Use when ratings are collected together to present an average rating of an object from the collective user set.

How

- Show clickable items (stars are used most often) that light up on rollover to infer clickability.
- Initial state should be "empty" and show invitational text above to invite the user to rate the object (e.g., "Rate It!").
- As the mouse cursor moves over the icons, indicate the level of rating (through a color change) and display a text description of the rating at each point (e.g., "Excellent").
- Once the user has clicked the rating (fifth star, third star, etc.), the rating should be saved and added to the average rating, which should be displayed separately.
- The saved rating should be indicated with a change in final color of the items and a text indication that the rating is saved.
- An aggregate or average rating should also be displayed.
- Users should be able to change their ratings later if they change their mind.

Considerations

Consideration should be made for presenting the call to action for a rating if a user is not logged in.

Labels are important because they help the user decide which rating to select and how that compares to the average.

Why

Rating an object provides a lightweight model for user engagement. Ratings are often tied with reviews to encourage richer user contributions and activity.

Accessibility

Use DHTML and CSS for displaying the rollover states and for instant collection of the rating. In cases where this is not possible, a Save Rating button may be added to confirm the final selection of the rating.

Related patterns

"Reviews" on page 280

"Vote to Promote" on page 266

Sources

Yahoo! Pattern Library and the Yahoo! Platform design team

As seen on

Amazon.com (*http://www.amazon.com*)

Yahoo! Local (*http://local.yahoo.com*)

Yahoo! Shopping (*http://shopping.yahoo.com*)

The Lifespan of Content and What Should Be Rateable

What type of items are rateable?

Items that should be rateable by the community share some common traits.

Rateable items should have some intrinsic value.

We should never ask users to provide metadata (basically "add value") to an item whose own apparent value is low. Or, more specifically, we should be careful to only ask for user participation in a way that acknowledges an item's intrinsic value: it might be OK to ask someone to give a thumbs-up rating to someone else's blog comment (because the "cost" to do so is low, basically a click), but it would be inappropriate to ask for a full-blown review of the comment. There would be more effort and thought involved in writing the review than there was in the initial comment!

—continued—

The Lifespan of Content and What Should Be Rateable

Rateable items should persist for some length of time.

Rateable items must remain in the "community pool" long enough for all members of the community to cast their votes. There's also little use in asking for a bunch of metadata for an item if others cannot come along afterward and enjoy the benefit of that metadata (Figure 10-9).

Figure 10-9. *The content-lifespan spectrum.*

A rateable item's lifespan

Highly ephemeral items, such as News articles that disappear after 48 or 72 hours, probably aren't good candidates for rating.

Juxtapose this with TiVo (which is kind of the canonical example) where thumbs (up and down) are used to rate TV shows for recommendation purposes. The programs being rated have high value (i.e., they cost money to produce, and we get entertainment value out of them), and they're highly persistent (they'll recur at the same time next week, and in reruns, and in syndication, etc. etc.; for all intents and purposes, TV episodes are immortal). And TiVo's whole user experience (including user-education movies that ship with the unit, its printed manual, and, heck, the dang remote has 'em hardcoded on there) is oriented around the thumbs-up and -down voting. I'd venture that thumb-voting and the recommender system are a huge part of why many people buy TiVo in the first place. (OK, that plus "pause live TV.")

Items with a great deal of persistence (on the extreme end are real-world establishments, such as restaurants or businesses) make excellent candidates for rateability. Furthermore, the types of ratings we can ask for may be more involved. Because these establishments will persist, we can be reasonably sure that others will always come along afterward and benefit from the work that the community has put into the item.

When it comes to explicitly input recommender systems, we should acknowledge the limitations of folks' interest in "feeding the machine." If they understand the benefit, and they think that the work they'll put in will at some point be worth something to them, then folks will play along.

—Bryce Glass, coauthor,
Building Web Reputation Systems
(http://buildingreputation.com)

Comments

What

A user has a comment or opinion about an item she is viewing on the site and wants to share it (Figure 10-10).

Figure 10-10. *Flickr comment field associated with the asset a user is viewing.*

Use this pattern when:

- You want comments associated with an object (place, person, thing) on your site.
- You want to allow users to express an opinion in relation to an article or blog post or begin a public conversation.

- Provide a text entry field for the comment that is large enough for several lines of text.
- Associate the comment field in close proximity to the item (image, article, blog post) that is being commented on.
- Ask for an identifier in order to attribute the comment (username or nickname).
- Provide a method for anonymous commenting, through either a drop-down selection or by allowing the user to leave the identifier blank and then automatically noting that as anonymous.
- If the user is already registered in the system, then autofill the attribution field.
- Link the user attribution to the user's site profile. If there is no profile system, allow the name to be linked to a website entered by the user (see "Attribution" on page 113).
- To reduce spambots, present some type of validation option (captcha, image captcha, etc.) that only a real person can answer.
- To further cut down on spambots, require user registration before a comment can be left on the site. Use this as an opportunity for progressive registration (see "Sign-up or Registration" on page 45).
- Consider some community moderation to filter out trolls, spam, and other bad participants who post spam or illegal or hateful comments (see "Group Moderation" on page 391).
    - Make sure that the community Terms of Service and rules of conduct are clearly articulated for users in advance.
    - When comments are removed, be clear about the reason and make sure it falls within the guidelines for the site.
    - Don't remove comments just because you disagree with them. Dissent and opposing opinions make for a lively discussion.
    - Don't be afraid to ban someone and shut down his account if he is continually abusive and inappropriate. However, this action should only come after an appropriate warning had been issued.

  – Consider utilizing the technique of disemvoweling (*http://en.wikipedia.org/wiki/ Disemvoweling*) to censor unwanted comments or spam without having to actually delete the posts or comments. By using the practice in public, the site sends a message that this behavior is unacceptable, and the bad apple looks stupid.

Why

Comments are an easy way to allow user participation on your site and can be a conduit for multiuser conversation. Comments associated with an item give context to the conversations and the participation.

Related patterns

"Reviews" on page 280

As seen on

The New York Times (*http://www.nytimes.com/2008/12/08/opinion/08kristol.html?ref=opinion*)

Most blogs, including those using Blogger (*http://blogsofnote.blogspot.com/*), WordPress (*http://wordpress.com/*), TypePad (*http://www.typepad.com/*), Moveable Type (*http://www.movabletype.org/*), and other blogging tools

Reviews

What

A user wants to share her opinion with others about an object (place, person, thing) in greater detail than a simple rating or comment (Figure 10-11).

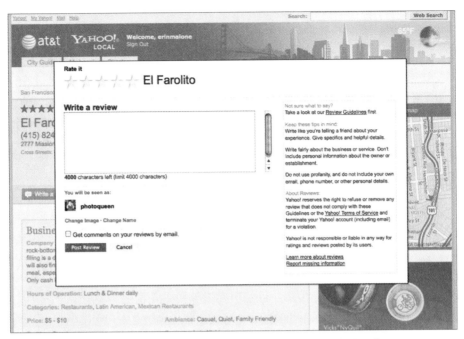

Figure 10-11. *Review form on Yahoo! Local for a restaurant. Note the tips for how best to write a review on the right of the screen.*

Use when

Use this pattern when:

- A user wants to write a review of an object.

- You want to supplement the content of a product/website with user-generated reviews.

- You are also using the "Rating an Object" pattern (see "Ratings (Stars or 1–5)" on page 274). Combined, they will help to obtain better review feedback.

- You are also using reputation rankings (for encouraging quality user-generated content).

How

- Provide contextually relevant links that allow the user to initiate the process of writing a review.

- Provide a clear call to action in your text, like "Write a Review" (Figure 10-12).

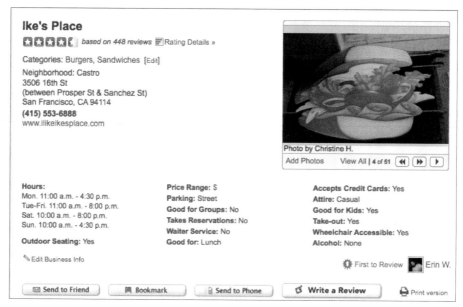

Figure 10-12. *Yelp uses a slightly larger button in a brighter color (red) for the "Write a Review" call to action.*

- Include the following five fundamentals in the review form:
    - Ability to input a user's quantitative (rating) assessment
    - Field to enter the user's qualitative (review) assessment of the object
    - Guidelines for helping the user write a review
    - Any legal disclaimers
    - User identity, most often a required field or pre populated if the user is signed in
- Clearly indicate which fields are required.
- Organize the fields to be most conducive to completing the review, rather than exactly how they will appear when published.
- Utilize maximum and minimum character restrictions on fields to encourage the desired field length (short and concise versus narrative).
- After the user has completed her review, allow the options of submitting (primary call to action), previewing, or canceling it.
- If the user submits the review and has filled out the required fields, consider showing a confirmation page or message.
- Set expectations regarding when the review will be published.
- Provide a clear path back to the review's initiation point.

- Provide additional, relevant objects for review if possible.
- Provide appropriate in-line error messaging on the review form if required fields are not filled.
- If a user previews the review, display how it will appear when published, and then allow the user to either edit or submit his review.
- If a user cancels a review, return him to the review's initiation point.

Accessibility

- Allow the user to move through the fields by pressing the Tab key.
- Allow the user to submit the review by pressing the Enter key.

Why

Qualitative fields such as Pros and Cons seem to be easier for users to create than a full narrative. They do not need to think in complete sentences, and they have more specific direction regarding what to write (positives and negatives). Additionally, readers find them easier to scan than a narrative.

Related patterns

"Ratings (Stars or 1–5)" on page 274

Sources

The Yahoo! Pattern Library

As seen on

Yahoo! Local (*http://local.yahoo.com*)

Yahoo! Shopping (*http://shopping.yahoo.com*)

Yelp (*http://www.yelp.com*)

Soliciting Feedback

What

The site owners want to be able to collect feedback about the site from its users (Figure 10-13).

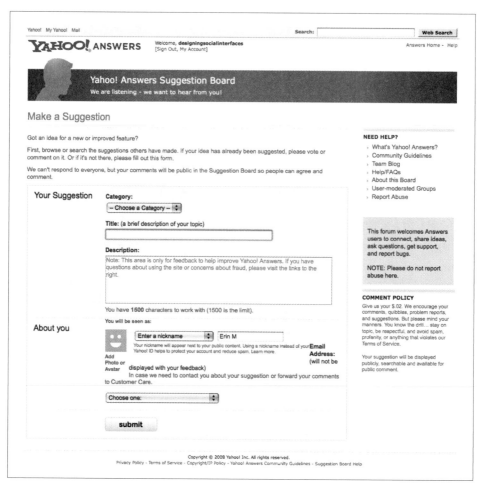

Figure 10-13. *Yahoo! Answers has a robust suggestion board that allows users to give feedback on the product.*

Use when

Use this pattern when:

- You need a mechanism to collect user feedback about your site or service.

- You want to capture feature improvements or new feature ideas.

- You want to better understand your users and how they interact with your site.

How

- Provide a clear "Give Feedback" or "Leave Feedback" call to action (Figure 10-14).

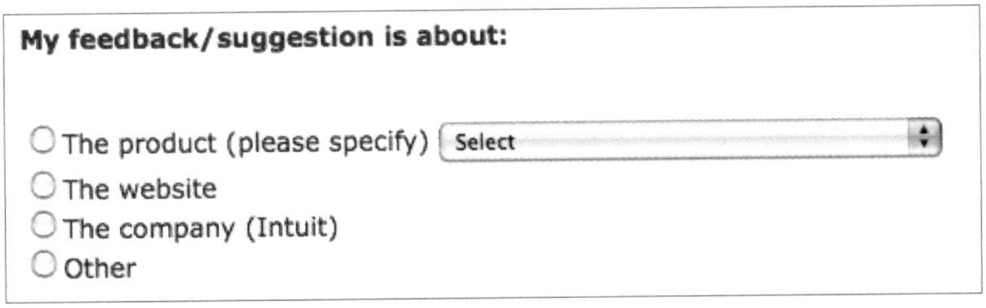

My feedback/suggestion is about:

○ The product (please specify) [Select ▾]
○ The website
○ The company (Intuit)
○ Other

Figure 10-14. *Allow the user to scope what the feedback may be about. This can be done through a drop-down selection or radio button selection.*

On many sites, the feedback link is relegated to the footer of the site. This means that only the most tenacious people end up finding the link. If you are actively soliciting feedback, consider a different placement (Figure 10-15).

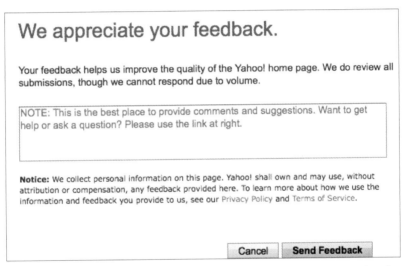

Figure 10-15. *When the link is global, if possible, glean from the context of the page under what scope the user may want the feedback to be classified as a default. For example, the feedback link on the Yahoo! home page is specific to that page, and the text on the page refers to the scope being just the Yahoo! home page.*

- Provide a free-form field for the user to write out and explain her feedback.

- Be clear about the intent of the feedback form. If no one associated with Customer Support or Help will ever see this information, say so, and give the user an opportunity to access help.

- Provide a way for the user to identify himself. This is especially important if the feedback is presented in a public forum.

- Allow the user to select a method for a company representative to get in touch. Keep that contact information private.

- Consider aggregating all user suggestions together and letting users browse through the comments, feedback, and suggestions of the community.

- Consider allowing users to rate other people's suggestions. The highest-rated feedback can be used to help inform new features and prioritize product improvements (Figure 10-16).

Figure 10-16. *User suggestions for ReadWriteWeb, which uses the service UserVoice for feedback, are ordered based on community voting and then later used to inform new features.*

- If the feedback or suggestion is really a bug or a help question, allow the user to filter scope in the interface, and then behind the scenes send the request, help, or bug to the right people in the organization. If a user knows that someone is listening to a channel, she will use that channel for all her issues, regardless of your intent or labeling.

Considerations

Providing a feedback mechanism for your site, whether you build it yourself or use a third-party service, requires a commitment on your part.

If you build the feedback mechanism yourself, you need to create a system to filter the feedback into a few buckets for action. Feature requests should be separated from bugs. Bugs need to be triaged and compared against an existing list of bugs. Acknowledgment of the feedback should happen in some form so that users know they aren't speaking into a black hole.

When you create your own system, you own everything and can adjust and manage the flow as time and people permit, but the support of this part of the software can often take an amount of effort that may not have been anticipated.

Leaving your feedback system to a third party, such as Get Satisfaction, still requires manpower to filter and engage with the community, but the management of the operations of the system is covered. On the other hand, any changes to the system are out of your control, and the feedback site is not integrated with your service.

Either way has issues and benefits and should be weighed against staffing, operational costs, and long-term goals.

Why

Allowing your users to give feedback and suggestions gives them a sense of ownership over the site. If the site is extremely social and houses a person's online identity (see Chapter 4), then users already have a sense of ownership for the site. They are using the site frequently and most likely in ways that you had never predicted. Tap into that passion.

Tapping into the community is a way to gather new ideas for improvements and future features, and can give insight into how your users perceive the site experience and your brand.

As seen on

Get Satisfaction (*http://www.getsatisfaction.com*)

UserVoice (*http://www.uservoice.com*)

Yahoo! Answers (*http://answers.yahoo.com*)

Yelp (*http://www.yelp.com*)

Further Reading

"The Digg Effect," ReadWriteWeb, December 6, 2007, *http://www.readwriteweb.com/archives/the_digg_effect.php*

"Revenge of the Know-It-Alls: Inside the Web's free-advice revolution," by Mark Frauenfelder, *Wired Magazine*, July 2000, *http://www.wired.com/wired/archive/8.07/egoboo.html*

Satisfied Customers Tell Three Friends, Angry Customers Tell 3,000: Running a Business in Today's Consumer-Driven World, by Pete Blackshaw, Broadway Business 2008

Chapter 11

Watson, Come Quick!

The great secret of succeeding in conversation is to admire little, to hear much; always to distrust our own reason, and sometimes that of our friends; never to pretend to wit, but to make that of others appear as much as possibly we can; to hearken.

—Benjamin Franklin

There are several different types of communication that can be utilized among users, and these should be considered when putting together the tools for enabling a social site. Each has its strengths and its specific kind of behaviors.

One-to-many, or broadcast, communications—blogs, video blogs, microblogs—offer users the opportunity to author and publish. The author is presenting her opinion about something, an article read, new music to hear, thoughts about a specific topic, or recent activity status. There is no expectation of conversation, but adding comments and tools such as Twitter replies creates an opportunity for indirect conversations to take place.

Many-to-many communications—message boards and forums, listservs, chat—allow multiple people to discuss multiple topics, usually bound by a parent topic. Anyone can start a conversation, and everyone can read it and participate. These are often public, but listservs generally require membership to participate.

One-to-one communication—instant messages, Twitter direct messages, Skype—provides communication between two people (or a small group), usually in real time and often in private.

Meaning-Making Machines

Grandma Powazek once told me why she stopped making cucumber salad. She'd been chopping cucumbers when her hands started to hurt. She thought the cucumbers caused the pain.

It's logical, of course. Her hands hurt when she was chopping, and felt better when they weren't. It's also completely wrong. Her hands hurt because she was developing arthritis. But no amount of lecturing from my dad could change her mind.

In Yiddish this is called **bubbe maisse**, literally "mother stories," but we all do it.

Our brains take a ton of input and turn it into narrative stories to help us understand the world. Imagine your brain sitting in a movie theater, watching the flashing screen. It takes those separate images and creates a story around them, just like you're taking these individual words and turning them into something more than a string of definitions.

What's interesting is that if you take away some of that input, our brains work twice as hard to fill in the gaps. In one of my favorite episodes of Radiolab (a podcast aired on NPR), the hosts talk to fighter pilots who have had out-of-body experiences (*http://www.wnyc.org/shows/radiolab/episodes/2006/05/05/segments/59026*) and find that, when the brain is deprived of input, it can create elaborate virtual realities on its own.

This is relevant online because we have much less input than in real-life social situations. Virtual communications such as email, blog comments, and instant messages come without the associated social data our brains are used to. In the absence of context, our brains fill in the rest. What we fill it in **with** is a byproduct of our own insecurities.

In the October 2008 edition of **Science**, a researcher named Jennifer Whitson published a study called "Lacking Control Increases Illusory Pattern Perception" (*http://www.sciencemag.org/cgi/content/abstract/sci;322/5898/115*). She did an experiment with two groups that were given a test. The "powerless" group members were told that their answers were half right, half wrong, no matter what they said. The "in-control" group members were told that their answers were right.

Both groups were then shown a series of images of random static. Here's the interesting part: the people in the "powerless" group were more likely to see images in the static—to find meaning in chaos—than the people in the "in-control" group. So, while all our brains are meaning-making machines, the results of this study show that stressed-out brains work harder to find meaning. They literally see things that are not there.

I think this is fascinating because it begins to explain the old question: why do normal people become jerks online? Sure, people are more likely to act out when they think they're not being watched, and the screen contributes to that. But why is that so? Maybe it's because their brains are working harder to create meaning in the online chaos, and the meaning their stressed-out brains see is one where they're justified in lashing out. After all, every child's first excuse for a fight is to insist that the other kid started it.

All of this is just biology. You can't tell a person that what he's seeing or feeling is not real and expect him to believe you. So what to do? The NPR story on Whitson's study contained this juicy bit at the end:

—continued—

Meaning-Making Machines

"In a different experiment, she asked volunteers who were feeling a lack of control to talk about a personal value that they consider important. When these people were shown fuzzy, meaningless images, they did not see imaginary objects. Maybe this could help in real life, Whitson says. When you're feeling powerless, maybe you should stop and think about what you really care about—something you do have control over."

In addition to being a great tip for individuals, this is something community designers should think about. How can the interfaces we create to collect community participation give the user an "in-control" feeling? If they did, I believe the user's participation would be more positive.

Everything we experience in life is a story we tell ourselves. As a creator of, or participant in, online community, remember that you're much more in control of your story than it sometimes seems.

(This essay was originally published at *http://powazek.com/posts/1263* on October 4, 2008.)

—Derek Powazek, Community Media Maven

Synchronous Versus Asynchronous Communication

Thinking about time as part of designing conversation systems is a critical consideration when deciding what type of communication tool to add to your social framework. Public conversations in forums and streams (Twitter, for example) are often asynchronous and take place over extended periods of time. Individuals can be online at different times, participating in the conversation when it is convenient. Comments on a blog post that all refer to a single starting object are generally very easy to follow and can drift in and out of activity over a long period of time. These types of conversations might benefit from threading or other tools to help users follow the conversation. This adds complexity for the system as well as for end users, but it can aid in following the conversation across multiple users. Many of these types of conversations are public. The real-time conversations in instant messaging tools are synchronous and rely on all participants being present and engaged at the same time. These types of conversations can be followed easily because the conversation is happening in real time and is usually between a small number of participants. These conversations are often private.

Sign In to Participate

Most communication and activity tools in social contexts require signup before participating (see "Sign-up or Registration" on page 45 and "Sign-In Continuity" on page 54). This serves multiple purposes. Users trade something of value for the privilege of participating. Registration information is used for monetization and advertising by site creators. Additionally, requiring sign-in lets site owners save the contributions of each user. Without the registration information associated with the user, the user's participation is lost once the session ends. Finally, having an account associated with a particular username helps build a reputation based on that participation and allows others to form an opinion about that user and his contributions.

Communicating

Forums

What

A user wants to participate in a discussion with other people on a focused topic (Figure 11-1).

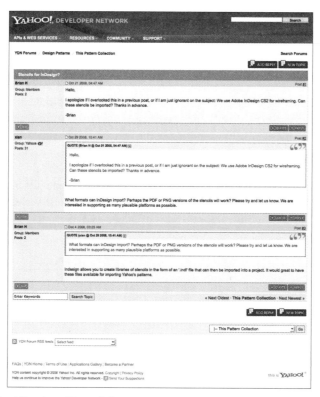

Figure 11-1. *Yahoo! Developer Network forums.*

Use when

Use this pattern when:

- You want to allow users to create topics for discussion.
- You want to give users the opportunity to respond to those topics.
- You want to allow users to respond to other users' responses.

How

- Consider pre seeding topics for discussion on sites that have a specific context.
- Allow users to create new topics for discussion.
- Provide a clear call to action for posting a message within a topic.
- Provide a clear call to action for posting a reply to a message (Figure 11-2).

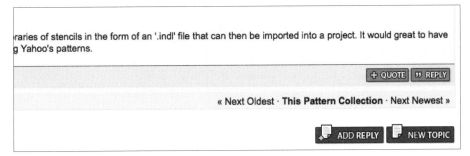

Figure 11-2. *Large buttons provide the call to action for adding a reply to the current message or adding a new topic to the forums.*

- Clearly indicate if there is a character limit in the reply or topic fields.
- Allow the user to preview before posting.
- Time- and datestamp posts and topic creations.
- Present attribution with each message and link the username to that person's public profile (see "Attribution" on page 113 and "Profile" on page 86).
- Indicate if the poster is an "official" representative of the site, as in Figure 11-3 (see "Norms" on page 384 and "Role Model" on page 388).

Figure 11-3. *Yahoo! Developer Network forums indicate Yahoo! employees with a small Y! icon near the username.*

- Allow users to edit their own posts in case of errors and typos. Indicate that the post has been edited with a time-/datestamp indicating an edit.

- Consider indicating presence as part of the attribution (see "Attribution" on page 113) for posts, as in Figure 11-4. If sharing presence, allow users to communicate in real time via a chat or IM mechanism.

Figure 11-4. *Yahoo! Finance message boards indicate whether a message poster is currently online.*

- Indicate when a topic is new.

- Indicate when a topic is hot.

- Allow topics and posts in public forums to be crawled and searched via the major search engines.

- Allow users to follow discussions via RSS (Figure 11-5).

Figure 11-5. *Yahoo! Developer Network message boards offers RS feeds of conversations.*

- Present messages in a threaded format so that users can follow a conversation throughout its lifecycle.

Moderation

- Moderate the discussion lists with a light but firm hand. Too much, and people will take their discussion elsewhere; too little, and the community can become fractured, be overrun by trolls, or veer into flame wars and violate legal and ethical norms (see "Community Management" on page 384).

- Allow users to report abuse or inappropriate posts to the moderator or site owner, as shown in Figure 11-6 (see "Report Abuse" on page 394).

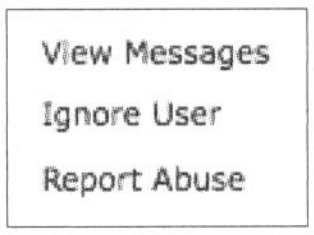

View Messages

Ignore User

Report Abuse

Figure 11-6. *Yahoo! message boards allow users to Ignore User or Report Abuse on every post.*

- Allow the ability for a discussion topic to be closed, and clearly indicate that no more posts will be allowed.

Why

Forums and message boards are a more controlled method for conversations around a topic of interest than comments. Message boards allow multiple topics to be created within the context of a larger topic of interest and can create a rich community on websites.

Related patterns

"Attribution" on page 113

"Comments" on page 278

"Community Management" on page 384

"Groups" on page 376

As seen on

Flickr (*http://www.flickr.com*)

vBulletin (*http://www.vbulletin.com*)

Yahoo! Developer Network (*http://developer.yahoo.com*)

Yahoo! Finance (*http://finance.yahoo.com*)

Public Conversation

People want to have a conversation in a public environment and don't mind others watching or overhearing (Figure 11-7).

Figure 11-7. The conversation on Twitter is primarily public with side conversations between people, much like a cocktail party.

- Use this pattern to create a framework for public conversations.

- Use this pattern to differentiate public from private conversations.

- Allow users to create a dialog among themselves. Provide a framework that is flexible enough to support two or more people in conversation. Clearly indicate through the interface that the conversation is public and can be seen by others.

- Provide people the opportunity to add a comment to a statement, item, or other comments. This creates a conversation in an asynchronous method (Figure 11-8).

Figure 11-8. *Comments on posts or activity allow micro-conversations to happen asynchronously.*

- Provide a form field for text entry. Clearly indicate the character count for conversing. Comments on a blog or a post in a message board generally have a large character limit. Microblogging has set the trend for short character counts. For example, Twitter limits its character entry to 140 (see "Microblogging" on page 138).

- Consider allowing the option for content-free communication. The Phatic Poke, as popularized by Facebook, brings a sense of play and whimsy into the online communication arena and allows one user to let another know that she is thinking about her (Figure 11-9).

> Send Sheila a Message
> Poke Sheila

Figure 11-9. *Poke someone in your network with just a click on Facebook.*

- If the public conversation is around an item (e.g., a photo or news article) or in a site-sponsored forum, periodically moderate to warn against bad behavior or to remove spam.

- If the public conversation is in a personal environment or in a framework specific to the conversation, allow users to self-moderate by letting them delete or edit their own words. Additionally, allow users to block or ignore specific users that they don't want to hear from, without disrupting the flow of conversation to other participants (see "Report Abuse" on page 394).

Why

- Sometimes people want to have conversations in the context of the social situation they are in and don't want to move to email or an offline situation.

- Providing options for public conversations allows the conversation to become the content and a shared activity.

- There will always be lurkers, but open, public conversations are more likely to entice folks who otherwise might not chime in and participate.

Related patterns

"Comments" on page 278

"Forums" on page 292

"Private Conversation" on page 298

As seen on

Facebook (*http://www.facebook.com*)

FriendFeed (*http://www.friendfeed.com*)

Twitter (*http://www.twitter.com*)

Private Conversation

What

People want to have a private conversation in the context of a social or interest-based online situation (Figure 11-10).

Figure 11-10. *Facebook allows you to see who's online when you are visiting the site, and allows you to privately message someone in an instant message chat.*

Use when

Use to create a private environment for people to talk.

How

Allow people to send private messages to each other for both synchronous and asynchronous conversations.

Creating an in-context inbox for private messaging can compound a fractured online identity. Consider allowing users to use their previously set-up email for messaging as an option. But don't break email—let people reply directly from an email message to keep the conversation going.

Younger users are less likely to use email for conversations, so an in-context messaging system may be more appropriate for the younger demographic.

Provide a "nudge" capability. Allow one user to send another a canned message of encouragement or a nudge for more participation or conversation (Figure 11-11).

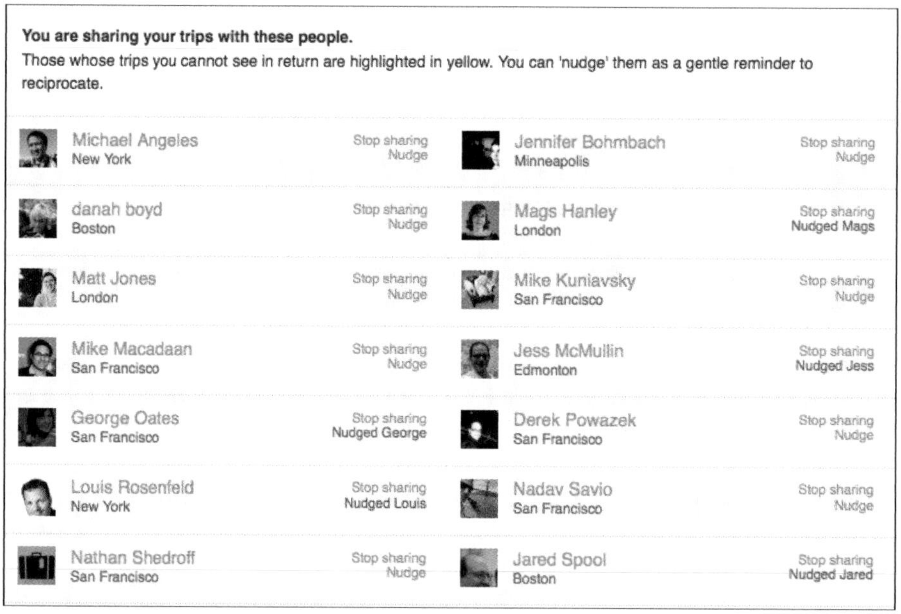

Figure 11-11. *Dopplr provides a simple "Nudge" link for one user to communicate with another in an easy, low-effort way.*

Sometimes just the ability to have a backchannel from the public arena may be all that's needed, rather than a heavy messaging system. Twitter provides the ability for its users to send a direct message to each other within the system (Figure 11-12).

Direct Messages Sent Only to You

cwodtke when I try to phone you I get a MSG you aren't receiving calls now
11:49 AM yesterday

cwodtke heading up now.
11:47 AM yesterday

Figure 11-12. *Twitter allows users to send private messages to each other.*

Consider an inline chat capability when also displaying online presence (see "Availability" on page 127).

Nudging

Providing simple tools for one user to nudge another can get a conversation going, especially if one person is shy or not as confident online as the other (Figure 11-13).

Figure 11-13. *Match.com offers users the ability to wink at someone. Low-effort, low-risk in the stressful arena of online dating.*

Backchannel

A backchannel for a private conversation within a public conversation tool will keep people engaged in the service for longer periods of time.

Twitter's direct message feature allows people to message each other within the same interface as the main one by simply adding the letter D in front of a user's handle.

Why

Sometimes people want to have an "offline" conversation away from the public venue. Giving people tools for private conversations—whether asynchronous (such as email, direct messages, or notes) or synchronous (such as instant messaging)—can help strengthen ties in relationships and increase participation in the social environment.

Related patterns

"Presence Actions and Facets" on page 125

"Public Conversation" on page 296

As seen on

Facebook (*http://www.facebook.com*)

Match.com (*http://www.match.com*)

Twitter (*http://www.twitter.com*)

Group Conversation

What

Multiple people want to have a discussion together about a topic of interest (Figure 11-14).

Figure 11-14. *Yahoo!'s short-lived video chat program allowed groups of people to chat both in text and video.*

Use when

- Use to enable multiple users to converse in real time.
- Use within communication tools to expand the opportunities for conversation.

How

- Show the user a large enough window to keep up with the ongoing conversation.
- Provide a field for the user to enter his thoughts.
- Fields should be flexible, and users should be able to resize them.
- Provide tools for text shortcuts, such as emoticons, to visually impart emotions: laughing, sarcasm, sadness, etc. If possible, show the graphic interpretation of the text symbols.

- Clearly indicate who is saying what. Show the speaker's name and consider showing a timestamp for each part of the conversation.

Private group conversations

- Allow one person to initiate a conversation and invite other participants on the fly (Figure 11-15).

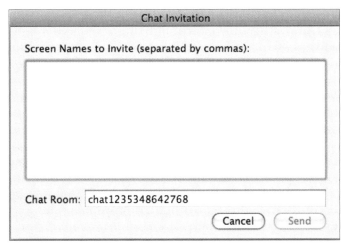

Figure 11-15. *Any user can initiate a group chat in AIM by inviting others from his buddy list.*

- Provide a URL to the group creator so that she can easily invite others into the conversation.
- Provide a list of people for creating group conversations.
- Allow the user to save a transcript of the chat as a text file.

Public group conversations

- Allow users to create public conversation spaces on the fly.
- Provide a search mechanism so the user can easily discover public conversations.
- If the conversation space is initiated by a user, allow her to name the room so that it can be found by others through searching or browsing.
- Allow the space to be stored for later or repeat use.
- Consider promoting or featuring interesting group discussions.

Related patterns

"Groups" on page 376

"Private Conversation" on page 298

"Public Conversation" on page 296

As seen on

Acrobat Connect (*http://www.adobe.com/products/acrobatconnect/*)

AIM (*http://www.aim.com*)

Skype (*http://www.skype.com/*)

WebEx (*http://www.webex.com/*)

Yahoo! Instant Messenger (*http://messenger.yahoo.com*)

Yuuguu (*http://www.yuuguu.com/*)

Arguments

Flame Wars

Flame wars break out when a person responds in a volatile manner to a negative, hostile, or otherwise personal attack against him by another person (usually a *troll*, a person trolling for a reaction). These usually happen in forums or message lists, but can also take place in online chats, in IM, and in comments on an object.

A flamer often starts out espousing an opinion as the only valid opinion on the topic being discussed. The conversation then devolves as others challenge that opinion and the flamer begins making personal attacks.

In most social contexts, flame wars are not welcome and are against the terms of service. The flame war hijacks the conversation away from the majority. In many cases the flame war will die down as the community moderates itself and makes it clear that this kind of behavior is not tolerated. In more extreme cases, a community moderator, site owner, or those who uphold a company's Terms of Service have to be brought in to address the situation. Community moderation can cut a flame war off at the knees by censuring the participants or throwing the participants off the service (see "Community Management" on page 384).

Vendettas

Vendettas can happen within an online community when one person or a group of people takes retaliatory, vengeful, or hostile actions against another person or group of people. Vendettas should be dealt with through community moderation and possibly termination of the offenders' accounts. Vendettas, as with flame wars, can hijack and destroy a community if not dealt with swiftly and firmly.

Sock Puppets

Sock puppets are fake users whose identity is fabricated by another user for the sole purpose of deception in an online space. These fabricated identities, or sock puppets, are often created for the purpose of talking up or praising a product or another person or to support a cause, usually in support of the sock-puppet creator. A *New York Times* article claims that "sock-puppeting" is defined as "the act of creating a fake online identity to praise, defend or create the illusion of support for one's self, allies or company."

Sock puppets, if found out, can be dealt with through community blacklisting or community moderation by the site owners.

Further Reading

"Flame Warriors," by Mike Reed, *http://redwing.hutman.net/~mreed/*

"The Hand That Controls the Sock Puppet Could Get Slapped," by Brad Stone and Matt Richtel, *The New York Times*, July 16, 2007, *http://www.nytimes.com/2007/07/16/technology/16blog.html?ex=1342238400&en=9a3424961f9d2163&ei=5088&partner=rssnyt&emc=rss*

Chapter 12

Barnraising

I still remember the moment I saw a big piece of the future. It was mid-1999, and Dave Winer called to say there was something I had to see.

He showed me a web page. I don't remember what the page contained except for one button. It said, "Edit This Page"—and, for me, nothing was ever the same again.

I clicked the button. Up popped a text box containing plain text and a small amount of HTML, the code that tells a browser how to display a given page. Inside the box I saw the words that had been on the page. I made a small change, clicked another button that said, "Save this page" and voilà, the page was saved with the changes....

Dave was a leader in a move that brought back to life the promise, too long unmet, that Tim Berners-Lee, inventor of the Web, had wanted from the start. Berners-Lee envisioned a read/write Web. But what had emerged in the 1990s was an essentially read-only Web on which you needed an account with an ISP to host your web site, special tools, and/or HTML expertise to create a decent site.

What Dave and the other early blog pioneers did was a breakthrough. They said the Web needed to be writeable, not just readable, and they were determined to make doing so dead simple.

Thus, the read/write Web was truly born again.

—Dan Gillmor, Dave Winer: A Toast,
http://dangillmor.typepad.com/dan_gillmor_on_grassroots/2005/05/dave_winer_a_to.html

Collaboration

The first thing I put on the Web was personal: a story (*http://ezone.org/no/bird.html*). The next thing I made was collaborative: a magazine (*http://ezone.org*). This was 1994. We knew we wanted to engage newcomers more fully than the traditional letters to the editor, and many of the letters (and email messages) we received at the time were submissions. People wanted to work with us and we wanted to work with them, and they came from all over the world. We managed for four years with no system in place besides a series of personal understandings, but any form of collaboration requires some form of orchestration, and our ad-hoc approach didn't scale.

In the earliest days of online social networking applications (think SixDegrees and Friendster), there eventually came the "so what" problem: you could make an account, register your name, find people, connect to them, and then…what? There was no *there* there. You might be able to form groups and discuss things, but of course you could already do that through a lot of other interfaces (such as email lists and Usenet, for Pete's sake), even if they weren't explicitly noted as social.

No, it's only when you start enabling people to "do things" together that the real power of online social networks kicks in.

Today, it's possible to orchestrate collaborative groups through a series of time-worn, well-proven design patterns. Provide people with a shared space, give them a way to invite others, provide the means for managing tasks, use version control, and take care of people's rights.

Wiki projects, such as the omnipresent Wikipedia; open source software development using tools such as Sourceforge, Collabnet, and Github; Yahoo! Groups; and charismatically driven groups of people such as Ze Frank's (*http://zefrank.com*) fanbase have all demonstrated the power that can be unleashed when you give people interfaces for working together on their shared concerns (Figure 12-1).

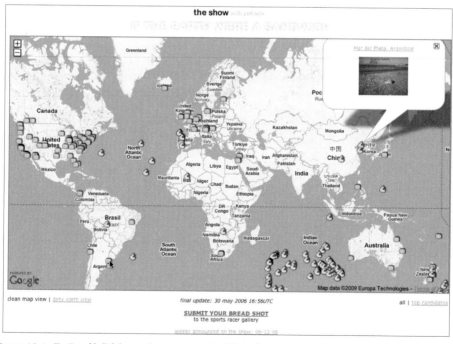

Figure 12-1. *Ze Frank's "If the earth were a sandwich" challenge recruited numerous participants into attempting to place slices of bread at antipodes, to turn the planet into a sandwich.*

Manage Project

When people get together and form groups, they often discover a shared desire to accomplish something tangible or complex, frequently something with a real-world (offline) impact (Figure 12-2).

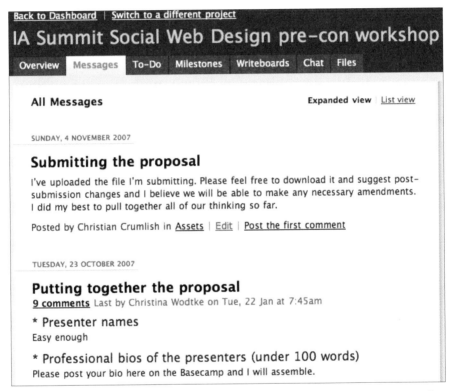

Figure 12-2. *You can use most social interfaces to organize projects by sheer force of effort, but it's easier if you've got at least the fundamentals of project management available, such as tasks, calendars, file upload, and collaborative editing.*

Also known as a "Workspace" pattern.

Use this pattern when you have enabled group formation and wish to host and support group project activities. If you don't have the bandwidth (literally or figuratively) to support this, consider supporting third-party services.

- Support your members' ability to orchestrate projects by coordinating goals, tasks, and deadlines among multiple participants with varying degrees of commitment and availability.

- Provide a workspace for connecting all the facets of the project (people, tasks, dates, collateral) and, if possible, offer a summarized dashboard view linking to more detailed inventories by facet. This enables asynchronous communication (see "Synchronous Versus Asynchronous Communication" on page 291) across disconnected geographies.

- Enable the creator of the project or a participant to bring in collaborators with "Send Invitation," and possibly to assign varying rights by individual or group (Figure 12-3).

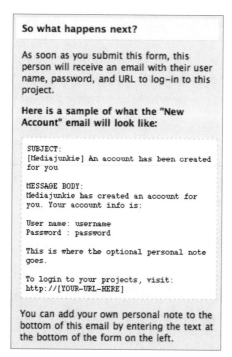

So what happens next?

As soon as you submit this form, this person will receive an email with their user name, password, and URL to log-in to this project.

Here is a sample of what the "New Account" email will look like:

```
SUBJECT:
[Mediajunkie] An account has been created
for you

MESSAGE BODY:
Mediajunkie has created an account for
you. Your account info is:

User name: username
Password : password

This is where the optional personal note
goes.

To login to your projects, visit:
http://[YOUR-URL-HERE]
```

You can add your own personal note to the bottom of this email by entering the text at the bottom of the form on the left.

Figure 12-3. *With Basecamp, you can add an entire company (team) to your project or invite individuals by adding them to an existing company.*

- Support task management with the ability to assign tasks, accept tasks, and distribute processes among multiple participants by breaking them down into individual tasks. Optionally support the ability to declare that one task is dependent on another and possibly calculate the critical path to the end goal.

- Provide a calendar on which deadline and milestone dates can be scheduled and then verified.

- Offer the ability to send messages to project participants, as well as reminders and notifications.

- Provide a means for "collaborative editing" of documents or source code, including version control (Figure 12-4).

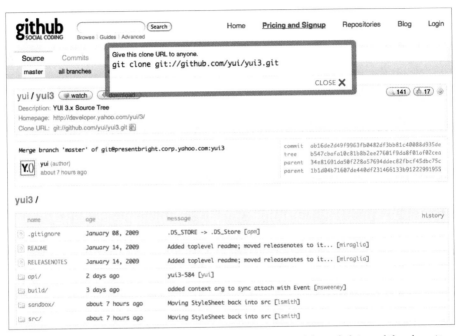

Figure 12-4. *At github, I can make my own clone of the YUI 3.0 codebase, fork it, and then have it merged back into the main trunk.*

- Enable project participants to make and keep track of decisions.

- Optionally provide an interface for project blogging (see "Blogs: Ownership" on page 245) or statuscasting (see "Statuscasting" on page 137) so that project participants can report on their progress and anyone can see at a glance what has been happening lately on the project. Or, provide a timeline view (see "Updates" on page 139) on the dashboard to roll up all recent events in chronological order.

Why

Enabling your community members to work together or comanage their own efforts increases the utility of your service and the culture of the social environment.

However, your users can often do this effectively via email and phone and perhaps a filesharing system. Do you have anything more to offer? Do you need to?

As seen on

Basecamp (*http://basecamphq.com*)

Bugzilla (*http://bugzilla.org*)

Collabnet (*http://collab.net/*)

Github (*http://github.com*)

Groove (*http://office.microsoft.com/groove/*)

Publicsquare (*http://publicsquarehq.com*)

SharePoint (*http://www.microsoft.com/sharepoint/*)

Socialtext (*http://socialtext.com*)

Traction (*http://tractionsoftware.com/*)

Voting

What

In order to make decisions, the members or stakeholders of a group need a way to give their opinions, and project leaders need to know which options have the most support from the participating community (Figure 12-5).

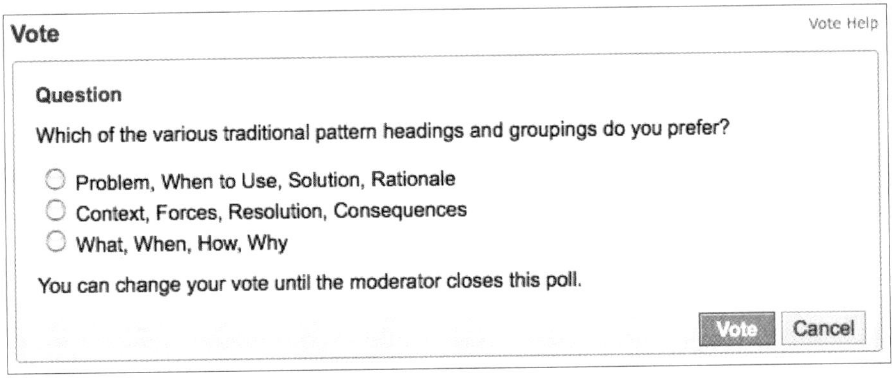

Figure 12-5. *Polls are one way to gather directed input from collaborators.*

Also known as "Polls" or "Surveys."

Use when

Use this pattern to collect the opinion of a group of people around a topic (with facets).

It works best when groups are large enough that only a core subgroup is doing most of the collaboration, to provide a voice to the less fully engaged members of the group.

This may be in an enterprise or workgroup context, or it may equally well be in a consumer context, in which a group of people freely associating with one another need ways to discern their preferences and make collective decisions.

How

Provide a form by which a group moderator or participant can suggest a question or topic to be voted on and then a series of possible votes (anything from "yes" or "no" to a multiple-choice option).

Optionally, provide configuration choices governing such issues as how long the voting will remain open, whether a vote can be changed, whether votes are anonymous or open, whether a person may vote for a single choice or more than one, or whether a ranking of choices is preferred (Figure 12-6).

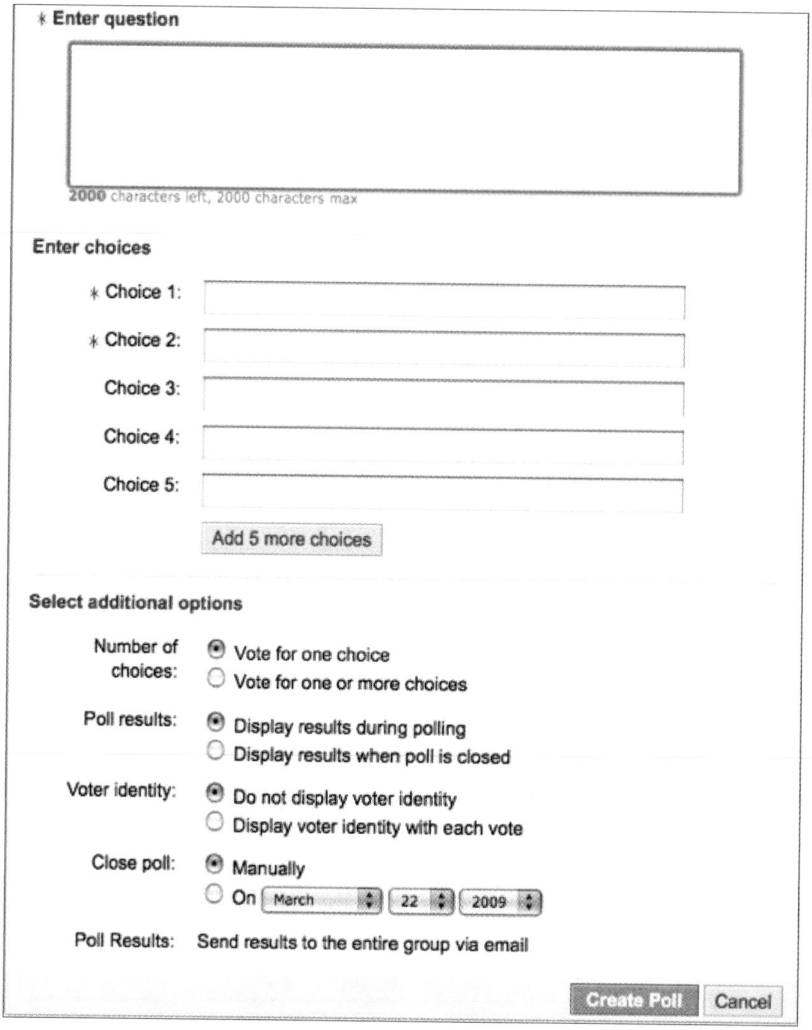

Figure 12-6. *Yahoo! Groups makes it easy to create an instant poll and invite the members of the group to vote in it, with the ability to change their vote up to a deadline.*

Why

Voting and surveys provide a means of soliciting feedback (see Chapter 10) about specific questions from a wider participating community.

Note that voting systems can potentially be gamed, especially if no fixed identity is required or authenticated before voting (see "Identity" on page 82); voting can provide perverse incentives in much the way that a leaderboard can (see "Leaderboard" on page 174); and there are many competing voting algorithms out there, each with its own pros and cons.

Related patterns

"Ratings (Stars or 1–5)" on page 274

"Reputation Influences Behavior" on page 154

"Thumbs Up/Down Ratings" on page 269

"Vote to Promote" on page 266

As seen on

Evite (*http://evite.com/*)

SurveyMonkey (*http://surveymonkey.com/*)

Yahoo! Groups (*http://groups.yahoo.com/*)

Collaborative Editing

What

People like to be able to work together on documents, encyclopedias, and software code-bases (Figure 12-7).

Figure 12-7. *Asynchronous editing enables multiple people to work on the same document.*

Use when

Use this pattern when you wish to enable your site members to work together to curate their collective wisdom or document their shared knowledge.

- Provide a repository for hosting documents with version control. Give users a way to bring in additional collaborators with an invitation to participate, as in Figure 12-8 (see "Send Invitation" on page 59).

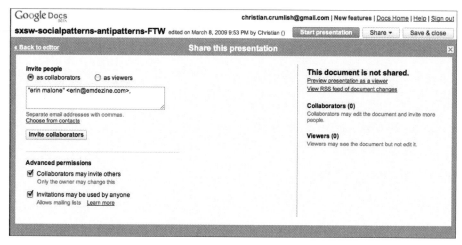

Figure 12-8. *The "invite to participate" pattern is used to enable people to invite collaborators to work together on a document.*

- Provide an Edit This Page link (see "Edit This Page" on page 319) directly on the document to be edited, or enable uploading of incrementally updated versions of a stored document.

- For direct editing, provide an edit box, much as in a blog or comment interface (Figure 12-9).

Figure 12-9. *It doesn't get more meta than this: here I am editing this very pattern in the collaborative wiki where it lives outside of the book.*

- Optionally, give contributors mechanisms for tracking changes, through notifications or with RSS feeds.

Why

Collaborative editing is better suited to the web medium than the alternative: emailing documents to multiple participants and then orchestrating the proliferating multiple, asynchronous updated copies of a document, with aspirational filenames ending in "finalFinalfinal" (Figure 12-10).

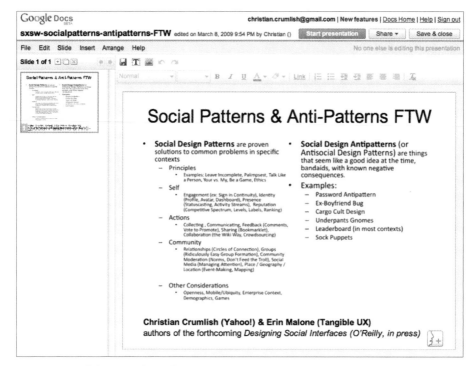

Figure 12-10. *Collaborative editing does away with multiple copies of files, unreconciled changes, and email overload.*

Related patterns

"Comments" on page 278

As seen on

Drupal (*http://drupal.org/handbook/modules/book*)

Google Docs (*http://docs.google.com*)

Mediawiki (*http://mediawiki.org/*)

SocialText (*http://socialtext.com*)

SubEthaEdit (*http://www.codingmonkeys.de/subethaedit/*)

Twiki (*http://www.twiki.org*)

Wikipedia (*http://wikipedia.org/*)

Writeboard (*http://writeboard.com*)

Numerous FAQ documents that accompany active Usenet newsgroups

Edit This Page

What

The more difficult it is to edit a shared document, the fewer people will bother to do so. Even forcing people to switch contexts (to an "editing mode") will create a barrier to participation for a significant fraction of potential contributors (see Figure 12-11).

Figure 12-11. *A button or link inviting the reader to edit this page encourages collaboration (and lowers the threshold for making improvements by reducing the friction involved in offering edits).*

Also known as "Edit This," "Universal Edit Button," "Inline Editing," "Read-Write Web," or "Two-Way Web."

Use when

Use this pattern in interfaces for editing shared or personal documents. May be used in contexts that permit universal editing, anonymous editing, or registered, authenticated, and privileged editing.

How

- Provide a button or link on any editable content that links directly to an edit box for the content, preferably without even loading a new page (Figure 12-12).

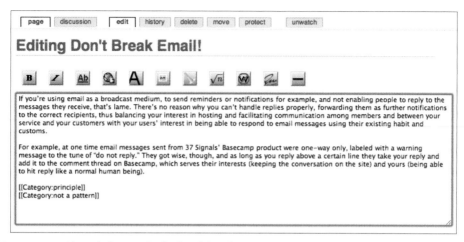

| page | discussion | edit | history | delete | move | protect | unwatch |

Editing Don't Break Email!

| B | I | Ab | | A | | | √n | W | | — |

If you're using email as a broadcast medium, to send reminders or notifications for example, and not enabling people to reply to the messages they receive, that's lame. There's no reason why you can't handle replies properly, forwarding them as further notifications to the correct recipients, thus balancing your interest in hosting and facilitating communication among members and between your service and your customers with your users' interest in being able to respond to email messages using their existing habit and customs.

For example, at one time email messages sent from 37 Signals' Basecamp product were one-way only, labeled with a warning message to the tune of "do not reply." They got wise, though, and as long as you reply above a certain line they take your reply and add it to the comment thread on Basecamp, which serves their interests (keeping the conversation on the site) and yours (being able to hit reply like a normal human being).

[[Category:principle]]
[[Category:not a pattern]]

Figure 12-12. *If an edit box can be displayed directly in the reader's original context, the experience of making and saving an edit and then resuming reading is smoother than if the editing must be done in a separate context.*

- Optionally, when restricting editing only to privileged groups, hide the button from anyone who has not been authenticated as a contributor.

- Consider providing a WYSIWYG (what you see is what you get) editing environment, to reduce one of the barriers to participation for the majority of people who are not comfortable using abbreviated markup languages to format and style text.

Special cases

When trying to cultivate a culture of collaborative editing, community moderators may need to make an extra effort to recruit, campaign, and encourage contributions. By default, many people are passive, even when invited to edit content, because they are afraid to break something or give offense to a preceding editor. The interface should be as inviting as possible, but be prepared to challenge incumbent behavioral patterns.

Offer a "sandbox" area for beginners where they can practice editing safely without worrying about damaging anything or exposing themselves to criticism (Figure 12-13).

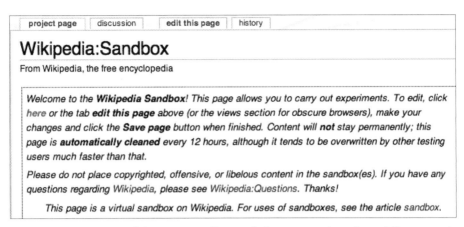

Figure 12-13. *Giving your collaborators a sandbox in which to practice their editing skills can ease the slope of the learning curve and take some of the fear out of inline editing.*

Why

The great promise of the Web draws in part from its facilitation of two-way communication and collaboration across geographical and other boundaries. An interface element that invites the reader to become an author goes beyond the "second-class" forms of participation, such as giving feedback and ratings. The easier you make it to edit content, the more likely people will bother to do so and potentially spur one another on to build knowledge stores and other projects that otherwise might never have come into being.

As seen on

Wikipedia (*http://www.wikipedia.org*)

Just about every wiki, everywhere

Social Networks and Managing Knowledge

Concepts like **knowledge management** and **learning organizations** have gained importance in the last decade and a half. Regardless of the size and nature of their business, organizations realize the importance of tapping into the collective skills and knowledge of their people to build competitive advantage. As people work their way through an increasingly complex decision-making process, navigating a tough regulatory framework, the knowledge they acquire forms the basis of what an organization can achieve. And since knowledge is notoriously "sticky," it tends to stay with them, even when they choose to leave the organization. Most organizations have been clueless on developing effective strategies and tools to capture, discover, and use this knowledge.

—continued—

Social Networks and Managing Knowledge

Traditional *profiling applications* and *skills databases* enabled organizations to build repositories of workforce skills and capabilities. While these captured key structured details about the workforce, they left a void in terms of capturing unstructured knowledge. In this traditional environment, "who you know" was as important as, if not more than, "what you know" for getting a task done. Avenues of sharing this knowledge were few, and so were the incentives. Rewards and recognition programs were tailored to favor people who "had" the knowledge. As an organization grew, it created islands of experience, and knowledge that led to duplicate and wasted effort and lost opportunities.

The very nature of knowledge makes it difficult to manage like other organizational assets. Knowledge assets can be *explicit*, easy to articulate and precise; or *tacit*, understood in context of an experience or a situation, and difficult to codify or articulate. An organization has to leverage both explicit and tacit knowledge inherent in its social networks, both within and outside organizational boundaries, to get jobs done. Organizations use this everyday knowledge to empower decision making, improve performance, reduce risk, and encourage innovation.

The popularity of social networks and user-generated content in organizations is gradually changing the way knowledge is created, shared, and utilized. With tools like employee blogs, corporate wikis, and social bookmarking, people within the organization have a way to capture and share their knowledge without letting technology get in the way. Blogs (and microblogs like Twitter) enable people to express themselves without being burdened by corporate content policies and multiple levels of reviews in a more traditional environment. Wikis enable employees to create and edit content in a collaborative environment. Social bookmarking and social ranking of content (as exemplified by Delicious and Digg) enable an entire community to organize what it knows in a single repository, enabling users to define and manage what is relevant and useful.

Access to knowledge assets is provided with information push (as in alerts), pull (for instance, search), or a combination of these models (as with RSS feeds). Coupled with effective metrics, organizations can then monitor the creation and use of knowledge assets and identify most valuable links in the entire organization that go beyond organizational hierarchy charts.

This free flow of communications not only promotes knowledge creation and sharing but has also completely altered traditional group dynamics. Where traditional models incentivized having knowledge, the new social models actively promote sharing what you know. Social standing in this environment is determined by the extent to which an employee contributes to the community. This further encourages creation of knowledge assets and enables the community to gain value by virtue of the knowledge assets it contains within its repositories. An HR manager today can tap into the power of social networks to find new recruits; a sales manager can find a way into a customer account tapping into the connections of his network; and management can implement decisions faster by focusing on key executives and influencers throughout the organization.

—continued—

Social Networks and Managing Knowledge

Where consumer social networks are largely community-managed, organizations can choose to exercise varying degrees of control over the communities of knowledge they create. From content administration to the classification of knowledge assets, organizations can decide what degree of control works best for them, and help people within the organization to achieve more with technology as an enabler.

As more businesses see the value of social networks in capturing a lifetime of experiences inherent in their workforce, a continually changing landscape will demand new ways to manage knowledge. Social networks are gaining in popularity because they don't get in the way, unlike traditional knowledge management systems. Rather, by forming communities of interest, social networks enable the entire community to define, moderate, and evolve knowledge management frameworks to meet new needs as they arise. This is what social networks are all about, anyway!

—Harjeet S. Gulati, President,
Netsoft Global Services

The Wiki Way

What

Collaborative editing can get bogged down in conversational mode, and when contributors become too attached to their own individual contributions, this can impede the development of the collaborative document (Figure 12-14).

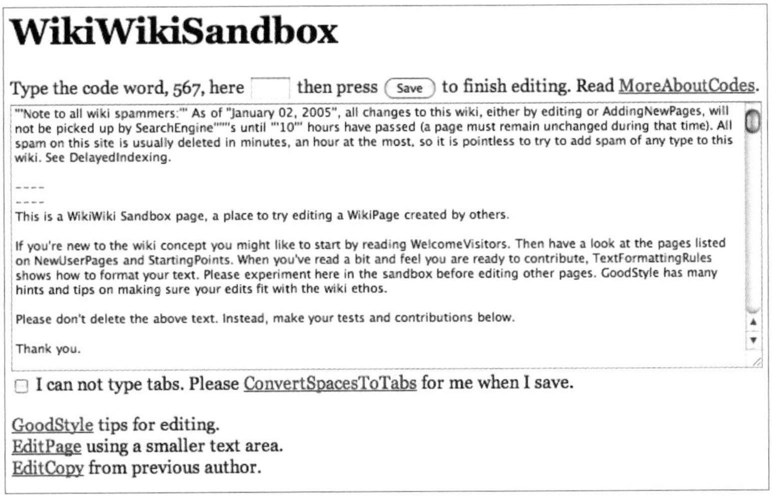

WikiWikiSandbox

Type the code word, 567, here ☐ then press (Save) to finish editing. Read MoreAboutCodes.

"'Note to all wiki spammers:'" As of "January 02, 2005", all changes to this wiki, either by editing or AddingNewPages, will not be picked up by SearchEngine"'"s until "'10'" hours have passed (a page must remain unchanged during that time). All spam on this site is usually deleted in minutes, an hour at the most, so it is pointless to try to add spam of any type to this wiki. See DelayedIndexing.

- - - -
- - - -
This is a WikiWiki Sandbox page, a place to try editing a WikiPage created by others.

If you're new to the wiki concept you might like to start by reading WelcomeVisitors. Then have a look at the pages listed on NewUserPages and StartingPoints. When you've read a bit and feel you are ready to contribute, TextFormattingRules shows how to format your text. Please experiment here in the sandbox before editing other pages. GoodStyle has many hints and tips on making sure your edits fit with the wiki ethos.

Please don't delete the above text. Instead, make your tests and contributions below.

Thank you.

☐ I can not type tabs. Please ConvertSpacesToTabs for me when I save.

GoodStyle tips for editing.
EditPage using a smaller text area.
EditCopy from previous author.

Figure 12-14. *Many of the principles underpinning Ward Cunningham's original wiki (created to house the Portland Pattern Repository) should be kept in mind when you're trying to facilitate effective collaborative editing in a community setting.*

Use when

Use this pattern when providing an interface for collaborative editing.

How

Encourage anonymous editing, use version control, and enable refactoring of document content by contributors.

Here are the original principles Ward Cunningham cited when recalling the design principles that underpinned the first wiki:

Open
> Should a page be found to be incomplete or poorly organized, any reader can edit it as he sees fit.

Incremental
> Pages can cite other pages, including pages that have not been written yet.

Organic
> The structure and text content of the site are open to editing and evolution.

Mundane
> A small number of (irregular) text conventions will provide access to the most useful page markup.

Universal
> The mechanisms of editing and organizing are the same as those of writing, so that any writer is automatically an editor and organizer.

Overt
> The formatted (and printed) output will suggest the input required to reproduce it.

Unified
> Page names will be drawn from a flat space so that no additional context is required to interpret them.

Precise
> Pages will be titled with sufficient precision to avoid most name clashes, typically by forming noun phrases.

Tolerant
> Interpretable (even if undesirable) behavior is preferred to error messages.

Observable
> Activity within the site can be watched and reviewed by any other visitor to the site.

Convergent
> Duplication can be discouraged or removed by finding and citing similar or related content.

There are many wiki authors and implementers. Here are some additional principles that guide them, but were not of primary concern to me:

Trust

This is the most important thing in a wiki. Trust the people, trust the process, enable trust-building. Everyone controls and checks the content. Wiki relies on the assumption that most readers have good intentions (but assume that there are limitations to good faith).

Fun

Everybody can contribute; nobody has to.

Sharing

Of information, knowledge, experience, ideas, views....

Why

The wiki approach has unleashed a torrent of creativity on the Web and seems to have captured in its principles the fundamental grain of digital, electronic, web-enabled collaboration.

Related patterns

"Learn from Games" on page 36

"Ongoing Sharing" on page 239

Chapter 17

As seen on

WikiWikiWeb (*http://c2.com/cgi/wiki*)

Crowdsourcing

What

Some jobs are too big for the immediate group of engaged collaborators to manage on its own. The community will benefit if the interface provides a way to break a large project into smaller pieces and engage and give incentives to a wider group of people (or "crowd") to tackle those smaller pieces (Figure 12-15).

Figure 12-15. *Amazon's Mechanical Turk plays matchmaker to people looking for distributed help in solving problems or answering questions, and other people willing to do said work for a fee.*

Use when

Use this pattern when you wish to enable your active core community members to engage with the wider set of people participating in your social environment and get their help accomplishing ambitious projects that would not be possible with fewer people.

How

- Provide a method for splitting up a project into individual tasks so that each task may be advertised individually. Also, provide a venue for announcing crowdsourced projects.

- Give community members a way to "shop for," review, and claim individual tasks for the project (Figures 12-16, 12-17, and 12-18).

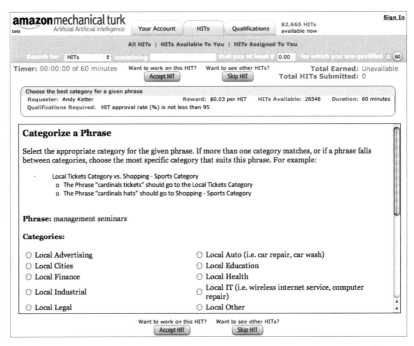

Figure 12-16. *At Amazon's Mechanical Turk, one can easily sign up and start reviewing human intelligence tasks (HITs) before deciding whether to do any of the work for the offered pay.*

Figure 12-17. *When designing a t-shirt for Threadless, you can volunteer to have others critique your design for you, and then iterate the design based on the feedback.*

Figure 12-18. *Anyone can sign up to start reviewing existing designs at Threadless.*

- Provide an upload interface or submission form to enable participants to contribute their completed work (assuming the work isn't accomplished directly in your interface).

- Keep track of tasks that have been claimed but not completed by their deadline, so that they may be returned to the general pool and reassigned.

- Ideally, offer a dashboard view for management of the project.

- Where appropriate, incorporate a mechanism for compensation for the participants (Figure 12-19).

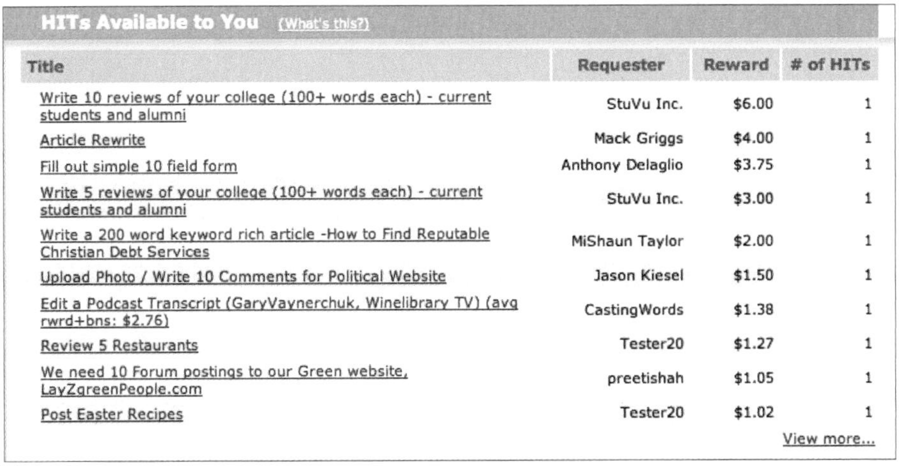

HITs Available to You   (What's this?)

Title	Requester	Reward	# of HITs
Write 10 reviews of your college (100+ words each) - current students and alumni	StuVu Inc.	$6.00	1
Article Rewrite	Mack Griggs	$4.00	1
Fill out simple 10 field form	Anthony Delaglio	$3.75	1
Write 5 reviews of your college (100+ words each) - current students and alumni	StuVu Inc.	$3.00	1
Write a 200 word keyword rich article -How to Find Reputable Christian Debt Services	MiShaun Taylor	$2.00	1
Upload Photo / Write 10 Comments for Political Website	Jason Kiesel	$1.50	1
Edit a Podcast Transcript (GaryVaynerchuk, Winelibrary TV) (avg rwrd+bns: $2.76)	CastingWords	$1.38	1
Review 5 Restaurants	Tester20	$1.27	1
We need 10 Forum postings to our Green website, LayZgreenPeople.com	preetishah	$1.05	1
Post Easter Recipes	Tester20	$1.02	1

View more...

Figure 12-19. *Tasks for Amazon's Mechanical Turk all come with price tags, so it's easy to decide if you're willing to do the work for the payment offered.*

Why

Crowdsourcing breaks large jobs into pieces that can be tackled with a much lower commitment threshold, taking advantage of the loose ties in social networks.

As seen on

Amazon Mechanical Turk (*http://www.mturk.com/mturk/welcome*)

Assignment Zero (*http://zero.newassignment.net/*)

The ESP Game (*http://www.cs.cmu.edu/~biglou/ESP.pdf*)

iStockphoto (*http://istockphoto.com*)

ReCAPTCHA (*http://recaptcha.net/*)

SETI@home (*http://setiathome.ssl.berkeley.edu/*)

Threadless (*http://threadless.com*)

Further Reading

"Berners-Lee on the read/write web," BBC News, August 9, 2005, *http://news.bbc.co.uk/2/hi/technology/4132752.stm*

Cross Cultural Collaboration, *http://crossculturalcollaboration.pbwiki.com/*

"Deriving Process-driven Collaborative Editing Pattern from Collaborative Learning Flow Patterns," by Olivera Marjanovic, Hala Skaf-Molli, Pascal Molli, and Claude Godart, *http://www.ifets.info/journals/10_1/12.pdf*

"Edit This Page," by Dave Winer, *http://www.scripting.com/davenet/1999/05/24/editThisPage.html*

Edit This Page PHP, *http://sourceforge.net/projects/editthispagephp/*

Paylancers blog, *http://paylancers.blogspot.com/*

The Power of Many, *http://thepowerofmany.com*

Regulating Prominence: A Design Pattern for Co-Located Collaboration (*http://www.ida.liu.se/~matar/coop04arvola-web.pdf*)

"The Rise of Crowdsourcing," by Jeff Howe, *Wired* 14.06, *http://www.wired.com/wired/archive/14.06/crowds.html*

"The Simplest Thing That Could Possibly Work," by Bill Venners, *http://www.artima.com/intv/simplest.html*

Universal Edit Button, *http://universaleditbutton.org/Universal_Edit_Button*

Wiki Design Principles, *http://c2.com/cgi/wiki?WikiDesignPrinciples*

"The Wiki Way," by Jon Udell, *http://weblog.infoworld.com/udell/2004/10/19.html*

Wired Crowdsourcing blog, *http://crowdsourcing.typepad.com/*

Chapter 13

Social Media Junkies Unite!

Some commons-based peer production efforts are less self-conscious on the part of the users, and emerge more as a function of distributed coordinate behavior, like del.icio.us or Flickr. The critical defining feature of these "enterprises" is that they rely primarily on social information flows, motivations, and relations to organize the group. Individuals self-identify, mostly, for tasks, and through a variety of peer-review mechanisms contributions get recognized by the group and incorporated into what emerges as the collaborative output.

—Yochai Benkler interview in OpenBusiness (about his book *The Wealth of Networks*)

Keeping Up

As with "Web 2.0" and "synergy," the buzzphrase "social media" has taken on a life of its own, and has already spawned its own mutant bastard: "social media marketing." As with those other terms, and much Internet jargon, "social media" means different things to different people. As noted at the beginning of this book, we prefer to use the term to refer to social production and consumption of media objects, and not merely as a lazy synonym for social networking in general. This entire chapter is devoted to the collecting, sharing, and creation of social objects. As Hugh MacLeod put it in a post on his weblog, called "Social Objects for Beginners" (*http://www.gapingvoid.com/Moveable_Type/archives/004390.html*):

> *The Social Object, in a nutshell, is the reason two people are talking to each other, as opposed to talking to somebody else. Human beings are social animals. We like to socialize. But if you think about it, there needs to be a reason for it to happen in the first place. That reason, that "node" in the social network, is what we call the Social Object.*

So how do these social media objects swirling around us add up to an ecosystem or even a marketplace? How do people discover them, subscribe to them, and share them across networks? (See Figure 13-1.)

Figure 13-1. *Take any classic or interactive medium, add social interaction to it, and you've got social media, whether it takes off or fizzles in a vacuum.*

Social Metadata and Future Uses

Social metadata today

Much has been made of this trend labeled as *Web 2.0*, which places social web tools and services in the forefront of open, collective, and collaborative interaction in and around content and other media objects. One of the benefits of the shift is the by product of semi structured information and metadata in and around the objects and content. Information on the Web prior to this era was, at best, loosely structured, or heavily structured through the process of entry using form-field-heavy interfaces.

Semistructured information is created through the application of the HTML markup structures, human tagging, machine tagging, URLs, page titles, navigation structures, and inbound links. All of this creates metadata that gives some structure. Social tools, such as Yahoo! Answers and Wikipedia, all play a vital part in augmenting metadata around objects.

Much of the social metadata is not created by the people using the services, but is a mixture of user input and smart tools. The exception to this is tagging, but the value of this goes beyond metadata for the sake of metadata; it adds personal value for retrieval and contextualizes information for retrieval and aggregation. Most blogging and wiki tools use proper semantic HTML structures, and many augment these tools with microformats under the surface.

—continued—

Social Metadata and Future Uses

Today's metadata and future uses

Much of the future lies in an idea that has been around many years. This future is embracing the Semantic Web and similar tools, building on semantic information. Semantically relevant metadata improves relevance in information and media retrieval. The Semantic Web has had a chicken-and-egg problem, as it has the tools to do fantastic things with structured information, but it has been held back by the lack of that structured information at a scale that will make a difference. Today's social semi structured information gives enough of a boost that Semantic Web tools can begin to provide their long-promised power.

The Semantic Web is based on triples of information: subject, predicate, and object. Using what we have today, this turns into: Thomas uses the resource tag; Thomas's resource tag points to web page X. This pairing of two triples gives us fairly good information that becomes a building block for future uses.

Using the social tools of today, we are setting up a very nice semi structured foundation for tomorrow. We do this in a variety of ways, but all are built through the patterns required for interaction on social tools. The primary element in social architectures is identity within the service. This allows an understanding of the subject, or who is making a statement. Most services are focused around some sort of social object (link, photo, video, statement, document, etc.) that is shared, pointed to, described, and/or central to a collective effort through conversation or collaborative capturing of a description. These social environments offer rich fodder for the subject (who) and predicate (descriptors) about an object (social object).

Additionally, many of the social tools are capturing ancillary metadata and exposing it. This ancillary data is something Flickr calls *machine tags*, which include things such as the date the photo was taken, the date the photo was added to the Flickr service, the camera type that took the photo, the geographic location where the photo was taken, etc. This metainformation is not something that is generated by the individual using the service, but by the tools the person uses. This is not only prevalent in tools like Flickr, but also in blogs and community services that have profile information associated with an identity, as well as what others in the service have stated about that identity or activities that identity has participated in.

This richness of metadata can then be used by the tools to serve up better understanding of the objects to improve search, surface highly probable similar items, build highly probable synonyms, as well as help discern meaning of ambiguous terms and statements. This will help us understand, for example, the probability that the Apple Macintosh being discussed in a podcast in the second week of January 2008 in San Francisco is likely different than the Apple Macintosh photographed in roughly the same place seven months later. Our tools can discern that the January 2008 Macintosh is a computer-related discussion because the MacWorld convention is held in San Francisco then, but the July 2008 Macintosh is a fruit at a gathering of an American agricultural association's large meeting in San Francisco. The ancillary metadata around these social objects give clues to this discernment, but clues are also available in an aggregation of the interests of the people using the identities in the services.

—*continued*—

Social Metadata and Future Uses

Summary

In short, the social tools we are using today are letting us focus on what we care about, and through the use of lightweight connections and light form fields, are capturing and building a web of semi structured information. The web of semistructured information working as metadata provides enough of a foundation to be used as structured elements, which are the fodder for using Semantic Web tools. This use of the Semantic Web tools leads to better relevance and discernment providing drastically better search to find exactly what the seeker wants, not just what is good enough. This also provides much better capability for aggregating information people care about and would like to keep closer to them.

—Thomas Vander Wal, Principal & Sr. Consultant, InfoCloud Solutions (*http://infocloudsolutions.com*)

See Chapter 17 for a further discussion of microformats and semantic markup in general.

Tuning In

Social media is a two-way street: read/write. In addition to providing tools for sharing and publishing media, you can provide your users with interfaces for zeroing in on the streams they're interested in and then sifting through them for the most interesting and relevant objects (Figure 13-2).

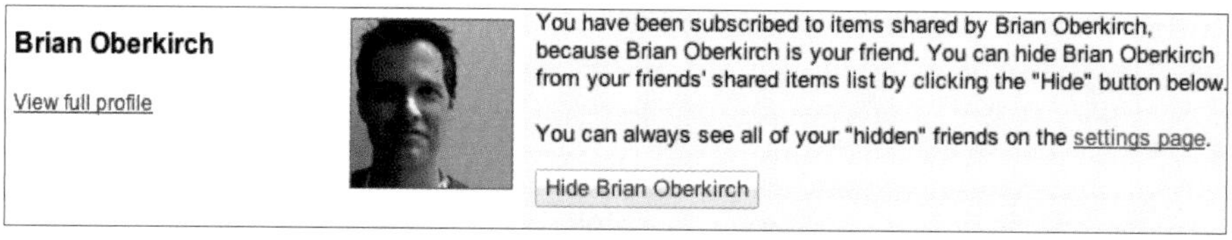

Brian Oberkirch

View full profile

You have been subscribed to items shared by Brian Oberkirch, because Brian Oberkirch is your friend. You can hide Brian Oberkirch from your friends' shared items list by clicking the "Hide" button below.

You can always see all of your "hidden" friends on the settings page.

Hide Brian Oberkirch

Figure 13-2. *Google Reader guessed I might be interested in the blog entries and other RSS objects that Brian Oberkirch shares. (Reader was right, but if it guessed wrong, I could "hide" Brian to tune my incoming feed that way.)*

Following

Also known as *asymmetric following* (and explored more thoroughly in Chapter 14), following is a way of expressing interest in someone else's activities and objects and subscribing to them. It does not require reciprocation, and although it might correspond with acquaintanceship or friendship, it does not necessarily imply a reciprocal relationship between the follower and the followed (Figure 13-3).

Figure 13-3. *I can choose to follow Anil Dash on Hunch without any obligation for him to approve, confirm, or reciprocate. Thus, following is a way of subscribing to or indicating interest in somebody's activities.*

Related patterns

"Add/Subscribe" on page 198

"One-way following (aka asynchronous following)" on page 364

"Updates" on page 139

Filtering

What

As Randy Farmer is fond of reminding us, "context is king." As human beings, we rely on context to derive meaning from our sensory inputs. One of the unfortunate side effects of augmented universal oversharing is that we get these streams (torrents, really) of updates and objects from all of our connections across multiple social facets, usually with most or all of the originating conceptual context stripped away.

This dissolution of context is alienating and disorienting for most normal people. Even those of us who are at times capable of surfing these unrestrained information feeds usually grow weary of the onslaught eventually.

The first resort for most people is "social filtering," which means relying on the pointers of friends and those we follow for deciding what to pay attention to (Figure 13-4). The ordinary follow and subscribe interfaces suffice for enabling users to "tune in" to the recommendations of others, but you can use this pattern to give people additional handles on which to filter for context.

Figure 13-4. *An arbitrary link to a blog post or comment thread is unlikely to get my attention, but if Mary Hodder takes the time to mention something, I'm much more likely to click through and check it out.*

Use when

Use this pattern when the potential for information overload and jumbling together of unrelated contexts grows intolerable (Figure 13-5).

Figure 13-5. *If I go to Robert Scoble's Friendfeed page, I get a jumble of his activities and objects across numerous contexts.*

How

Provide affordances for restoring (or, if necessary, imposing) contextual filters on data streams so that they can be parsed in more manageable groupings (Figures 13-6 and 13-7).

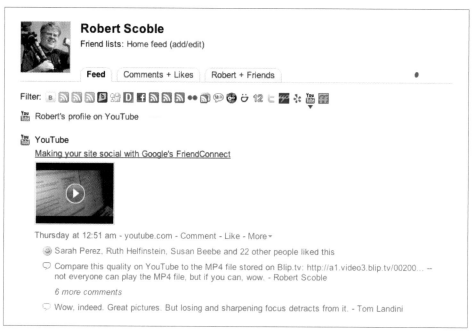

Figure 13-6. *When I choose the miniature YouTube icon, Robert's activity stream is filtered for me, to show just the most recent videos he has marked as a favorite (and the public conversations around them).*

Figure 13-7. *Facebook now offers a non-lossy activity stream (just like FriendFeed's) and provides you with a customizable list of filters for focusing the stream.*

Filtering can also be achieved by giving users a way to hide people or specific types of objects. Instead of singling out a context and showing just items in that context, which tends to be a temporary choice, hiding involves singling out a context and filtering items in that context *out* of view (Figure 13-8).

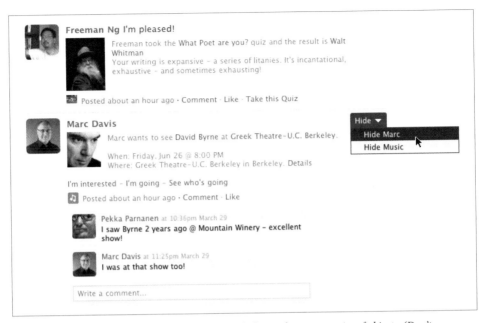

Figure 13-8. *Facebook also gives you the ability to hide people, or categories of objects. (Don't worry, Marc: I didn't really hide you!)*

People will also use leaderboards (see "Leaderboard" on page 174), favorites (see "Favorites" on page 193), and other "best of" tools as an attempt to filter on quality (Figure 13-9).

Figure 13-9. *Another way people manage their attention is by filtering on favorites or "best of," as with this tweet I found on Favrd.*

Why

Giving people the ability to filter incoming information based on various contexts (type of content, closeness of relationship to the sender, timeframes) enables them to establish a stable point of view from which to explore the rich, never ending stream of new objects and information.

As seen on

Facebook (*http://www.facebook.com/*)

FriendFeed (*http://friendfeed.com/*)

Google Reader (*http://www.google.com/reader/*)

Recommendations

What

In the search for relevancy and quality, people have a difficult time zeroing in on satisfactory content (Figure 13-10).

Figure 13-10. Amazon recommends media for me based on my past buying habits as well as on similarities between my behaviors and those of other customers.

Use when

Offer recommendations when you have a sufficient body of data about your user's self-declared and implied interests as well as a rich enough social graph to be able to identify similarities and make helpful guesses about likely interesting content (Figures 13-11 and 13-12).

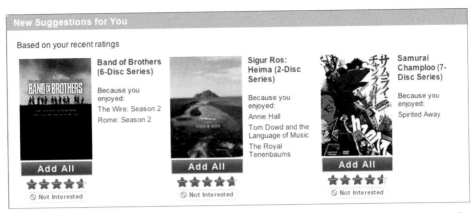

Figure 13-11. *Netflix bases recommendations primarily on your past behavior, but it factors in social data as well, when it has any.*

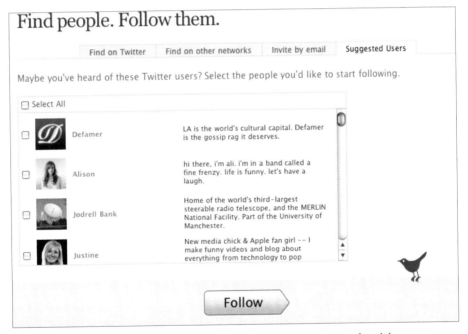

Figure 13-12. *Twitter suggests users for you to follow. If you're just starting, it doesn't know your preferences yet, so it's going either on popularity, some other quality metric, or paid placement.*

- Offer a call to action inviting the user to explore recommendations. Educate the user about how to obtain better recommendations (for example, by rating content).

- Display recommendations as a list, or if there is a large number, in a carousel or scrollable window.

Recommendations push objects toward people rather than relying on them to be passively discovered. If you can provide value to your users by making educated guesses about the type of objects they are interested in, then you may be able to capture their loyalty. The benefit to users is more readily finding the information and media they need without having to hunt around for it quite so hard.

Related patterns

"Testimonials (or Personal Recommendations)" on page 100

As seen on

Amazon (*http://www.amazon.com/*)

Digg (*http://digg.com/*)

The Filter (*http://www.thefilter.com/*)

Netflix (*http://www.netflix.com/*)

SeeqPod (*http://seeqpod.com/*)

StumbleUpon (*http://www.stumbleupon.com/*)

Twitter (*http://twitter.com/*)

Social Search

Social search is an emerging phenomenon, and there are a number of different aspects of search that can be enhanced with a social dimension (are you searching for people? are your searches facilitated by social behaviors? are you searching for social objects?). The phenomenon of finding content by searching on user-contributed tags is perhaps one of the most familiar social search experiences available online today.

The two most interesting forms of social search I've seen are real-time search and conversational search.

Real-Time Search

What

People can't always find breaking news and current topics of public conversation with ordinary keyword searches of indexed web resources, and already get frequent pointers to current information by the electronic equivalent of word of mouth (Figure 13-13).

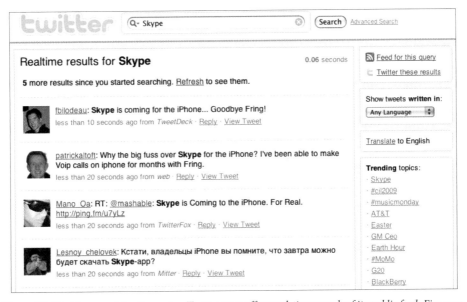

Figure 13-13. *After acquiring Summize, Twitter now offers real-time search of its public feed. Five new tweets came in while I was setting up the screen snap.*

Also known as "The Notificator" (*http://www.borthwick.com/weblog/2009/02/05/ creative-destruction-google-slayed-by-the-notificator/*).

Use when

Use this pattern with an activity stream service to enable people to find concepts in up-to-the-minute status updates and activities.

How

- Provide the familiar elements of a search interface (a text box and a search button), and make it clear to the person searching that the results will be ordered by recency (reverse-chronological order) and not by relevancy (Figure 13-14).

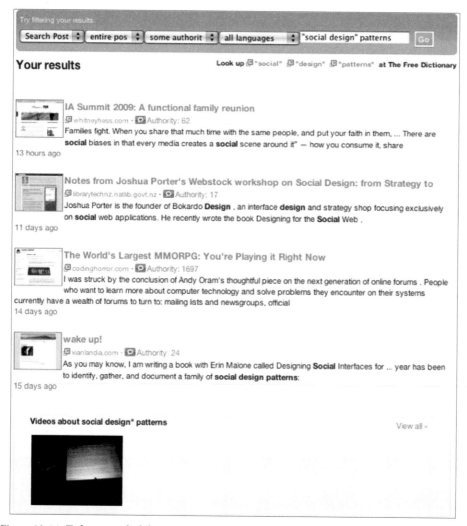

Figure 13-14. *Technorati, which began as a blog search engine, offers search results from what it calls "the world live web."*

- Optionally, give the user hints about the sort of things that can be profitably searched for in a real-time search interface. For example, Twitter Search lists the current top trending topics (Figure 13-15).

Figure 13-15. *Twitter offers hints about some of the most popular search topics of the moment.*

- Optionally, offer the ability to subscribe to search results, most commonly in the form of an RSS feed, to give people the ability to track a term or phrase and be notified almost immediately whenever it appears (Figure 13-16).

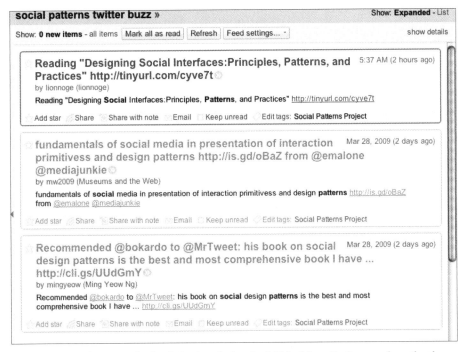

Figure 13-16. *While writing this book, I subscribed to the RSS feed for a Twitter search on the phrase "social patterns" as way of tracking the spread of this meme.*

Why

The world is moving too fast for "old-school" search engines to keep up with the leading edge. Real-time search tools that capture signals from the social web provide a method for finding extremely current information and news.

Related patterns

"Tools for Monitoring Reputation" on page 182

As seen on

Google Alerts (*http://www.google.com/alerts*)

Technorati (*http://technorati.com/*)

TweetNews, a mashup of Twitter and Yahoo! Boss running on the Google App Engine (*http://tweetnews.appspot.com/*)

Twitter Search (*http://search.twitter.com/*)

Yahoo! Alerts (*http://alerts.yahoo.com/*)

Conversational Search

What

People sometimes want information or advice that can't be found in a neutral, objective reference guide, and they would ask another human being directly if they could find someone interested in or knowledgeable about the topic of their question (Figure 13-17).

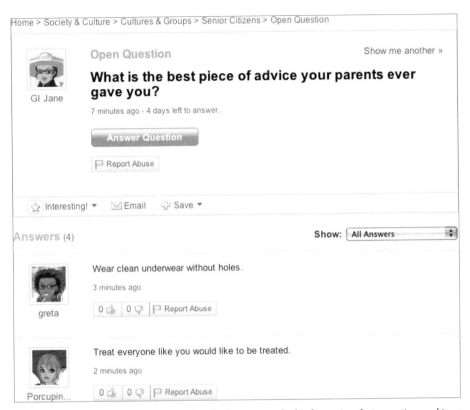

Figure 13-17. *Consulting a reference is often the best way to find information, but sometimes asking a person is better.*

Also known as "Subjective Search."

Use this pattern when you wish to foster communication and cooperation among the people using your social application.

- Provide a large, inviting text-entry box to encourage questioners to write full sentences (like a human being) instead of query strings or Boolean operators, and label the form button with a word such as "Ask."

At the same time, expose open questions to people as a way of inviting them to answer (or route questions to likely, willing answerers based on affinities you derive from the metadata in your social graph). See Figure 13-18.

Figure 13-18. *LinkedIn invites you to ask a question while showing you questions that you can answer at the same time.*

- Alternately, as Aardvark does, rely on existing conversational channels (in the case of Aardvark, primarily IM) for capturing questions, routing them to potential respondees, and delivering answers (Figure 13-19).

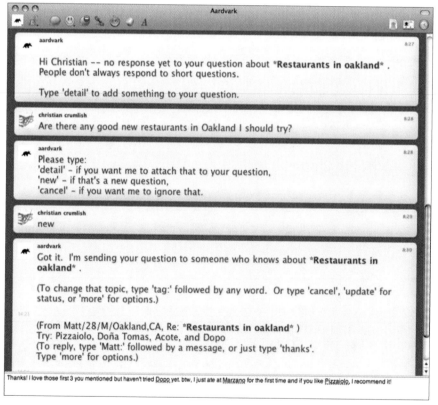

Figure 13-19. *Aardvark facilitates connections between askers and answerers and encourages conversation.*

- Optionally, embrace a reputation system to help ferret out the best contributors and the most helpful answers.

Directly querying an index of data is a great way of searching for information, with historical roots going back to the earliest libraries, archives, and repositories, but people have always gathered information in other ways as well. In fact, most people in the real world ask other human beings for information as a starting point.

Aardvark (*http://vark.com*)

LinkedIn (*http://www.linkedin.com/*)

Yahoo! Answers (*http://answers.yahoo.com/*)

Most mailing lists everywhere

Pivoting

Some people like to browse, others prefer to search, but most use a combination of both. And no one ever says to themselves, "Today I'm going to only browse and do no searching," or vice versa. A person may start by searching for information and then when he finds something juicy, begin browsing from there to related content. Similarly, browsing may lead to search and then back to browsing again.

Providing your users with ways to "pivot" between one form of discovery and another offers them the richest possibilities.

To do so, provide a persistent search box that is always in the same location (most commonly the upper-right or upper-left of the screen), and when displaying search results, offer related links, "more like this," and other opportunities for lateral exploration.

Further Reading

"Creative destruction … Google slayed by the Notificator?", by John Borthwick, *http://www.borthwick.com/weblog/2009/02/05/ creative-destruction-google-slayed-by-the-notificator/*

"Do your friends make you smarter? Exploring social interactions in search," by Brynn M. Evans, *http://www.slideshare.net/bmevans/ do-your-friends-make-you-smarter-exploring-social-interactions-in-search*

"Social Objects for Beginners," by Hugh MacLeod, *http://www.gapingvoid.com/Moveable_Type/archives/004390.html*

TweetNews, *http://tweetnews.appspot.com/*

"Why social search won't topple Google (anytime soon)," by Brynn M. Evans, *http://brynnevans.com/blog/2009/01/30/why-social-search-wont-topple-google-anytime-soon/*

Part IV

A Beautiful Day in the Neighborhood

So far we've looked into how to represent people in your application (and, perhaps more importantly, how to enable people to represent themselves), and we've examined the sort of activities people can do by touching social objects within your system. This brings us smack into the realm of relationships.

Without relationships between and among people, there is no social. Shared activities, like many of those discussed in Part III, naturally lead to the development of relationships in the real-world sense of the term: people meet through shared affinities, do activities together, make commitments to each other, and eventually find that they are in some sort of ongoing relationship.

In this part, we'll look at the mechanisms for labeling and declaring relationships, the community dynamics that can arise from multiple overlapping relationships (and particularly how to encourage healthy behavior and discourage parasites and vandals), and how to enable people to bring their virtual connections into the real world through local engagement and shared event creation.

Chapter 14

One of Us, One of Us

"I used to think of all the billions of people in the world, and of all those people, how was I going to meet the right ones? The right ones to be my friends, the right one to be my husband. Now I just believe you meet the people you're supposed to meet."

—Diane Frolov, *Northern Exposure*, "The Quest," 1995

Friendship is born at that moment when one person says to another: "What! You, too? Thought I was the only one."

—C.S. Lewis

Relationships

Having a group of people to hang out with, communicate with, and participate with is key to the successful social experience. One of the worst problems is to show up somewhere and find you're alone. The ability to find friends and make them a part of your circle for participation is one of the key interactions to design when building a social site. The first impulse is to simply import all contacts from the variety of address books a user may have. This process, like casting a large net into the ocean and hoping for the best, doesn't help filter out meaningful relationships. Not all contacts are equal. I may have my aunt and my accountant in my address book, but I don't necessarily want them as friends on Facebook.

The strength of ties in relationships and the type of site and network being encouraged all need to be considered when offering ways for users to build relationships. Additionally, the context surrounding these relationships needs to be considered when developing the circles of friendship.

Is the friend-of-a-friend potentially more helpful than the people I may know directly, like on LinkedIn, where that second- or third-degree connection may be the key to the next job?

Is the site a broadcast-type site, like Twitter, where following what a person has to say is more important than actually knowing him in real life?

Is knowing a person in real life important, like having a small circle of trusted friends to share family photos with on Shutterfly or using a site like Centerd to plan an evening out with the group?

The patterns in this chapter look at the ways to find and add friends to a user's network and the considerations you must make when creating the framework for relationships. The framework must equally take advantage of weak ties and strong ties; it must allow users to change their minds, back and forth, about following or friending others; and it must be graceful in how the system alerts both the user and the recipient of the follow or unfollow. After all, while the system may be mediating the connection, it shouldn't cause undue embarrassment or create a social faux pas.

Finally, we look at relationships in the context of groups. In these cases, the topic of interest is often the driving factor for belonging and the relationships people grow over time.

Relationships Terminology

Cohort: A number of people banded together or treated as a group (as defined by the Oxford English Dictionary).

Colleague: A person with whom one works (as defined by the Oxford English Dictionary).

Connection: A link or relationship; the action of connecting; (connections) influential people with whom one has contact or to whom one is related (as defined by the Oxford English Dictionary). In social networking (e.g., Flickr), a person to whom a user has connected. The connection may not necessarily be reciprocal.

Contact: A person who may be asked for information or assistance (as defined by the Oxford English Dictionary).

Family: A group consisting of two parents and their children living together as a unit; a group of people related by blood or marriage; the children of a person or couple; all the descendants of a common ancestor; a group united by a significant shared characteristic (as defined by the Oxford English Dictionary).

Fan: A person who has a strong interest in or admiration for a particular sport, art form, or famous person (as defined by the Oxford English Dictionary).

Follow: In social networking (e.g., Twitter), the act of marking a person or a person's content to have streamed into your experience. On Facebook, this is streamed into the NewsFeed, and on Twitter, into the activity stream.

Follower: A person who follows; a supporter, fan, or disciple (as defined by the Oxford English Dictionary).

Friend: A person with whom one has a bond of mutual affection, typically one exclusive of sexual or family relations (as defined by the Oxford English Dictionary). In social networking (e.g., Facebook), a friend is someone who a user has connected to and the connection is reciprocal and agreed upon by both parties.

Find People

The user wants to find people she knows so she can connect and interact with them on a site or social web service (Figure 14-1).

Figure 14-1. *Various methods are presented to add connections on Facebook.*

- Use when you want to help users find people they care about who may already be using this site.
- Use to expand user's circles of connections beyond friends and family.
- Use to encourage connections after the initial network-building exercise.

Provide a variety of ways for users to build out their connections.

Browsing for people

Allow users to browse friends of friends.

Consider presenting a user's friends and connections in a graphical grid that shows avatars, and allow others to browse through to their profiles. Provide visual clues to a person's identity (via the avatar) to help confirm that person's identity (Figures 14-2, 14-3, 14-4, and 14-5).

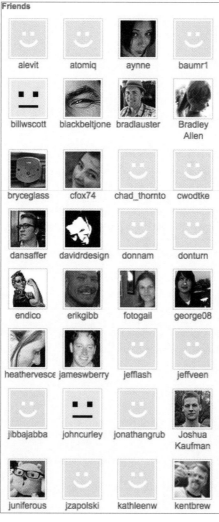

Figure 14-2. *Friend grid on Upcoming.*

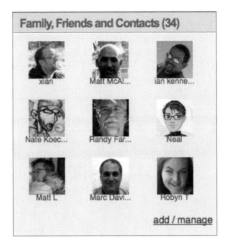

Figure 14-3. *Friend grid on myBlogLog.*

Figure 14-4. *Following grid on Twitter.*

Figure 14-5. *Contact grid on Flickr.*

Searching for connections

- Allow users to search for friends within the network on your site.

- Provide a keyword field. Clearly indicate what terms are accepted in the search query—name, email, or other identifying factors.

Facebook allows users to constrain a search by known information about the user. For example, users can search for people from their high school or college graduation years, or from companies they have worked for recently (Figure 14-6). Constraining the search in this way increases the likelihood of finding people a user really knows.

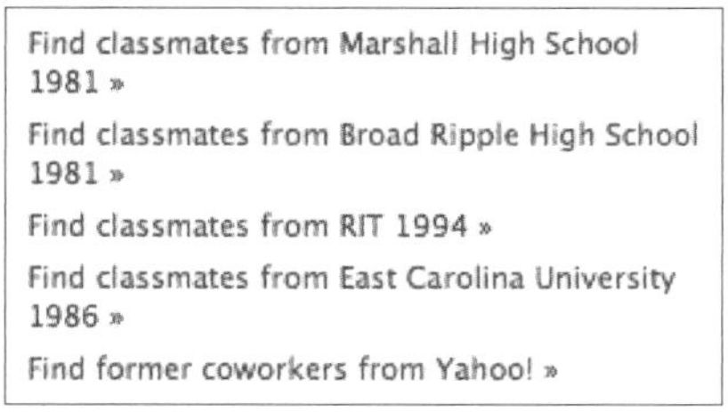

Find classmates from Marshall High School
1981 »

Find classmates from Broad Ripple High School
1981 »

Find classmates from RIT 1994 »

Find classmates from East Carolina University
1986 »

Find former coworkers from Yahoo! »

Figure 14-6. *Facebook offers constrained searches by a user's schools and workplace.*

Finding friends from email, IM buddy list/contacts, and other networks

- Allow the user to import contacts from his address book or instant messenger lists to use as a comparison list to find people already using the service.

- Allow users to import their connections from Facebook using Facebook Connect.

- Allow users to import their connections from Twitter using OAuth.

- Compare known data points—name, email address, or other reliable information— and then present to the user a list (with images for ease of identification) of relevant people who also use the service.

- Allow the user to select one or more names to make them connections.

- If reciprocity is required, present the message that will be sent to the user and the option to send the request for connection or an option to cancel the request (see "Adding Friends" on page 361).

- When bringing in people lists from an address book or address book service for a user to connect to, don't automatically spam the user's contacts asking to connect.

- Don't automatically spam the rest of the user's contacts with invitations to join the service.

Discovery/recommendations

- Consider presenting people the user may know as potential connections (Figure 14-7).

Figure 14-7. *LinkedIn regularly makes people recommendations to encourage fleshing out a user's network.*

- Use known connections and friends of friends to extrapolate potential connections for users.

Why

Having a circle of connections and friends is what makes the Web social. Building a network of connections is hard, and as more time goes by, becomes overly redundant as a user moves from site to site. Providing easy mechanisms for finding people and building their networks will encourage repeat use and prevent social-networking burnout.

Portable Social Graph

The easiest way to create a network upon joining a new site would be to bring your network with you. Although there are some contexts that may be very specialized and need only a small subset of people a user knows—for example, a fantasy sports site—for the most part, many current and future social sites are generalized enough that the network the user built on site A will be the same network of connections she wants on site B.

The *social graph*, the network of people the user has built around herself (Figure 14-8), wants to be portable. There is a growing movement encouraging openness (*http://bradfitz.com/social-graph-problem/*), just like with OpenID. The idea is to create a data standard that allows users to easily bring their network from one site to another without all the work involved in finding people and adding them into the network at each site.

—continued—

Portable Social Graph

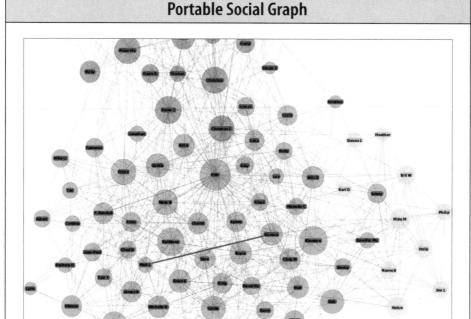

Figure 14-8. *The author's social graph on Facebook as visualized by TouchGraph.*

The logistics are far from resolved, but as new sites are being developed, being aware of this initiative and designing new sites and using data structures that play nice will encourage interplay between sites and help the users out in the long run.

Related patterns

"Adding Friends" on page 361

"Sign-up or Registration" on page 45

As seen on

Facebook (*http://www.facebook.com*)

Flickr (*http://www.flickr.com*)

LinkedIn (*http://www.linkedin.com*)

myBlogLog (*http://www.mybloglog.com*)

Plaxo (*http://www.plaxo.com*)

Twitter (*http://www.twitter.com*)

Upcoming (*http//upcoming.yahoo.com*)

Adding Friends

What

A user has found people she knows on a social site and wants to add them to her circle of connections (Figure 14-9).

Figure 14-9. *Recommended connections from Facebook, based on current connections and friends of friends.*

Use when

Use this pattern when:

- User connections are a core part of the site's experience.

- Relationships will be confirmed, providing a two-way reciprocal relationship.

- Allowing one user to follow another participant without reciprocity.

- Ignoring a connection request is allowed.

How

Once a user has found people he cares about on your site (see "Find People" on page 355), provide an easy way to add these people as connections:

- Provide a clear link (a button or text/icon combination) as the call to action to add this person as a friend (Figure 14-10).

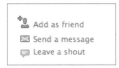

Figure 14-10. *"Add as friend" call to action on Last.fm.*

- Once the person has been added as a Friend, clearly indicate to the user that this person is now a friend (Figure 14-11).

Figure 14-11. *Flickr indicates when you are already connected with another user.*

Confirming friendship/two-way connections

Requiring two-way relationships encourages a network that more closely resembles real-world relationships:

- Clearly indicate when selecting "add as a friend" that the relationship must be confirmed by the other party before it will be recognized on the site (see Figures 14-12 and 14-13).

Figure 14-12. *Facebook shows the first confirmation screen, after selecting "Add as Friend", alerting the user that the recipient of the request will have to confirm the relationship.*

Figure 14-13. *Facebook shows a confirmation that the Add request has been sent and must be approved.*

- Likewise, alert users when a connection request is being made (Figures 14-14, 14-15, and 14-16).

Figure 14-14. *Facebook indicates friend requests in a "Requests" module on a user's personal dashboard.*

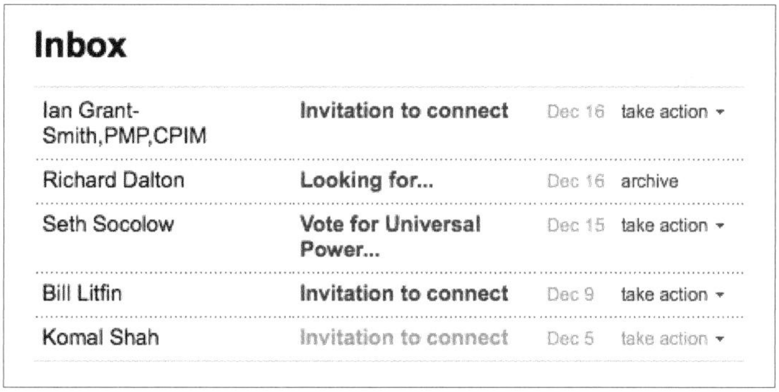

Inbox

Ian Grant-Smith,PMP,CPIM	**Invitation to connect**	Dec 16	take action ▾
Richard Dalton	**Looking for...**	Dec 16	archive
Seth Socolow	**Vote for Universal Power...**	Dec 15	take action ▾
Bill Litfin	**Invitation to connect**	Dec 9	take action ▾
Komal Shah	Invitation to connect	Dec 5	take action ▾

Figure 14-15. *LinkedIn alerts users to invitations to connect in the Inbox.*

Figure 14-16. *Twitter has both public and private status streams. If the stream is private, it effectively is a two-way connection and must be approved by the person who is the recipient of the request.*

- Allow the user to cancel the request at any time.

One-way following (aka asynchronous following)

An alternative to reciprocal relationships is the one-way connection. This type of connection is best used when the content is more important than a personal relationship. This is essentially a subscription to the person's activities and contributions within the system (Figure 14-17).

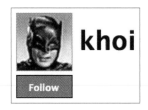

Figure 14-17. *Twitter has a simple large "Follow" button associated with the identity of the person to follow.*

- Label the action in a way that doesn't imply an intimate or real-life relationship, such as "friends" or "family." Instead, use terminology like "Contacts," "Fan," or "Follow" (Figure 14-18).

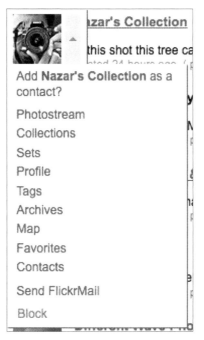

Figure 14-18. *Flickr uses the terminology "Contact" when adding a person to your network. This is a one-way relationship.*

- When a connection is made, alert the connected person that a connection has been made (Figure 14-19).

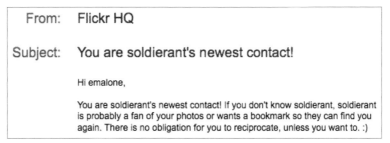

Figure 14-19. *Flickr sends a notice every time someone is added as a connection.*

- If two parties connect to each other—in a mutual one-way connection—acknowledge the connection (Figure 14-20).

Figure 14-20. *Flickr sends a message when a relationship is reciprocated.*

Implicit and explicit relationships

Most social networks require users to make explicit connections and declare their relationships publicly. But there are situations where the implied relationship will do. By subscribing to someone's blog or joining an interest group, there is an implied relationship between the user and the author of the blog or the person and the group of people involved in the group. The very nature of being involved in the group implies relationships that may or may not be very strong.

Expressing these implied relationships within the interface can help users make explicit connections as well as get a sense of the group they are involved with.

Allow users to become involved without having to explicitly declare relationships, and let the relationships evolve over time.

Fans and fame (aka asynchronous following)

Public websites such as blogs and microblogs (e.g., Twitter), and sites such as Flickr, where the default for photo posts is public, allow their authors to broadcast to the world. Include interactions in the interface that allow users to follow or subscribe to the author or the author's content. These one-way relationships are often initiated by people who are just fans of the author or their content. "Fan" has an implied difference from "friend," in that the relationship is usually one-way and there is often little or no direct interaction between the fan and the object of fandom other than consumed broadcasts. (See Figures 14-21, 14-22, and 14-23.)

Figure 14-21. *MyBlogLog allows users to add a widget to their blogs and track who visits. The widget declares the implicit community around the site, regardless of whether the site owner has any interaction with it.*

Figure 14-22. *Twitter's Followers grid and list is in essence a list of fans for a person or her tweets. To some, collecting followers has become a game or popularity contest.*

Figure 14-23. *Bands have long used MySpace to build up their fan bases. They offer music and information about gigs and new releases, and allow their fans to interact with them and declare to the world their fanhood. Although the service calls all connections "Friends," these are clearly fans.*

Ignore me

Allow users to ignore connection requests.

Clearly indicate what the consequences of "Ignore" will be; otherwise, the outcome will be a collection of neglected connection requests living in some sort of perpetual purgatory. Many people won't actively ignore someone, because it isn't clear what will happen if they select Ignore. They fear insulting the person who is making the request, even though this isn't a person they would consider connecting with.

Facebook's interface offers some good options, but they fall short in setting expectations for the user when the actions are selected (Figures 14-24 and 14-25):

- Does the requestor get a message that he is being ignored? If the requestor isn't notified, then the action is the same as no action.

- Does Ignore block this person from requesting a connection again? Or is that what happens with the Block link?

Figure 14-24. *Facebook offers Ignore as an equal option to Confirm, but doesn't tell you what happens if you click the button.*

You ignored a friend request from Sydelle Wiser. Report and/or block this person?

Figure 14-25. *Once the Ignore button is clicked, a confirmation of that action is presented, but it still doesn't say what happens with that action.*

Clearly set expectations for the user about the implications for each action. Add rollover messages to inform the user of the consequences of these actions.

Without setting clear expectations, you are wasting your design and development effort, building a feature that users will be too scared to use for fear of negative social implications.

Why

Allowing users to connect to one another encourages conversations and sharing among networks of people, resulting in viral growth of the site. People want to do things with their friends or with others who have similar interests, and allowing them to connect strengthens these ties.

Related patterns

"Find People" on page 355

"Unfriending" on page 373

Twitter (*http://www.twitter.com*)

Facebook (http://www.facebook.com)

Flickr (*http://www.flickr.com*)

Last.fm (*http://www.last.fm*)

LinkedIn (*http://www.linkedin.com*)

Circles of Connections

What

A user wants to indicate nuances in her relationships with other people. (See Figure 14-26.)

Figure 14-26. *Plaxo has six levels of connections built in and also allows users to add their own levels.*

Use when

- Use to distinguish levels of participation in a person's network.
- Use to set permissions for shared activity and content.
- Use to disambiguate real-life versus online and strong versus weak ties.
- Use to help users filter which content to consume.

- Depending on the context of your user experience, levels of granularity in describing connections may or may not be important.

- Consider allowing users to classify their connections along a continuum of influence or intimacy.

- Clearly articulate what the implications are for each level of classification (Figure 14-27).

Figure 14-27. *Flickr allows connections to be categorized as friends, family, friends and family, or contacts. When images are uploaded, visibility can be constrained based on the relationship indicated.*

- Don't add too many levels, or you risk confusing users about what each level permits. Users need to be able to easily separate what each level allows and how their actions and content will be consumed based on those levels.

Real-life relationships are complex, and context often changes how two people might interact. Online representations of relationships need to be presented in as simple a format as possible to aid in understanding and usability.

Providing mechanisms for users to create relationship groups avoids awkward social situations and puts the user in control of how his actions and data are consumed.

"Adding Friends" on page 361

"Blocking" on page 374

Flickr (*http://www.flickr.com*)

Plaxo (*http://www.plaxo.com*)

Publicize Relationships

To promote virality, the system announces, or publicizes, relationships between people (Figure 14-28).

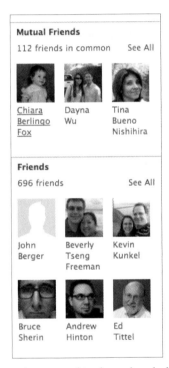

Figure 14-28. *Facebook shows a user how many friends are shared when viewing someone else's profile, in addition to showing how many friends that person has. Only a handful is featured at a time, and friends rotate on page refresh.*

- Use to announce new connections to people in shared networks.
- Use to show profile visitors who the person is connected to.

- Use to promote connecting by sharing new connections and enticing users to make them as well.

How

- As discussed in "Adding Friends" on page 361, consider publicly showing the group of people a user is connected with (Figure 14-29).

Figure 14-29. *Flickr indicates a person's connections with a contacts grid. Each picture and name is linked to that user's photo stream. Rolling over the picture brings up a contextual menu that allows the viewer to make that person a contact right there, inline.*

- Showing connections in a grid format of avatars is a space-saving way to publicize a person's relationships.
- When a new connection is made, consider announcing the new connection to each person's network via the activity stream (Figures 14-30 and 14-31).

Figure 14-30. *Facebook shows recent connections in the News Feed. Additionally, it shares how the two people connected if it was through one of the friend-finding tools.*

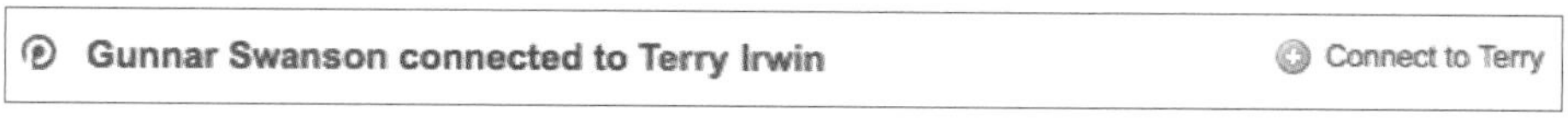

 ⓟ **Gunnar Swanson connected to Terry Irwin**   ⓒ Connect to Terry

Figure 14-31. *Plaxo shows a contact's recent connections in my activity stream and offers me the option of connecting to the same person.*

- When visiting a person's profile, display to the user whether or not she is connected (see "Profile" on page 86).

Why

Publicizing relationships helps a network grow through friends of friends browsing and connecting.

Announcing new connections to the group lets everyone know who's there and whom they know. Chances are, someone else in the group knows the new person and may want to connect as well. This is especially useful when the person is new to the service and can help alleviate the cold-start issue of having no connections.

Related patterns

"Adding Friends" on page 361

"Identity Cards or Contact Cards" on page 111

As seen on

Facebook (*http://www.facebook.com*)

Plaxo (*http://www.plaxo.com*)

Yahoo! Profiles (*http://profiles.yahoo.com*)

Unfriending

Relationships online are more ephemeral than in real life, and the desire to add and delete, friend and unfriend, follow and unfollow people is as fluid as people are complex.

What

A user has a collection of friends and then decides he wants to remove a person from his friends or connections list (Figure 14-32).

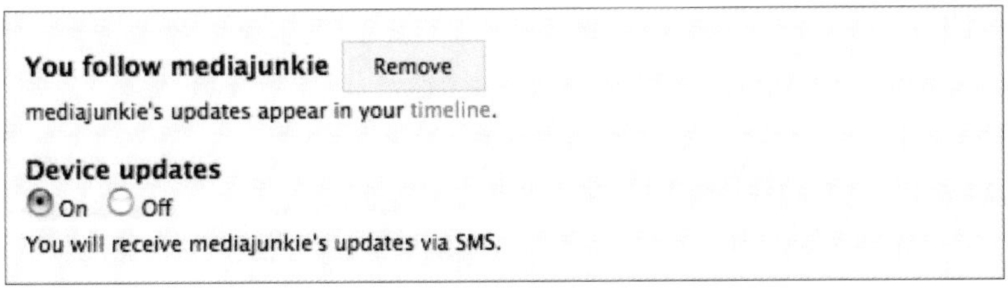

You follow mediajunkie   Remove

mediajunkie's updates appear in your timeline.

Device updates
● On ○ Off

You will receive mediajunkie's updates via SMS.

Figure 14-32. *Twitter offers a Remove function for every person you follow.*

Use when

• Use this pattern to allow users to remove connections.

- Use this pattern to manage unwanted relationships.

How

- Provide an easy way to remove connections without embarrassing the user.
- Provide a "Remove" or "Unfollow" call to action button or link near the connection's name or relationship status.
- Clearly indicate the consequences of each action.

Blocking

- Allow the option for users to block other users.
- Clearly indicate the consequences of blocking a user (Figures 14-33 and 14-34).

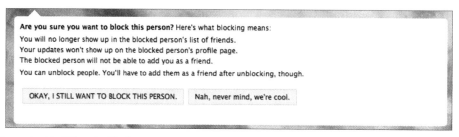

Are you sure you want to block this person? Here's what blocking means:

You will no longer show up in the blocked person's list of friends.
Your updates won't show up on the blocked person's profile page.
The blocked person will not be able to add you as a friend.
You can unblock people. You'll have to add them as a friend after unblocking, though.

OKAY, I STILL WANT TO BLOCK THIS PERSON.   Nah, never mind, we're cool.

Figure 14-33. When the block option on Twitter is selected, the site presents a screen that clearly defines the ramifications of this action and then allows a graceful way to back out or continue with the block action.

Accept   I don't know Bill   Archive

If you don't know Bill, click here and he/she won't be able to re-invite you.

Figure 14-34. LinkedIn offers an "I don't know XX" button to block a connection request. The rollover tip alerts you to the consequences of this action.

Ostracizing

Wiktionary defines *ostracize* as: "to exclude someone from society or from a community, by not communicating with or even noticing them, similar to shunning."

danah boyd writes about the Top 8 culture in MySpace and the social ramifications in real-life high schools when someone isn't added into this special class of friends, which functions as a shunning and ostracizing behavior. (See "Friends, Friendsters and Top 8: Writing community into being on social network sites" at *http://firstmonday.org/htbin/cgiwrap/bin/ojs/index.php/fm/article/view/1418/1336.*)

Age plays a role in the ensuing drama, so consider your target demographic when thinking about these types of tools or lack thereof on your site.

Some users inevitably will ostracize others. The ability to ignore and block are overt forms of ostracizing, whereas simply ignoring requests for connecting is a more passive behavior. Human behavior indicates that this is a part of group dynamics, and the systems we build need to be flexible enough to accommodate this.

Bozofilter

A "bozofilter" is a filter that allows a user to block email or messages from specific individuals.

Provide the ability for users to filter out specific posts or messages based on the poster or sender. This is especially helpful for blocking trolls and spammers in forums and groups.

Allow the "bozo" to still see his message in context even when others won't see it. This may help keep the person from creating another account.

Related patterns

"Adding Friends" on page 361

As seen on

Facebook (*http://www.facebook.com*)

LinkedIn (*http://www.linkedin.com*)

MySpace (*http://www.myspace.com*)

Twitter (*http://www.twitter.com*)

The Ex-Boyfriend Anti-Pattern

The boyfriend anti-pattern (also known as the ex-girlfriend bug) exists when the social system makes suggestions for connecting, based on friends-of-friends inference, to people who are not desired, such as an ex-boyfriend or ex-girlfriend.

The anti-pattern also presents itself when systems without connections grouping or filtering rely on location awareness and alert a user's network about where the user is or announces an event to her whole network, regardless of whether the user wanted that to happen (see "Mobile" on page 432; see also Figures 14-35 and 14-36).

> @ 13th St & Central Fwy, San Francisco, CA 00, United States ·
> 23 minutes ago · 3.2 km

Figure 14-35. *Without filters, Brightkite announces location to everyone in the user's network.*

Figure 14-36. *Brightkite allows you to mark a friend as a "trusted friend," which allows that person to see more specific information when in private mode.*

Consider this: in 2005, the mobile social networking software Dodgeball allowed people to broadcast their location to their network via SMS text messaging to encourage impromptu social gatherings. At first there was only one bucket for friends, but as people began hooking up, dating, and breaking up, there was a very strong need to filter out an ex without totally alienating that person through unfriending or blocking. The founders of Dodgeball called it "the ex-girlfriend bug," and created a feature called "manage friends" to address the issue. This functionality provides a level of filtering and permissions that allows only certain groups to receive specific updates and announcements. The exes who are on a filtered friends list never know you are in the same neighborhood, and social awkwardness is avoided by not having to "unfriend" them.

To avoid this issue, give your users more control over privacy and broadcast settings, and provide the ability to filter based on groups of people. Allow users to control their communications and information streams through the creation of buckets or circles of connections. This in turn avoids all those potentially awkward social situations (online and in real life) when information about whereabouts or actions appears to the wrong people.

Groups

What

A user wants to participate with a group of people, usually around a topic of interest (Figure 14-37).

Figure 14-37. *Groups on Flickr are often formed around specialty types of photos or techniques. The group page showcases photos, discussions, a description of the group, and rules of engagement within the community.*

Use when

Use this pattern when:

- You want to allow people to create groups around topics of interest.
- You want to create groups on the fly from a list of people.

Groups and clubs are generally closed, private networks of people. In many cases they have come together based on a shared interest or topic, such as photography or a school.

Ridiculously easy group formation

- Allow the creation of a group on the fly with a list of users.

- Allow one person to pull the group together and alert users that they either are invited or are automatically in the group.

- Automatically connect each person—in a mesh—and notify all members that the group has been created and they are now connected to everyone else in the group.

- Indicate what the benefits are and what activities can take place in the group (e.g., group chat, private communications among the members, shared content, etc.).

Create

- Allow users to create both public and private groups. Public groups should show up in search results and have a minimum amount of content that is viewable by the public to encourage joining.

- Consider threaded discussion boards as part of the group suite of tools.

- Consider an email list or RSS feeds for the discussion boards.

- Provide storage space as part of the group for centrally stored images and files.

- Allow a minimum level of customization for the group. Consider preset templates to choose from or skinning to create an environment specific to the topic or personality of the group.

- Allow group creators to mix and match the tools needed/wanted for the group.

- Consider a variety of group tools depending on the needs of the group. These might include photo albums, calendars, events, address books, maps, bookmarks, RSS feeds, discussion lists, polls, etc.

Finding groups

- Allow users to browse or search through public groups.

- Provide a "Join this group" call to action from within search results, as well as from the main group details page.

- Each group should have a home (details) page that describes what the group is about. Users should see enough information to make an informed decision about joining the group.

- Consider displaying an indication of activity level of the group (Figure 14-38).

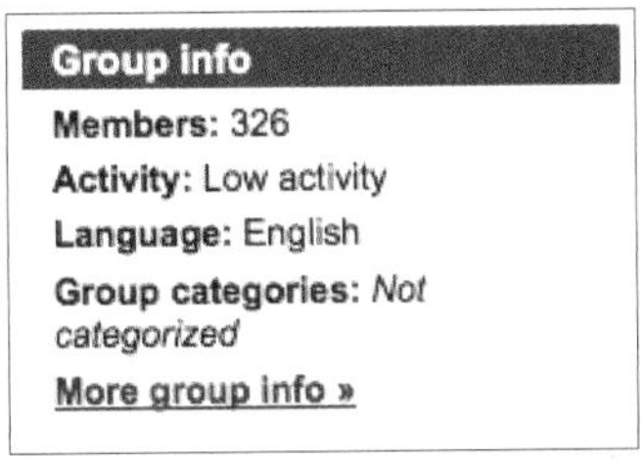

> **Group info**
>
> **Members:** 326
> **Activity:** Low activity
> **Language:** English
> **Group categories:** *Not categorized*
> **More group info »**

Figure 14-38. *Google Groups shows the number of members and activity level.*

- Display the number of members in the group.
- Provide a member list or roster of members.
- Allow users to browse the list of groups that is displayed on a friend's profile.

Participation

- Allow users to post and share images among group members.
- Allow users to post and share files among group members.
- Consider allowing members to invite other potential members to join the group.
- Allow users to build a contextual profile (see "Profile" on page 86) that is built with participation and group activity.
- On a user's home page or dashboard, provide a list of groups the user belongs to.
- Provide indication of recent activity in a group on the user's dashboard (Figure 14-39).

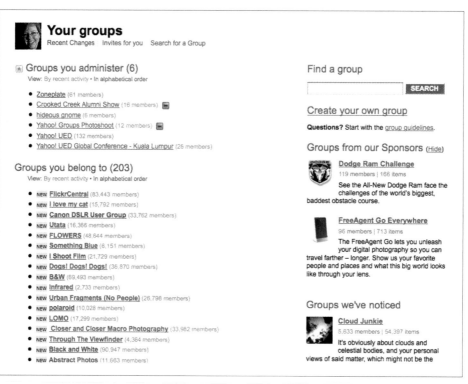

Figure 14-39. *Flickr groups are divided into sections based on administration/ownership versus membership. Groups with new activity have the NEW icon next to the group name, and the list is ordered by recent activity.*

Administration

- Allow the group creator to assign administrative duties to other members.

- Allow the group creator to assign moderator duties to other members.

- Allow the group creator to assign group ownership to other members. This is especially helpful if the original owner wants to leave the service but wants to allow the group to continue without her future involvement.

- Provide tools for managing and deleting spam.

- Allow admins, moderators, and group owners to kick out members who violate the group rules.

- Allow admins, moderators, and group owners to block users from posting if the group is public.

- Provide an option for membership approval.

- Allow admins, moderators, and group owners to invite members.

Related patterns

"Forums" on page 292

"Profile" on page 86

As seen on

Facebook (*http://www.facebook.com*)

Flickr (*http://www.flickr.com*)

Google Groups (*http://groups.google.com/*)

Multiply (*http://multiply.com*)

Yahoo Groups (*http://groups.yahoo.com*)

Further Reading

"Friends, Friendsters and Top 8: Writing community into being on social network sites," by danah boyd, 2006, *http://firstmonday.org/htbin/cgiwrap/bin/ojs/index.php/fm/article/view/1418/1336*

"Friends May Be the Best Guide Through the Noise," by Brad Stone, *The New York Times*, May 4, 2008, *http://www.nytimes.com/2008/05/04/technology/04essay.html*

Six Degrees: The Science of a Connected Age, by Duncan J. Watts, W.W. Norton and Co., 2004

Social Network Analysis: A Handbook, by John P. Scott, Sage Publications Ltd., 2000

The Strength of Weak Ties: A Network Theory Revisited, by Mark Granovetter, State University of New York, Stony Brook, 1983, *http://www.si.umich.edu/~rfrost/courses/SI110/readings/In_Out_and_Beyond/Granovetter.pdf*

"You are who you know," by Andrew Leonard, Salon, June 15, 2004, *http://dir.salon.com/story/tech/feature/2004/06/15/social_software_one/index.html*

"You are who you know: Part 2," by Andrew Leonard, Salon, June 16, 2004, *http://dir.salon.com/story/tech/feature/2004/06/16/social_software_two/index.html*

Chapter 15

Good Cop, Bad Cop

In the past I engaged in the whack-a-mole game against abusers. I spent many man months on algorithmic approaches for fighting abuse. My efforts focused on analysis of the content, sophisticated filters, and user "rehab" automation. In the end, the abusers (as a collective) have won. While I had given up and have left to engage in more fulfilling endeavors, the abusers have gradually figured out ways to bypass filters, create multiple accounts, and keep flooding message boards and public forums with spam.

Anyone who has ever tried seriously to block email spam knows that these kind of arms' races are very hard to win. We are very few, the abusers are many, and there always seems to be more of them. They have learned to share sophisticated tools (like breaking captcha) so effectively the pros and the least sophisticated script-kiddies are no longer two separate groups.

The good news is that there is a better way, but it requires a totally new and fresh approach.

In particular, I've become a true believer in community-moderation and collaborative filtering, after seeing the success of schemes like those of Y! Answers and Slashdot. What these successful sites are doing in essence is empowering their (good) users to take ownership of the abuse and quality-level goals. They create strong incentives for good users to put an effort into moderating the sites. Users who consistently exhibit good judgments and willingness to contribute, get "strength points" making them more and more powerful in the never ending game of stamping-out abuse.

In contrast, abusers have almost no power. The more they abuse, the more they lose points. New accounts start with zero reputation/power making them useless to engage in the game.

Once we get a critical-mass of good and willing users, the incentive system feeds itself. The abusers may bypass a filter, but they cannot fool an army of dedicated human beings.

—A Yahoo! "Paranoid" (security professional) who wishes
to remain anonymous,
Yahoo! Abuse Team, on an internal wiki (quoted with
permission)

Community Management

Administrators are people, too! And they deserve good interfaces. Far too often, since the earliest days of the Web, beautiful sites have been launched to the public with minimally functional content management and administrative functionality, or sometimes none at all. Similarly, a social website has an engine room, too: it needs an admin side where community managers can help cultivate the best contributions and downplay or discourage the worst.

But how can people be expected to behave well if they don't know what constitutes good behavior? Thus it's important to establish and clearly communicate the behavioral norms of the community and to actively participate in the community, particularly in its impressionable early days, modeling good behavior and demonstrating how to get things done.

Norms

In the context of managing social networks and information in the public domain, *Norms* refer to a pattern, and expected behaviors (in contrast to those established by law) when operating or working with a system.

Norms are socially enforced, and less restrictive than rules, although this does not quite reflect on the actual effectiveness of a Norm as compared to a legally established Rule. In many cases, Norms appear to be more effective in molding or directing user behavior as compared to rules because of greater visibility of actions in a broader community. This appears to align with the fundamental observation that a broad community involvement in management is far better than the management entrusted to a select few.

A key building block of any community interface is a published set of guidelines that is easy to find and crystal-clear (Figure 15-1).

Yahoo! Community Guidelines

Just like any other community, Yahoo! communities include people from a wide variety of experiences, backgrounds, and mindsets. We take pride in the fact that our communities give this diversity of membership an interesting place to interact, share, learn, and grow. In keeping with this spirit of community, we have a core set of principles that must be followed by all members:

- Use must comply with all applicable local, state, and federal rules, regulations, and laws.

- Do not post content protected by any intellectual property rights, including but not limited to copyright, trademark, or other proprietary rights, without permission from the owner.

- Adult content is permitted only in areas marked 'adult'. You must be 18 years or older to access these areas.

- Participation in all communities is subject to the Yahoo! Terms of Service.

- For specific rules, refer to the community guidelines of the service you are using – however nothing found elsewhere may override these basic principles.

Yahoo! does not edit content posted in our communities. Yahoo! may, in our sole discretion, take action against users who post material or engage in activity that violates these principles or the Terms of Service or is otherwise objectionable. Such action may include , without notice, termination of your Yahoo! ID and everything associated with it, including email accounts, groups, posts, pages, and profiles.

Please report any violations to our Customer Care Team.

Figure 15-1. *Yahoo! publishes and links to a clear, straightforward set of community guidelines that apply across the entire Yahoo! network. Specific Yahoo! sites may also have their own additional community guidelines.*

Explicit and Implicit Norms in Online Groups

Social interfaces are designed and deployed to support ongoing, geographically dispersed gatherings of people drawn together by common interests and the conversational power of textual exchange. Through this activity—in which participants engage in a process of writing for others and reading what others write in return—a number of complex phenomena are apparent: questions are asked and answered, information is sought and provided, people chat about matters both trivial and profound. And, as they come to know one another over time, participants can come to perceive the space where they interact as a kind of home, a place in which something like a community can take shape. As in other social contexts, such social groups develop their own sets of norms, which they use to define those behaviors and attitudes they accept as appropriate for their members. Over time, these norms become embedded within the very fabric of the community's interactions and expectations; they become a guide, a rubric for how to behave within the community, as well as a benchmark for the degree to which newcomers are perceived and either welcomed as full members or treated with the suspicion due outsiders.

Social norms may be defined as a set of values particular to a group, the purpose of which is to provide a sense of balance, a mechanism by which people may gauge what is "normal" and acceptable in a specific context or situation. Such norms are not defined by outside factors; rather, they emerge directly from the activities, motives, and goals of the group itself. Social interfaces function as settings within which such a process may take place. The sociologist Robert K. Merton, in a classic formulation of social norms, distinguished between *attitudinal* and *behavioral* norms. However, since attitudes are visible in online settings only through visible behavior—only, that is, through the medium of textual production—it seems more appropriate to think of norms in online interactions in terms of a different distinction. Online social norms can be divided into two types: explicit and implicit norms.

Explicit norms are codified in formal written documents such as FAQs, and user agreements that outline the purpose and expectations of the group. Such norms are distinguishable from rules in that, even though they are codified in FAQs, they often have no institutional *imprimatur* beyond the general agreement of group members; thus, they may lack formal mechanisms for invoking sanctions, and can be subject to debate and contention within the group they purport to govern. In online settings, explicit norms, since they are formalized and openly articulated, function as public expressions of a community's standards of rightness and wrongness in social behaviors. In ideal situations, explicit norms are directly linked to the group itself through some kind of formalized process of development and review (an example can be seen in USENET FAQ documents, which are typically re posted regularly for comments from group members). Thus, they can be distinguished from truly external norms such as rules or laws that may be imposed truly from outside. Typically, documents outlining explicit norms might address acceptable topics for discussion, defining a group's normative areas of interest, or might provide specific guidelines for behavior, such as the "dos and don'ts" of posting practices. They form what could be called the baseline normative expectations of the community, making explicit the fundamental conventions and parameters that govern behavior and interaction within the group. They both document certain definable aspects of the worldview a group holds of itself and paint a portrait of themselves through which they can present that worldview to the outside world.

—continued—

Explicit and Implicit Norms in Online Groups

Implicit norms, by contrast, are not formally codified, but emerge socially through the day-to-day interactions of the group. These norms may or may not ultimately be formalized, and often are not even explicitly voiced, but are widely understood and accepted by group members and are used informally to define and police acceptable behavior within the group. Often, documents delineating explicit norms make oblique reference to the existence of implicit norms (without defining those norms directly), acknowledging a give-and-take between explicit norms and actual normative behaviors, and encouraging newcomers to spend time observing group postings for some time before engaging in active interaction.

Because implicit norms are embedded in the discursive activities of an online group rather than being explicitly documented, they are tightly linked to the overall character of the group, giving it much of its discursive flavor and pushing its participants in the direction of certain topics of conversation and certain ways of engaging with one another. As a result, implicit norms can emerge in many different ways as a group persists over time; for instance, because newcomers may or may not enter the community with any kind of understanding of its implicit norms, responses to such an entry may reflect the potency of implicit norms as the newcomer is evaluated according to her influence. Implicit norms may also affect the ways in which participants establish their individual and group identities within their shared space, how they refer to one another, the degree to which they accept or reject pseudonyms or other expressions of creativity, the degree to which they tolerate flaming, humor, or off-topic posting, etc.

One of the most interesting impacts of implicit norms is the way in which they influence what could be called the "structure of the 'meta'," as groups spend time either dissecting their own discussions or directly focusing on issues related to acceptable behavior and group norms. Such "meta discussions"—discussions about discussions—can draw conversation and attention away from a community's nominal shared area of interest into long, often detailed, and sometimes seemingly interminable tangents devoted to the dynamics of interaction itself. While these discussions are often strongly disparaged by community members—who can view them as distractions from more interesting matters—they can also serve as a primary mechanism through which groups can interrogate the boundaries of what is acceptable, can construct norms through channels other than the formalized structure of the FAQ, and can enforce a certain degree of compliance to those norms. Note: a fuller discussion of these issues can be found as part of a study of norms in two Usenet newsgroups in the following article: Burnett, G., and Bonnici, L. (2003). "Beyond the FAQ: Implicit and explicit norms in Usenet newsgroups." *Library and Information Science Research*, 25, 333–351.

—Gary Burnett, Associate Professor,
College of Communication and Information,
Florida State University

Role Model

If you conceive of the founders or creators of a social website as a kind of external deity ruling with an iron fist, you conjure up one sort of image of a community, but if instead you picture the founders manifesting (or "incarnating"?) as ordinary users in the system, then they can walk among the common folk and demonstrate how life in this microcosm is really intended to be lived (Figure 15-2). This doesn't preclude attending to and learning from the innovations and revealing mistakes of your users, but it is a proven method for getting patterns and norms of behavior established from the get-go.

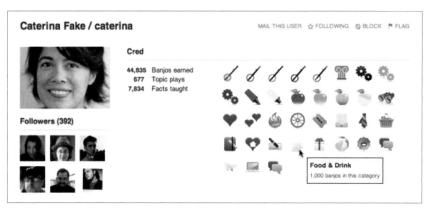

Figure 15-2. *By manifesting as a full participant, a founder can seed the community with great content while actively modeling the intended behavior and reinforcing the norms and expectations of a new community.*

Potemkin Village (Anti-Pattern)

Users may want separate areas for discussing separate topics, and site creators may have an elaborate vision of a complex arrangement of topic and groups, but instead of creating a complicated empty scaffolding in hopes of enticing community to take root (the "if you build it, they will come" fallacy), start small and compact, and then prepare to grow organically (Figure 15-3).

Create one main topic, a pinned (permanently on top) welcome topic, and perhaps a separate help topic, and nothing else. Resist the urge to anticipate the contours of the conversations and groups. Wait until people are begging for a subtopic, then fork the original group. Repeat.

This way, any pioneer community members will all interact in a single shared space, with no dilution of numbers. By the time they want to start sequestering topics from one another you'll have already reached critical mass.

Continue to resist calving off new groups until they are clearly and undeniably needed.

Building out a thorough structure of anticipated groups or discussions before a site has any real life in it creates a "Potemkin Village," an empty, fake site that dissipates any early momentum it might otherwise gather across too many cubbyholes.

	Me and My Day Job	2	262	My Gainful ... by noonie Mar 28 2009 - 2:31pm
	Most Life-Changing Show	4	335	Most Cosmic ... by J T Dutton Mar 25 2009 - 5:43am
	News and Talk Deadhead History lives here! along with everyday talk topics.	35	7691	spinnin' ... by johnman 3 hours 3 min ago
	Tapers	5	646	The Vindex by Sunshine-daydre... 19 hours 23 min ago
	The Vineyard This is where all the vines grow, along with related technical and other discussion. New to vining? See the New Vines 2009 topic for details on how to get started.	219	13543	Dylan-Dead ... by Phatmoye 49 min 8 sec ago
	The Scene WharfRats live here, along with free-topic discussions and our own Shakedown Street. Talk too, of the best and worst scenes, and the Unbroken Chain symposium.	6	119	The Summer of ... by lamagonzo Mar 27 2009 - 3:23pm
	Dancin' In The Street Topic-free discussion.	19	1044	Meet Me at ... by braygun 1 hour 55 min ago
	Shakedown Street The virtual parking lot to hawk your (legal, please) wares.	2	164	Your own ... by ccs tryin real ... Mar 28 2009 - 5:06pm
	Strangers Stopping Strangers Did you meet a fellow traveller in an offbeat kinda way?	5	111	As I was ... by Richard Vigeant Mar 27 2009 - 6:40pm
	Wharf Rats The folks, not just the song.	1	312	WharfRats Meet ... by Sparkling Clean Mar 27 2009 - 4:08am

Figure 15-3. *Instead of building a Potemkin Village, the architects of the relaunched dead.net site started with a judicious few groups and then let the community spawn the rest.*

Collective Governance

Determine how much self-governing you want your community members to do, and then give them the tools to do it with. They will want to make their own decisions. They may want to use voting to do so sometimes.

Also, confer with your users when deciding on the direction of the site. Don't necessarily bow to the majority's will, but some decisions are best made when given over to the community.

As Craigslist has wrestled with sustainable ideas for making money without damaging the "magic" of its community, the founder has frequently asked the community to help decide the direction of the site. For example, the decision to charge for rental listings in a few hot real estate markets and keep everything else free was made by consensus within the existing user community.

Building an Online Community

You want to grow a healthy and vibrant community. As you're designing the interface, think about the different kinds of participants. Of course you need to figure out who the influencers are in your online community (the people who will help it grow), and provide them with visibility and tools to spread their influence. For influencers, consider special badges that show off their status; prominent display of fan/friend stats; asynchronous follow; robust share tools; special member messaging capabilities; special access to community staff; roles in community governance, moderation, and policing; private influencer-only groups; and special highlighting of their content. If you want more good content from your community, highlight the highest-quality content and bury the low-quality content. You will get more of what you highlight. When building your community interface, don't assume that all user content you get will be great, so design with a content burial system in addition to a content highlighting system. Don't just cultivate the big fish. Look for up-and-comers who create great content or are especially passionate. Help them attain visibility as if they were already superstars. Listen to their feedback. Give them attention and advice and opportunities. If you have an automated way to surface great user-created content, make sure your algorithm does not just pull up existing influencers. Your community blog is a good place to give up-and-comers some love. Their stories will inspire others and create engagement as members follow their successes. At least some of them will actually become superstars, and they'll be grateful, and naturally draw more passionate members into your community's orbit. Don't forget about the lurkers, who may be 99% of your audience. You can reflect their presence in numerous ways, such as displaying reader views on a blog post or highlighting recently browsed or most-popular items. Some may not ever post, but may be wonderful aggregators—does your community have a way users can bookmark, tag, or make lists? Create a game plan for gently easing lurkers into participation. Use tactics such as a simple "recommend" link at the end of an article or a "like" button. Develop a system of alerts to remind users of new content, member actions, or tasks that need completing. If you have Q & A, surface relevant questions that need answering to users upon login or a profile visit. Make it super easy to participate. Consider integrating with existing social applications; if lurkers see that their friends are active on your site, they are much more likely to participate.

—Shara Kasaric, Social Strategy,
http://www.sharakarasic.com

Group Moderation

The goal of community moderation is to foster rich conversations, connections, relationships, and activities. Reward the kinds of participation you wish to see more of, and gently discourage the behaviors you believe are counterproductive.

When dealing with flame wars and sock puppets (see "Flame Wars" on page 304 and "Sock Puppets" on page 305), "don't feed the trolls." Whenever possible, de-escalate. Give problem users "time outs" (suspensions from posting privileges), and when necessary, freeze entire threads or topics to let emotions cool.

For incorrigible characters, consider banning them (but there's always the risk they will simply reregister with a new account), or put them in a "Hall of Mirrors" in which only they (and perhaps other spammers and trolls) can see their posts. They will wonder why no one is falling for their tricks anymore.

Official moderators (paid, employed staff) can do only so much. They will need to find allies in the community itself. Promote from within. Create labels (see "Labels" on page 163) and identify the most helpful community members. Grant moderation privileges to trusted users, and harness the feedback of all users to promote the best contributions and bury the worst.

The Community-Building Trifecta

One of the most common questions I'm asked is, "How do you build a community?" This question is usually followed by the asker explaining that he must build a community because either his boss wants him to do it, or because he thinks it's the fastest way to get the word out about a new product. Building a community takes a great deal of effort and is often impossible. I have no interest in extinguishing someone's genuine desire to be a part of a community, but building one takes a lot of work and is extremely difficult. To build a community, you need passion, commitment, and proper tools. If even one of these three components is missing, your efforts will not be successful.

The passion must come from both your side and from the community. Building a community around a product or idea that is not going to elicit passion is impossible. In other words, if your idea/product sucks, don't waste your time. You will not be able to manufacture passion. If you don't have passion, you don't have a community; it's that simple.

Committing yourself to months of continued nurturing is also required. This must come from you or your team, not from your burgeoning community. The time drain is significant, so don't be surprised to find that you must spend hours each day creating and responding to discussion topics. In the early days, almost all of the creation of content will be on your side. Do you have the resources and desire to do this? Without this significant commitment of time, your "soon-to-be-community" will die a quick death.

—continued—

The Community-Building Trifecta

Tools are the final part of the community trifecta. Don't ask new community members to stumble through a complicated registration process or spend more than the minimum amount of time interacting with your interface. Reputation should be considered. How a user receives information should be well thought out. The tools you employ should make talking to you, and to other members of the community, easy and fast. Don't create barriers because you failed to properly plan, create, and test a vital area of the user's experience.

In short, if you don't have the time, the money, the desire, and the dedication to create a community, don't bother. It's much faster/cheaper/easier to locate a great community and take part there. As well, if your product or idea is just bad, and you still need to get the word out, do what people in your situation have been doing for years: spend a great deal of money marketing it. Community is precious, and it's great when it works, but it's not viral marketing.

—Robyn Tippins, Yahoo! Developer Network,
http://developer.yahoo.com

Collaborative Filtering

What

People need help finding the best contributions to online community (Figure 15-4).

Figure 15-4. *Slashdot popularized the idea of harnessing the preferences of the site's readership to vote articles up or down and (in theory) bring the highest-quality articles and comments to the surface while burying the worst.*

Use this pattern when you have a large base of contributors and a wide range of quality.

Enable authenticated users to vote up or down, or otherwise rate content. Optionally give users with higher reputation status more privileges to highlight or hide content. Aggregate the votes, and use this to determine sorting and display order (Figure 15-5).

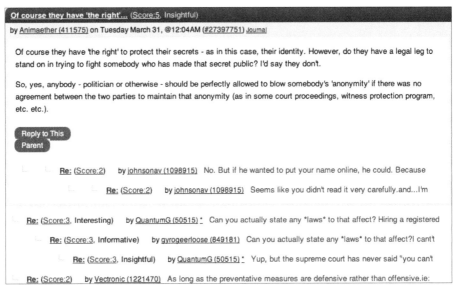

Figure 15-5. *At Slashdot, only comments above a rating threshold are displayed automatically in the thread. A reader can still expand a hidden comment to read it, or change her preferences to move the threshold.*

The collective wisdom of the community can help filter out the best contributions and conversations.

"Reputation Influences Behavior" on page 154

"Thumbs Up/Down Ratings" on page 269

"Vote to Promote" on page 266

Kuro5hin (*http://www.kuro5hin.org/*)

Slashdot (*http://slashdot.org/*)

Yahoo! Answers (*http://answers.yahoo.com/*)

Report Abuse

What

Any active, successful social system online is subject to abuse. We know it will occur, so we need to have processes in place for identifying and mitigating it. People need a way to report it that isn't too inconvenient and doesn't require them to type in or restate information that we could glean from context.

In a growing community, abuse reporting scales up faster than human beings can handle it, so an escalation strategy is needed to deal with the consequences of popularity.

Use when

Use this pattern to allow your users the ability to self-moderate content that is contributed by the community (Figure 15-6).

Figure 15-6. *To safeguard a thriving community, you must pay attention to any signals of abuse, and enabling your participants to flag abusive content helps the community moderate itself.*

How

The experience of reporting abuse should be as simple and transparent as possible. Do not ask the user to enter data that could have been captured automagically. Make it clear to the user how the report will be handled, without overpromising, and then deliver the user cleanly back to the context from which he reported the abuse. Where possible, immediately hide the reported content from the user who reported it:

* Offer a Report Abuse link on any community-generated content (optionally include the standard flag icon).

* Reporting abuse should take the user to a simple form.

* Abuse reports should be tracked as signals along with other evidence of abuse.

For highly granular user-generated content (such as a stream of vitality updates on a page), the Report Abuse affordance must be made available individually for each item, without overwhelming the page with a stream of Report Abuse links or little flags.

Report Abuse link

Use consistent terminology for labeling the report link. Some sites prefer "Report Abuse," and others use "Flag."

Optional icon

Optionally, include a consistent icon to mark the link for reporting abuse. (Reporting abuse is sometimes colloquially referred to as "flagging" abusive content, hence the iconic symbol for the abuse report button is a flag.) It should be easy for the user to spot a Report Abuse flag icon and click it to initiate the abuse reporting process:

- Avoid the flag icon in contexts where it will conflict with existing terminology or symbols (as in Mail, where "flagging" a message indicates that it is important and not that it is abusive).

- Likewise, if the icon doesn't suit the design, then use only the "Report Abuse" link text.

- Do not use the icon without text. (It's OK to use text without an icon.)

Abuse report form

The form should be as simple as possible (but no simpler):

- Clicking the Report Abuse link should take the user to a form where he can select the type or nature of the abuse and optionally fill in more context.

- The user should not be required to manually enter the relevant URL or page title or any other metadata we can glean from the source page.

- If possible, use an inline short form for people who are already signed in (they just choose from two categories—offensive or illegal—optionally make a comment, and they're done).

- Signed-out users will need a full-page form where they can indicate how they can be contacted.

Confirmation

Submission of the form should generate a success message that does not promise any specific action, and then should return reporting users to the original context where they initially started the abuse-reporting process. Optionally, hide the offending content from them while the response to the report is pending.

Abuse tracking

After a user submits an abuse report, it must be reviewed by a customer care agent (unless a reputation system is in place to track signals of abuse). As a site scales up, additional considerations have to be factored into the abuse-reporting process:

- Just provide a way for a user to report abusive content and send the request to a support team for review.

- Add priority to different requests by allowing users to choose whether this abuse violates community guidelines or is illegal.

- Take into consideration whether you should inform the original poster about the abuse report.

- Take into consideration whether an appeal mechanism should be provided.

Why

Providing users a standard way to report abusive content and behavior complements any algorithmic and behavioral signals of abuse gathered.

Related patterns

"Reputation Influences Behavior" on page 154

As seen on

Craigslist (*http:// craigslist.org/*)

Yahoo! (*http://www.yahoo.com/*)

Most social sites

Sources

This pattern is based on the Report Abuse component pattern written primarily by Micah Alpern at Yahoo!.

What's the Story?

Shara Kasaric says, "Good stories are the glue of the strongest online and offline communities. Every group, from hunter-gather tribes to modern physicists, has a story that binds them together with history, mission, and purpose. Weave your story into your interface and interactions, and let your users become the main characters in that story."

Further Reading

"Community Lessons from Flickr's Heather Champ," from Brian Oberkirch's Only Connect blog, *http://www.brianoberkirch.com/2008/03/07/ community-lessons-from-flickrs-heather-champ/*

Derek Powazek's posts on community, *http://powazek.com/posts/category/community*

"The Virtual Community," by Howard Rheingold, *http://www.well.com/~hlr/vcbook/*

Chapter 16

Where in the World?

It's a beautiful day in this neighborhood. A beautiful day for a neighbor.
Would you be mine? Could you be mine?

—*Mr. Rogers' Neighborhood*

TUBBS: I haven't seen you before. Are you local?

MARTIN: No, I'm meeting up with a friend actually—going hiking.

TUBBS: Don't touch the things! This is a local shop for local people, there's nothing for you here!

TUBBS: Edward! Edward!

EDWARD: Hello, hello? What's going on? What's all this shouting, we'll have no trouble here!

TUBBS: I caught him stealing from the shop.

EDWARD: Who is he? Is his identity known?

TUBBS: He's not local.

—"This is a Local Shop," sketch by League of Gentlemen, BBC

The Local Connection

One of the things we like to do as social creatures is to plan events and gather in groups. Lunches, meetings, playdates, parties, weddings, even funerals—mundane events, and events to punctuate the week and celebrate milestones and major life events. Events have become easier to plan with a variety of online tools, and with the explosion of social tools, they can be more collaborative than ever. Invitation tools and calendaring are two of the oldest applications available online. The addition of the social graph and other rich social tools continues to keep these tools relevant, and we see these features creeping into mainstream social networking sites such as Facebook and LinkedIn.

GPS capabilities are available in more and more of our devices and applications, and the proliferation of mobile devices means we can be connected and location-aware regardless of where we are. Location tools such as geo-tagging, geo-mashing, and even neighborhoods provide a context of place around what we are doing online. Although people may be generally drawn together based on interests or on activities, the natural progression of a community will eventually lead people to get together in real life. The crossover of interests and desire for face-to-face meetings is powerful and really useful. Without explicit interactions to facilitate meeting in person integrated into interest sites, people will still figure out how to bring groups together—only it will be cumbersome and may require the use of multiple sites, along with email, texting, and old-school phone calls. Building in event-creation tools makes this much easier for people.

The following patterns—when added to things like identity, presence, and activities such as forums, collections, and groups—create a rich suite of tools that can be combined to help bring people together, whether they actually know one another or not.

Being Local

What

The user wants to use online social tools to facilitate offline events and meetings in her location (Figure 16-1).

Figure 16-1. *Upcoming.org focuses on local events.*

- Use the following patterns to bring people together at real locations, offline.
- Use to plan around real locations, utilizing addresses and maps.

Face-to-Face Meeting

The user wants to meet offline with people from his network, in a nearby location (Figure 16-2).

Figure 16-2. *Meetup facilitates people meeting in their local areas for a variety of events.*

Use this pattern to help facilitate face-to-face meetings between people.

Allow users to create events and invite participants.

Pre-event creation

- Allow users to enter full details of an event, including location, time, date, details, and special considerations (Figure 16-3).

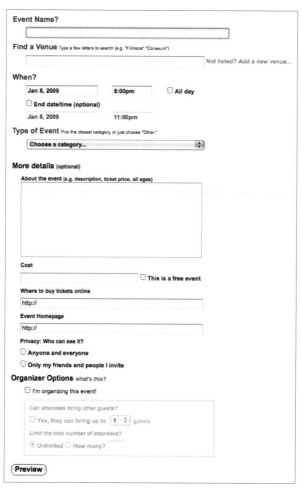

Figure 16-3. *Event creation form on Upcoming.*

- Integrate a calendar (see "Calendaring" on page 416) for scheduling time-based events (Figure 16-4).

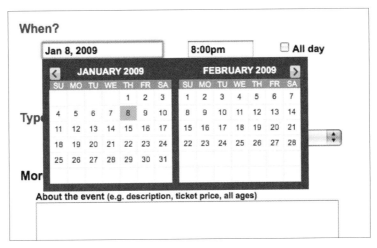

Figure 16-4. *Calendar picker on Upcoming.*

- Allow event creators to mark an event as public or private (Figures 16-5 and 16-6).

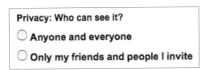

Figure 16-5. *Privacy options on Upcoming.*

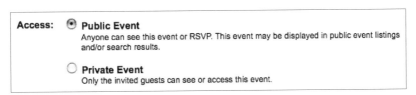

Figure 16-6. *Privacy options on Socializr. Secondary text clearly articulates what each choice means.*

- Allow users to select locations from a list of places: from city guides, yellow pages, or other directories.
- Consider indicating nearby establishments, like restaurants, parking, coffee shops, ATMs, or other relevant businesses, which allows for comprehensive planning (Figure 16-7).

Figure 16-7. *Upcoming provides a map indicating the venue of the event and shows nearby parking, restaurants, ATMs, or a user-entered item.*

- Provide the full address, phone number, and other relevant details, such as costs, hours, restrictions, or ambiance.

Pre-event attendees

- Allow users to RSVP to events. Consider showing RSVPs to other users and indicating attendees from a viewer's network (Figures 16-8, 16-9, and 16-10).

Figure 16-8. *Upcoming shows who from your network is also attending or thinking about attending an event.*

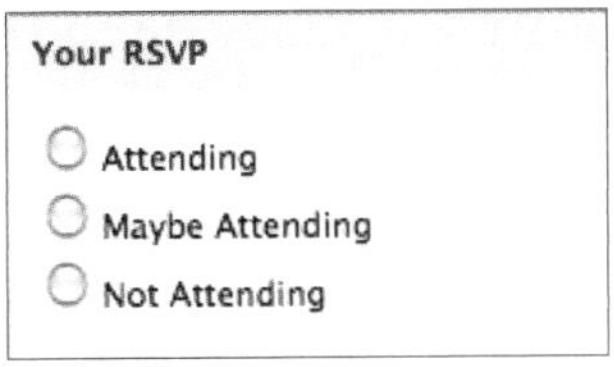

Your RSVP

○ Attending
○ Maybe Attending
○ Not Attending

Figure 16-9. *Facebook offers three choices of RSVP for events.*

Figure 16-10. *Showing attendees can encourage others to RSVP "yes" if they see someone they know in the list.*

- Consider allowing public events where users invite themselves or follow an event.

- Consider adding wiki software for collaborative content creation.

- Integrate maps for selecting and displaying locations (see "Geo-Mapping" on page 425).

- Allow users to indicate a method for receiving alerts or reminders for events (see "Reminding" on page 420).

- Allow users to easily invite their network or a subset of their network to an event (Figure 16-11). Consider a batch invite process, such as multiselect, for sending invites.

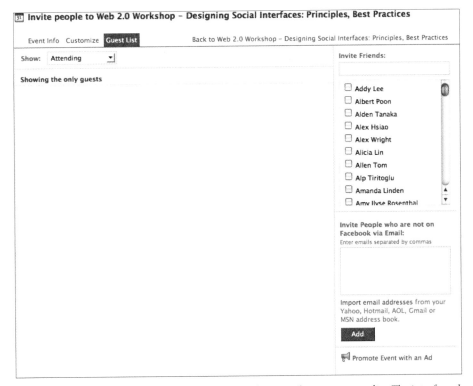

Figure 16-11. *Facebook presents a user's network in order to easily create a guest list. The interface also offers the ability to add email addresses for those not on the service.*

Post-event attendees

- Allow users to attach photos to the event (Figure 16-12).

Figure 16-12. *Upcoming creates a "scrapbook" for each event attended or watched. Photos from the event are associated with the event through a mashup with Flickr.*

- If the user attended (or RSVP'd "yes"), show the event in his calendar of past events.
- Consider asking the attendees to rate the event afterward (Figure 16-13).

Figure 16-13. *Meetup offers a rating option to attendees of recent events.*

Public events

- Allow events to be searchable by keyword/category, tags, and date.
- Allow users to browse through events and filter by keyword/category, tags, and date (Figure 16-14).

Figure 16-14. *Upcoming filters events by date first.*

- Show users a list of events being attended by friends in their network (Figure 16-15).

Jan 14 2 weeks away	San Francisco, California, United States	**DIYcity San Francisco** PariSoMa Coworking Space Twitter bots, aggregators, social software, mobile apps - we use these things more and more in our daily routines to make our lives better. But can we also use them to remake our cities altogether? ...	Joshua Kaufman
Jan 16 2 weeks away	San Francisco, California, United States	**Book Signing** Stacey's Bookstore	peterme
Jan 20 3 weeks away	San Francisco, California, United States	**End Bush** Bush and Presidio Regardless of whether McCain or Obama wins the election, on January 20th 2009 at noon Eastern time, 9am Pacific time, George W. Bush will no longer be President of the USA. Meet at Bush & Presidio by...	endico
		Simulcast of Presidential Inauguration Civic Center Historic District NextArts Presents: The Inauguration of the 44th President of the United States of America - Simulcast (The Sock It To Me Concert) Where: Civic Center, San Francisco When: January 20, 2009 7:00AM-12No...	endico
Jan 27 4 weeks away	San Francisco, California, United States	**IxDA SF Presents: Tap is the New Click with Dan Saffer** Adobe San Francisco Please RSVP on the IxDA-SF Ning site: http://ixdasf.ning.com/events/ixda- sf-presents-tap-is-the-1 Tap is the New Click Even though touchscreen and gestural technology has been around for decades, Nin...	dansaffer
Jan 28 4 weeks away	San Francisco, California, United States	**The Album Leaf** Bottom of the Hill The Album Leaf is the solo endeavor of Tristeza's Jimmy LaValle. He incorporates ambient noise, field recordings, taped conversations, radio transmissions and other unique sounds to create a sound and...	endico
Jan 31 over 1 month away	San Francisco, California, United States	**Teens in Tech Conference** Microsoft San Francisco Office The Teens in Tech Conference is bringing youth and technology together in San Francisco. Learn from teenagers what they think about the current trends of teenage technology. Feel inspired to create te...	fotogail, samtripodi

Figure 16-15. *Friend's events on Upcoming sorted by date first.*

Semi-public events

- Indicate whether the user must be part of the network in order to RSVP or attend the
  event (Figure 16-16).

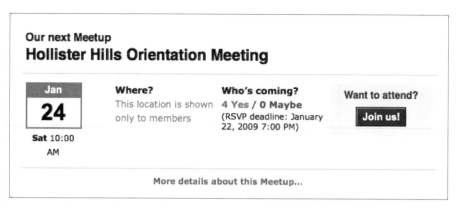

Figure 16-16. *Meetup combines small interest groups with public events. Users must join the group first in order to RSVP for an event or activity.*

"Party", described next

Facebook (*http://www.facebook.com*)

Meetup (*http://www.meetup.com*)

Socializr (*http://www.socializr.com*)

Upcoming (*http://www.upcoming.org*)

Party

The user wants to plan an event and invite friends to join the party (Figure 16-17).

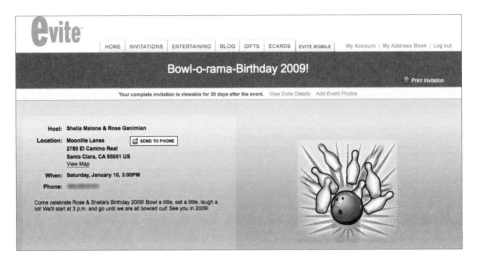

Figure 16-17. *Evite party invitation.*

Use when

- Use this pattern to allow users to create customized and personal invitations for events such as parties.
- Use this pattern to replace regular email for party planning.

How

Pre-party planning

Allow users to enter full details of an event, including location, time, date, details, and special considerations (Figure 16-18).

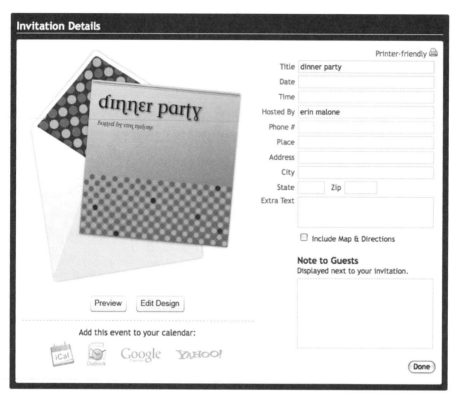

Figure 16-18. *Event details on MyPunchbowl.*

- Use a calendar picker for easy date selection and minimization of data entry errors (see "Calendaring" on page 416).

- Offer to add the event to the user's calendar (Yahoo!, iCal, Google, etc.).

- Allow event planners to poll invitees through the use of simple polls.

- Provide templates for invitation display. Allow the event creator to choose a theme that is appropriate to the theme of the party (Figures 16-19 and 16-20).

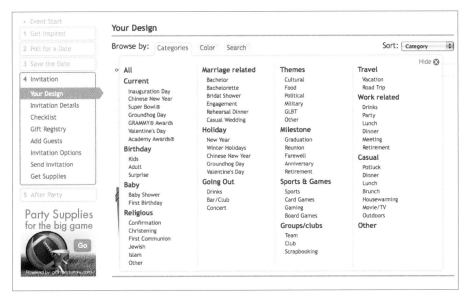

Figure 16-19. *Theme selection on MyPunchbowl.*

Figure 16-20. *Template section on MyPunchbowl.*

- Allow the event creator to invite multiple people at a time. Provide a field for adding multiple email addresses.
- Allow selection from the user's desktop address book (Figure 16-21).

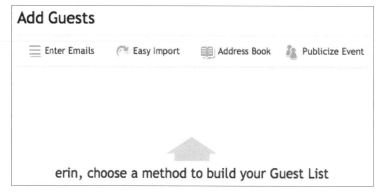

Figure 16-21. *MyPunchbowl offers the invitation creator a variety of ways to build a guest list.*

- Consider allowing selection from online address books, such as Plaxo and Yahoo!.
- Allow the event planner to save the email addresses for later use.

Invitees

- Offer to add the event to the user's calendar (Yahoo!, iCal, Google, etc.).
- Consider showing RSVPs to others and indicating attendees.
- Show the event on a map (Figure 16-22).

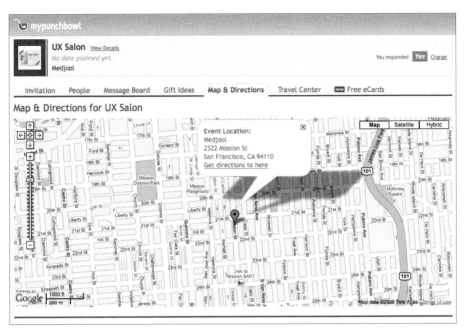

Figure 16-22. *MyPunchbowl integrates maps into the invitation.*

- Allow users to get directions to the event.
- Consider indicating nearby establishments, such as restaurants, parking, coffee shops, and ATMs, to allow for comprehensive planning.
- Show the full address and phone number of the location.
- If the event is at a public location, such as a restaurant or park, show details about the location: hours, ambiance, restrictions, etc.

After party

- Allow users to upload photos from the event.
- Consider allowing users to leave comments about the party.

Why

Giving users the tools to create offline events enhances relationships that previously may have existed only online. People want to gather, and they will use whatever tools are available to coordinate the event. Bringing this functionality into your site (if appropriate) will keep users engaged and can create a holistic experience that moves seamlessly from online to offline and back online again.

Related patterns

"Face-to-Face Meeting" on page 401

As seen on

Evite (*http://www.evite.com*)

Facebook (*http://www.facebook.com*)

MyPunchbowl (*http://www.mypunchbowl.com*)

Calendaring

What

A user wants to find or submit an event (public or private) based on a date or within a certain date range (Figure 16-23).

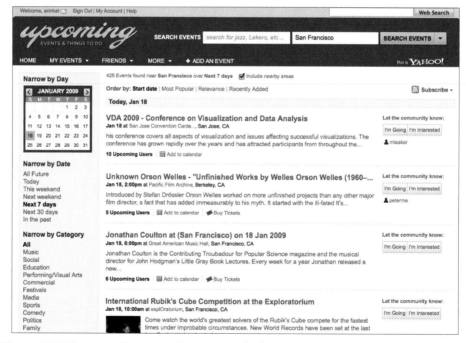

Figure 16-23. *Upcoming allows user to browse events by date.*

Use when

- Use this pattern to create date-driven events.

- Use this pattern to find events by date.

- Use this pattern with "Face-to-Face Meeting" on page 401 and "Party" on page 410.

How

- Allow users to associate an event with a date. This can be done through an event-planning interface or within a calendar interface (Figures 16-24 and 16-25).

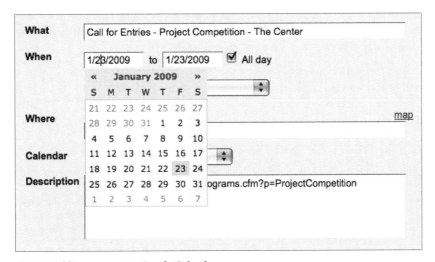

Figure 16-24. *Adding an event to Google Calendar.*

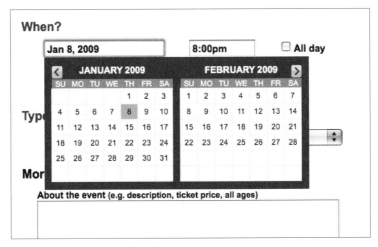

Figure 16-25. *Associating an event with a date on Upcoming.*

- Allow the event creator to indicate whether the event is public or private.

- Allow the calendar event to be shared, whether through direct selections from the user's network, through email, or through RSS, blogs, or other social offerings.

Selecting a specific date

When selecting an associated date for an event, allow the user to either type in the date or choose the date with a calendar picker. See the Calendar Picker pattern in the Yahoo! Pattern Library for detailed interaction specifics (*http://developer.yahoo.com/ypatterns/ selection/calendar.html*) and the Calendar component in the YUI Library for implementation code (*http://developer.yahoo.com/yui/calendar/*).

Providing the calendar picker allows the user to see the date in the context of other dates and the day of the week, and it ensures fewer data entry errors.

Calendar details

- Provide a title and description field (Figure 16-26).

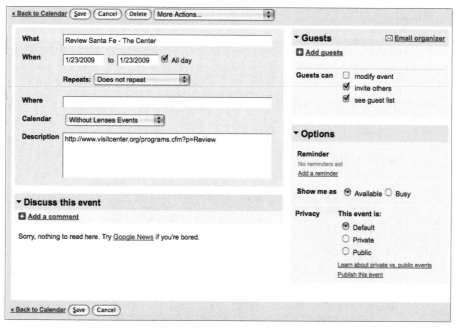

Figure 16-26. *Calendar entry on Google Calendar.*

- Provide a notes field for URLs and other information.

- Allow the user to associate a location to the event.

- When the details are complete, present the event in all presentations of the calendar (i.e., list view, day view, week view, and month view).

- Present the title, location, and as much of a description as appropriate for the display. For example, the list view would display most, if not all, of the description, whereas the month view may show only a truncated title.

- Use rollover panels to display the full calendar event without forcing the user to click.

Why

Events are time constrained, and including robust online calendaring tools will make creating parties, events, and face-to-face meetings easier to plan.

Provide enough functionality to be useful without creating a whole enterprise-level application.

Related patterns

"Face-to-Face Meeting" on page 401

"Party" on page 410

As seen on

30 Boxes (*http://www.30bxes.com*)

Evite (*http://www.evite.com*)

Facebook (*http://www.facebook.com*)

Google Calendar (*http://www.google.com/calendar*)

MyPunchbowl (*http://www.mypunchbowl.com*)

Upcoming (*http://www.upcoming.org*)

Yahoo! Calendar (*http://www.yahoo.com/calendar*)

Reminding

A user needs to know when an event is happening (Figure 16-27).

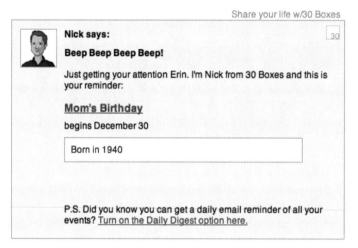

From: 30 Boxes <mail@30boxes.com>
Subject: **Reminder: Mom's Birthday (December 30)**
Date: December 29, 2008 12:00:01 AM PST
To: Erin Malone

Share your life w/30 Boxes

Nick says:

Beep Beep Beep Beep!

Just getting your attention Erin. I'm Nick from 30 Boxes and this is your reminder:

Mom's Birthday

begins December 30

Born in 1940

P.S. Did you know you can get a daily email reminder of all your events? Turn on the Daily Digest option here.

Figure 16-27. *30 Boxes sends out email reminders about events on the calendar.*

- Use this pattern to alert others where an event is happening.
- Use this pattern to encourage sending reminders to a mobile device or email account.

- When creating an event, allow the user to set reminders or alerts about those events (Figure 16-28).

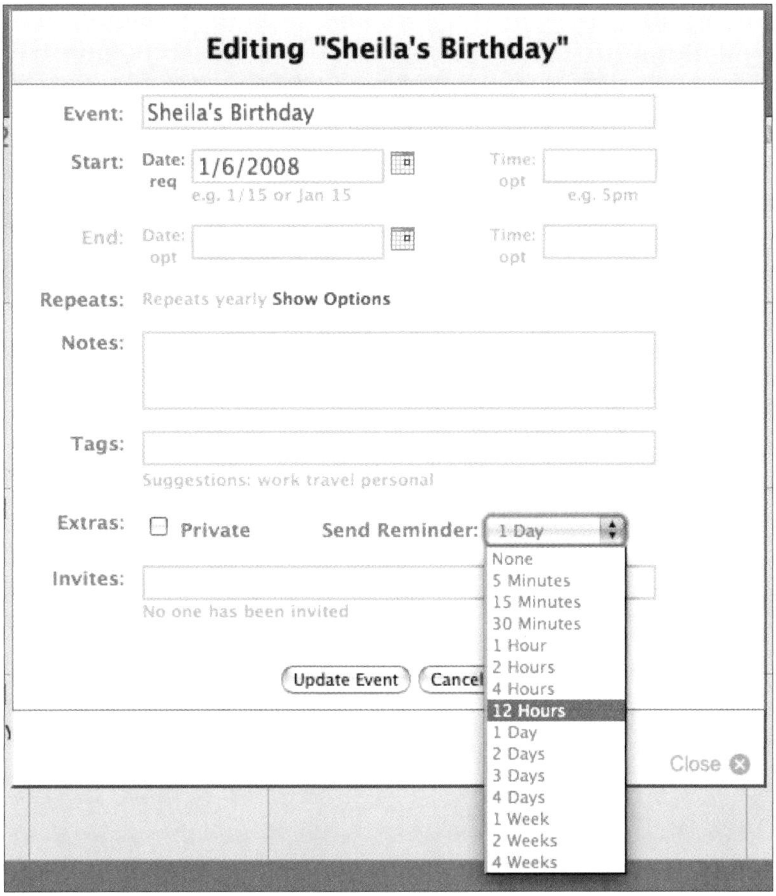
Editing "Sheila's Birthday"
Event:
Sheila's Birthday
Start:
Date: req
1/6/2008
e.g. 1/15 or Jan 15
Time: opt
e.g. 5pm
End:
Date: opt
Time: opt
Repeats:
Repeats yearly Show Options
Notes:
Tags:
Suggestions: work travel personal
Extras:
Private
Send Reminder:
1 Day
None
5 Minutes
15 Minutes
30 Minutes
1 Hour
2 Hours
4 Hours
12 Hours
1 Day
2 Days
3 Days
4 Days
1 Week
2 Weeks
4 Weeks
Invites:
No one has been invited
Update Event
Cancel
Close

Figure 16-28. *Setting up a reminder on 30 Boxes.*

- If the event creator is inviting attendees, set the reminder to automatically send alerts to the attendees.
- Give the user the ability to select from a preset list of reminder times. For instance, Yahoo! Calendar offers to send reminders from 14 days before the event all the way to 5 minutes before the event, and Google Calendar allows you to specify an exact number and then qualifies it with minutes, hours, days, weeks, months, etc. (Figures 16-29 and 16-30).

Reminder
Email
10
minutes
remove
Add a reminder

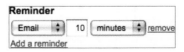

Figure 16-29. *Google Calendar reminder setup widget.*

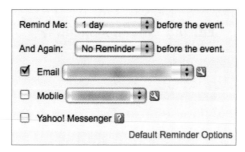

Figure 16-30. *Yahoo! Calendar reminder setup widget.*

- Reminders should be able to be sent to an email address and to mobile devices or added to a social networking profile.

- Consider allowing two reminders to be set, for example, 14 days and 5 days before the event.

- For public events, allow people to set their own reminders.

"Calendaring" on page 416

"Face-to-Face Meeting" on page 401

"Party" on page 410

30 Boxes (*http://www.30bxes.com*)

Facebook (*http://www.facebook.com*)

Google Calendar (*http://www.google.com/calendar*)

Yahoo! Calendar (*http://www.yahoo.com/calendar*)

Geo-Tagging

A user wants to annotate a person, place, or thing with a geographic tag, usually in the form of latitude/longitude, which is then translated into an address that can be placed on a map (Figure 16-31).

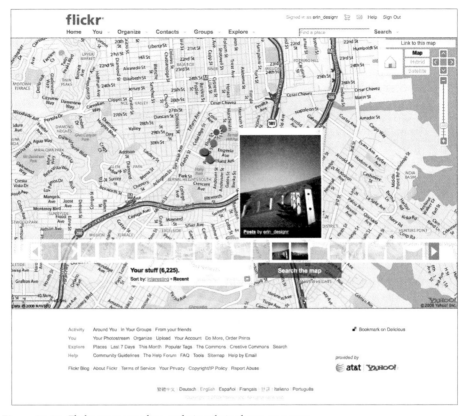

Figure 16-31. *Flickr users can place and view their photos on a map.*

Use this pattern when you want to place objects (people, places, or things) on a map.

- If the item is a photo and there is exif data that includes lat/long information, associate that location string with the object (Figure 16-32).

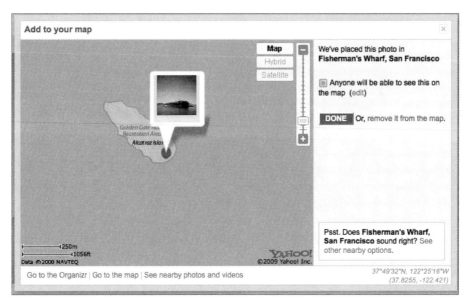

Figure 16-32. *Adding a photo to a map on Flickr through selection on a map. Lat/long coordinates are presented in the lower right of the interface, but an easy-to-understand real place translation of the location is presented in the top right of the interface.*

- Automatically place the item on a map.

- If the item has an address associated with it, such as a business, automatically place the item on a map.

- Allow the user to associate an address with an object.

- Consider allowing users to drag and drop items (photos, listings, friends) onto a map and associating a location with the item.

- Allow the user to refine the location by offering an address form. Allow the full address, a city/state combo, or even a zip/postal code. Fields should be optional.

- Allow users to enter specific latitude and longitude numbers indicating a point on a map as an alternative to picking a spot on a map.

- Use the emerging format for geo data, e.g., geotagged geo:lat=57.64911 geo:lon=10.40744. The first item is the tag "geotagged", allowing all items to be searched from a common tag. The other tags are "geo:lat" and "geo:long", which was established by geobloggers and has been popularized by sites such as Flickr, Panoramio, and Delicious.

- Convert geotags into user-friendly addresses when presenting locations in the interface.

- Clearly indicate how the information will be used.

Why

Offering geo-tagging capabilities for assets, particularly photos, allows them to exist not only in time but also in a context related to the real world. Placing images on a map gives people a sense that this image really exists and that they might see this, too, if they went there. Geo-tagging also announces to a person's network that she was there, at this spot.

Related patterns

"Face-to-Face Meeting" on page 401

"Geo-Mapping", described next

"Geo-Mashing" on page 428

As seen on

Flickr (*http://www.flickr.com*)

Upcoming (*http://www.upcoming.org*)

Geo-Mapping

What

A user wants to see where he is (or where his stuff is) in relation to other people and places (Figure 16-33).

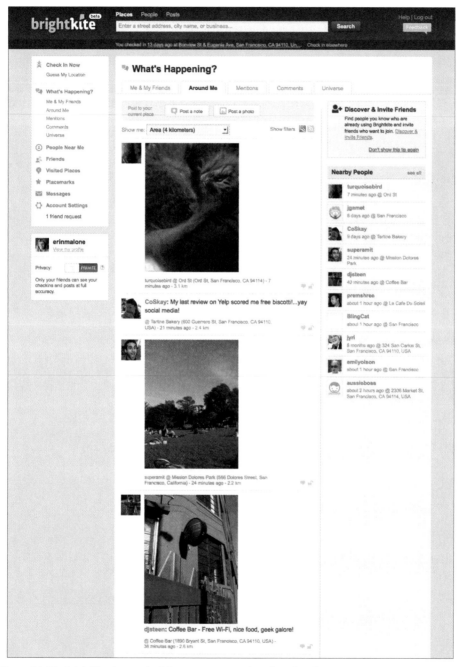

Figure 16-33. *Brightkite shows what's happening around me based on location.*

Use this pattern to automatically place people, status updates, photos, and other objects on a map.

- Present the item location with a graphic pointer on the map (Figure 16-34).

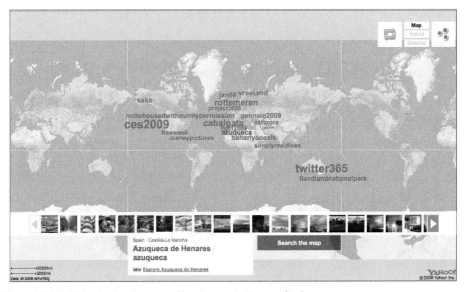

Figure 16-34. *Flickr displays tags as well as images in its map display.*

- Allow the user to see other people or items on the map in relation to himself (if the user is on a mobile device or has indicated his location).
- Allow the user to search for items based on location.

Providing easy drag-and-drop tools for placing items on a map can offer alternative ways to filter objects on a site. Additionally, showing items on a map can provide contextually relevant information and can help support local, face-to-face meetings and gatherings between people.

"Face-to-Face Meeting" on page 401

"Geo-Mashing" on page 428

"Geo-Tagging" on page 422

Brightkite (*http://www.brightkite.com*)

Flickr (*http://www.flickr.com*)

Geo-Mashing

Geo mashups are applications and tools that pull together map APIs from map providers such as Yahoo!, Google, and MapQuest and geotagged content, such as photos, user blogs, news articles, real estate data, videos, status casts, and any other data that can have geotags associated with it (Figures 16-35 and 16-36).

Figure 16-35. *EveryBlock pulls together mapping and content from government records (liquor licenses, zoning permits), real estate listings, photos, media and news articles, and police calls to create a local neighborhood information portal.*

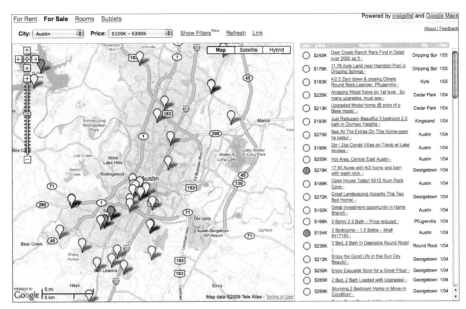

Figure 16-36. *HousingMaps mashes up Google Maps with Craigslist Housing information and shows homes for sale, rent, or share on a map.*

Neighborhood

What

A user wants to know what's going on around her neighborhood (Figure 16-37).

Figure 16-37. *Outside.in presents news and other content based on neighborhoods.*

Use this pattern when pulling together geographic or place-specific content.

- Allow users to select a neighborhood for filtering information. The neighborhood boundaries should include relevant location definitions, including zip code and school districts, and explicit metadata and location keywords (Figure 16-38).

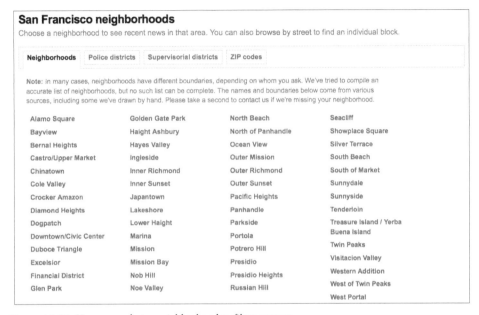

Figure 16-38. *Users can select a neighborhood to filter content.*

- Allow people to explicitly identify with a neighborhood, through selection of a specific neighborhood or entry of a zip code.

- Present the option to connect to people from the same neighborhood or in nearby areas.

- Allow people to search by neighborhood, zip code, or other relevant location data (Figure 16-39).

Figure 16-39. *Nearby neighborhoods and other area definitions available for filtering content.*

- Provide an easy mechanism for users to switch neighborhoods.

- Consider mashing up a variety of interesting and relevant content related to the selected neighborhood. The types of content that can be pulled together include photos, news items, business listings, real estate listings, police blotter announcements, ratings and reviews of businesses, parks and public places, events, and people.
- Display the user's location on a map.
- Display relevant content on a map to indicate proximity to the user.

Why

Bringing together local information around neighborhoods provides a more relevant experience for people who want to keep tabs on what's happening nearby. The tools can also support bringing people together who are already close in proximity.

Related patterns

"Geo-Mapping" on page 425

"Geo-Mashing" on page 428

"Geo-Tagging" on page 422

As seen on

EveryBlock (*http://www.everyblock.com*)

Outside.in (*http://www.outsidein.com*)

Yahoo! Local Neighborhoods (*http://local.yahoo.com/neighbors/?csz=South+San+Francisco%2C+CA*)

Mobile and Location

Mobile phones are becoming more ubiquitous in the U.S., and in Asia and other parts of the world they are often the primary mode for connecting to the Internet and with other people. Tools and applications for enabling social experiences need to be designed for the mobile experience as more and more people use the phone exclusively or move seamlessly between the computer and the phone for their social transactions.

What

A user wants to connect with friends or post content while on the go (Figure 16-40).

Figure 16-40. *Zannel offers users the ability to see themselves as well as their network on a map.*

Use this pattern when you want to enable users to:

- Share photos and/or videos from their mobile devices.
- Plot themselves on a map or announce their locations.
- Meet up with other people nearby.

Content

- Provide one-click upload of photos and videos.

- Allow the user to do his setup on the Web as an option. More complex setup that requires typing and data entry is easier with a keyboard than a phone interface.

  But, with that said, the setup and upload of content should be easy on the phone for those not equipped with a computer. (See Figure 16-41.)

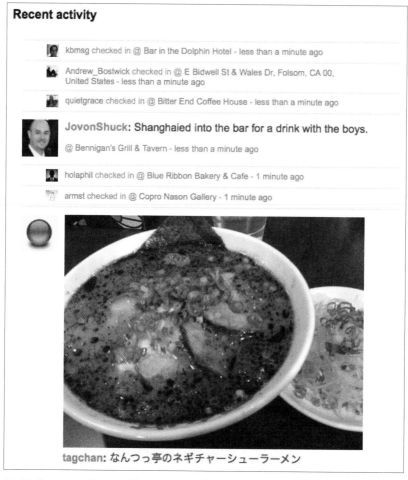

Figure 16-41. *Recent activity posted by users of Brightkite also shows up on the website.*

- Provide one-click ability to share items of interest to others.

Geo

Most mobile phones are now being equipped with geo-location features, which means more and more applications and tools can bring together location and people in interesting ways:

- Utilize the built-in features of geo-mapping to allow users to share their locations with a trusted network.

- Allow users to turn off presence or location indicators.

- Use a user's location to show nearby businesses or events of interest.

Gatherings

Using a combination of geo-location and text messaging, users can easily pull together an impromptu gathering. Services such as Foursquare and Loopt offer the ability to see yourself and those in your network plotted on a map (Figure 16-42).

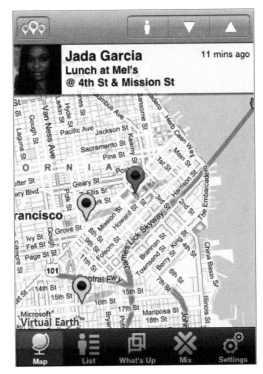

Figure 16-42. *Loopt allows users to broadcast to their network for impromptu meetups.*

- Allow users to easily see where their network is located (with permission, of course; see "The Ex-Boyfriend Anti-Pattern" on page 375) and send out a message or invitation to meet up to those people.

- Allow users to send out one message to a predefined group of people.

- Consider the option of allowing users to send out one message to a group pulled together on the fly that is based on proximity.

Mobile statuscasting

The social mobile person will utilize a variety of tools to announce her current actions and activities for her network and the world to see:

- When considering a status tool for mobile, allow users to plug into their existing social networks, such as Twitter or Facebook (Figure 16-43).

Figure 16-43. *Twittelator is a client that taps into the user's existing Twitter account.*

- Consider pulling in the activity stream from the user's existing network onto his mobile device.

- Allow the user to indicate how often to pull data. User should be able to easily turn off the stream to save on data charges and battery life.

- Allow users to indicate whether their outgoing message is sent via an application, into an existing network, or as an SMS or text message to their network.

Considerations

The CTIA, an international mobile industry body, has published a set of best-practice guidelines for location-based service applications (*http://www.ctia.org/content/index.cfm/ AID/11300)*. Two fundamental principles guide the document:

User notice
> Location-based service providers should inform consumers as to how their location information will be used, disclosed, and protected so users can make informed decisions about whether or not to use the service or authorize disclosure.

User consent
> Once users have selected location-based services or authorized disclosure of their location information, they should have choices as to when or whether location information will be disclosed to third parties, along with the ability to revoke any such authorization.

Related patterns

"Activity Streams" on page 135

"Geo-Mapping" on page 425

"Neighborhood" on page 429

"Presence Actions and Facets" on page 125

As seen on

Foursquare (*http://playfoursquare.com/*)

Loopt (*http://www.where.com/*)

Treemo (*http://www.treemo.com*)

Twitterific (*http://iconfactory.com/software/twitterrific*)

Where (*http://www.where.com/*)

Zannel (*http://www.zannel.com*)

Further Reading

Best Practices and Guidelines for Location Based Services, International Association for the Wireless Telecommunications Industry, *http://www.ctia.org/content/index.cfm/AID/11300*

"Digital Hide and Seek: Are you ready for social mapping?," by Barrett Sheridan, Newsweek Web Exclusive, originally published August 14, 2008, *http://www.newsweek.com/id/153197/*

"Take Your Geo-Mashups Beyond Google Maps," by Scott Gilbertson, WebMonkey, originally published October 17, 2008, *http://www.webmonkey.com/blog/Take_Your_Geo-Mashups_Beyond_Google_Maps*

Part V

But Wait...There's More!

The world of social media software is constantly changing. Increases in bandwidth, web technology advances, the browser becoming the operating system, and mobile devices that give users instant online access wherever they are all provide more opportunities for creating interesting, viral, sticky applications that people can't live without. In the time we have taken to write this book, hundreds of new sites and applications have launched in the hopes of spreading and growing like Facebook or Twitter.

What we are seeing is an ever-increasing amount of people experimenting and making mashups with different kinds of social features, interwoven into just about any kind of content or service you can imagine. Some of them are amazingly inventive, and others are downright weird. With all these different opportunities and rehashes of social features, just where should designers be paying attention?

The breadth of software being developed for consumers today is only half the story. Opportunities lie with mashups and open software. Areas that traditionally have been ghettoized in traditional web software design are mobile and enterprise. Often forgotten or addressed as an afterthought, these areas provide rich and interesting challenges to creating social experiences.

If you want to see the future of interactive interfaces, look to gaming. Game designers have the liberty to experiment and Darwinian competitive pressures. The ideas they come up with and prove out in the market are setting expectations for a large number of people who may eventually become, or may already be, your users. With more and more consoles appearing in homes, families playing together, and games becoming a standard offering on mobile devices, designers need to consider how social intersects with gaming and how that changes the nature of play.

Cutting across it all is the need to understand how different age groups are negotiating digital life.

The collection in this book is presented as an evolving language, and as such is fluid. The patterns can be used one at a time or selectively mixed together to create a rich social experience. We end with a reminder that the subjects of our interfaces are human lives and aspirations, and ethical dilemmas are never far away as we create these frameworks within which people gather, play, commune, and—we hope—thrive.

Chapter 17

Open for Business

Instead of authority-based decision-making, we relied on a process we called "rough consensus and running code." Everyone was welcome to propose ideas, and if enough people liked it and used it, the design became a standard.

After all, everyone understood there was a practical value in choosing to do the same task in the same way. For example, if we wanted to move a file from one machine to another, and if you were to design the process one way, and I was to design it another, then anyone who wanted to talk to both of us would have to employ two distinct ways of doing the same thing. So there was plenty of natural pressure to avoid such hassles. It probably helped that in those days we avoided patents and other restrictions; without any financial incentive to control the protocols, it was much easier to reach agreement. This was the ultimate in openness in technical design and that culture of open processes was essential in enabling the Internet to grow and evolve as spectacularly as it has. In fact, we probably wouldn't have the Web without it. When CERN (http://topics.nytimes.com/top/reference/timestopics/organizations/c/cern/index.html?inline=nyt-org) physicists wanted to publish a lot of information in a way that people could easily get to it and add to it, they simply built and tested their ideas. Because of the groundwork we'd laid in the R.F.C.'s, they did not have to ask permission, or make any changes to the core operations of the Internet. Others soon copied them—hundreds of thousands of computer users, then hundreds of millions, creating and sharing content and technology. That's the Web.

—Stephen D. Crocker, author of the first RFC (Request for Comments) building block of the Internet, from an Op-Ed in the *New York Times* (*http://www.nytimes.com/2009/04/07/opinion/07crocker.html*)

Play Well with Others

A friend of a friend told me that "APIs are the biz dev of Web 2.0," and there's some real truth to that, especially if you mean open APIs. (An *API*, or *application programming interface*, is a set of protocols for interacting with an application from without.)

Internal APIs are essential to the development of any true platform, but open APIs unlock the potential of a third-party developer community, taking your project into realms far beyond what you could commission or build yourself.

The Internet has always thrived on openness: the open (and social) process by which its fundamental protocols (such as the TCP/IP stack) were developed (on the basis of "rough consensus and running code"), the open source operating systems and programming languages that have fueled and sustained its growth, the open interlinking of netnews nodes to create the anarchic and resilient Usenet, the open linking customs of the World Wide Web, the open editing norms of successfully wikis…. I could do this all day.

Of course, today everybody pays homage and lip service to the concept of openness. Everyone says they're open, or trying to be open, or getting more open, but there are many ways to be open and there are many degrees of openness, and frankly, "open" isn't the ultimate value that inherently trumps all other concerns. As with any software architecture of a user experience design project, there are inevitable trade-offs. Great fortunes have been built on lock-in, by keeping switching costs high, and by not allowing users complete control over their own data.

What Does It Mean to Be Open?

The word "open" is jam-packed with meaning for those in the software/web services landscape, and as the term proliferates, it can be increasingly difficult to find two folks who agree on its definition. For some, "open" is associated with "free"; for others, it is associated with flexibility and utility outside of its original location.

Because of the lack of agreement on its definition, it can be useful to think of "openness" as a construct with various edges. These edges follow a 13-point spectrum that begins on the technology side (and the developer experience), moves into the world of data, and then ends with the user experience.

It is important to note that none of the following points described on this spectrum are meant to be independent or incompatible. Rather, think of this spectrum like time theory: it can be bent, twisted, and collide with other points on the spectrum so that any product or service could be none, one, many, or all of the facets described.

1. **Open source:** Free to use, decentralized, and (generally) highly reliable, this software movement seems to drive most folks' definition of "open." (Examples include projects such as PHP, OpenOffice, and Hadoop.)

2. **Open infrastructure:** Emerging as a new kind of openness, "cloud computing" has opened a pay-as-you-go, only-what-you-need approach to technology. (Examples in this area include Google App Engine and Amazon's EC2 and S3 services.)

3. **Open architecture:** By defining a spec for how others can plug into your product, anyone can mod and extend your product. (A popular example of this is Firefox's plug-in framework.)

4. **Open standards:** A community-powered, consensus-driven approach aims for a goal of interoperability, whether for software or hardware. (Examples of these standards can be found throughout the Web's very fabric: HTML, CSS, XML, and JSON.)

—continued—

What Does It Mean to Be Open?

5. **Open ontology:** Add value to the Web by surrounding your data with semantic meaning, so that software can make meaningful connections. (RDFa, aka Resource Description Framework in attributes, and microformats best exemplify this element.)

6. **Open access:** By providing APIs, third-party developers and partners can take your data/service into their products. (Examples of open access include Twitter, Yahoo! BOSS, and eBay.)

7. **Open canvas:** Your product can become a vehicle for third-party content by opening portals into other products (while keeping users on yours). (The most popular example of this element is Facebook's application platform and the ever-growing usage of OpenSocial APIs.)

8. **Open content:** The user becomes the editor by programming self-relevant content that comes to you when it's ready. (My Yahoo! pioneered this space, but other RSS readers such as Google Reader, NetVibes, and NetNewsWire are similar strong examples.)

9. **Open mic:** The product's content is populated entirely by users, not by the product team. Users own their content, and products support the making/discovering of content. (YouTube and WordPress share both an affinity for mid-name capitalization and an approach that centers almost exclusively on user-generated content.)

10. **Open forum:** Users form a rich web around content by contributing ancillary data, ratings, reviews, ranking, conversations, and link submissions. (Examples of community-driven content layers of significant user value include Netflix's ratings/reviews and Digg's content-ranking system.)

11. **Open door:** The user is welcomed and embraced as a product decision-maker in this corporate bizarro world. (Think Get Satisfaction's customer-driven customer service or Craigslist's revenue model determination process.)

12. **Open borders:** Settings and configurations become portable. Import/export is the requirement, and users are not locked into a single product, and can come and go as they please. (As an example, OPML, aka Outline Processor Markup Language, is used extensively to manage the export and reimport of users' RSS feed subscriptions and groupings.)

13. **Open identity:** The user is the owner of her identity and information, meting out bits to services/products as she finds it appropriate. This is in opposition to the near-universal approach of surrendering control of user information at every service with no central means of management. (OpenID, fittingly, best illustrates the idea of Open Identity, alongside its Attribute Exchange extension.)

The 13 points illustrate many of the different concepts that flesh out the term "open." And, although many are compatible and complementary, it is rare to find any one product or service that exemplifies all of these elements.

Why is that? Although being open can be a competitive advantage, it can also have what some would list as disadvantages. It may force constraints by which the competition isn't hindered, determine product direction, outsource key infrastructure, or free previously proprietary information. Fortunately, there are no horror stories available of companies who bet the bank on open only to be cannibalized by the competition; rather, there are many success stories to the counter.

—continued—

What Does It Mean to Be Open?

It is also important to note that all these points require a level of investment and effort beyond what not being open entails. One could easily argue, however, that this time/cost is quickly recouped (in terms of PR, customer support, brand affinity, product extension, and more). Existing companies and products attempting to move toward any of these facets will therefore face more hurdles and obstacles (whether real—i.e., technology—or imagined—i.e., internal politics) than those with no existing baggage.

In the end, being open can mean a number of different things, some of which are dependent on the nature of the product and some of which are the choice of the product's owners. Regardless, though, product owners should understand the marketplace's open vocabulary, and consciously steer that messaging to users and the press around the points it has embraced (and have articulate answers in response to those points it does not embrace).

Doing so can keep open as the intended advantage for a product, rather than as a weapon against it.

—Micah Laaker, Director, User Experience,
Yahoo! Open Strategy

For the sake of this discussion, let's look at four clusters of open patterns and principles:

- Embracing open standards
- Sharing data outside of the bounds of your application
- Accepting external data within the sphere of your application
- Two-way interoperability

To be clear, we're not religious about any of this: if a proprietary protocol or technology or model works best for you, then use it in good health and gain whatever benefits you can get, but be aware of what you may be giving up in exchange. Where possible, though, we've found that the more you can build your app upon the rock of proven, well-implemented, open standards and technologies, the easier it is to participate fully in the social potential of the Web and the always-on digital environment we now live in.

The Open Stack, the Social Stack

Throughout this book, we've lamented the Password Anti-Pattern and the pain of re-friending the same people on multiple networks. Over the last few years, many community-developed protocols have arisen to facilitate interoperability, building upon each other wherever possible. There are several ways to visualize this stack, and it's still a work in progress (Figure 17-1). But to the extent that you can leverage the solutions that are already out there, you'll be able to focus on the value you're trying to add to the ecosystem: the unique killer service your app provides.

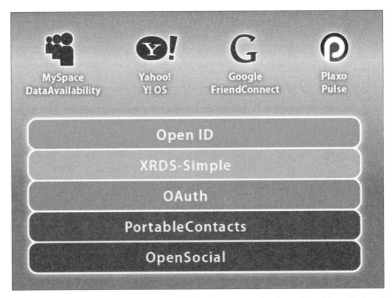

Figure 17-1. *One articulation of the "open stack" (also known as the "social stack" to distinguish it from the existing open stack that already powers the Internet).*

Open Source

What can I say about open source technology that hasn't been said before? The Internet thrives on open source, and many of the most successful startups and powerhouses run open source languages on open source operating systems. But even if you're fully convinced to use free software that you can patch yourself instead of expensive, opaque software, you still have choices. Will you contribute your code back to the community or essentially create a forked-off cul-de-sac that you'll end up maintaining single-handedly? Will you pay employees to contribute to open source projects that may benefit your competitors? These decisions aren't easy to make, and there's no single answer for everyone, but take the time to think these puzzles through.

Opening Out

Often the first step in "going open" is to open out to the rest of the Web, to make your content and features available elsewhere. It can be easier to sell the idea of extending the reach of your data than perhaps to permit others to play in your own sandbox. As always, there are trade-offs.

When you enable your content to appear in contexts you don't control, you lose a little bit of mastery over the presentation of your brand. You'll have to weigh the pros and cons to determine what to do, but recent history—as in the great success of RSS as a simple syndication format—tells us that limiting your expanse to the servers and hosts and sites you control directly is a risky proposition when the rest of the Web feels more and more like a free-for-all.

Successfully opening out means providing ways for external applications to consume and add value to your data, either public data or data your users have affirmatively authorized for this additional service.

Badging

Badging out is one of the easiest openness patterns. It involves packaging up information, frequently personalized information, in a portable format that can be copied and pasted into the template of another site so that content from your service can cleanly appear elsewhere on the Web (Figure 17-2).

Figure 17-2. *Generating a badge is a simple way to make your content available away from your own site.*

Perhaps the canonical example of this pattern's success is the way YouTube's simple embedding code enabled it to piggyback on the popularity of MySpace as members of the latter site shared videos with one another (having found it much easier to embed YouTube videos than those from any other service). MySpace briefly considered banning YouTube embeds from its service, but by then it was too late.

Also known as "(External) Module," "Badges," "Badging Out," "Embed Codes," "Codes," and "Widgets."

Use this pattern when the user wants a way of taking his content from your social site and sharing it elsewhere.

- Allow your user to collect the data that he wants to share on another site.

- Generate a snippet of sanitized code that contains access to the data from your site.

- Let the user cut and paste the code from a textbox to paste into the other site.

- Later, when another user accesses the other site and the page loads in the browser, the embedded, sanitized code executes and retrieves the personally selected data from your site for display as an embedded module or widget.

Giving your users a simple snippet of code for embedding in another site is one of the easiest ways to facilitate organic awareness of your site. Any user who creates a badge and embeds it on her blog or Facebook page is in effect advertising your site for you. Users provide an invitation for their visitors to explore the data or content being shared from your site by clicking through the badge and visiting.

"Embedding" on page 236

Open Standards (Semantics and Microformats)

Microformats and other established semantic markup and data-structure formats enable third-party developers to write applications that consume and manipulate the data you're generating (Figure 17-3).

Sample vCard

Here is a sample vCard:

```
BEGIN:VCARD
VERSION:3.0
N:Çelik;Tantek
FN:Tantek Çelik
URL:http://tantek.com/
END:VCARD
```

and an equivalent in hCard with various elements optimized appropriately. See hCard Example 1 for the derivation.

```
<div class="vcard">
  <a class="url fn" href="http://tantek.com/">Tantek Çelik</a>
</div>
```

This hCard might be displayed as:

Tantek Çelik🖉

Figure 17-3. *By the simple virtue of marking up your presented data with microformats, you can enable machine reading and semantic interpretation of that data by third-party developers.*

Use when

Use when designing templates and parsers for your data feeds, streams, sources, and pages.

How

- Wrap any data you publish on the Web with semantic markup, using the common emerging standards (notably, RDF and microformats), as a ready way of sharing it in a structured format.

- Broadcast your public content in a readily consumable format by marking up with commonly accepted semantic formats, including but not limited to RDF, microformats, and POSH.

- Another site accesses your site using arbitrary URLs to read your public content.

- Wrap the content in a standard, sanitized format so that the other site can blend it with its own data.

Why

Third-party developers will improvise unreliable screen-scraping routines in order to consume, structure, mash up, and distribute your content if it is displayed in public dressed in semantically meaningless markup.

Related patterns

"Authorize" on page 63

Opening In

Incoming interoperability is the mirror image of outgoing. It involves the ways in which you support bringing in and building on data generated externally to your system and either found in public or authorized by your own users.

Import

Just as providing badges enables site users to export content from your site and have it appear elsewhere on the Web, openness is a two-way street, so you can strengthen the appeal of your own environment if you enable your users to import their own data from elsewhere on the Web into your site (see Figure 17-4).

Figure 17-4. *An application on Facebook enables status updates from Twitter to be imported systematically, consumed, turned into Facebook status updates (with some rules and exceptions), and displayed on Facebook, giving Facebook users the benefit (or annoyance) of additional information that would otherwise not flow to them.*

Also known as "Consume Feeds."

What

Much as we may dream of building one site to rule them all, it's much more likely that our site participants will continue to live at least part of their lives elsewhere, creating content and forming relationships outside of our site.

Use this pattern when designing the formats and structures of your social objects. Allow the flexibility of open content and data modules to enhance the overall user experience. Allowing offsite content to intermix (even if only with side-by-side widgets) lets your users truly make the experience their own.

- Invite your users to provide credentials (or simply URLs for public data) to retrieve third-party data from a third-party site.
- Use the credentials or URL to connect to the third-party site, authenticate and/or authorize if required, and retrieve the third-party data.
- Optionally blend the incoming data with your existing data.
- Present the data to the user.

Instead of trying to fight or ignore the sad fact that our users have lives outside of our site, we can instead invite them to aggregate their content inside of our site by providing easy ways for them to import content generated elsewhere.

Hosted Modules

Making your own content and services available "off network" is beneficial, but it's only half the story. Without opening your own environment to third-party modules, you deny your users opportunities for experiences that can be improved by greater inventiveness and competition (Figure 17-5).

Figure 17-5. *Hosting a module from an external site on yours can feel risky. It's the reverse of the badging out role, but the experience for the user is the same.*

Use this pattern when your core services are strong and healthy, you've given outside developers the ability to build on and enhance all of your incoming and outgoing hooks, and you feel confident enough to permit external developers to create services mixing your sources with others that are hosted on your own site.

Another site creates a module/app that includes access rights to data.

The module is uploaded to your site, scanned for safety, and stored for later use.

Going Both Ways

As you can see, opening out and opening in involve much of the same thinking, but from the opposite side of the table. To fully embrace the "flow" of the Web (and perhaps avoid being routed around), explore the possibility of being open in *and* open out.

Be the Glue

Don't try to own everything. Create more value than you capture. Don't build an application when a feature will do. (See Figure 17-6.)

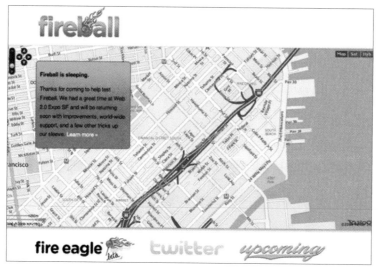

Figure 17-6. *Fireball, a prototype that mashed up Twitter for its social graph, Upcoming for its calendar of Web 2.0 Expo events, and Fire Eagle for its location-awareness.*

Open APIs

What

You have a suite of interesting solutions and a collection of data. You recognize that others can create new and unforeseen solutions with the data if it is exposed through an API (Figure 17-7).

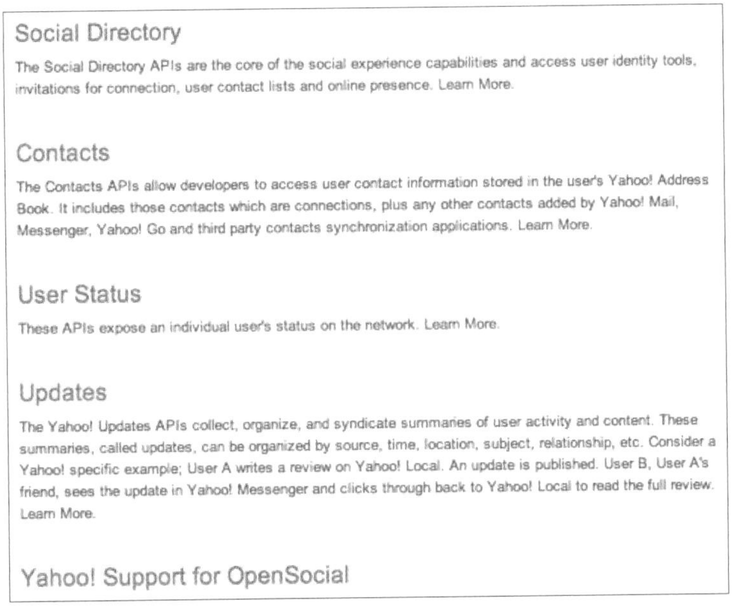

Figure 17-7. *Exposing your APIs to outside developers is a fundamental form of openness that can enable your social service to operate as part of a larger ecosystem, rather than as a backwater unto itself.*

Also known as "Data Sharing."

Use when

Use this pattern when developing your site's architecture, when conceptualizing the ecosystem your service will live in, and when deciding which APIs or which aspects of your existing APIs to expose to the public.

How

Wherever possible, expose APIs that enable outside developers to extend the value of your core service.

Each case will have its own issues of data security, privacy, what gets shared, authentication, authorization, and so on. Terms of Service provide a legal framework for safe data-sharing practices, but a rule-based permission system must be in place to enforce rules mechanically.

Some services must be opened on a read-only basis. This may frustrate your third-party developers, but if it can be justified as better than no access at all to data and connection information, then it may still be worth offering.

Why

What's good for the goose is good for the gander. If your site can be enriched by the import of data from outside sources, your data can also provide value to your users when you allow them to take it into their environments and experience it in convenient contexts.

As seen on

Facebook API (*http://maps.google.com/help/maps/getmaps/advanced.html*)

Flickr APIs (*http://www.flickr.com/services/api/ and http://code.flickr.com/*)

Google Maps APIs (*http://apiwiki.twitter.com/*)

Twitter API (*http://wiki.developers.facebook.com/index.php/API*)

Yahoo! APIs (*http://developer.yahoo.com/everything.html*)

Honest Broker

What

Many opportunities for social design experimentation online involve adding incremental new features to existing services, but the effort involved in duplicating those services just to add one more feature is prohibitive or wasteful. (See Figure 17-8.)

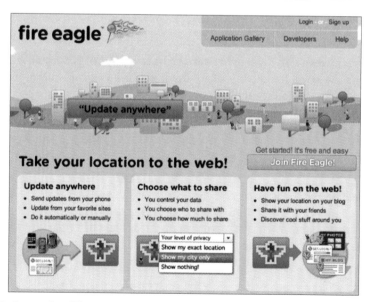

Figure 17-8. *A trusted middleman can broker data exchanges and profit by understanding the flow of information and social gestures that pass through the utility.*

Also known as "Middleman, "Middleware," and "Utility."

Use when

Use this pattern when you are designing a system that can enhance existing social behaviors but you don't see the value in trying to launch your own ecosystem just to support your idea, because it's more of a feature than a complete application.

How

Build an open, interoperable service with clear opportunities for data input and retrieval, clear privacy and security rules and permission structures, and adequate documentation. Then, support the developer community as if it is your primary customer (because it is).

Why

If you want to be seen as a utility (as Facebook describes itself), then you cannot be perceived as self-dealing. Bakers put that 13th cookie in the bag to prove to you that they don't have their thumb on the scale.

Generation Open

I recently attended an event called TransparencyCamp, modeled after BarCamp and focused on government transparency and open access to sources of federal data (largely through APIs and web services). The event was conceived in the context of a government-wide directive to embrace social media and to shed a decades-long romance with obfuscation and secrecy. Throughout the affair, "open source," "open access," and "transparency" were spoken of ceaselessly, as though a prohibition against the concepts had recently been lifted and people were eager to regain mastery of, if not familiarity with, the terms.

Clearly something has changed since I worked on the Spread Firefox grassroots marketing project in 2004—when Mozilla was easily dismissed as an outpost for "modern communists" (where meritocracy and distributed work somehow suggested communist leanings).

Indeed, the culture of "openness" has infected even the most "free market" companies, such as Microsoft, with behemoths such as Yahoo! and Google (among others) falling over one another to claim the mantle of being the most open of all.

So we won, right? We can go home now?

Hardly.

Just as the organic and green movements have been challenged to retain the integrity of their original goals and ideals, so too must the open movement wrestle with those who wish to be "open" in name only, without making real changes to how they conduct business.

—continued—

Generation Open

Fortunately, we have in our corner one of the world's largest social networks, and fortunately for us, Facebook features a preponderance of leaders and employees from Generation Open.

What defines Generation Open isn't age; it's maturing during a time when all your cultural references come from the Web, rather than TV, where bilateral communications are the norm, having obsoleted the unidirectional broadcast forms of the previous age. Once upon a time, authority figures could silence dissent with a word; now Generation Open can turn to Twitter and let the whole world know what it thinks.

Those who adopt a networked mindset will flourish; those who do not will struggle to remain relevant. It's not just that the means of publishing have been democratized and the new medium is being mastered; change flows from the events that have shaped Generation Open's understanding of economics, identity, and freedom.

Maybe it started with Pearl Jam and grunge and getting bored with the banality of "tuning out." Maybe it was finding the Web, only to watch one company after another try and fail to monetize human relationships during the bubble, and then witnessing Google succeed by becoming a residue on the Web itself, as a lichen seduces a redwood, becoming inseparable from its host, demonstrating a more organic and sustainable approach to commerce.

People who hack on Drupal or Firefox take openness in their work for granted. They thrive on the output of those who have come before and, in turn, pay it forward. To them, it's beyond comprehension why their work *wouldn't* be open—indeed it would imperil their continued success to attempt to lock it down.

In many of my conversations with Facebook employees, I see the same attitude. Not so with Microsoft, which now claims to love open source and yet lacks the genetic makeup to bear products that prove this claim. It wants so badly to be open and to derive success from openness, and yet all its learned instincts betray it. You simply can't buy your way into openness. You have to be created by openness.

The people who are building Facebook are largely from Generation Open. They've grown up (many still growing up!) in an era where open source is how you get things done, and how you make your name on the Web. It wasn't just a bygone conclusion; your first accepted patch was a right of passage into the world of meritocratic collaboration.

That Zuckerberg et al. talk about making the Web a more "open and social place" is no surprise. It's the open, social nature of the Web that has brought them such success, and will be the domain in which they achieve their magnum opus. They are the original progeny of the open Web, and its natural heirs. And to think that we're just getting started.

—Chris Messina,
Citizen Agency (*http://citizenagency.com*)/
Diso Project (*http://diso-project.org*)

Further Reading

How to Build the Open Mesh (presentation),
http://www.slideshare.net/marccanter/how-to-build-the-open-mesh-09-1427980

How to Build the Open Mesh (unbook wiki), *http://buildtheopenmesh.com/*

Joseph Smarr at Web 2.0 on the New "Open Stack,"
http://therealmccrea.com/2008/09/19/joseph-smarr-at-web-20-on-the-new-open-stack/

Microformats.org, *http://microformats.org*

OpenSocial, *http://code.google.com/apis/opensocial/*

The Open Stack: An Introduction (YDN blog),
http://developer.yahoo.net/blog/archives/2008/12/the_open_stack.html

The Open Web Foundation, *http://openwebfoundation.org/*

Chapter 18

Other Contexts

Thinking Mobile

The proliferation of mobile devices worldwide, especially after the introduction of the iPhone a couple of years ago and other smart phones released on the market more recently (294 million mobile devices were sold in the first quarter of 2008 alone), means that every designer is going to be a mobile designer. As of December 2008, nearly 10% of U.S. customers and 34% of customers in Western Europe were using social networks from their mobile device, and this is expected to grow over the next few years. As Jenifer Tidwell recently said in a talk at Interactions 09 in Vancouver, "We're all going to be mobile designers soon enough. If you're a web designer, chances aren't bad, you're already doing it."

When considering social interfaces, remember that the mobile device is inherently a social device. Build easy, one-click opportunities for connecting people with others and their content. Remember that people, especially teens, want to be connected to their network all the time. Mobile devices are along for the ride and are generally always available, whereas computers are not.

If you are designing a web service that is going mobile, bring the features that are most popular into the mobile space (Figure 18-1). But remember that screen size differences and bandwidth issues need to be addressed in order to make the experience appropriate for the medium. It is also important for designers to understand whether their service is going to be consumed through a browser in the mobile device, or as a unique application installed on the device with its own interaction conventions, rather than standard browser conventions.

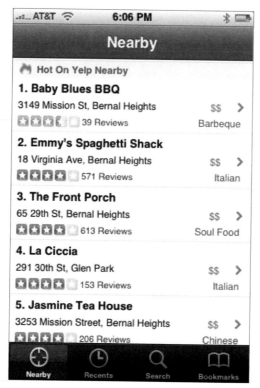

Figure 18-1. *Yelp has translated its successful web service to the iPhone. This screenshot shows a listing of "Hot on Yelp" restaurants near the location of the phone and user.*

General interface factors to consider are:

- Infinite lists that load only as needed to cut down on download costs.

- Auto complete within forms as much as possible to avoid typing.

- Graceful interpolation of intent when typing on small keyboards.

- Making the ability to share everything and anything, from anywhere, as easy as possible.

- Larger clickable targets, especially for smart phones that support gestural interactions.

- Take advantage of time and location (see "Mobile" on page 432) to add extra dimensions to social experiences not usually appropriate for the more asynchronous web experiences.

- Leverage existing data. For example, utilize the common information from the user's address book and location rather than duplicating or requiring new data to be input.

Mobile devices are turning into small computers, but the rules are different and the interaction patterns need to adjust accordingly. There are emerging patterns for mobile (see *http://patterns.design4mobile.com/index.php/Main_Page*), and designers should become familiar with the basic principles that are common across all devices. The complexity, though, lies in the fact that there are no standards in screen size, in type (keypad, touchscreen, pen-based), or in how the hardware interacts with the software.

Most of the social patterns discussed here can be combined to create interesting and rich social experiences in the mobile environment with minor modifications. Others may need to be connected through the Web for an expanded experience. For the most impact, designers should make sure that the experience on the device is not dependent on a web interface for cohesion, as many people may only have a phone and not a computer.

Designing for Mobile

People often ask me how I can stand designing for mobile. How can you do anything on those tiny screens? When you add in all the weird industry rules—hardware constraints and differences, carrier requirements—it sure can seem daunting. I tend to think of these less as annoying constraints and more as just skeleton or structure. Mobile design to me is like writing sonnets—or better, haiku—as compared to writing free poetry. The structured nature of the mobile environment can lead designers directly to what I think is the number one guiding principle of design decision-making for this medium: thinking critically about which end-user tasks to optimize and which features to include in our mobile applications or websites.

The following are my "Dos and Don'ts" for designers getting into mobile (or those who already live here).

Do:

- Use the 10-minute rule. Or maybe 5 minutes. Mobile users are, well, mobile; they're going to use your application while standing in line at the Chinese takeout/standing at the bus stop/sitting on the couch waiting for the commercial to be over. Make sure that whatever your mobile app or site's raison d'être is, it breaks down easily into short bursts of activity. Even better if those bursts of activity are super-entertaining or super-useful.

- Some focused research. Figure out what your user is really going to use your app for in those 5–10 minutes—and make sure your designs do that well.

- Make sure it works out of the box with very little setup. Sure, your engineering and design geek buddies might have fun tinkering with the guts of the settings on their phones, but this is the global consumer mobile market we're talking about. (Oops, here comes a don't in my dos!) You don't have to dumb it down, but don't rely on settings or setup flow wizardry, either.

- Get familiar with the mobile ecosystem. Take a field trip to a local shop or three and play with the display models. Develop a habit of watching people texting and playing mobile games on the train and reading their email in the elevator. Immersion can quickly make you a local in Mobile-landia, rather than a tourist.

—continued—

Designing for Mobile

Don't:

- Think that shrinking a desktop app down to mobile size is going to work—especially on a touchscreen. Most mobile designs that fail do so because the designer (or engineer) who built them assumed that a mobile phone was just a very small computer. Ever tried to click that little "X" to close a window in Windows Mobile without a stylus?

- Pare down the feature set too much. If you're converting a successful desktop app to mobile, it's not only important to determine which features to take out, but also to figure out which are the key features to leave in for the mobile context. I mean, mobile Gmail without search? Even if it's technically hard to do the right thing in Mobile-landia, I say work with the engineers to figure out what it takes.

- Do stuff because it's always been done that way. Just because every mobile phone you've ever seen has an application launcher full of icons/options menu/ton of pop-up confirmation windows, doesn't mean you have to design that way. Sure, if you're designing "on-deck" applications to be shipped with the phone (rather than sexy app-store downloadables), you might have to worry about carrier requirements. But if cutting-edge mobile designers weren't challenging those requirements, all of our phone UIs (rather than just some of them) would still look like it's 1999.

Speaking of mobile carriers, being a successful designer in the mobile space also requires an understanding of the industry and its business models—maybe even more so than design work in other media. I'm not saying that business acumen doesn't always help a designer, but in Mobile-landia you need to be thinking about the business aspects of the designs, especially when it comes to social networking apps. For instance, if you're building a new social network ("people interested in X can download this app and connect with others who have it"), you'll have to think about how your users will find one another. You can't have a community of two—and you can't rely solely on viral marketing. If you're designing an "on-deck" application that the nice sales people at your company will be pitching to carriers, you have to think not only about how great your design will be for the actual people who end up using the phone, but just as much about how that improved experience will make money/increase sales or subscribership for your customer.

Designing social interfaces for mobile is its own unique opportunity. Contextually speaking, mobile phones are by definition social networking devices. Breaking out of the classic phone/phone book mental model and transforming that experience to include 21st century–style social networking, though—that's where the fun challenge is for designers. Asking ourselves some mobile-specific questions can lead us as a community to create some exciting, disruptive social interfaces for mobile. I'll leave you with a few to think about:

- What can I do with all of my friends' contact information, a GPS, and a relatively high-powered computing device in my pocket that I couldn't do before?

- What social experiences are enabled by the power of a global population with increasingly ubiquitous connectivity?

- What does the intimacy my user has with his/her phone mean for how s/he experiences mobile social networking? (Think about the difference between the majority of the people I follow on Twitter, as opposed to the ones whose updates I set to vibrate in my pocket.)

- How can I work with this intimacy to further shape my users' experience?

—Billie Mandel, Director,
User Experience at Myriad Group AG

Inside the Enterprise

The enterprise market is a slowly waking giant. Enterprises are gradually moving toward the use of social experiences to enable and empower their organizations. This market has traditionally been ill-served by software that is hacked together from competing providers. Many IT and HR groups figure that their users (their captive employees) can just learn the software and make do. With companies tightening their belts and cutting costs and waste as much as possible, time spent "learning" bad software shouldn't be tolerated. Alternatively, some teams would like to use consumer tools for their work, but many of those services host the user's content and data and are not secure or usable with other tools inside a corporate firewall. In most cases, the IT departments can't sanction this practice for a variety of security and legal reasons. In large corporate environs, using tools outside the firewall for business purposes and storage can get an employee fired.

With teams geographically dispersed, tools with social features are needed more than ever inside the enterprise environment. The challenge, however, is that these tools must work behind firewalls, are generally private and used by a discrete set of people on a smaller scale than many consumer software experiences, and must be secure in ways that a lot of consumer software doesn't have to be.

Some of the core differences lie in the patterns for sign-up, login, identity, profile, friends/relationships, status streams, and community moderation. Activity patterns, such as blogs, wikis, forums, and collaborative calendars, should adjust to work inside the firewall—perhaps with no additional login other than the intranet—and usage may be bound by the roles within a given workgroup.

These requirements provide some interesting challenges for the designer to consider when looking at the array of social patterns to combine into a rich and useful set of enterprise tools.

Implementing Knowledge Management with Social Knowledge in Mind

Early knowledge management solutions treated the organization like a machine. They saw the knowledge itself as information to be squeezed from people's heads, rather than complex memories of cause and effects that are best recalled in response to specific problems or situations.

The failure of many of these early projects highlighted an interesting fact: that much of knowledge work is actually done socially as part of a community. This doesn't mean that information technology community (ICT) tools don't work. It suggests that instead of the tools being central, they should act as enablers of the community, both for communication and collaboration.

Enterprise 2.0 solutions such as wikis, blogs, and tagging are some ways in which the social exchange of knowledge can not only be captured in the transfer process, but also expanded in scope, allowing remote employees to enjoy the same level of connection to the community as local members do.

Implementing these tools is not the same as putting in an enterprise resource planning system (ERP) or document management system (DMS). It requires a more adaptive approach, including:

- An evolutionary framework that is modified based on the changing business requirements and participation rates. Which applications are being used often indicates which are fittest for the local environment.
- Safe-fail pilots of new solutions. This means small, carefully planned experiments. If they succeed, then they can be duplicated. If they fail, then their design allows the failure to highlight the cause and point to better solutions.
- Security is also slightly different in this area. A combination of clear guidelines and structured zones or domains for internal and public information should be provided for. Security breaches should be dealt with in a positive way that encourages proper use and doesn't discourage participation.

One of the key productive outputs of enterprise-based social computing is that of serendipity. Often the need for clear ROI to justify IT projects fails to distinguish between quantity and quality content. As such, those who produce the most content are considered more important. Alternatively, social computing tries to make use of Clay Shirky's "Long Tail," i.e., tapping into those people who have little to do with a project or operation, but who could add the one thing that might be the difference between success and failure.

To make the best use of this requires high levels of involvement. The project design and implementation should aim to avoid factors that can discourage participation, such as bad usability and lack of management support. The first one is right in the domain of designers and IT managers. The second should be championed by the project manager through gaining executive support early on, preferably before the implementation begins.

"One solution fits all" is a best-practice mantra from the area of high-volume, low-variability solutions used in mass manufacturing and the like. In knowledge work, where variability and change are the norm, top-down or waterfall solutions are usually not the best way forward. By matching both the applications and the implementation methodologies to the culture of the business unit, you will stand a much greater chance of success.

—Stuart French, Knowledge Manager, Delta Knowledge
(*http://www.deltaknowledge.net*)

Sign Up and Login (Sign In)

In the corporate environment, there should be no need for signing up, as the user is already an employee and part of the system. Designers should leverage existing security and signup mechanisms, including username, password, and any security measures, such as RSA tokens. Once the user is signed in, the social tools should reflect his identity to himself and to others (see "Identity" on page 82).

The Corporate Identity and Profile

First of all, the designer should consider how much of the basic social networking foundations need to be a part of the system. In most corporate environments, there is an intranet and an internal employee lookup system, such as LDAP, which gives employees information about role, title, email address, phone number, location, and other information about their fellow colleagues. This information is often managed and generated by the HR and IT departments and is a source of truth in terms of data.

Any social tools built for this environment should pull in this existing profile and identity information rather than duplicate it (Figure 18-2). Users should not be required to create another profile.

Figure 18-2. The user experience design (UED) team at Yahoo! has its own intranet, but taps into the main Yahoo! internal system for identity information, including username, reporting structure, phone numbers, and email. The UED intranet itself allows users to add more personal information to help build teams and strengthen relationships across workgroups.

Friends and Relationships

In many corporate intranets, employees can see where a person falls in terms of her reporting structure or workgroup. There is an inherent set of relationships available in the reporting structure information, but this is not necessarily the most useful people list for users in terms of collaborative software.

The useful people list in an enterprise social context is the listing of the relevant workgroup, regardless of reporting structure. In most cases, this can be put together by the group or project leader. The functionality of walking the social graph to find and add friends to the list is not as vital in the enterprise situation, but there can be value in being able to pull together a network that is divergent from the hierarchical reporting structure or workgroups. Displaying the work group or members list in a collaborative situation is useful, and "Publicize Relationships" on page 371 can work for this situation.

The Status/Activity Stream

A shared dashboard for the workgroup that shows the latest changes or activity within the context of the enterprise solution is a good way to utilize the status or vitality stream in the corporate environs.

Users of the system will want to know at a glance where activity is happening, what conversations are happening, who last worked on a document, or whether a collaboration event has been scheduled.

Designers need to be mindful of the delivery mechanisms for the status stream within the enterprise environment. People get a lot of email already, and consideration needs to be made for whether an action pushes out both a vitality notice to the stream as well as an email, or whether the user will be responsible for continually checking in to see what's happening.

Administration and Moderation

Administrators and moderators of these types of social experiences don't have to deal with the large amounts of bad behavior that can often disrupt a discussion or other social environment in the public at large, but this kind of behavior can still take place in the enterprise world. The difference here is that users cannot hide behind a pseudonym, and their interactions are tied to the workplace and often to work performance.

Tools for various levels of permissions and roles may still need to be developed. In this context, different levels of authorship or ownership may be tied to the hierarchical role in the company and some data-editing may be limited to certain levels in the system. For legal reasons, many companies never delete anything. They may archive it or hide it, or that option may be given only to the highest level of administration in the system.

Wikis and forums and other collaborative tools still need to be moderated, if only to clean things up, keep files and documents organized, and generally keep projects or tasks moving.

In short, features such as favorites, ratings, reviews, and reputation are not necessarily needed within the enterprise. Users are captive, so they don't need to be led along the social ladder of participation, but many of the tools may be helpful. Features such as tagging and collecting may be valuable for finding and sharing information in an ongoing fashion, or for finding people in the organization who might be experts on a specific topic.

Ratings, reviews, and reputation should be scrutinized for their value in the specific organization. There are potential social and cultural barriers for utilizing and participating in ratings and reviews in the enterprise. People may be hesitant to proactively rate or review work or documents in a public forum for fear of repercussions affecting their status, their employment position, and their annual reviews. The ramifications of these tools for the people and the business should be carefully considered before spending the time and effort to implement them.

Other Tools

Communication tools—text, video, and voice—play a bigger role than in consumer software and should be integrated into the everyday workflow.

Collaborative tools— wikis, blogs, and group calendars—should be at the forefront of an enterprise social experience (see Chapter 12).

Ultimately, people are there to get work done together, and the enterprise tools should help facilitate that collaboration and sharing, regardless of the organizational structure.

What's Age Got to Do with It?

As we look to the future of connected software, designers need to consider and understand what is happening with both ends of the age spectrum. The youth market has grown up using the Internet, cell phones, and other digital devices. It is savvy in ways that most of us cannot even comprehend. For every way that we may consider designing a service, the youth market will find ways to mix it up and combine it with something else that we might never have dreamed about.

There is a lot to learn from how the youth demographic uses technology and how it shapes their lives, both online and off. The Digital Youth Project (November 2008), funded by the MacArthur Foundation, studied hundreds of youth in different social, economic, and interest groups over several years. It found that teens often have to work around the interfaces that we are designing in order to make them work for their social norms. From the P. 37 Digital Youth Project Whitepaper:

For example, the issue of how to display social connections and hierarchies on social network sites is a source of social drama and tension, and the ongoing evolution of technical design in this space makes it a challenge for youth to develop shared social norms. Designers of these systems are central participants in defining these social norms, and their interventions are not always geared toward supporting a shared set of practices and values.

Youth are much more aware of the nuances involved in the processes of "friending," and how the display of these friends and the messages they send to others relates to their place in the social hierarchies offline. They spend their time online using communication tools such as IM and chat, and exchanging notes in comments on social networks like MySpace and Facebook with their friends from the real world. They use these tools to enhance their already existing relationships and to show newly "friended" others the peer group with which they are associated. This isn't as important to adults, although the ramifications of "ignoring" and "unfriending" are of concern to all ages.

Designers need to be aware of what kinds of messages will be sent to a user's community when certain actions are taken (i.e., how and whether this kind of information will be publicly displayed). They should also understand how rule sets developed for relationships and connection circles have an impact on how an individual is perceived among his peer groups.

Additionally, designers should be concerned with levels of privacy, balancing the desire for openness and ease of use with the need to filter and group relationships to mirror the real world.

Teen Strategies for Friending

Teens have different strategies for choosing whom to mark as Friends. By and large, the teens I interviewed "Friend" those they know—friends, family, peers, and so on. Yet, even within the confines of this general rubric, there is immense variation. Teens may choose to accept requests from peers they know but do not feel close to, if only to avoid offending them. They also may choose to exclude people they know well but do not wish to connect with on Facebook or MySpace. This category rarely includes peers, but it often involves parents, siblings, and teachers. Both MySpace and Facebook offer many incentives for adding people other than close friends. Many of the privacy features that were introduced during the course of my study limit non-Friends from profile viewing, leaving comments, and, in some cases, sending messages. Teens who wish to talk with peers or friends of friends are encouraged to accept requests from peers so as to open the channel of communication.

—continued—

Teen Strategies for Friending

Teens must determine their own boundaries concerning whom to accept and whom to reject. For some, this is not easy. Generally, there are common categories of potential Friends that most teens address in deciding how to structure their boundaries. The first concerns strangers. While many early adopters of MySpace gregariously welcomed anyone and everyone as Friends, the social norms quickly changed. For most teens, rejecting such requests is now the most common practice. Although teens who accept Friend requests from strangers rarely interact with these people online, let alone offline, the same concerns that keep teens from interacting with strangers online also keep them from including strangers in their lists of Friends. Like many teens, Guatemalan-Pakistani 15-year-old Ana-Garcia from Los Angeles adds only people she knows as Friends. She does not want strangers on her Friends list, and she is adamant that her sister does not have strangers on her list either. Her approach reifies MySpace's claim that it is "a place for friends."

Although most teens focus on Friending people they know, some teens actively connect with strangers. Teens commonly send Friend requests to bands and celebrities. They do not believe that such connections indicate an actual or potential friendship, but they still find value in these Friends. Other teens seek strangers who share their interests, primarily around music. For example, Eduardo, a Hispanic 17-year-old from Los Angeles, leverages MySpace Music to make his rap music available to a wider audience. He loves that he can share his music with his friends, but he especially likes that there is the potential to meet other musicians or people who might help him produce his music. Another musician, Dom, the 16-year-old from Washington, has actively used MySpace to connect to other musicians. Through MySpace, he found another musician who shared his musical interests and they recorded music together. Teens who have passionate interests can and do use social network sites to meet others who share their interests.

Connecting with strangers is controversial, but there is little social cost to rejecting Friend requests from strangers—because these people are unknown, teens do not worry about offending them. Rejecting known individuals, on the other hand, is much more complicated. So while teens differ on whether or not to connect with strangers, they generally accept Friend requests from all known peers, including all friends, acquaintances, and classmates, regardless of the quality of the relationship. Jennifer, a white 17-year-old from a small town in Kansas, upholds this social convention because "I'd feel mean if I didn't." She sees Friend requests as a sign of niceness and the opening of potential friendships. She also thinks it is important to be nice because she would be "mad" if someone rejected her attempt to be nice.

Social network sites take this to the next level because Friending can be both a symbolic display of popularity and a functional way of gaining access to what is being said.

While Friending classmates can lay the groundwork for building a friendship out of an acquaintanceship, not all such Friend requests are attempts to deepen the relationship. Often teens send requests to everyone they know or recognize, and no additional contact is initiated after the Friend request is approved. This only adds to the awkwardness of the Friend request. As Lilly, the 16-year-old from Kansas, explains, getting Friend requests from classmates does not mean that they even know who she is at school, making it difficult to bridge the online-offline gap: "It's just on Facebook, you're friends. At school, you don't have to talk if you don't want to…. It's kind of nice, but then at the same time it's not because you know they're your Friends…. You don't say hi in the hall 'cause maybe they just added me because somebody else had me added and they'd be like, 'I don't know who you are. Hi.'"

—continued—

Teen Strategies for Friending

Lilly accepts requests from all classmates, even those who she is not sure know who she is, but her friend, the 15-year-old Melanie, prefers to mock the dynamic that this sets up. Melanie will approach classmates who send her Friend requests with comments such as "Hey Friend from Facebook" simply because she thinks it is funny. Melanie's approach to Facebook is quite unusual. Not only is she willing to call out the absurdity of being Friends online but not talking at school, but she is also willing to buck the norms by rejecting people she does not like and deleting people who annoy her. Melanie notes that Facebook "is better than real life" because while there is no simple mechanism to formally indicate disinterest in school, it is possible to say "No" on Facebook by rejecting Friend requests. Likewise, when people annoy her on Facebook, she is comfortable deleting them. While Melanie and Lilly both find the online Friending practices to be "fake," Melanie is more outraged. Both girls are in the top classes at school and involved in many activities, but neither is particularly popular. I get the sense that Melanie's resentment stems from her frustration with the status games and peer pressure that take place at school. Melanie is adamant to point out that she does not drink or party; she thinks teens should be more focused on what is "important."

Most teens find deleting people discomforting and inappropriate. Penelope, the 15-year-old from Nebraska, says that deleting a Friend is "rude…unless they're weird." Yet while she will do it occasionally, the process of deleting someone is "scary" to Penelope; she fears that she will offend someone. Generally, it is socially unacceptable to delete a Friend whom one knows. When this is done, it is primarily after a fight or breakup. In these situations, the act of deletion is spiteful and intentionally designed to hurt the other person. Teen awareness of malicious deletions adds to the general sense that deleting someone is socially inappropriate. Thus, it can be problematic when teens accidentally delete people they know. Ana-Garcia, the 15-year-old from Los Angeles, faced this problem when her brother decided to log into her account and delete two pages' worth of Friends. Luckily, those she did know understood as soon as she explained what happened. Although deleting known people can be seen as malicious, it is socially acceptable to delete strangers. In fact, there is often social pressure to do so. Lolo, the 15-year-old from Los Angeles, says: "At the beginning, I was just adding people just to get Friends and just random boys living in New York or Texas. Then my boyfriend [was] kinda like, 'You don't know them…' so I deleted them and then I had 300 and I really knew them."

By forcing them to articulate relationships, the Friends feature forces teens to navigate their social lives in new ways. While teens are developing a set of shared social practices for Friending, the norms for these practices are still in a state of flux and interpretive flexibility. The process of adding and deleting Friends is a core element of participation on social network sites. It allows teens to negotiate who can gain access to their content, but it also means that teens have to manage the social implications of their decisions. Because the peer groups that teens connect with on social network sites are the same as those they socialize with in everyday life, decisions about whom to accept and reject online directly affect their offline connections. By facing decisions about how to circumscribe their Friends lists, teens are forced to consider their relationships, the topology of their peer group, and the ways in which their decisions may affect others.

—danah boyd, Researcher at Microsoft Research
New England and a Fellow at the Harvard University
Berkman Center for Internet and Society

While teens may adapt interfaces and social tools to fit and augment the social behaviors happening offline, they still fall into similar patterns of use as their adult counterparts when it comes to consuming, creating, and then contributing to the community.

Various age groups can be found participating in communities of interest across the Internet and in every type of experience. When people are motivated to contribute and share, and meaningful tools are available to promote discussion, offer feedback, and share ideas, age differences between users are less meaningful.

For the aging population, adoption of technology and social spaces has meant more connectedness and the ability to stay independent, even if their physical selves have slowed down.

Seniors and boomers moving into senior citizen status are one of the fastest-growing netizen populations. Because their kids and grandchildren are using social tools to share their lives, these users have had to learn these tools as well, to stay engaged and active in the family circle. This adoption spreads out to their other social circles, and suddenly we have the baby boomer generation taking over Facebook. My mother, who is on Facebook and is at the leading edge of the boomers, has almost as many connections as I do ranging across multiple generations.

There are some general best practices to consider for interfaces that may cater to the aging population. Keeping this group of users in mind during the design will create easier-to-use interfaces for all age groups:

- Create larger target areas.
- Provide better contrast in object/ground (text or iconography).
- Create legible interfaces (consider type size and readability issues).
- Make choices clear.
- Include confirmation messages to increase the user's confidence in her success. Many older people are newly engaged with these types of interfaces and consider themselves at fault when things don't work right.

Consideration of alternative interfaces for seniors, such as voice or gestural, becomes more realistic as devices for the home become intertwined with social interfaces. These bring with them a whole host of other issues and design challenges that we don't have room to address here, but designers should educate themselves on the specific difficulties in these areas for all users.

For the Win

Gaming has become big business in the context of social networks, reaching over 150 million players on Facebook alone. The merging of social interactions with games is not a new phenomenon. Multiplayer games have always had social aspects to them—forming groups, chat and conversations among players, points and leaderboards, and player reputation, to name a few features.

There is a set of core gaming interactions, described by Amy Jo Kim as "Game Mechanics." Specifically, they are:

Collecting

> Players can create collections of things. This gives the user bragging rights for those who complete the whole collection or find everything there is to find in the game (see "Collecting" on page 189).

Points

> Most games have a points system built in, and points can be awarded by the system or other players. Points are usually presented in a leaderboard fashion and drive behavior. They can punctuate key parts of the experience through unlocking new features or giving rewards when certain levels are attained (see "Leaderboard" on page 174 and "Rankings" on page 171).

Feedback

> From other players, feedback drives engagement and enjoyment in the group play (see "Soliciting Feedback" on page 283, "Comments" on page 278, "Public Conversation" on page 296, and "Private Conversation" on page 298).

Exchanges

> These are the structured social interactions, such as gifting. Most experiences have both implicit and explicit exchanges built into the game (see "Give Gift" on page 223, the Sharing patterns in Chapter 8, and "Comments" on page 278).

Customization

> Allows users to express themselves and create unique identities associated with their personas within the game. This can be the interface or their characters within the interface (see "Profile" on page 86 and "Avatars" on page 115).

These elements of games are super-important to making games social, but are also powerful key principles and patterns for general social experiences. Making sure your experiences utilize aspects of these patterns together with a compelling social object or reason for participating will help create a fun and engaging platform for your users.

You get a double hit of social engagement when games are embedded into the social networking experience (Figure 18-3). They are an entertainment alternative to television and allow users to engage in fun ways with their network that go beyond comments, sharing photos, and poking (Figure 18-4).

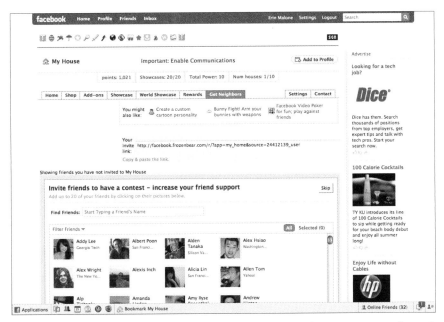

Figure 18-3. *Games embedded into Facebook enable people to pull in their existing network into the gameplay.*

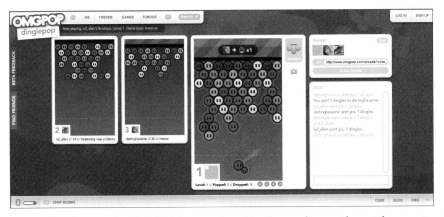

Figure 18-4. *Social games site OMGPOP lets you play with other random people or with your network of friends.*

Social games are growing in popularity and appeal to all demographics. There is tremendous growth in game use on social networks by women and older people. Social games have an advantage over traditional video games in that they are much more available and can be played anywhere you have a computer or an Internet-enabled mobile device. The barrier to entry is lower, and these new casual users are more likely to play a game on Facebook than install an unknown gaming application on their computer.

Developing games within an existing social environment should build upon the tools and experiences that already exist in the host environment. Leverage the user's existing network of friends, and use that to your advantage to promote and spread your game virally. But make sure to do it in a nice way that doesn't spam the person's network (see "Send Invitation" on page 59). Don't require users to create a new login. Most people have status and reputation built upon their identity—take advantage of that, but be respectful of appropriate context. Share rewards and points notifications within the activity stream if there is one, and notify users when something cool happens, like one of their friends reaching a new level or beating a bunch of other friends in a game. Provide a chat or threaded comment experience that can be woven into the regular part of the host site or filtered out of the host site. If you build on what already exists and provide a framework for users that they already know how to use, they will become engaged or even addicted to the games you provide.

Further Reading

"Challenges of Interface Design for Mobile Devices," by Lucas Pettinati, YUI Blog, originally published October 2, 2007,
http://yuiblog.com/blog/2007/10/02/challenges-of-interface-design-for-mobile-devices/

"Living and Learning with New Media: Summary of Findings from the Digital Youth Project," by Ito, Mizuko, Heather A. Horst, Matteo Bittanti, danah boyd, Becky Herr-Stephenson, Patricia G. Lange, C.J. Pascoe, and Laura Robinson (with Sonja Baumer, Rachel Cody, Dilan Mahendran, Katynka Martínez, Dan Perkel, Christo Sims, and Lisa Tripp). The John D. and Catherine T. MacArthur Foundation Reports on Digital Media and Learning, November 2008,
http://digitalyouth.ischool.berkeley.edu/files/report/digitalyouth-WhitePaper.pdf

"Putting the Fun in Functional: Applying Game Mechanics to Social Media," a presentation by Amy Jo Kim for Startup2Startup Gathering, 2009,
http://www.slideshare.net/amyjokim/fun-in-functional-2009-presentation

"Social Networking Goes Mobile," by Olga Kharif, *Business Week*, originally published May 31, 2006,
http://www.businessweek.com/technology/content/may2006/tc20060530_170086.htm

"Social Networking Leaves the Confines of the Computer," by Brad Stone and Matt Richtel, *The New York Times*, originally published April 30, 2007,
http://www.nytimes.com/2007/04/30/technology/30social.html?emc=eta1

"Taken Out of Context: American Teen Sociality in Networked Publics," by danah boyd (PhD thesis), 2008, *http://www.danah.org/papers/TakenOutOfContext.pdf*

"Teens and Social Media," Pew Research Report, by Amanda Lenhart, Mary Madden, Aaron Smith, Alexandra Macgill, 2007,
http://www.pewinternet.org/Reports/2007/Teens-and-Social-Media.aspx

Epilogue

Limitations encourage creativity.

Never rue the limitations of a design problem—a too-small site, an inconvenient topography, an overlong space, an unfamiliar palate of materials, contradictory requests from the client...Within those limitations lies the solution to the problem.

—Matthew Frederick, *101 Things I Learned in Architecture School*, #97

And in the End...

In the preceding pages, we have covered patterns about self (Identity, Presence, Engagement, and Reputation), patterns about social objects (Collecting, Sharing, Broadcasting and Publishing, Feedback, Communication, Collaboration, and Social Search), and patterns about the social graph and location (Personal Connections, Community Management and Place, Geography, Location). We have shared patterns about community management, licensing, and open standards. We have also given you some food for thought in a set of overarching principles: Talk Like A Person, Design for Everyone, Be Open, The Ethical Dimension, and others.

And finally, we acknowledge in this book's last chapter that not everyone is designing social web interfaces for the average consumer in the United States. There are facets and contexts of delivery medium (web, mobile, device); business or consumer; age (youth, elderly, everyone in between); and other factors that will color how you approach your design and what patterns to pay attention to and which to leave in the toolbox.

The landscape of social interactions is as broad as it is deep, and—as we have touched on briefly in the last chapter—complicated and flavored by different delivery mechanisms, contexts, and user types. Designing for this space is complicated but also a lot of fun. It's important to remember that the social experience can be quite extraordinary, even with the simplest of interfaces (remember the BBSes we mentioned in the beginning?). Pick and choose thoughtfully, and put the patterns together like a recipe or a poem, knowing that you can always start simple and expand as you go. Much of what we can do as designers is really about building a space for something to happen and then getting out of the way.

Are We Building a Better Internet?

When was the last time you fought for a good user experience against shortsighted business goals? How about delaying a development schedule to get a feature right? Or redesigned a major section of your site to make tomorrow's Internet a better place? I bet you were with me until the last question.

The Internet has no absolute authority on right or wrong. No Pope, Czar, or Commander in Chief. Yet, like the flutter of a butterfly's wing that creates a hurricane halfway around the world, the small design decisions we make today shape tomorrow's Internet. Our decisions can welcome a new digital utopia or reinforce an Internet that teaches its citizens to be jaded, narcissistic, and paranoid. The choice is ours.

For a long time, the ever-expanding Amazon.com top-tab navigation was the Internet's most successful design meme. Although Amazon.com abandoned it, many sites still employ top-tab navigation doppelgangers. This was a fairly harmless design meme in the scheme of things. I was never a huge fan, but, besides offending my sense of good design, it probably didn't do much to damage the overall Internet. Until the advent of social applications, most design memes fell into this category: at worst, they were a drag. Now we're facing a different worst-case scenario. Users are storing their most intimate data in the cloud, social media is incestuously interconnected, and application creators (like yourselves) are eager to reuse design elements across the Internet. We're creating hyper-replicating design memes with the potential to do real harm. Replace "design meme" with "evil alien virus," and you've got yourself a pitch for an action-packed Hollywood blockbuster.

The first design meme I encountered with true deleterious power was the opt-out checkbox for marketing emails on sign-up forms. Our argument for it to be opt-in instead was user-experience-focused with a nod to the business folks. Undesired emails would hurt the brand, annoy the user, and not necessarily generate qualified leads. What we didn't consider back then was how that small decision would help create today's Internet. These undesired marketing emails—along with the invention of V1@gra—contributed to the cacophony of commercial noise that now pollutes the Internet. As far as I know, this noise hasn't killed anyone. Yet most of us would prefer the Internet to feel a little more like relaxing on a secluded beach with a good book and less like Times Square on a muggy Saturday night.

Imagine for a moment what today's design decisions will do to mold the Internet's future. What if every product decision you made last week became a successful design meme? Would that create an Internet where you'd want your kids to play?

Sometimes we get lucky and it's not difficult to discern the difference between right and wrong. Don't sell user data because you're short on beer money. Don't keep emailing users after they unsubscribe. Don't read user emails to find the next great stock pick. These are certainly over-simplified dilemmas, and sadly, most ethical dilemmas aren't as clear-cut.

—continued—

Are We Building a Better Internet?

One of the great advances in the Internet was integrating disparate systems to produce new products. The early Google Maps mashups opened the door for complex social applications that found new uses for personal information stored in the cloud. Gathering this personal social data is not as simple as displaying Craigslist apartment rentals on a Google Map. Social sites secure user data using credentials, such as a unique ID and password, a design pattern introduced in the earliest computer systems. Some products allow third parties to securely access user data, although the experience is often frustrating. Many don't even bother to make such allowances. When it's a choice between no access and a poor user experience, it may seem reasonable to request a user's credentials from another site. After all, can't you create a better user experience if you can control the experience? Sadly, this design meme is training users to feel comfortable giving out their passwords to anyone who asks nicely. Identity theft is already a major problem, and training users to be sheep certainly won't help.

The ethical solution for accepting other sites' credentials is easy. All products should be built on open standards with a complete set of secure APIs using common design interfaces. Let's universally employ an un hackable icon to denote that entering your credentials is 100% guaranteed secure. Any site that refuses to participate will be shut down instantly. Then we can all hold hands on a picturesque hillside and sing "I'd like to buy the world a Coke."

Unfortunately, what is truly best for the Internet's future may not always be realistic. The challenge in this case is to develop standard interfaces to allow third-party access while teaching users responsible identity protection. The solutions become even more onerous when we consider that not every site will adopt the ethical standard. Tomorrow's Internet relies on sharing data across products. However, we don't want to achieve this at the expense of our user's security. A sense of security breeds trust, and trust breeds openness and understanding—all valuable attributes for tomorrow's Internet.

To complicate matters, sometimes it's a decision between two undesirable outcomes. A user's freedom of speech is wonderful until it's focused on making another user miserable. I tend to lean anti censorship, but am I willing to design the systems to ensure that my site doesn't make cyber-bullying worse? Will I take the time to consider nascent destructive trends and go out of my way to build systems to prevent them from maturing? Is this even a good use of my time, considering I may mistakenly choose to address an ultimately innocuous trend?

Even when the perfect solutions don't exist, we need to add the ethical questions to our product conversations. Will this decision do anything to make the Internet worse? Better? If everyone else did the same thing, would I ever log on? These conversations should certainly occur in the greater industry (and in fine books like this one). More importantly, we need to include the ethics discussion in our everyday product design meetings.

There's a lot of guesswork involved. We need to put on our futurist hats and look into our crystal balls to see what we're creating. Our predictions may fall flat. We may not always comprehend the full extent of our decisions. But to ignore ethics in our product discussions is the equivalent of accepting that we have no power or influence over the future. I, for one, am in this industry to create products that help people fulfill their personal potential and ultimately make the world a better place. It's a lot of gravitas for seemingly insignificant product decisions, but I believe in the power of the Internet, and I want to be on the right side of history.

—continued—

Are We Building a Better Internet?

Today's Internet has revolutionized the way the world communicates. We are living in a time of unprecedented access to information, and so many barriers of the past are receding. Conversely, today's Internet not only replicates atrocities from the offline world, but it makes them easier to commit. Child abuse, sexual predators, bullying, and identity theft come quickly to mind.

Skynet may be waiting around the corner to render all our efforts moot, but until that day we need to accept the responsibility to build an Internet that can make us all proud. Critically examining our decisions on ethical grounds alone won't solve all the problems of tomorrow's Internet. But acknowledging that seemingly small design decisions are the foundation of tomorrow's Internet is a valuable first step in accepting ownership of the future.

—Matte Scheinker, matte.org (*http://matte.org*)

The collection of patterns in this book is just the beginning of a conversation. What started on whiteboards, in barcamps, and on listservs is collected in this book and on our site wiki. We invite you to join us at our website, *http://www.designingsocialinterfaces.com,* to continue the conversation. We are interested in hearing your stories about designing for this space and what patterns have been most successful, which ones need more work, which should be tossed out entirely because the world has moved beyond them, and which new and emerging interactions might be added to the library.

As we mentioned in the beginning, we approached this as a pattern language, and like any language, this is a living, evolving, and ever-changing beast.

As Christopher Alexander writes in *A Pattern Language*:

> *This language, like English, can be a medium for prose or a medium for poetry. The difference between prose and poetry is not that different languages are used, but that the same language is used differently. In an ordinary English sentence, each word has one meaning and the sentence too, has one simple meaning. In a poem the meaning is far more dense. Each word carries several meanings; and the sentence as a whole carries an enormous density of interlocking meanings, which together illuminate the whole.*

> *The same is true for pattern languages. It is possible to make buildings by stringing together patterns in a rather loose way. A building made like this, is an assembly of patterns. It is not dense. It is not profound. But it is also to put patterns together in such a way that many many patterns overlap in the same physical space; the building is very dense; it has many meanings captured in a small space; and through this density, it becomes profound.*

Why not try for that lyric quality, the quality without a name, in the spirit of Alexander?

Index

H

Hess, Whitney, 72
Hinton, Andrew, 231
Honest Broker pattern, 454–457
Hosted Modules pattern, 450–452
Hughes-Croucher, Tom, 19

I

identity, 82–118
    account identifier, 85
    Attribution pattern, 113–115
    Avatars pattern, 115–118
    Facebook privacy settings for profile, 84
    Identity Cards or Contact Cards pattern,
        111–113
    LinkedIn profile, 83
    login identifier, 85
    MySpace customized profile, 83
    Personal Dashboard pattern, 104–108
    Profile pattern, 86–100
    public identifier, 85
    Reflectors pattern, 108–111
    Testimonials (or Personal
        Recommendations) pattern, 100–104
    Tripartite Identity Pattern, 84–85
Identity Cards or Contact Cards pattern,
    111–113
ignoring connection requests, 368
iLike.com, 62
Implementing Knowledge Management with
    Social Knowledge in Mind, 464
implicit and explicit relationships, 366
Import pattern, 449–450
Inline Editing pattern, 319–323
interaction design, xv
internationalization, 253
invitations, 58–80
    Authorize pattern, 63–66
    onboarding, 70–72
    Password Anti-Pattern pattern, 61–63
    Private Beta pattern, 66–72
    Receive Invitation pattern, 58–59
    Reengagement pattern, 75–79
    Send Invitation pattern, 59–61
    Welcome Area pattern, 72–75
invitees, 414
iPhone, 460
iPhoto, 235

J

Jones, Matt "blackbeltjones", 23, 25

K

Kasaric, Shara, 390, 396
Kharif, Olga, 474
Kim, Amy Jo, 472, 474
Kirigin, Abby, 26, 225
knowledge management, 321–323
    Implementing Knowledge Management
        with Social Knowledge in Mind, 464
Kulikauskas, Andrius, 259

L

Laaker, Micah, 444
Labels pattern, 163–166
Last.fm, 362
Leaderboard pattern, 174–178
Leaderboards Considered Harmful, 175–177
Leonard, Andrew, 381
levels, 157–165
    Labels pattern, 163–166
    Named Levels pattern, 157–159
    Numbered Levels pattern, 160
Lewis, C.S., 353
LibraryThing
    tag cloud, 206
    tags, 202
licensing, 254
Lifecycle pattern, 249–252
Lifespan of Content and What Should Be
    Rateable, 276–277
lifestreaming, 144–145
LinkedIn
    blocking connection requests, 374
    friend alerts, 363
    photo cropper, 110
    profile, 83, 98
    promoting new features, 77
    questions and answers, 348
    recent activities, 148
    recommendations, 102, 103, 104
Logic of the Global Brain, 257–259
login identifier, 85
Loopt, 435

About the Authors

Christian Crumlish has been designing and writing about interactive applications since 1994. He is the curator of the Yahoo! Design Pattern Library, treasurer of the Information Architecture Institute, and a member of the Open Web Foundation. He is the author of *The Power of Many* (Wiley) and *The Internet for Busy People* (McGraw-Hill Osborne Media). He lives in Oakland, California, with his wife, Briggs, and his cat, Fraidy.

Erin Malone, a Principal with Tangible UX, has over 20 years of experience leading design teams and developing social experiences for Yahoo!, AOL, Intuit, and others. She is the founder of the Yahoo! Pattern Library and a founding member of the IA Institute.

Colophon

The image on the cover of *Designing Social Interfaces* is a king bird of paradise (*Cicinnurus regius*). Members of the *Paradisaeidae* family, these small passerine birds can be found on the New Guinea mainland and on the surrounding islands of Aru, Missol, Salawati, and Yapen. They inhabit lowland rainforests and build their nests in tree cavities. Their diet consists of fruit and insects.

The smallest and most vividly colored of the birds of paradise, the king bird of paradise has been called a "living gem." Males are a brilliant red with a white underside, a green band across the chest, and a black spot above each eye. They are further distinguished by two long, wirelike tailfeather shafts tipped with a swirl of emerald-green feathers. By contrast, females are a subdued shade of olive or brown with a buff-colored chest. Both sexes have blue legs and feet and are on average six to seven inches long (not including the males' tailfeathers, which can be as long as their bodies).

The colorful feathers of birds of paradise were popular in women's fashion over a century ago, and in fact, their population was almost decimated in the late 1800s due to the practice of using the feathers to decorate women's hats. As many as 50,000 skins were exported each year until the 1920s, when exportation of the birds out of New Guinea was prohibited. Although the skins and feathers of male king birds of paradise are still sometimes used by native New Guineans in their dress and rituals, the species is abundant and no longer at risk of extinction.

The cover image is from *Cassell's Natural History*. The cover font is Adobe ITC Garamond. The text font is Adobe Minion Pro, and the heading and note font is Adobe Myriad Pro Condensed.

Get even more for your money.

Join the O'Reilly Community, and register the O'Reilly books you own. It's free, and you'll get:

- 40% upgrade offer on O'Reilly books
- Membership discounts on books and events
- Free lifetime updates to electronic formats of books
- Multiple ebook formats, DRM FREE
- Participation in the O'Reilly community
- Newsletters
- Account management
- 100% Satisfaction Guarantee

Signing up is easy:

1. **Go to: oreilly.com/go/register**
2. **Create an O'Reilly login.**
3. **Provide your address.**
4. **Register your books.**

Note: English-language books only

To order books online:
oreilly.com/order_new

For questions about products or an order:
orders@oreilly.com

To sign up to get topic-specific email announcements and/or news about upcoming books, conferences, special offers, and new technologies:
elists@oreilly.com

For technical questions about book content:
booktech@oreilly.com

To submit new book proposals to our editors:
proposals@oreilly.com

Many O'Reilly books are available in PDF and several ebook formats. For more information:
oreilly.com/ebooks

O'REILLY®

Spreading the knowledge of innovators   www.oreilly.com

Buy this book and get access to the online edition for 45 days—for free!

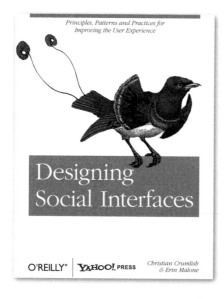

Principles, Patterns and Practices for Improving the User Experience

Designing Social Interfaces

O'REILLY® YAHOO! PRESS *Christian Crumlish & Erin Malone*

Designing Social Interfaces
By Christian Crumlish & Erin Malone
August 2009, $49.99
ISBN 9780596154929

With Safari Books Online, you can:

Access the contents of thousands of technology and business books

- Quickly search over 7000 books and certification guides
- Download whole books or chapters in PDF format, at no extra cost, to print or read on the go
- Copy and paste code
- Save up to 35% on O'Reilly print books
- **New!** Access mobile-friendly books directly from cell phones and mobile devices

Stay up-to-date on emerging topics before the books are published

- Get on-demand access to evolving manuscripts.
- Interact directly with authors of upcoming books

Explore thousands of hours of video on technology and design topics

- Learn from expert video tutorials
- Watch and replay recorded conference sessions

To try out Safari and the online edition of this book FREE for 45 days,
go to *www.oreilly.com/go/safarienabled* and enter the coupon code BFOZGAA.
To see the complete Safari Library, visit safari.oreilly.com.

Spreading the knowledge of innovators   safari.oreilly.com